STATECRAFT
BY STEALTH

STATECRAFT
BY STEALTH

Secret Intelligence and
British Rule in Palestine

STEVEN B. WAGNER

CORNELL UNIVERSITY PRESS

Ithaca and London

First published 2019 by Cornell University Press

Printed in the United States of America

Library of Congress Cataloging-in-Publication Data

Names: Wagner, Steven, 1985– author.
Title: Statecraft by stealth : secret intelligence and British rule in Palestine / Steven B. Wagner.
Description: Ithaca : Cornell University Press, 2019. | Includes bibliographical references and index.
Identifiers: LCCN 2019002330 (print) | LCCN 2019003969 (ebook) | ISBN 9781501736483 (pdf) | ISBN 9781501736490 (epub/mobi) | ISBN 9781501736476 | ISBN 9781501736476 (cloth ; alk. paper)
Subjects: LCSH: Palestine—History—1917–1948. | Palestine—Politics and government—1917–1948. | Intelligence service—Great Britain—History— 20th century. | Great Britain—Foreign relations— Palestine. | Palestine—Foreign relations—Great Britain.
Classification: LCC DS126 (ebook) | LCC DS126 .W26 2019 (print) | DDC 956.94/04—dc23
LC record available at https://lccn.loc.gov/2019002330

Contents

PREFACE

This title represents my own work. All errors and omissions are my responsibility alone. Translations, unless otherwise indicated in endnotes, are my own work. I have not used any standard form for transliterations from Hebrew and Arabic, since the source material provides a varied range of methods. I have attempted to avoid confusion through the use of consistent spelling outside of quotations, and by using ' for ʿayin and ' for hamza. In some instances, I have spelled the same name differently to distinguish between prominent figures, such as Feisal bin Husayn and Faysal bin ʿAbd al-ʿAziz. Finally, for consistency, British English spelling has been changed to US English, except in quotations.

This research was supported by the Social Sciences and Humanities Research Council. I am grateful for the financial support of the Alberta Heritage Fund and the Beit Fund at Oxford, Derek Penslar, chair of Israel studies, and Anne Knowland, senior tutor at University College, which ensured the procurement of key documents. Travel grants from the University College Old Members' Trust and the History Faculty's Arnold Fund provided important support for this research. I must thank the staff and services of the National Archives at Kew, the British Library, the Israel State Archives, the Middle East Centre Archive, Givat Haviva and the Yad Yaʿari Archive, the Zichron Yaʿakov Council Archive, and Beit Aaronoshn. I am particularly grateful to the Central Zionist Archive for graciously discounting copies, and for enabling me to retrieve some of the most important material in this book. I am especially indebted to Orly Levy for her interest in and assistance with this project.

I am grateful to the Oxford Intelligence Group, especially Michael Herman and Gwilym Hughes, who have provided me with community and mentorship at Oxford. I am also grateful for the advice and help of Margaret MacMillan, Eugene Rogan, and John Darwin. Robert Johnson has been a zealous supporter of this project, for which I am thankful. I would also like to express my appreciation to Laila Parsons at McGill, whose guidance has been invaluable. I must also acknowledge my new home at Brunel's Department of

Social and Political Sciences, which supported the completion of this book. Thank you to my colleagues for your help and understanding. Thanks especially to Matthew Hughes for your feedback on certain parts of the book.

I must offer my deep thanks to the Steinitz family of Herzliya for accommodating me on several research trips, as well as Ariella Kimmel for hosting me on my final visit to Jerusalem. I also thank the staff and teachers at Givat Haviva, whose support was crucial to my Arabic training. Dawn Berry's friendship and advice helped me to get this book project on track. I especially thank Dawn for introducing me to my editor, Emily Andrew, to whom I am also grateful for taking me on.

My parents have been my most important source of moral and financial support. Their encouragement, interest, and care helped to see me through to completing this book. My brother, Daniel, looked after me as I wrote. My wife, Kira Blumer, patiently supported my career aspirations and made this book possible. Her faith in me and in this project has sustained me throughout my work. For all this, and for Ari, from the bottom of my heart, thank you.

My eternal gratitude belongs to John Ferris, my teacher and mentor, without whom I never would have begun this journey in 2006, when I first went to London to investigate newly released MI5 files. John has been a priceless source of feedback, providing expert advice and tutelage. His care for my success is that of a true friend. For these reasons, this book is dedicated to him.

ABBREVIATIONS

AOC	Air Officer Commanding
ASC	Arab Supreme Committee
ASI	Air Staff Intelligence
AWS	Arab Workers' Society
CID	Criminal Investigation Department
CO	Colonial Office
CS	Chief Secretary
CUP	Committee of Union and Progress
ECPAC	Executive Committee, Palestine Arab Congress
EEF	Egyptian Expeditionary Force
Exco	Executive Council
FO	Foreign Office
GC&CS	Government Code & Cypher School
GCHQ	Government Communications Headquarters
GOC	General Officer, Commanding
GSI	General Staff Intelligence
HC	High Commissioner
HMG	His Majesty's Government
IB	Information Bureau
I/C	Intercepted
IPC	Iraq Petroleum Company
JA	Jewish Agency
JAPD	Jewish Agency Political Department
JB	Joint Bureau
JIC	Joint Intelligence Committee
MCS	Muslim-Christian Society
MNA	Muslim National Association
MPS	Miflaget HaPoalim HaSocialistim—Socialist Workers' Party
NILI	Netzach Yisrael lo Yishaqer ("The eternity of Israel shall not lie")
NPL	National Political League
OETA	Occupied Enemy Territory Administration

OETS	Occupied Enemy Territory Administration—South (Palestine military government)
PAC	Palestine Arab Congress
PAD	Palestine Arab Delegation
PAP	Palestine Arab Party
PAWS	Palestine Arab Workers Society
PIC	Palestine Information Centre
PICA	Palestine Jewish Colonization Association
PKP	Palestine Communist Party
PLL	Palestine Labor League
PMC	Permanent Mandates Commission
Pubsec	Public Security Committee (Tegart)
PZE	Palestine Zionist Executive
RAF	Royal Air Force
RAN	Rigul Negedi
RMP	Rural Mounted Police
SAD	Sudan Archive, University of Durham
SHAY	Sherut HaYediot
Sigint	Signals Intelligence
SIS	Secret Intelligence Service
SMC	Supreme Muslim Council
SNS	Special Night Squads
SOE	Special Operations Executive
SSO	Special Service Officer
TAP	Temporary Additional Police
TJFF	Transjordan Frontier Force
WO	War Office
YMMA	Young Men's Muslim Association
ZC	Zionist Commission

STATECRAFT
BY STEALTH

Introduction

The Life and Death of Joseph Davidescu

On an August evening in 1945, in the hill town of Zichron Yaʿakov, Palestine, Joseph Davidescu put his son Jack to bed and returned to chat with his neighbor at the kitchen table. A car pulled up to the window. Gunmen opened fire and killed Davidescu—a Zionist pioneer, Arabist, spymaster, and British intelligence officer.

During the First World War, Davidescu acted as an undercover scout behind enemy lines, providing intelligence to Britain on the human and physical landscape ahead of the British Army between the British and Ottoman front lines. He continued work for British and Zionist intelligence after the war, monitoring Arab villages and politics in the region. He joined the Haifa police, but resigned in late 1921 after a perjury conviction during an arms smuggling trial: he lied to protect the Zionist smuggling ring that his own department had dismantled. The incident nearly cost him his Medal of the Order of the British Empire (OBE), awarded for gallantry for his intelligence gathering behind enemy lines during 1917–18, but Winston Churchill intervened on his behalf.[1] Convicted by French authorities in Lebanon for smuggling arms in 1929, Davidescu joined British intelligence upon his return to Palestine the following year. His work for the British and his cooperation with the Zionists illustrate a pattern central to the arguments of this book—namely, simultaneous Anglo-Zionist cooperation and competition in intelligence. And it is this pattern that explains many things: how Britain ruled

Palestine during 1917–40, the growth of Zionist intelligence capabilities, and the Palestinians' relative disadvantage in that field.

Davidescu also represents key British and Israeli approaches to intelligence gathering. He was one of the original Mistaravim, agents who disguised themselves as Arabs. It is possible that he was known to Arab nationalists as an Arab Jew, rather than the son of Romanian immigrants of the First Aliyah (or first wave of immigration to the land). In fact, he even adopted the Arab moniker, or *kunya*, "Abu-Djaj," or "father of chickens," for his livestock business, which served as a cover for his clandestine work. In 1938, during the Palestinian revolt, Davidescu managed a network of informers based in Damascus that supplied British intelligence with crucial information on rebels and their political leadership.

Davidescu's life story, from the First World War until his death, speaks to the peculiarities of British rule in Palestine and the regime's deep reliance on intelligence. Davidescu often was a key actor in the intelligence mechanisms that shaped policy. Britain depended on the support of Zionist intelligence, and Davidescu was, from the beginning, an important liaison in that process. Anglo-Zionist intelligence cooperation is central to the story of British rule in Palestine. It underpinned British rule as part of a quid pro quo wherein Britain, in return, supported Jewish immigration and settlement in Palestine.

Like Davidescu, the Anglo-Zionist intelligence partnership did not survive the Second World War. From 1939, British policy severely limited Jewish immigration during Hitler's genocide. This deeply divided the Jewish community of Palestine, or Yishuv, and transformed the nature of Anglo-Zionist intelligence cooperation. That partnership ended shortly after Davidescu's death—symbolic, perhaps, of the changing relationship. His assassination was an act of revenge by Jewish terrorists from the Stern Gang whose comrade had been captured by British police thanks to Davidescu's work as a British security officer.[2] Controversy over Davidescu's assassination persists; it is widely believed among veteran residents of Zichron Ya'akov that former Israeli prime minister Yitzhak Shamir was among the gunmen.[3]

This book focuses on other controversies. It examines the influence of intelligence on British policy, and its role in the evolution of the triangular conflict between Britain, the Palestinians, and the Yishuv. It covers the period beginning with the inception of Britain's occupation during the First World War and ending with the fall of France in 1940, which forced Britain and the Yishuv into a life-or-death struggle against Nazi Germany. These were the years of Britain's Zionist policy, first articulated in the Balfour Declaration of 2 November 1917 and then reinterpreted and included in Palestine's legal constitution under the League of Nations.

Throughout this period, intelligence was fundamental to British power and policy in Palestine. It shaped British policy in Palestine on fundamental issues: governance, security, Zionist immigration and settlement, and Arab self-government. Intelligence records shed new light on the story of British rule and misrule, but also on the development of the Arab-Zionist conflict after the First World War. Guided by intelligence, British policy strangled Palestinian aspirations and strengthened those of the Zionists.

On Intelligence

In this book, intelligence refers to information relevant to security, communal relations, and administration, obtained from open or secret sources, and normally kept secret from other competitors. Intelligence served as a currency for exchange between collaborators. Zionists in particular sought to trade intelligence for British political support, while Palestinians tended to emphasize secrecy. Intelligence also refers to institutions: those bodies responsible for stealing secrets, keeping them, and deploying them as an arm of policy, through anything from covert action to propaganda, disinformation and deception, and clandestine diplomacy.

By the time Britain conquered Palestine, its intelligence services were still relatively underdeveloped by today's standards, and the profession was immature. Founded in Britain just before the First World War, the Security Service, or MI5, and the foreign intelligence-gathering Secret Intelligence Service (SIS, or MI6) grew into global centralized intelligence agencies to meet wartime demands. That growth was rolled back beginning in 1920, as budget cuts limited the agencies' global reach. British ministries, which used to gather intelligence on an ad hoc basis, received a regular stream of reports from MI5, SIS, and, from late 1919, the Government Code and Cypher School (GC&CS, today's GCHQ). GC&CS continued Britain's wartime practice of reading the world's cable and wireless communications. Access to these communications, deciphered and translated into English, was invaluable to British diplomacy and to this book. These agencies affected policy at high levels, and chapter 9 in particular shows how GC&CS shaped Britain's Palestine policy.

In the colonies, things worked differently. In India, for example, Britain had maintained a permanent intelligence service since the mid-nineteenth century.[4] India was the main example of security intelligence for other British colonies. Since colonial governments often ruled against the wishes of at least part of the local population, most had political police to gather security intelligence. Colonial police forces often wielded responsibility for gathering internal security intelligence. Various special branches, or Criminal Investigation Departments (CIDs), combined intelligence gathering with law enforcement, aiming to prevent local resistance from dragging troops into another "small war." Finally, although not exhaustively, security services received intelligence through liaison with local colonial auxiliaries and other European powers.

Throughout the empire, intelligence agencies engaged in more than just information gathering. They also served in an enforcement role. Colonial states depended on security services to censor local populations, and to catch foreign and local agitators. In some instances, especially during wartime, they performed foreign espionage roles in addition to their normal colonial security functions. While communications or signals intelligence was normally Britain's best source, human intelligence, or humint, played no small part in colonial security. Human agents feature throughout this book. Davidescu, for example, played various roles on behalf of British security, including undercover operative, analyst, and liaison officer, and he later handled other agents as a case officer, in today's terms.

However, today's standards do not apply to the interwar years in Palestine. Intelligence was a burgeoning profession. British officers and their associates brought with them the normal prejudices that affected other aspects of colonial rule. Orientalism, antisemitism, and racism prominently feature in the colonial worldview. Such prejudices created calamity. As will be seen in chapter 1, racial prejudice underpinned British policy, whether it favored Arabs or Jews. British policy discriminated between Jew and Arab, usually favoring the Yishuv's political and economic interests over those of the Palestinians. However, racism and prejudice do not explain the whole story. British observers were capable of seeing nuance. In part, the rise of professional analytic qualities correlated with the maturity of the intelligence organization. During the First World War, most British intelligence offices were new, and struggled to separate myth from their assessments. During the 1930s, British assessments often demonstrated a surprisingly rich understanding of Palestinian and Zionist politics, and the various conflicts that swirled within and between those communities. Officers could become emotionally attached to either community. Often, different agencies produced competing assessments of the same problem. The cognitive biases of policymakers and intelligence analysts each affected decisions.

While authorities in Palestine adopted other colonial examples, and communicated closely with London's intelligence agencies and ministries, the story of British intelligence in Palestine is unique. Examining Britain's security policy, governance, and relationships with Jewish and Arab communities, this book argues that secret intelligence—in both informational and institutional forms—was central to the story of British rule in Palestine: to the machinery of the colonial state in Palestine, and to the policy that governed it. This story has not been told until now because the evidence has only recently become available. Using newly declassified intelligence records from the United Kingdom and Israel, alongside other government records and Hebrew and Arabic sources, it is now possible to piece together a new and detailed picture of statecraft in Mandatory Palestine. Once a "missing dimension" of history, intelligence evidence illuminates the story of the Palestine Mandate's birth, life, and first symptoms of death.[5] Britain's support for the Zionist policy is central to that story: its intelligence partnership with Zionism was an important component of British power in Palestine. When Britain abandoned the Zionist policy in 1939, it sacrificed its long-term ability to govern.

Intelligence records must be approached as though seen in a magnifying mirror. They clearly reflect British policy, enabling one to trace how intelligence influenced policymakers (or was ignored by them), which issues mattered to them, and how they perceived events. But these records also offer a new and expanded view on the subjects of intelligence reportage: the Arab nationalist and Zionist communities. Simultaneously, this book offers a new reading of political developments in these communities, as well as of the colonial state, and revises our understanding not only of the foundation and growth of the mandate as a special form of British colonial state, but also of developments in the power and challenge of the Arab nationalist and Zionist communities.

Intelligence evidence illuminates more than just the machinery of British rule. It also sheds light on the Zionist and Palestinian national stories. In the early days of British rule, Palestinians hoped for self-government and legislative control over immigration to Palestine. They hoped that the liberal aims of the League of Nations mandate would check Britain's support for Jewish immigration, which, they feared, would displace them in their homeland. However, Britain's improvisational approach to Palestinian demands entertained discussion but never gave them what they wanted. Since diplomacy had delivered little success, the Palestinians escalated their demands and their pressure tactics. Palestinian political life progressed rapidly during 1921–36, as leaders mobilized the public to resist British policy and Zionist immigration. By the mid-1930s, most Palestinian parties were demanding independence. Palestinian resistance to British policy culminated in revolt from 1936 to 1941. That resistance faced the might of the empire and was crushed. Intelligence evidence reveals the many disadvantages facing the Palestinians in both diplomatic and military terms, and sharpens our understanding of their failure to achieve independence. The laws of the mandate were structured against their interests, and Britain preferred to negotiate with Zionists rather than any Arab party. Anglo-Zionist intelligence cooperation was at the heart of those disadvantages. To defeat the revolt, British military intelligence created a security state and devastated Palestinian society.

Anglo-Zionist intelligence relationships also contribute to our understanding of key issues in the Yishuv, such as the domination of Labor Zionism in Palestine's political and economic life. Partnership with British intelligence also highlights the growth of the Yishuv's stately capabilities during the interwar years, which ultimately equipped the Yishuv for independent statehood. The Zionists learned from the best intelligence professionals, while the British enjoyed the benefits of augmenting their resources with other expertise and alternate perspectives. Anglo-Zionist intelligence cooperation was tied—by both parties—to British support for Jewish immigration and settlement in Palestine. The end of Britain's Zionist policy in 1939, on the eve of the Second World War, was itself driven by intelligence and secret diplomacy. That moment transformed the Anglo-Zionist intelligence partnership and created a new conflict between the sides. The Anglo-Zionist conflict was set aside by the fall of France, when the Nazi German onslaught threatened the survival of both Britain and world Jewry.

Despite the calamity after 1939, the Yishuv enjoyed many triumphs under the cozy protection of British policy during the interwar years: it gained military might and freedom of decision, and achieved its policy aims. Of course, Zionism did not achieve statehood during this period, but it did make enormous strides toward that end. The British occupation introduced the possibility for mass immigration of Jews to Palestine—a core Zionist objective. Before Britain, the Yishuv had little ability to defend itself, and lacked a central autonomous governing body to develop stately institutions. After twenty-two years of British rule, the Yishuv's population had approximately quintupled, and Jewish land ownership had more than doubled.[6] The Yishuv's defensive militia, the Haganah, and its intelligence agencies became competent forces. They worked closely with British authorities, who trained and equipped them to secure the Yishuv. The growth of these capabilities paved the way toward Zionism's ultimate objective—independent statehood. While this book is not about the founding of Israel in May 1948, or the Palestinian catastrophe (the Nakba), it does explain the path to that destination. British intelligence shaped a security state and offered incredible advantages to its junior Zionist partners in their conflict with the Palestinians. This is the story of how Britain used intelligence to rule Palestine. In Palestine, as in other colonies, it ruled through local actors. Yet nowhere else in the empire did Britain depend so heavily on intelligence. Nowhere else were its policy options so limited.

Intelligence about environment and enemies shaped British policy and actions. One cannot understand how Britain ruled and lost Palestine without assessing these factors. Five themes come into focus throughout this exploration of intelligence and policy: the "intelligence state"; Britain's governance of Palestine; the Palestinian revolt of 1936–41; the mufti of Jerusalem, Amin al-Husseini; and the 1939 White Paper policy.

The Intelligence State

This book borrows the notion of an "intelligence state" from Martin Thomas, who discusses it in his characterization of British and French colonies in the Middle East during the interwar years, when they depended on intelligence for their security. Intelligence mattered both to the day-to-day workings of the administration and as an arm of policing.[7] Thomas also emphasizes a colonial-client relationship: "Colonies," he notes, "may have exhibited both the defined territoriality of a state and a single, central authority, but they lacked any voluntary associational basis between rulers and ruled to help underpin the state."[8]

Consent of the governed is significant to the story of Mandatory Palestine, and relates directly to the book's next major theme—governance. Intelligence tried to facilitate British governance since it could not reconcile the mandate's liberal-democratic aims while enforcing Jewish immigration against the will of the majority. Intelligence supported normal colonial governance: European powers ruled colonies through the cooperation of local elites and the recruitment of junior auxiliaries. British colonial authorities and local elites needed each other to survive. The various rival parties, interests, governments, elites, and others each sought influence in the colonial state. Intelligence was a medium for these competing interests, and simultaneously, these interests were the chief subject of colonial intelligence. In Palestine, Britain had unusually few options in how it approached local elites and junior auxiliaries. Thus, intelligence—whether overt or covert—was all the more important as a tool to negotiate those relationships.[9]

This is complicated by the conflicting roles of intelligence officers, since in the Middle East, British intelligence officers conflated their roles as intelligence providers and agents of state violence.[10] In Palestine especially, the line between these activities was blurry. Intelligence officers collected information and spread disinformation. They monitored security threats and countered them. Between 1918 and 1947, their roles varied according to leadership, administration, and conditions. Complicating matters, local elites and junior auxiliaries were not passive. Arab and Jewish factions competed among themselves and with the British for their own interests. The two communities' interest in governance and policy shaped their competitions with intelligence agencies and officers. So, whether subjects of surveillance or enthusiastic informers to the British, both Arabs and Jews participated in British rule and its hidden hand.

Thomas's model of an intelligence state applies unevenly in Palestine. The British intelligence officers who created the mandate saw some version of an intelligence state as vital, even if they never articulated the concept as such. Yet the intelligence state did not always dominate British governance, which had to comply with League of Nations obligations, the general principles of responsible government, and a prevalent liberal internationalist ideology.

The intelligence state underwent three major transformations during the period under examination. In 1920, the intelligence state embodied by the military government was remodeled into a civil government. The appearance of a civil government was deceiving, as many key government posts were filled by former army intelligence officers, who continued to handle intelligence as they had during the military administration and the war. They filled important roles as civil secretaries, district governors, and other officials. It was a "civil" intelligence state in name only. It lacked the structure and organizational benefits of the army's centralized intelligence, but comprised bright and talented ex-officers with wartime experience. By 1927–28, most seasoned intelligence-hands-cum-administrators had left the country, taking their habits and a ghost intelligence state with them.

The second transformation occurred in the wake of the 1929 disturbances, when two parallel intelligence states were rebuilt. The government expected the first of them, revolving around the police CID, to dominate political intelligence, and to conform to the high commissioner's policy. Operating in parallel, the Royal Air Force (RAF) reintroduced Staff Intelligence—a wartime innovation. Military intelligence was responsible for defense and military security and, as such, also examined Palestinian and Zionist political affairs. Military intelligence assessments of local politics differed from those of the CID and civil state. These services competed for attention and validation from the high commissioner and the civil secretary. Although military intelligence provided more nuance in its assessments of Arab and Zionist politics, they were ignored because the military had a weaker relationship with the government.

That competition was exacerbated during the Palestinian rebellion in the late 1930s. The military intelligence state was enlarged with reinforcements from Britain and the empire, while the CID and police began to crack. Arab policemen and civil servants faced incredible pressure not to go to work, or to assist the rebels. Families of officers who refused were threatened. This compounded the problem that CID assessments about the revolt had proven optimistic, even naive. By 1938, the police service had collapsed and had been rebuilt by the army under emergency laws. This was the third transformation of the intelligence state. Its civil manifestation was extinguished and replaced by a security state.

In all, the "intelligence state" was more of a security state in Palestine, since intelligence rarely affected the core of policy. There were two notable exceptions. The first, during 1919–20, took place when it secured a mandate over Palestine for Britain and cemented the Jewish national home into the bedrock of British policy. The second and final time that intelligence affected high policy occurred in 1938–39, when signals intelligence (sigint) led Britain to abandon its Zionist policy. During the interwar years, intelligence mainly served to augment British force: it was fundamental to the defeat of the rebellion, and occasionally mitigated violent disturbances, but not their political underpinnings. Intelligence could not solve the basic contradictions that underlay British rule in Palestine, but it could manage them for two decades.

Governance

Palestine was mandated to Britain by the League of Nations. Britain committed itself to providing self-government to its people, and to fostering a Jewish "national home," while protecting the "civil and religious" rights of Arab residents. The contradictions derived from Britain's notorious conflicting wartime commitments to Arabs, Jews, and France. Britain could not reconcile these claims with its own interests, or with its commitment to allow Jewish immigration against the wishes of the Arab population, which created an additional challenge for colonial government in Palestine. These issues are elaborated in chapter 1. The inherent contradiction between self-government and the Zionist policy was not acknowledged until late. It compounded the contradiction between Britain's liberal self-image and its colonialism in other parts of the empire. Intelligence shaped these contradictions and helped to manage them.

British colonial administrators preferred to rule through prestige, manipulation, and the minimum use of force. When those aims failed, they turned to the exemplary use of force, relying on reserves from elsewhere and the guidance of intelligence services.[11] According to Robert Johnson, the tactic of "divide and rule" was a common outcome of this strategy, especially where societies were already divided, but it was not Britain's only, or even its preferred, option. After the First World War, British policymakers sought to expand local autonomy throughout the empire, especially in India. Autonomy also was a league aim for mandates, but it proved impossible to implement in Palestine because it conflicted with the competing constitutional commitment to support Jewish immigration against the will of the Arab majority. In Palestine, as elsewhere, when Britain could not grant autonomy, it strived for "responsible" or good government. Britain did not trust local elites to govern themselves.[12]

Ideological, financial, and military limitations also were at play. Liberals and legalists—powerful forces in British ideas—desperately sought constitutional solutions to the Palestine problem. Financial limitations made rule through force impossible and hindered effective intelligence work, which required staff and cash for agents. In order to balance all of these commitments and conflicts, Britain relied more heavily in Palestine than elsewhere in its empire on intelligence, improvisation, and political relationships with local elites. These approaches sought to boost Britain's prestige, enable its policies, and supplement the military force that it could not afford to maintain and could not use easily. Secret intelligence and diplomacy were essential for Britain to manage relations between Arabs and Jews, and to preserve its interests and rule in Palestine.

When facing riot and revolt, intelligence guided the use of hard power and served as a force multiplier. Exemplary force hit hard, devastating Palestinian military and political organization by 1940. To these ends, administrators required political and security intelligence, and collaboration with local forces and elites. In this way, Britain's junior Zionist partners played a vital role in the maintenance of security, and were rewarded with immigration and settlement, as well as unusual freedom to develop a sophisticated internal security apparatus. Britain's dependence developed because of its inability to follow "normal" colonial practices in Palestine, and led to the creation of an *imperium in imperio*, or a state within a state. This process prepared the Yishuv's self-governing institutions for statehood.

The Revolt

The Palestinian revolt of 1936–41 was the greatest challenge to British power in Palestine during the interwar years, and one that transformed the balance of power between the three sides. Although conventionally the revolt is dated 1936–39, this book marks its end with the reoccupation of Iraq and Syria during April–June 1941. The revolt's leadership relocated to Syria in 1937, and continued to organize resistance from over the border until they were captured or fled to Axis territory in 1941. Although these latter events are beyond the scope of the book, the revised dating supports a new understanding of both Palestinian resistance and Britain's drastic responses to it.

Much of the book is dedicated to a series of questions relating to the origins, development, and defeat of the revolt and its consequences. An examination of intelligence records on the Palestinian national movement reveals important issues about both intelligence and the Palestinian national story. Although Palestinians were frustrated by Britain's commitments to Zionism, the story of the Palestinian national movement's development until 1936 was one of extraordinary and surprising success, far more so than is conventionally realized. Within fifteen years, Palestinian society overcame its divisions of class, ideology, religion, and other allegiances, and united against a common foreign threat. British observers did not understand this process as it took place, and only began to try during the revolt. Debates between intelligence officers and policymakers about Palestinian national organization illuminate how policymakers used or ignored intelligence. On the other hand, the Palestinian national story after 1936 is one of successive disasters.

The mandate was irreversibly altered by the revolt and its suppression. Britain defeated the revolt as it slid steadily toward a "dirty war" in which intelligence officers mobilized support from Jewish and Arab paramilitaries, and coordinated a vicious campaign to retake the country. The consequences were far reaching. These events tipped the balance between the two main political and demographic developments in Palestine between 1917 and 1936: the increase in the Jewish population and the expansion of the Yishuv's political organs, and the corresponding rise in Palestinian and pan-Arab nationalist organization and activity under the mufti, the British-appointed Palestinian leader. The power of Jewish military and intelligence agencies surged. Palestinian society was left shattered, divided, and leaderless. Any hope for a civil government, as guaranteed by Britain and the League of Nations, imploded under the strains of civil disobedience, the threat and use of violence, armed rebellion, and unprecedented Arab-Jewish tensions. A militarized form of rule remained in place until 1948.

The Mufti

If there is one key player in this account, it is the Palestinian leader Hajj Amin al-Husseini, mufti of Jerusalem from 1921 to 1937. The mufti was the key subject whom British intelligence and policymakers needed to understand in order to appreciate the security and governance problems they faced. This book assesses British intelligence in part by examining its assessments of the mufti. Comparing their views with other evidence helps to evaluate British intelligence services and their influence, or lack thereof, over policymakers. Of all Arab leaders, al-Husseini posed the greatest challenge to British policy in Palestine. This was complicated by his tendency to act indirectly, and by his official policymaking role from 1921 to 1937. While Britain gave him the powerful position of mufti, it nevertheless maintained a watchful eye on the Palestinian leader and his connections with the nationalist, pan-Arab, and pan-Islamic communities until 1927–28, when it lost intelligence resources and expertise. During the 1930s, British intelligence services and policymakers underrated the mufti's influence and ability to mobilize the population to demand a halt to Jewish immigration.

Recently declassified intelligence records offer a new understanding of how the mufti exercised his power, disputing historians who have argued that he did not direct armed resistance, and those who accuse him of genocidal ambitions (at least before 1941). With his multiple interests and frequent clashes with his compatriots, al-Husseini's role in armed resistance during the interwar years was hard for British observers to identify. On the one hand, he was a loyal government officer, a reliable and collaborative local elite, and a stabilizing force in Palestinian society. On the other, working through intermediaries, he mobilized nationalists in Palestine to assert their political rights and try to end the Zionist policy. Beginning in 1929, his opponents faced increasing risk of murder. His pan-Islamist activity brought him close to leading anti-imperialist voices. British administrators could reasonably see him as an ally until 1937; likewise, intelligence officers reasonably interpreted evidence to see him as hostile. This disagreement was at the core of British policy's approach to Palestinian demands during the 1930s. It explains why policymakers were slow to treat him as hostile and why they pursued constitutional negotiations and high diplomacy instead of succumbing immediately to the military's demand for martial law in 1936.

The White Paper

Finally, this book offers new explanations for Britain's decision in 1939 to abandon its Zionist policy in its White Paper, which limited Jewish immigration and land purchases for the first time since the beginning of the mandate. The intelligence record offers a new and more complete explanation for the end of Britain's twenty-two-year Zionist policy, and its abandonment of a junior partner on the eve of the Second World War. Intelligence had long monitored the communications of the founding king of Saudi Arabia, 'Abd al-'Aziz Ibn Sa'ud. He was a hero in the pan-Arab theater, and since 1915 had been a key player in Britain's Middle Eastern empire. Saudi Arabia was independent but in need of protection by a great power. Ibn Sa'ud's relations with Britain improved steadily, especially during the 1930s. The Foreign and Colonial Offices, along with the prime minister, chose in 1939 to use the Palestine question as a means to bolster the Arab leader and buy his support and widespread influence. They let the Saudis lead the other Arab delegations to London in offering new proposals for a future Palestine policy, and take the credit for this victory over Arab nationalism's Zionist enemy. Britain's relationship with Zionism was sacrificed on the altar of Anglo-Saudi diplomacy and Britain's hopes that Ibn Sa'ud would influence the region in a pro-British light—as he did. This faith in Ibn Sa'ud was based mainly on records of his intercepted communications—over the span of a decade, he proved himself to be dependable, and to share Britain's interests and enemies.

Source and Methods

Important intelligence sources on Palestine and the Middle East began to be released in 2006. Since then, the UK National Archives and the archive of the Palestine Police CID in Tel Aviv have released much material. These records contain everything from tactical intelligence against terrorists and rebels, to political intelligence on Zionism and Arab nationalism, to the structure of British security in Palestine, augmented by personal papers of soldiers, administrators, and intelligence personnel who served in Palestine or led the counterinsurgency. The Yad Ya'ari Archive at Givat Haviva, Israel, possesses personal papers of Zionist intelligence officers, including correspondence with Arabs, Zionist leaders, and British officers, while the Aaronsohn House archive in Zichron Ya'akov holds the papers of Alex Aaronsohn and Joseph Davidescu, who intermittently served British intelligence throughout the period.

The great problem is the paucity of records on Arab politics. Publicly held Arabic sources are few, located mostly at the Israel State Archives in its "Abandoned Documents" collection, or in memoirs. The lack of Arabic state records is partly relieved by the availability at the National Archives at Kew of signals intelligence intercepts of Saudi, Egyptian, and Iraqi diplomatic cables, translated into English. This material often addresses the interaction between events in Palestine and pan-Arab and pan-Islamic politics. These are rare and unique Arab accounts of important events. The sparse

Palestinian sources can be augmented by coordinating the record of British and Zionist intelligence liaison with and surveillance of Arabs. Comparing what each says about Arab contacts illuminates their secret diplomacy, albeit filtered through the viewpoint of British and Zionist observers, who were not omniscient.

Further intelligence records are available at the Haganah Archives in Tel Aviv, the Israel State Archives, and the Central Zionist Archives in Jerusalem. They contain British documents, varyingly stolen, shared, or left behind. Along with other Hebrew materials, they highlight Zionist secret diplomacy, and liaison with British and Arab contacts. These records shape the overall picture of the relationship between intelligence and policy. Hebrew and Arabic materials serve as a check on British reportage, revealing the accuracy of intelligence and the competency of its assessors. Sometimes these checks show that intelligence accurately presented issues or events but could still misconstrue their meaning. Within these gray areas we find some of the most important insights about intelligence and policy in Palestine. These issues are elucidated throughout this book's ten chapters.

Chapter Summary

Chapter 1 examines the origins of British rule and its conflicting commitments to Arabs, Jews, France, and the League of Nations. Most British officers never realized that they were creating conflicts and contradictions through these commitments. Partly this derived from the way they expected the war to end, and how that expectation was shattered by the collapse of the central powers. The misalignment of expectations also derived from British prejudices about Jewish power and Arab conspiracy. In the end, the intelligence officers who created these problems became responsible for managing them.

Chapter 2 explains how those officers sought to manage conflicting issues during military government in Palestine between 1918 and 1920. They had to convince the League of Nations to grant Britain a mandate over Palestine, and that this was best for the local population and the league's liberal-internationalist aims. Only after the league recommended a British mandate in August 1919 did British intelligence realize that they would have to use military force to uphold their commitment to Jewish immigration and settlement against the will of the Arab population. Zionist intelligence made important contributions to Britain's hold over the mandate, and was rewarded in turn. The intelligence state took shape in this discordant environment, but it had not discovered a way to reconcile Britain's conflicting commitments.

Chapter 3 covers the transition from military to civil government, and the relative peace that prevailed from 1922 to 1928, and describes the intelligence response to the disturbances in Jaffa in May 1921. Working closely with Zionists, the CID eliminated the Communist threat. Its approach to Arab nationalists, however, was different. The high commissioner appointed Amin al-Husseini as mufti of Jerusalem and later president of the Supreme Muslim Council and its land trusts. The government hoped that the mufti would use his newfound powers of patronage in its favor. Intelligence worked with Zionists to exacerbate conflicts between Palestinian parties. The government refused to negotiate with Palestinian leaders on the basis of these disagreements, accusing elites of not representing the population. Unable to secure legitimate self-government, Palestinians resisted outside the country, using connections in London, Geneva, and the broader Middle East to coordinate their protests and support the Syrian revolt. The intelligence state realized by 1921 that it was managing a stalemate in a zero-sum conflict. It guided decision makers' improvisation, but could not change the mandate's contradictions, which underpinned the conflict.

Chapter 4 is about the 1929 Buraq revolt. It examines the outbreak and consequences of the disturbances, and the security weaknesses that led up to them. It also examines the security reforms that followed, creating two parallel intelligence states. The clash of Arab and Zionist demands revolved around holy sites during 1928–29. In August 1929, tensions led to violence, which expanded and began to spiral toward revolt. British forces crushed this movement, but Palestine's security and policy failings were exposed. Postwar cuts could no longer be sustained, and security in Palestine would have to be maintained at a price.

Chapter 5 discusses the mufti and his place in pan-Arab and pan-Islamic networks. It assesses his role as leader of the Palestinian national movement, his motivations, and his modus operandi. Al-Husseini had a long history of working with transnational networks, and following the 1929 disturbances, he exploited those connections to bolster his own leadership and to elevate the Palestinian cause abroad. He allowed local activity to be led and managed by close associates, who fostered the growth of youth-led mass movements. In this way, the Palestine Istiqlal (Independence) Party was founded to resist British policy. The mufti supported Istiqlal, but kept his distance and absorbed its criticisms of his role as a colonial government officer. A comparison of intelligence evidence about these issues with other original sources reveals the nature of the mufti's leadership and demonstrates that intelligence assessments were complicated by the government's collaborative attitude toward him.

Chapter 6 looks at the tests facing British rule and its two parallel intelligence states. On the road to rebellion, it examines how intelligence assessed the mufti and Palestinian mass movements. The civil intelligence state embodied by the CID was strong on the facts and sources in Arab politics but failed to understand the mufti's role in the transnational networks that began to plan the liberation of Palestine. The military intelligence state, while ignored by the high commissioner, prepared for revolt. The army drilled a simulated revolt, and supported the police when disturbances broke out in 1933 and afterward. British security was, however, politicized. Not all crime was equal, as the police ignored murder within the Arab community but strived to prove their competence through their investigations of high-profile murder in the Yishuv, whether committed by Arabs or Jews. This unequal treatment exacerbated the basic problems of governance in the mandate. Those contradictions brewed revolt.

Chapter 7 examines the outbreak of the Arab revolt, its intermission during the Royal Commission, and its renewal upon the announcement of partition plans, and looks at how decision makers treated intelligence as the revolt escalated. Staff intelligence pressed for military escalation, but the high commissioner sought to give the mufti and his colleagues a face-saving way to end the general strike and revolt. Guided by signals intelligence, the Foreign and Colonial Offices authorized negotiations with the independent Arab states: Saudi Arabia, Yemen, and Iraq. Britain hoped that the intervention of leading Arab statesmen could persuade the Palestinians to end the revolt. Thanks to the Saudi king, the scheme worked, but not before the revolt escalated into a guerrilla campaign between rebel forces and two divisions of the British Army. Saudi Arabia was now a permanent consultant to the Foreign Office on the Palestine question. The mufti was at the peak of his influence, but could not deliver an acceptable result without escalating tensions. The second phase of the revolt made him an enemy as Palestine descended into chaos.

Chapter 8 is about how the military intelligence state sought to end that tumult. Staff intelligence organized the counterrebellion in the first centrally organized intelligence institution since the First World War. Handling intelligence and policy, military leaders reformed the police and built a security infrastructure that permanently changed the landscape of Palestine. This process also further empowered and equipped the British-Zionist intelligence partnership, which now included paramilitary cooperation against rebel units. The goals of reform were to make it possible for Arabs to serve the government. Those goals were met at a high price. Palestinian leaders were either interned or exiled, and the countryside was devastated by rebel looting and British occupation. Although bright and resourceful intelligence officers solved many security problems, Britain still had not addressed the basic contradictions of its rule. It was blind to the inevitable: Palestinians would resist Jewish immigration and make Britain pay a price to enforce it.

Chapter 9 details Britain's way out of that bind. It discusses various historiographic approaches to the 1939 White Paper policy and the retreat from partition proposals. It argues that, although prompted by the revolt, Britain's abandonment of its support for Zionism was motivated by its Middle East strategy on the eve of world war. Signals intelligence records reveal the close collaboration between Britain and Saudi Arabia in the crafting of unprecedented limits on Jewish immigration and land transfers, and the first concrete proposal to create self-government in Palestine under a single, federal, Palestinian state.

The final chapter discusses the consequences of that move. It created a conflict with the Zionist movement that British security was not prepared for. That conflict coincided with the first year of the Second World War, and was only superseded by the fall of France in June 1940. The Yishuv's response to these crises was disorganized and mixed. Right-wing revisionist Zionists launched a campaign of sabotage and propaganda while the larger, dominant Labor Zionist movement organized mass protests. Terrorists were rounded up with relative ease, largely thanks to the close relationships between British and Zionist intelligence. They would be released after the fall of France prompted a "cease-fire," or a pause in the sabotage campaign. The Colonial Office strove to disarm the Yishuv and the Haganah, but this proved impossible, as Zionist military contributions became a life-or-death necessity. The new Anglo-Zionist conflict was set aside. It could be managed by the intelligence state, but as before, the situation could not be sustained forever. This was the beginning of the end of British rule.

This book is the first to study the role of intelligence in the British Mandate of Palestine. Intelligence was a key tool in British policy and influenced its formulation. The intelligence record enables new conclusions about how the Palestine Mandate made its decisions and implemented them. As an intelligence state, the mandate faced enormous security challenges with small forces. Intelligence sustained the mandate's constitutional conflicts for over two decades. This story provides a closer look not just at the mandate, but also at Zionist and Palestinian political development. It is a story of concurrent success and failure and reflects the processes by which Britain maintained the mandate, and then lost its grip.

CHAPTER 1

Britain's Wartime Policies

Perceptions of Jewish Power and Arab Conspiracy

Between the first and final hundred days of the First World War, Britain and France witnessed few "good" days. Britain's capture of Jerusalem was an important exception. It offered citizens of the Entente a glimmer of hope after three years of butchery, which had culminated in the collapse of Russia and Germany's imminent return to a one-front war against Britain and France. The lack of progress against Germany, Austria-Hungary, and the Ottoman Empire, which persisted for most of the war, had led a desperate Britain to seek alternate pathways to victory.

Throughout the conflict, decision makers assumed that the war would end with a peace conference where they would negotiate with enemies not vanquished, able to strike again. To gain advantage at such a conference, and to limit their enemies, Britain and France resorted to propaganda. A form of psychological warfare or mass intellectual persuasion, propaganda became an important weapon in the struggle to win over the support of populations caught between loyalty to empire and their own national sentiments.

In an effort to demoralize enemy armies and populations, British war aims evolved to include the right of self-determination for small nations such as the Poles, Czechs and Slovaks, and Serbs, Croats, and Slovenes.[1] During the war, British propaganda sought to undermine the social, military, and political cohesion of the German, Austro-Hungarian, and Ottoman Empires, and to win over US support by influencing voters who had emigrated from

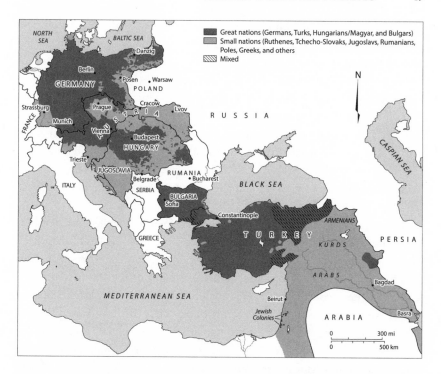

MAP 1.1. Subject nationalities of the German Alliance. This map was included in Britain and France's rejection of Woodrow Wilson's attempt to mediate peace at the end of 1916. They argued that small nations deserved representation at any peace conference. "Subject Nationalities of the German Alliance: From the Allies' Peace Terms as Stated in Their Reply to President Wilson's Note of 19th Dec. 1916: [Eurasia]," map, Library of Congress, accessed 29 November 2016, https://www. loc.gov/item/2004628224/.

those "small nations." During the final hundred days of the war, Britain's enemies collapsed. Filling the void, small nations that supported the Entente's war effort forever reshaped European borders.

The same processes reshaped the Middle East. Seeking to weaken their enemies, British war strategists undertook a propaganda campaign to champion the national movements of the Armenians, Arabs, and Zionists, with inflated assumptions about the capabilities and influence of those national movements. Intelligence officers, perhaps overoptimistically, saw Arab and Jewish conspiracies as powerful weapons to be aimed at the Ottomans and Germans. Britain's wartime Arab and Zionist policies, driven by racism and conspiracy theories, would shape British rule in Palestine. Moreover, they would define Britain's approach to managing the conflict between Arabs and Zionists for the following two decades.

Britain's wartime pledges were based on an inflated estimate of the power, capability, and influence of both nationalist movements. Britain believed that world Jewry was powerful—a force to be reckoned with, and a powerful potential enemy to Germany. Likewise, British estimates of the Arab nationalists assumed that they composed a monolithic movement united in purpose. Arab nationalism was thought capable of providing a counterblast to Ottoman and German pan-Islamic propaganda, which aimed to undermine British authority in India and Egypt. Both pledges assumed that Germany and the Ottoman Empire would survive the war, and that Arabs and Zionists would continue to be Britain's allies against those powers after it ended. The emergence of the Arab-Zionist conflict was as surprising as the stunning collapse of Britain's enemies, and the circumstances that underpinned its pledges.

Likewise, Britain's two key policymakers for the Middle East, Herbert Kitchener and Mark Sykes, did not live to see the consequences of their decisions and would not have recognized the Middle East of 1919, as revolutions raged against Britain. British intelligence estimates of the Zionists' military and intelligence contribution were inflated, but produced a partnership that lasted two decades—the scope of this book. They also overstated the potential for Arabs to subvert the Ottoman army. However, largely because of the postwar events discussed in the following chapters, Britain's partnership with Arab nationalism never manifested the way intelligence officers had imagined during the war years.

Britain's contradictory promises to Sherif Husayn bin 'Ali of Mecca in 1915, to France in the Sykes-Picot Agreement of 1916, and to Zionism in the Balfour Declaration of 1917 are infamous but misunderstood. Britain agreed to support an Arab revolt against the Ottomans and, in return, would support the establishment of an Arab kingdom under Husayn. Britain then divided the region into spheres of influence with its main war ally, France, and later included Russia in that division. Finally, Britain promised to establish in Palestine a Jewish national home. It is easy to see these as deliberate contradictions, and proof of British treachery. Yet the evidence complicates that perspective. Intelligence officers and decision makers saw no conflict between these pledges until it was too late, after Britain had secured its future in Palestine. The consequences of the contradictions were devastating to Arab aspirations, but proved foundational to Zionist dreams for a Jewish state.

The British intelligence officers who handled these issues, under pressure to achieve some alternate means of victory, acted hastily, even desperately. They engaged in wishful thinking, and their views of Jews and Arabs were shaped by prejudice and conspiracy theory. Moreover, they planned to use Arab nationalist and Zionist claims as bargaining chips with Germany and the Ottoman Empire. Those plans never met reality, as Britain's enemies had imploded by late 1918, and did not participate in peace conferences as British officers had anticipated during the war. After the war ended, small European nations achieved varying degrees of self-determination, while in the Middle East, the result was unprecedented direct rule by European powers.

Palestine in British Strategy and War Aims

British strategy in the Middle East evolved through 1915 in response to failures and successes on the battlefield. Palestine became a target for British occupation for several reasons. It was a front line in the war, but also offered the prospect of territorial security. The disaster of Gallipoli meant that there would be no short end to the war against the Ottomans. The Ottoman campaign in Sinai, which nearly destroyed the Suez Canal, convinced all policymakers that Herbert Kitchener, war minister and former high commissioner of Egypt, was right to seek a territorial buffer east of Suez to protect Britain's lifeline to India, and to prevent any future threat to this vital strategic asset. Only the India Office feared Muslim backlash to British occupation. Kitchener had long anticipated the need for some form of occupation, and had backed surveys of Sinai and the Negev in the years before the war. His maps were used during the war by the army and planning staff.[2]

The rise of airpower increased the attractiveness of the Middle East as a location for British airbases as further links to India. The conversion of the Royal Navy from coal to petroleum was a more immediate attraction. Kitchener and officers in Egypt did not want to colonize the area, but rather sought a pro-British Arab kingdom in Arabia, Syria, and Iraq as a buffer state. Ronald Storrs, Oriental secretary in Cairo, envisioned the Arab kingdom as, akin to Afghanistan, "uncontrolled and independent within, but carrying on its foreign relations through us." If achieved, Storrs argued, "we should be giving a maximum of satisfaction and assuming a minimum of responsibility; but this plan is not feasible unless we hold Syria."[3] Such wishful thinking was common at the time. Anglo-Arab negotiations were premised on the good that could result for the British Empire and war effort, and also on winning over the Hashemites—the powerful Ottoman client rulers of the Islamic heartland of Hejaz containing the holy cities Mecca and Medina. Before the war, they sought from Kitchener "an agreement similar to that existing between the Amir of Afghanistan and the Government of India, in order to maintain the status quo in the Arabian Peninsula and to do away with the danger of wanton Turkish aggression."[4] By 1922, Britain would be far more responsible for the region, and far less satisfied, than Kitchener had predicted.

Mark Sykes was another key architect of British policy in the Middle East. The scion of a wealthy but dysfunctional English family, Sykes traveled the Middle East with his parents during his youth, and returned many times as a Cambridge undergraduate and as an attaché to the British embassy in Constantinople. He took to travel writing in classic orientalist style, wherein he objectified poverty and tradition and described a region in decline, ripe for rescue by the British Empire. Such descriptions of the region were welcomed by Whitehall (the British government), which needed a new approach to the war and to the "Eastern question"—the future of the decaying Ottoman Empire, which had proved surprisingly resilient during the war. Kitchener placed Sykes on the Cabinet Committee for Eastern Affairs.[5]

In December 1915, the cabinet invited Sykes to discuss Middle East policy and his negotiations with France. Among other things, he recommended holding territory beyond the Sinai Peninsula, which Arthur Balfour said was normally regarded as a stronghold of Suez. Moreover, Sykes recommended a large-scale invasion of Ottoman territory east of Suez.[6] By this time the cabinet was well disposed to the idea of occupying Palestine as a buffer state.

British strategists had to contend with the failing campaign in Gallipoli as well as a possible two-front war in Egypt, as the Senussi—a collection of tribes who were adherents to a pro-Ottoman Sufi sect—launched their campaign in November 1915. The British feared that Muslims in Egypt and India might respond to the Ottoman call to jihad. During 1916, Britain's campaign in Mesopotamia came to an embarrassing halt with the surrender of the besieged force at Kut al-'Amara. Britain's campaigns in the Middle East did not begin to advance until 1917, nearly a year after the outbreak of the Arab revolt in Hejaz. Regrettably, success in the Middle East coincided with ongoing disaster in Europe.

Even Sykes, for all his biases, understood that Britain's wartime pledges aimed to shorten the conflict and advantage Britain's negotiating position. Sykes argued that Britain must win over the Middle East's small nations in order to end Ottoman influence in Egypt and German rail communications to Iraq. Failure to do so, he said, would "land us (Great Britain) in a bad peace position in the Middle East, lacking both control and future security. . . . I want to see a permanent Anglo-French Entente allied to Jews, Arabs and Armenians which will render pan-Islamism innocuous and protect India and Africa from the Turco-German combine, which I believe may well survive the Hohenzollerns."[7]

This view referenced German and Ottoman pan-Islamic propaganda designed to raise jihad against Christian forces in the Middle East: it was meant to consolidate Islamic unity within the Ottoman Empire and to obstruct

British mobilization in Egypt and India.[8] Even though the pan-Islamic threat to the British war effort proved to be less potent than imagined, British observers still feared pan-Islam's ability to arouse hostility and separatism in the empire through propaganda—hence Britain's decision to promote Arab nationalism. Aiming to defeat the enemy, or at least limit its ability to influence the Middle East after a peace conference, policymakers steeped in conspiratorial views of the region sought to wield nationalist propaganda against the Germans and Ottomans.

As Field Marshal Edmund Allenby advanced through Palestine during 1917, decision makers became increasingly confident that Britain would hold it. Imperial security needs drove this objective.[9] So did desperation to bring home good news. Palestine was one of Britain's few gains during the war, and by late 1917, policymakers were hoping that British influence would dominate the Middle East. Control over the Holy Land positively affected Protestant Christian and liberal sentiments. According to James Renton, "The capture of Jerusalem was to be the biggest propaganda spectacle of the war."[10] It would boost morale at home and, Eitan Bar-Yosef observes, would consolidate British support among "such diverse communities as Irish-Americans, Russian and Greek Orthodox, Indian and Algerian Muslims, and of course, 'Jews throughout the world.'"[11] Britain's occupation of Palestine was intended to secure British interests, but the impetus was conspiracy theories about the power and influence of international Jewry and the ability of Arab nationalists to conspire against the Ottoman army. The sources of those views help to explain Britain's wartime commitments.

The Zionist Policy

Historians tend to classify British opinion as having been "pro-Zionist," "anti-Zionist," or "pro-Arab," yet British officials rarely used such terms in policymaking, or even to describe their own views. On the contrary, all that mattered was the Zionist policy, outlined in the Balfour Declaration of 2 November 1917, which read, "His Majesty's government view with favour the establishment in Palestine of a national home for the Jewish people, and will use their best endeavours to facilitate the achievement of this object, it being clearly understood that nothing shall be done which may prejudice the civil and religious rights of existing non-Jewish communities in Palestine, or the rights and political status enjoyed by Jews in any other country."[12]

The notoriously vague wording was deliberate, as was the distinction of the "civil and religious rights" from the political privilege Zionism would receive. This book will use the term "the Zionist policy" as British officials did, meaning political and legal support for Jewish immigration and settlement in Palestine. When the Balfour Declaration was issued, Britain's conquest was far from complete. Britain still had not determined that it would rule Palestine directly, although it seemed increasingly likely. Regardless of what followed, the Balfour Declaration was not intended in 1917 to be the constitutional basis for British rule in Palestine, through a mandate or otherwise. British policy certainly never sought a Jewish state. For other complicated reasons, the Zionist policy ultimately did become the legal basis for British governance in Palestine—an outcome not expected by all decision makers in 1917.[13]

The Balfour declaration stemmed, ironically, from antisemitic assumptions about Jewish power and influence and the belief that world Jewry would be a vital ally in the war effort. Policymakers thought Jews able to harm the enemy on two fronts: Europe and the Middle East. Zionist colonists could be instrumental to the establishment of a territorial buffer east of Suez. Moreover, Zionist and Jewish support for Britain over Germany solved a glaring contradiction in British propaganda. The Russian czar—Britain's ally and Germany's enemy—was hated by most Jews for oppressing their coreligionists. Germany promoted emancipation in Eastern Europe, and the British cabinet sought to preempt a German Zionist declaration.[14] British propagandists and policymakers were attracted to the prospect of countering pro-German sentiment among world Jewry with a declaration in favor of Zionism. Zionism was one of many approaches to the "Jewish question," or the status and citizenship of European Jewry during the age of emancipation. Importantly, Zionism competed with socialism's answer to the Jewish question—perhaps one of its key virtues in the eyes of British elites.

The Zionist policy was rooted in common beliefs about national or ethnic stereotypes, which also applied to Jews—seen as a "people apart" in Edwardian Britain. Race and nationalism were central to political identities during this period. British elites, including wartime prime minister David Lloyd George, admired the Zionist aspiration to found a Jewish national home. Lloyd George saw it in a similar light to his own Welsh national romanticism.[15] Yet British Jews—let alone world Jewry—were not a homogeneous entity. Many British Jews abhorred the Zionist argument that Jews were unassimilable outside Palestine. A key success of the Zionist movement was that it won over British elites, including some Jewish members of that class. Jewish British elites had previously influenced foreign policy where it affected Jews abroad—for example in the Balkans or Russia.[16] As leader of Britain's Zionist Federation, Chaim Weizmann successfully capitalized on his elite social connections.

In 1915, Weizmann's patent on acetone, a vital ingredient for shell powder—
then in severe shortage—proved to be a potent catalyst for Zionism in British policy. It brought him closer to British policymakers, including Lloyd
George, then minister for munitions, and gave a platform to the Zionist
voice, which overwhelmed the majority of British Jewish elites who resented Zionism's threat to their Britishness.[17] With his financial windfall
and new social connections, Weizmann leapfrogged his way into the British
aristocracy.

During 1915–16, the British cabinet cemented its belief that world Jewry
must be mobilized to the Entente's cause. This would require persuasion,
as Jews were thought to be sympathetic to Britain's enemies. These views
were rooted in antisemitism and conspiracy theories. For example, before
the war, the British ambassador in Constantinople reported on the role of
Jews and Dönme, or "crypto-Jews," in engineering the Committee of Union
and Progress's 1908 coup, and reinforced conspiracy theories about Jewish
intentions to dominate the Ottoman Empire for the sake of Zionism.[18] During 1915, reports from the United States about the effect of German propaganda among US Zionists and Jewish communities reinforced the notion of
Jewish political and financial power. Such views, shared by antisemites and
Judeophiles alike, were more widespread in the Foreign Office than was justified by any rational interrogation of the facts, but they strongly influenced
British strategy.

For his part, Weizmann made no effort to disabuse British policymakers
of their stereotypes—in fact, he reinforced them.[19] He affirmed that Jews
were a nation, that Palestine was their natural home, and that by helping
Jewry achieve the Zionist dream and establish a settlement community in
Palestine, Britain and the Entente would win over a powerful ally and harm
its enemies. In doing so, he hijacked the largely German-speaking Zionist
movement to the British cause, and won support for his movement at the
British cabinet. The Balfour Declaration, like all of Britain's wartime pledges,
was issued with the aim of winning the war. It was based on a deeply flawed
understanding of Zionism and Jewry, but also on wartime desperation. When
the Zionist policy was issued, Germany was poised to occupy most of Eastern Europe, then in the throes of the Bolshevik Revolution. Britain assumed
that Zionists had more power in Russia as what James Renton calls a "latent
force" than was true.[20] From the time the Balfour Declaration was issued in
November 1917 until mid to late 1919, there remained little skepticism about
the virtues of Zionism within intelligence and policymaking circles.

Intelligence officers did not notice the contradictions in the document,
which in retrospect were inherent to its Arab and Zionist pledges. At first,

Gilbert Clayton, director of intelligence at the Cairo-based Arab Bureau, doubted the merits of the Zionist policy.[21] In his new role as head of the Zionist Commission (ZC), deputed by Britain to investigate how to implement the Zionist policy, Weizmann met Clayton and Allenby at Egyptian Expeditionary Force (EEF) headquarters in April 1918. There, he impressed them with his intelligence and openness. Weizmann persuaded Clayton that Arab-Zionist reconciliation was possible.[22] Clayton then attempted to promote early Zionist-Arab détente, and asked T. E. Lawrence, the most famous member of his Arab Bureau, to convince Feisal, Sherif Husayn's third son and the head of the Arab Army on the northern front, that the Arab movement depended on alliance with the Jews.[23] He also planned a meeting between Weizmann and Feisal. Weizmann, for his part, reported that he intended to tell Feisal that he could depend on Jews to help him build his Arab kingdom: "We shall be his neighbors and we do not represent any danger to him, as we are not and never shall be a great power. We are the natural intermediaries between Great Britain and the Hedjaz."[24] Clayton told Gertrude Bell, still working for the Arab Bureau but now Oriental secretary in Baghdad, that the meeting resulted

> in the establishment of very cordial relations and far more mutual sympathy than I had hoped was possible. . . .
>
> There is little doubt that the Zionist Policy has been of very considerable assistance to us already and may help us a great deal more not only during the war, but afterwards. A Palestine in which Jewish interest is established and which is under the aegis of Great Britain will be a strong outpost to Egypt.[25]

Bell was one of very few Arab Bureau officers who doubted the prospect of reconciling Britain's Arab and Zionist policies. Based in Iraq, she was distant from Weizmann's persuasive charm. She had closer contact with the Arab nationalist movements and doubted their compatibility with Zionism, or even the durability of Hashemite leadership. The ZC clarified to Clayton and other officials that its aims were not, for the present, to build a state. Arabs could be reassured by British control. Yet Clayton emphasized that "local feeling has to be studied and conciliated . . . as it might re-act on the more important Arab elements on whom our Arab policy is based and who are a great military and political asset."[26]

Clayton's changing attitudes illustrate not only Weizmann's powers of persuasion, but also the tendency for British intelligence officers to embrace conspiracy theories and then craft policy based on their flawed understanding of Jewry. Britain was desperate to turn the tide of the war, and the Balfour

Declaration was not the only British policy to be based on such a deep misreading of evidence and fact. Similar processes led to Britain's Arab policy.

Antecedents to Britain's Arab Policy

The Zionist policy might be contrasted with Britain's "Arab" or "sherifian" policy, which was based on correspondence between Sir Henry McMahon, the high commissioner of Egypt, and Sherif Husayn, patriarch of the Hashemite family and chief Ottoman authority in Mecca. In late spring 1916, they agreed that in exchange for leading an Arab revolt in Hejaz, Husayn would gain Britain's support for the establishment of an Arab kingdom roughly encompassing Arabia, Iraq, and Greater Syria (that is, modern Syria, Israel/Palestine, Jordan, and Lebanon). The details of the correspondence and the meaning of McMahon's commitments are the subject of many studies. Here, the conspiracy theories about Arab nationalism and Islam held by intelligence officers, as well as their ignorance about those issues, help to explain the emergence of Britain's Arab policy and the contradictions that ensued.

Like the Zionist policy, Britain's Arab policy rested on prejudicial assumptions and desperate responses that afterward proved to have little foundation in fact. British negotiators assumed that Sherif Husayn was the natural standard-bearer for Arab nationalism. They also assumed that Husayn and his sons were nationalists, and that they led a vast movement of separatists composed of various parties and secret societies in Greater Syria, Iraq, and Istanbul. In fact, Husayn and his family were latecomers to the Arab national movements.[27]

Arab national movements comprised a plethora of parties, clubs, publishers, artists, and secret societies that, from 1908 to 1918, were part of a burgeoning but heterogeneous national movement. They emerged during the latter phase of the Ottoman Tanzimat reforms, which centralized authority in Istanbul and sought to modernize the military, law, and education.[28] These reforms coincided with a boom in Arabic literature and educational and cultural reform known as the Nahda, or Arab "renaissance."[29] Arabism, or Arab protonationalism, was not the only political identity on the rise at this time. Ottomanist ideology, while imperialistic, was popular because it supported reform and equality of nations within the empire.[30] It might have been a potent antidote to British propaganda. Arabism burgeoned in an environment of social and legal reform, political centralization, and growing Western-Christian imperialism. Clubs in the Arab capitals and Istanbul, such as al-Muntada al-Adabi, the Literary Forum, provided venues for discussion of Arab literature, and played host to more secretive political organizations.

Among the many Arabist parties and societies, three come into focus here: al-Hizb al-la-Markazia, or the Decentralization Party; al-Jami'at al-'Arabiya al-Fatat, or the Young Arab Society (henceforth al-Fatat); and Jami'at al-'Ahd, or the Covenant Society (henceforth al-'Ahd).[31]

The Decentralization Party was founded in 1913 in Cairo by Syrian expatriates, and had affiliated branches in Damascus, Beirut, and elsewhere in Syria. This party, like others, mainly comprised elites whose social and political status was changing due to Ottoman reforms. It was based on the earlier Liberal Union party, an Ottomanist competitor to the established Committee of Union and Progress (CUP).[32]

Al-Fatat was founded in Paris by expatriates during the 1913 Congress of Arab Societies. Its network extended to Constantinople, Beirut, Damascus, and other Levantine cities. Its 1913 reform program for the Ottoman Arab provinces emphasized "Westernization" as an approach to modernization, and the decentralization of Istanbul's authority. Al-Fatat sought to defend Arab interests in the face of Ottoman decline and the rising Turkish nationalism of the CUP. Most authors agree that al-Fatat, like the other Arab movements, did not seek independence for Arabs before October 1914. Either way, the congress facilitated closer connections between al-Fatat and the Decentralization Party.[33]

Al-'Ahd was a secret society founded by Ottoman army officers returning from a campaign of irregular warfare against the Italians in Libya in 1913. Like the other Arab movements, it sought to reverse Ottoman decline and secure Arab interests within the empire. Al-'Ahd's members were predominantly Iraqi, and did not cooperate well with other Arab societies before the revolt in 1916.[34]

Until the Ottomans joined the war in late October 1914, the Arab movements largely were loyal to the empire and the sultan. The outbreak of war caused these parties, and other Arab movements, to coalesce for their own survival.[35] Together, they increasingly inclined toward separatism. This change, and the circumstances of the war and Arab revolt, gave rise to Arab nationalism, as it became known after the war.[36] Yet many Arab elites supported the Ottomans and sultan, as did the vast majority of soldiers and the broader population. The political picture was also complicated by pan-Islam—yet another response to Ottoman decay and Western imperialism.

During the late nineteenth century, a journal called *al-'Urwa al-Wuthqa* promoted the campaign of Jamal al-Din al-Afghani and Mohammad 'Abdu, which sought to promote pan-Islamic unity against the forces of Christian imperialism in the Muslim world.[37] Following the closure of the journal, al-'Urwa al-Wuthqa continued as a secret society, and taught its members that the prestige of Islam could only be rescued by the rebirth of the Arab nation. This contradicted Arabism and Ottomanism.

A minority of Arabists differed in strategy from their compatriots by promoting the transfer of the Ottoman caliphate to an Arab descendant of the Prophet Muhammad. ʿAbdu's student, Rashid Rida, was a chief proponent of this idea. Since 1911, Rida had worked to achieve unity among Arab chiefs in the peninsula to counter the CUP, to little avail. He founded and headed a Cairo-based Arab society and belonged to others, such as the Decentralization Party. Rida's ideas about transferring the caliphate to an Arab were possibly encouraged by British policy, which saw the under-construction Berlin–Baghdad railroad as a threat. Scholars have emphasized Rida's caliphate scheme as a defiant response to Ottoman weakness before the war.[38]

Rida used journalism to mobilize opinion for his reformist objectives, which were more political than religious.[39] After the war broke out, he and his compatriots began to work toward Arab independence. He secured funding from British authorities in Egypt to send emissaries to Syrian secret societies, and to the chiefs in Arabia. Although the British were hostile to Rida, they believed it was better to manage him this way and limit pan-Islamic influence in Egypt. Confirming their suspicions of Rida, his emissaries in the Persian Gulf were arrested by the British in Basra for possession of subversive anti-Christian propaganda.[40] Rida's anti-Ottoman activism would not serve British interests, it seemed.

British officers who handled Anglo-Arab negotiations during the war had a weak appreciation for how the war reshaped loyalties in the Arab world. They overlooked the anti-imperialist objectives shared by Arab nationalism and pan-Islam. Their fears about pan-Islam drove their reluctance to embrace initial overtures from the Arab movements, which were carried by prominent pan-Islamists including Rashid Rida and also Sheikh Kamil al-Qassab.

Al-Qassab was the first emissary sent by al-Fatat to feel out Britain's willingness to support an Arab revolt. He traveled from Damascus to Egypt to contact British authorities on the outbreak of war, only to discover their unwillingness to make commitments to him or to challenge France's ambitions in Syria. He left Egypt empty handed, was arrested by the Ottomans upon his return to Damascus, and was released without charge after nearly a month. The next year, in what would be the first of many diplomatic actions over the following decades, al-Qassab was instrumental in pressuring Husayn into alliance with Britain.[41] British officials had also been approached before the war by other figures, most famously ʿAziz ʿAli al-Misri, cofounder of al-ʿAhd and a hero to Arab nationalists for his participation in the Senussi campaign against the Italians in Libya during 1911–13. He too was rebuffed.[42]

British authorities still doubted the capabilities and intentions of Arab secret societies, especially after Husayn's first letter to Henry McMahon, which clearly reflected Rida's Islamist platform for an Arab kingdom, led by a caliph with both political and spiritual authority.[43] British policy would not support Husayn's revolt if its objectives were pan-Islamist, or at all shaped by Rida.

Toward an Arab Revolt

During the war, Arab secret societies such as al-Fatat, al-'Ahd, and the Decentralization Party did not have the opportunity to consider their aims or joint initiatives. Only in Damascus in spring 1915 were elements of the three main Arab societies able to coalesce. Husayn's third son, Feisal, went to Istanbul on government business in March 1915 and secretly met with al-Fatat in Damascus along the way. Feisal told them about his brother 'Abdullah's prewar correspondence with Lord Kitchener, former high commissioner in Egypt. This included Kitchener's offer to support the transfer of the caliphate to "an Arab of true race" in Mecca.[44] Throughout the Muslim world, the Ottoman sultan was considered the caliph, or khalifa—the Prophet Muhammad's successor. This issue was complicated, needless to say, by divergent definitions of the caliphate and competing claims over the title. D. G. Hogarth of the Arab Bureau warned against recognizing Husayn as caliph in 1918: "We should never, as I think, in any diplomatic or in any other way acknowledge the existence of a Caliph, and no hope of conciliating Indian Moslems ought to modify this rule. The more caliphs there are recognized by the Moslem world at one time the better for us. At present there are virtually three, the Ottoman, the Arab and the Morocan [sic]."[45] In 1915, British officers believed the sultan wielded more power and influence beyond his borders than proved true.

Such complications aside, Kitchener's overture aimed to counter Ottoman pan-Islamic propaganda with a British-sponsored variety, but did not advance far. Interference of this kind in Muslim affairs troubled the India Office, since it ruled over such a large proportion of the world's Muslims. To ease fears of provoking a pan-Islamic disturbance about the caliphate, the Foreign Office notified McMahon that "the question of Caliphate is one which must be decided by Mahommedans themselves," without foreign interference.[46] Of course, should Muslims establish an Arab caliphate, British policy would not object.

On his way back to Mecca in May 1915, Feisal saw al-Fatat in Damascus once more. Fearing Ottoman plans to supplant his family, Feisal now embraced the possibility of organized revolt. Members of al-Fatat, al-'Ahd, and the Decentralization Party identified Husayn as the organizational rallying point for their movement. They gave Feisal the "Damascus Protocol," a charter that called for an Arab revolt to be led by Husayn and armed by Britain.

The Damascus Protocol provided for Britain's recognition of Arab independence along specific boundaries, the abolition of foreign capitulations, the conclusion of a defensive alliance between Britain and the Arab state, and the granting of economic preference to Great Britain. Feisal handed the Damascus Protocol to his father and recommended that he lead the revolt. Through secret emissaries, Husayn then launched negotiations with Britain.[47] Meanwhile, the Arab officers who were members of al-Fatat and al-'Ahd were sent to the Gallipoli front with the Ottoman Arab divisions after their mutinous plans were discovered by the Ottoman secret service. This delayed the possibility for revolt, but left time for British authorities and Husayn to develop terms of agreement.[48]

Husayn was not necessarily al-Fatat's first choice for standard-bearer, according to the historian Eliezer Tauber, but "his noble ancestry, his status as guardian of the holy places of Islam, and the distance of the Hejaz region from the main Ottoman forces made him a suitable candidate to lead the planned revolt."[49] Witnessing centralization reforms and the extension of the Hejaz railway, the Hashemites had worried for years that the Ottomans aimed to limit or replace their control in Hejaz. Thus, Husayn's son 'Abdullah reached out to Kitchener during 1913–14 in search of protection of the status quo. He was not acting for nationalism, but to protect his family's interests, and was, Mary Wilson notes, operating "well within the bounds of normal central-peripheral tensions of the Ottoman systems."[50]

Although desired by both the Arab movements and Britain, this connection was not enough to cause a change in British policy toward supporting Arab revolt. Since 1914, the idea had been dismissed by most quarters. Change came in October 1915, after one Arab officer at Gallipoli defected to the British. This was 1st Lt. Muhammad Sharif al-Faruqi, a junior member of al-'Ahd. Al-Faruqi told the British everything about his secret society—its membership and leaders, their enciphered communications, and their ambitions. He exaggerated the capabilities and unity of the Arab movements, describing them instead as a single party. Records of al-Faruqi's debriefing at the Arab Bureau in Cairo illuminate his role in changing British minds about Arab revolt. Underlined in the text was the society's wish to "establish an Arab Caliphate in Arabia, Syria and Mesopotamia." Also, significantly, the Arab Bureau recorded that al-Faruqi's movement was open to a process of increasingly autonomous government, "under British guidance and control," in Palestine and Mesopotamia. "Syria is of course included in their programme," McMahon wrote, "but they must realize that France has aspirations in this region, though el Farugi [*sic*] declares that a French occupation of Syria would be strenuously resisted by the Mohamedan population."[51]

Wishful thinking began to dominate intelligence, which ignored the obvious contradictions between Arab and French objectives. Al-Faruqi's revelations supported what was known from other sources about the Arab movements, and seemingly provided objective confirmation of a widespread anti-Ottoman conspiracy. For the first time, British observers could see how Arab secret societies in Syria were connected to Husayn, as, according to McMahon, "the Arabs in Syria were under a signed compact to follow [Feisal]."[52] Moreover, the Ottoman military leader Jamal Pasha had hanged fifteen leading members of the Arab movements in Syria—a move that pushed al-Fatat and al-'Ahd closer to the Hashemites as their main lifeline to Britain.

Al-Faruqi eased British fears about Rida's influence over Husayn, or Arab hostility to the British Empire. Report of his debriefing spurred Kitchener and the foreign minister to authorize McMahon's favorable reply to Husayn, without consulting the government of India. Suspicious, the India Office noted McMahon's sudden emphasis on Al-Faruqi's modern, secular plans: "Interesting, if only because it may be merely a bait for us, is the idea that the Arab 'Empire' is to be 'national' and not religious in 'accordance with the spirit of this century' and again 'although the new Empire we wish to establish is to be headed by a Khalifa, its basis will be national and not religious. It will be an Arab not a Moslem Empire.'" Importantly, the minute concluded, "This is in striking contrast with the fanatical Islamism of Rashid Riza's [Rida's] memorandum."[53] British observers overstated the divisions between Arab nationalist and Islamic sentiments. All were affected by their modernist views that religion was a reactionary dying force, and that nationalism and modernity were inherently linked. Although some doubts persisted in the Indian and Foreign Offices, they eventually supported a revolt and McMahon's promises to Husayn as a means to hasten an end to the war.[54]

What is most astonishing is that British policymakers assumed al-Faruqi was telling the truth from November 1915 until the new year, when Sherif Husayn confirmed the matter. This covers the beginning of the Sykes-Picot talks, meaning that Britain entered negotiations with its main war ally on the basis of al-Faruqi's word alone. This best illustrates both the impetuous tendencies of intelligence officers and policymakers and their faith in the power of Arab secret societies to contribute to a British victory in the war. Through back channels, al-Faruqi communicated to Husayn that, in his communications with Britain, he should verify al-Faruqi's claims to represent the Arab movements. On New Year's Day, 1916, Husayn did just that.[55]

Al-Faruqi confirmed for intelligence officers what they previously had been told by al-Misri, al-Qassab, and Rida, while mitigating suspicions about their hostility to British imperialism. Al-Faruqi told them what they wished to hear—that the Arabs were pragmatic and could be reasoned with.[56] He confirmed the existence of al-Fatat and al-'Ahd, described their connections to Sherif Husayn and their desire for independence from the Ottomans, and emphasized their ability to support Britain's war effort. He presented the movement as united, separatist, and anti-Ottoman.

Yet al-Faruqi oversimplified these issues. British officers never fully understood how the Damascus Protocol emerged, or Husayn's late affiliation with Arab secret societies. Most misleading of all, al-Faruqi told British officials that his movement saw the future Arab state as a secular one when there was no such consensus. British soldiers and diplomats alike believed this because they had long been searching for a way to neutralize the Ottoman pan-Islamic weapon. Now it seemed that Arabs were promising to form a state—part of the British Empire—governed according to modernizing principles, which particularly impressed British officials. Once al-Faruqi had been debriefed in Cairo, no British official questioned the influence of pan-Islam among the Arab movements.

Image versus Reality: Britain and the Arab Movements

The mismatched expectations of Britain, France, and the Arab movements collided after the war. Officers who believed they had crafted a united Arab-Zionist-Armenian front against pan-Islam confronted ongoing conflict after 1918, defying their preconceptions. In 1919 members of al-Fatat founded the Istiqlal (Independence) Party in Syria to expand its influence over other classes of society. In early 1920, the independence movement split in three: a faction of dissenters rejected British and French imperial designs altogether, Feisal's faction sought cooperation with Britain in exchange for some autonomy in the Syrian hinterland, and the third faction hoped for a US mandate over Syria, but that possibly evaporated by late summer 1919. 'Izzat Darwaza led the dissenters with many other prominent nationalists, including Kamel al-Qassab, who in 1914 had risked much to approach Britain for an alliance. By 1919, al-Qassab rejected anything short of full Arab independence, and accused the Damascus administration under Feisal of "neglect of national interest."[57] This original pan-Syrian Istiqlal Party was the inspiration for the Palestine Istiqlal Party, founded over a decade later. In the meantime, Ottomanism and pan-Islamism resurged in reaction to the nationalists' disunity and the escalating claims of Britain and France.[58]

Intelligence officers never expected these outcomes. They failed to foresee the role that members of al-Fatat would play in the Arab kingdom. They assumed that the Hashemites would be another imperial client in Arabia, loyal and influential, and did not anticipate the anticolonial ambitions of Feisal's government in Damascus, or the influence of al-Fatat or al-'Ahd over the broader national movement. In Palestine, the Arab national movement—dominated by elites—also began to found self-representative institutions. Since the armistice with the Ottoman Empire enabled free expression, secret societies in Palestine emerged in the open. Arab nationalists partnered with notable families, mainly from Jerusalem, Jaffa, and Nablus, to found Muslim-Christian Societies (MCS). The various branches of the MCS coalesced in early 1919 to form the Palestine Arab Congress (PAC), whose executive committee (ECPAC) later advocated in Jerusalem, London, and Geneva against Britain's Zionist policy and for independence.

Open political associations such as the MCS, the Nadi al-'Arabi (the Arab Club), the revived Muntada, and other constituent parties at PAC were the successors of secret societies such as al-Fatat. PAC leadership included members of al-Fatat and other decentralization movements from the Ottoman period. Many had worked with Feisal and his family since 1916.[59] The first PAC sent its resolutions to the peace conference at Paris in 1919. It advocated self-determination under Wilsonian principles, posing a political problem for Britain, which sought to contain the influence of the al-Fatat-inspired independence platform. PAC challenged British ambitions in Palestine, but MCS delegates to PAC did not all agree on policy, with the result that diplomats and intelligence were quick to dismiss the MCS as a group of unrepresentative, self-appointed troublemakers.[60]

J. N. Camp, the British military intelligence officer in Jerusalem, reported the names, towns, and differing sympathies of each PAC delegate. Pan-Arab nationalists from the Nadi and the Muntada supported union with an independent Syria, while Christians supported French rule. "There were also many pro-British delegates at once anti-French, anti-Zionist, and anti-Sherif," Camp observed.[61] The one point of agreement was anti-Zionism: "I am convinced," he noted, "that if it were not for Zionism ninety per cent of the people of this country would come out without qualification in favor of a British administration or protectorate."[62] According to the Arab Bureau's Gilbert Clayton, the congress was inspired by Zionism's aggressive pace with its own propaganda "to capture Jewry for Zionism."[63] Clayton believed that if Weizmann could tone down Zionist rhetoric, the Arabs would be more conciliatory. Moreover, he had long doubted whether Syrian or Palestinian Arabs, whom he saw as backward, would accept "Meccan Patriarchalism" under a Hashemite king.[64] He thought the Arab kingdom would rule the no-madic Bedouin, and Britain would guide settled Arabs, who were not ready for self-government. His views were widespread in the military bureaucracy in Palestine and Egypt, and contradicted the aims of Arab nationalists.

Surprised by PAC's demands for self-government and its rejection of British or French rule, British intelligence officers attacked the legitimacy and representativeness of PAC and other institutions in their reports. The wishful thinking of the war and the hastily assembled and bizarre foundation of the Anglo-Arab alliance led officers to overlook how British and Arab aims might conflict. So did the rapid implosion of Britain's enemies, and the vacuum they left behind. British officers fought a war aiming for a multilateral peace conference, but suddenly had to dictate terms to vanquished enemies, their former territories, and their peoples. It is understandable how mismatched perceptions emerged. From 1914 to 1915, Britain had to contend with the possibility of competing great powers such as Germany dominating the Middle East. Assessments from the Arab Bureau never anticipated that the Arab movements might demand absolute independence, with no foreign influence. They assumed these movements would stand with Britain against Ottoman and German threats, and that those threats would outlast the war. When those threats dissolved, it was no longer possible to overlook the anti-imperial views of leading nationalists. It also brought Zionist support for the British Empire to the spotlight.

Intelligence and Transnational Threats to Empire

Intelligence officers continued to believe in conspiracy theories after the war. These views affected important decisions as the roots of British rule were planted. From 1917 to 1922, British intelligence and policymakers saw transnational issues such as pan-Islam and Bolshevism as the main threats to the empire. Although British officers saw these issues through a distorted lens, it is important to take their assessments seriously. By looking at events through their eyes, it is possible to understand British strategy and decision making during the riots and revolutions that rocked the Middle East between 1919 and the 1923 Lausanne Conference. Salient mistakes of interpretation in intelligence reports affected assessment and policy at high levels.[65]

According to the historian John Ferris, intelligence officers "did not distort (as against, mistake) the facts about conspiracy, revolt, Pan Islam and nationalism. Their interpretations were reasonable, but often wrong. . . . They suffered from the professional deformation of alarmism. They overemphasised the power of conspiracies."[66] They were influenced by the Ottoman and German Empires' use of pan-Islam as a propaganda centerpiece during the war, and overstated that threat. In 1919 and 1920, British analysts erroneously attributed political disturbances in India, Iraq, and Egypt to the influence of a secret German-Bolshevik alliance. Whitehall unfortunately took this information seriously. In Palestine, it led intelligence officers to attribute anti-British resolutions at PAC to ex-members of al-Fatat, which they described as a leading stream of Arab nationalism with Turkish pan-Islamic connections and inspirations. Thus, Arab nationalists were portrayed as being on the wrong side of Britain's new global situation.[67]

The views of the British Security Service, or MI5, illuminate the relationship between Islam and imperial security. In a discussion of its role in the world, and in order to justify a higher level of funding, MI5 described the emerging threats facing the British Empire. It maintained the wartime tendency to see the world as a series of conspiracies. The first threat, according to MI5, was Japan's military autocracy and its "pan-Asianism, or 'Yellow Peril.'" Closer to home, the CUP was still thought to be a "live political force" and would continue to sway "the ignorant masses, not only in Turkey but in other Muhammadan countries." MI5 warned that exiled CUP leaders had allied themselves with Russian Bolsheviks, "who after all are quite Oriental in their ideas and terrorist methods, and we have thus arrayed against Western civilization the three motive forces. Pan-Islamism, Pan-Turanianism, and Communism on the Bolshevik plan."[68]

MI5's notion of global security rested on countering an alleged transnational conspiracy between Bolsheviks and pan-Islamists to spread revolution around the world. Predictions of German and Russian officers leading "Muhammadan hordes" did not come true, but Britain's fear that transnational movements could cooperate against the empire shaped intelligence assessments in the Middle East. In part, this helps to explain why British officers were slow to realize that Britain's Zionist and Arab policies would be irreconcilable. Even during the Paris Peace Conference of 1919, it was assumed that national movements would be a bulwark against pan-Islam and Bolshevism. These mistaken interpretations were foundational to British rule in Palestine, as officers downplayed the strength of Arab nationalism after the war and justified cooperation with Zionists.

As a modern profession, intelligence was only in its infancy, and would have to mature quickly after 1918. This story demonstrates how intelligence could be simultaneously successful and wrong. Intelligence officers had initially forged partnerships with Arab nationalists and Zionists, believing they would contribute to British victory in the war. Their hasty and drastic responses to information were driven by wartime pressures and stereotypes of the power of world Jewry and Arab secret societies.

When Britain conquered Palestine in 1918, it had never produced a plan for Anglo-Arab relations in an environment without a German or Ottoman threat. British intelligence became responsible for reconciling the problems it helped create during the war. Arab nationalism and Zionism shared few interests, and would prove to be incompatible elements of British policy.

Like the Arab policy, the Zionist policy also was founded on Britain's flawed perception of its negotiating partners. The capabilities and unity of world Jewry were inflated in the imaginations of decision makers. Britain's commitments to Jews were not thought to contradict the commitments to Husayn. British intelligence officers equated Husayn with Arab nationalism, overlooking the more complex composition of that movement. But unlike Arab nationalists, Zionists would continue to persuade British officials about the merits of their movement. Cooperation with Zionist intelligence was key to Britain's early hold over Palestine.

CHAPTER 2

Intelligence, Policy, and the Emerging Modern Middle East

British decision makers viewed the League of Nations mandate as the best way to secure their rule in Palestine—a new strategic foothold. Interpreting the political allegiances and identities of Palestinian Arabs was one of Britain's main challenges before and during the mandate period. These interpretations impacted the shaping of the mandate itself. Unfortunately, political habits predating British rule sometimes masked the intentions of Palestinian leaders. One report stated, "In the words of one notable at Nablus, 'We are a polite nation, and we tell the young government Officials what we think they wish to hear. If they had a better knowledge of our customs and language they might get more out of us.'"[1] Indeed, cultural barriers could be bridged through close relations, both overt and secret, which Zionist intelligence facilitated during these early years.

Intelligence first shaped British policy, and its implementation, from the end of the First World War through the fallout from the 1920 Nabi Musa riots in Jerusalem, when Arab-Jewish tensions escalated into fighting, injury, and death. As the bubble of Anglo-Zionist-Arab relations burst, British intelligence was charged with enforcing British interests despite the emerging conflict. Anglo-Arab relations became more confrontational, and in response, the Zionist intelligence partnership found new purpose. Weizmann capitalized on Zionist intelligence contributions to British security during 1919–20. He tied Zionist intelligence work to British gains, and considered

Britain's support for Zionist immigration and settlement in Palestine to be quid pro quo. British decision makers agreed, and enshrined their protection of the Zionist policy in international law through the League of Nations mandate. This achievement was the basis of Anglo-Zionist relations until 1939 and was the most significant milestone for Zionism on its path to Jewish statehood.

Intelligence officers who had served under Field Marshal Allenby during the conquest of Palestine took on key administrative positions in the military government, or the Occupied Enemy Territory Administration (OETA; the OETS, the Occupied Enemy Territory Administration—South, governed Palestine). Through smoke and mirrors, they helped to secure League of Nations approval for British rule in Palestine. They created three interconnected illusions for the peace conference: First, Zionists and Arabs would cooperate with British leadership. Second, British rule brought security and stability. Finally, British rule was welcomed by the population. Three measures supported these illusions: the Feisal-Weizmann agreement, security intelligence, and censorship.

Britain's future possession of Palestine depended on the acquiescence of the peace conference. British, French, and US war aims came to include Wilson's Fourteen Points. By the end of the war, Germany's overseas empire and large swaths of Ottoman territory were occupied by the victorious powers. Yet they had championed liberal war aims, including the rights of small nations to self-determination, an impartial adjustment of all colonial claims, and the establishment of a League of Nations to settle disputes. The victorious powers could not annex new colonies, but instead had to take on international trusteeships, or mandates, which would guide small nations to self-government. Internationalization made sense to the British and US delegations, but the French demanded Syria as a prize for the war. This demand could unravel the mandate system, as could Arab objections to French rule. Britain needed a US ally at Paris, and Weizmann helped them secure Wilson's sympathy. However, throughout 1919, US interest in the problem dwindled as the French and British asserted their colonial interests. Mandates ultimately resembled colonies with some international oversight.[2]

That outcome was unexpected. During December 1918 and January 1919, British strategy assumed that US support for a British mandate over Palestine was vital. In advance of the conference, at Gilbert Clayton's instigation, Weizmann and Feisal met again. Overstating the case, Weizmann cabled the Zionist Commission in Tel Aviv about his successful encounter with Feisal: "[Feisal] assured Weizmann that he would not spare any effort to support Jewish demands at [the] Peace Conference where he would declare that

Zionism and Arab movement were fellow-movements and complete harmony prevailed between them."[3] In fact Feisal's support was conditional on the fulfillment of his own case and seemed instead to support British demands at Paris more than those of Weizmann.[4]

Their written agreement was used as evidence that Arab self-government and the Zionist policy could be reconciled. Louis Mallet, Britain's prewar ambassador in Constantinople who was attached to the British delegation in Paris in 1919, watched Weizmann work his magic with Wilson in Paris, and encouraged the FO to champion the Zionist policy as a reward, and because of the same prejudicial beliefs about Zionist influence discussed in the previous chapter.[5] Disillusioned with the French delegation, Weizmann and Wilson bonded as they disparaged France's position on Palestine and the mandate system. Wilson promised to support Weizmann at Paris. Arnold Toynbee, an undersecretary at the FO, minuted, "If the President's mood is that described by Dr. Weizmann, the present moment is very favorable for securing his sympathy for the British case in the Middle East."[6] Britain had Wilson's and Feisal's support. The Feisal-Weizmann accord also helped counter French suspicion about British ambitions, as T. E. Lawrence helped Feisal prepare his case in Paris.[7]

Although Britain and France tussled over policy at first, cooperation was the rule. In March 1919, David Lloyd George conceded a Syrian mandate to France, while the FO held that "no one contests France's right to rule in Syria."[8] Meanwhile, before the peace conference or the League of Nations had approved of any Middle Eastern mandates, the British Army began to hand Syria to the French. The withdrawal was methodically planned and coordinated.[9] Borders were settled through negotiations between the British and French general staffs.[10] One of the British negotiators during that process, Col. (later Brig.) Walter Gribbon, who had been part of the Arab Bureau, handled the Zionist spy ring NILI, a Hebrew acronym for "Netzach Yisrael lo yishaqer," from 1 Samuel 15:29, meaning "The eternity of Israel will not lie." He prioritized British interests, which he thought were aligned with those of the Zionists. Although he admired Feisal, he did not think the Arab kingdom worth defending. Feisal's family was showing weakness in Syria, but also in Hejaz against the expansion of 'Abd al-'Aziz ibn Sa'ud and his Wahhabi Ikhwan followers. The Arab movements in Syria were hostile to Britain and France, so Gribbon thought that Britain "need not be too respectful of their feelings." In the pursuit of British interests, Gribbon argued, "It will be seen that the Zionist question drops out and merely becomes a matter for adjustment as between the Jews and Arabs behind the British line."[11] There, Zionism would help Britain control Palestine, and could be handled independently of Arab demands. Feisal showed weakness. Intercepted communications revealed to Gribbon and his colleagues that Feisal ordered his forces to raise arms and prepare for battle, even as he reached short-term agreements with the French.[12] This intelligence convinced British officers not to exceed their previously agreed-on support for Feisal.

Meanwhile, the Feisal-Weizmann charade achieved its purpose; the prospect of reconciling Zionists and Arab nationalists enabled Britain to secure its interests in the Middle East during the Paris peace negotiations. British officers calculated that partnership with Zionist colonists would be worth more than upholding Feisal's kingdom in Damascus against France's wishes. However, other issues could have torpedoed British control. Revolutionary violence threatened to convince the peace conference that the locals resisted British rule, which might have put the mandatory system in jeopardy.

Intelligence, Peace, and War

As the OETA improved its grip on Palestine, British intelligence became increasingly dependent on its Zionist counterparts, continuing cooperation that began in 1915. The main source of intelligence cooperation were survivors of the NILI spy ring, run by the Aaronsohn family of Zichron Ya'akov, and an important part of Zionist history and mythology.[13] Alongside the Aaronsohns were Joseph Davidescu and Liova Shneerson, both decorated by Britain for their service.[14] Although the NILI ring was broken by the Ottoman security service, its remnants served the military governor of Jaffa during the final year of the First World War by running the Jewish Bureau. Alex Aaronsohn was employed within the intelligence staff of the EEF from 1918 to 1919, when he ran an Arab intelligence network. He was decorated for his work, which served dual purposes for the British and the Zionists. From 1919 he served in the General Staff Intelligence (GSI) of the British Camel Corps in Aleppo.[15] His brother Aaron served with the ZC delegation to Paris in early 1919, until his death in a plane crash in May of that year. On their journey to Palestine in March–April 1918, Aaron Aaronsohn and Weizmann discussed the need to establish a Jewish secret service.[16]

By the end of 1918, Liova Shneerson had developed a scheme with Vladimir (Ze'ev) Jabotinsky, a founding member of the Jewish battalions of the British Army. Once a roommate and close collaborator of Weizmann, Jabotinsky would leave the Zionist executive in March 1919 and oppose his policy. According to Shneerson's plan, Zionist intelligence could operate in Palestine and Syria for both British and Zionist needs. Its purpose was overlapping, without conflict of interest: the organization would examine the possibility of acquiring lands, and survey Arab politics and affairs and their relationship to Zionism and Britain. It would serve the ZC, and share intelligence with the British government.[17] This plan was the basis for the first Yishuv intelligence service, the Information Bureau (IB), which was headed mainly by members of NILI and the Jewish Bureau.

Here, and throughout the mandate period, ideological and partisan divisions plagued attempts within the Yishuv to develop intelligence and defense organizations. The socialist HaShomer (The Guard) organization offered itself to Weizmann as a source of intelligence on Arab movements opposed to Zionism. Alex Aaronsohn, Joseph Davidescu, and other prewar immigrant families tended to prefer independence from the institutional organs of the Zionist movement, and returned to British service. Such intransigence was noticed by the governor, Maj. Gen. Sir Arthur Wigram Money, who reported that although his ZC interlocutors were reasonable, they were managing a "difficult team, or rather a number of opposing teams," over which they exercised little control. Weizmann had to manage socialists, Jabotinsky's militant followers, and the independent-minded former NILI members.[18]

Despite this friction, Zionist intelligence officers monitored and analyzed the MCS and PAC. They were Britain's main source of information on Arab matters; documents in Israeli and British archives demonstrate that British reports were authored by Zionist intelligence or at least based on their analyses. For example, the text of Alex Aaronsohn's summary of the first PAC closely aligns with British military intelligence coverage of that event. However, the lead British officer in Jerusalem, J. N. Camp, attributed anti-British resolutions at the congress to French propaganda, while Aaronsohn emphasized the role of secret societies in promoting anti-Jewish feeling. He indicated that Britain should pay more attention to the youth, who were organizing extremist measures, mainly under the secret society Ikha wal-'Afaf (Brotherhood and Purity)—which, according to Yoav Gelber, "operated according to the direct instructions of the Literary Forum and caused most of the problems. . . . Trouble could break at any moment and unexpectedly even by the instigators themselves." A violent outbreak was expected immediately after the peace conference.[19] Both Aaronsohn and Camp noted the rising influence of the Nadi and Muntada.[20]

Aaronsohn's perspective came from his encounters while based in Aleppo. His source, Farid Pasha al-Yafi, discussed emerging nationalist movements, especially the "Parti des jeunes nationalistes," a clear reference to al-Fatat. Farid, a Damascus notable, had opposed the CUP, and was imprisoned for most of the war. His fearful reports of al-Fatat and the Nadi considered their leadership to be chauvinists, "drunk with independence. . . . The party also is made of countryside notables, journalists, and does not cease to propagate its ideas throughout the population." These people had formed the central Nadi in Damascus, which sought independence in all Arab countries, and cooperation with the CUP.[21]

Aaronsohn described the cooperative work of the Arab associations and their connections with Sherif Feisal's army in Syria. Other members of the IB, such as Shneerson, highlighted divisions that emerged at the first PAC in February 1919. Shneerson indicated frustration with the British military government, particularly Ronald Storrs in Cairo. He attributed the rise of Arab movements to British encouragement, and reported that Storrs had used an Arab agent to foment division at the first PAC. This probably derived from Zionists' frustration with British officers who had developed misgivings about the Zionist policy.[22]

Yet despite these petty quarrels within and between Zionist and British intelligence, this cooperation proved invaluable as it prevented organized nationalist violence from occurring in Palestine during 1919, even as it exploded in Egypt and Syria. Clayton warned the FO that anti-Zionist propaganda led Muslims and Christians to fear that Jews would receive political and economic advantage at the peace conference. Strangely, Zionist propaganda directed at Jewry contributed to those fears even though the intention was simply to create more Zionist immigrants. Clayton wrote, "There are considerable grounds for belief that anti-Jewish riots are being prepared in Jerusalem, Jaffa and elsewhere. Precautions are being taken but an announcement that Jews will be given any special privileges might precipitate outbreak."[23] Such violence might have embarrassed Britain at the peace conference and jeopardized its claim to a mandate over Palestine, which rested on the Feisal-Weizmann agreement and the premise that Arabs and Jews needed Britain for development.

The warning originated from Comdt. Angelo Levi Bianchini, a Jewish Italian naval officer and member of the ZC. A polyglot with experience in military liaison, he was Italy's attaché to both Allenby's staff and the ZC, and reported back to the Italian foreign minister. With Alex Aaronsohn, Bianchini built an intelligence network to monitor nationalists in Jerusalem. Importantly, this intelligence was shared with the British.[24] His ties with the ZC brought him closer to British intelligence, but their trust in Bianchini was based not just on that connection, but also on observation of his activities. A report that appears to be based on cable intercepts confirmed that Bianchini sent benign but accurate reports to the Italian Foreign Ministry. It also highlighted his independence, and his role as peacemaker within the quarreling ZC.[25] Robert Szold, an American member of the ZC, forwarded

Bianchini's report about impending disturbances to Weizmann so that he could deliver it to the British Foreign Office. "Some Arabs," Bianchini said, "are very well organised, weapons, signals, leaders are ready, they wait for action against Jews only a signal." Clayton, Money, and Storrs feared a massacre after the peace conference. Szold added that all the reports "confirm an increasingly alarming situation with bloodshed threatened."[26]

After receiving the warning, Major General Money placed a British battalion in Jerusalem and warned Arab notables, including the future mufti, Amin al-Husseini, against any subversive activity. The leadership would be held responsible for violence.[27] Bianchini's intelligence may have prevented violence coinciding with the Palestinian Nabi Musa (Prophet Moses) Festival in 1919, but the story would be different one year later, as the festival became the setting for the first major Arab-Jewish violence since the armistice.

Although it cannot be known for certain, by preventing revolution, Bianchini and Weizmann likely strengthened Britain's case for a mandate over Palestine against the contesting claims of other delegations and PAC's petitions. Intelligence led the military government to suppress resistance to foreign rule in 1919. Intelligence sharing also led to increased British sympathy for Zionism, despite growing signs that the Arab population was hostile to it. These warnings were also well timed since, in Paris, staff intelligence officers had begun to negotiate borders and administration of mandates with France. Clayton told the FO that "the Palestinians desire their country for themselves and will resist any general immigration of Jews however gradual, by every means in their power including active hostilities."[28] Britain needed to demonstrate that Zionist immigration would not be imposed against the wishes of the population. Since Weizmann's program precluded immediate mass immigration and statehood, Britain's partnership with him became all the more important.[29] Britain's support for Zionism became contingent on Weizmann's leadership, while his influence within the Zionist movement rose dramatically.

Meanwhile, the United States, Italy, and France approved Britain's policy to establish a Jewish national home. Clayton reminded the FO that this development was not without costs: "Unity of opinion among the Allied Governments . . . is not a factor which tends to alleviate the dislike of non-Jewish Palestinians to the Zionist policy."[30] He thought Arabs could be reconciled to Weizmann's moderate program, which emphasized British protection for Jewish colonization and development rather than immediate Jewish autonomy or statehood. Arabs began to lose confidence in Britain, as they realized its policy was constrained by French interests and the Zionist policy.[31] Perhaps to counter this development, in May 1919, Clayton attempted to

revitalize the Weizmann-Feisal accord. Feisal reportedly had told the Arab
congress in Damascus that Arabs and Zionists were compatible. Feisal invited some members of the ZC to Damascus and considered also inviting,
according to Clayton, "a few leading Palestinian Arabs to attend with a view
to rapprochement."[32] Clayton urgently insisted that the Zionists adopt a conciliatory attitude. He and the ZC approached Bianchini to liaise with Feisal.
The attempt to renew Zionist-sherifian relations failed, as Bianchini needed
official Italian approval to act, which the British government preferred not
to pursue. The ZC never sent a delegation. Though Clayton met Feisal himself, his inability to arrange a seemingly simple meeting illustrates the growing complexity of Britain's conflicting policies. Only now, by spring 1919,
was it clear that there was no future for an Arab-Armenian-Jewish combine,
as envisioned by Mark Sykes during the war. Meanwhile, Bianchini worked
in Paris with Col. Richard Meinertzhagen, an avowed Zionist, and then returned to Italy.[33] On his third and final visit to the region in the summer of
1920, at the height of the Franco-Syrian War, brigands hijacked his train to
Damascus. Mistaking him for a French officer, they removed him from the
train and executed him.[34] This valuable intelligence liaison was lost. He could
not have known how his actions during 1918–20 helped to pave the way for
the Jewish national home and the rise of Israel. Unlike most countries, Israel
commemorates its spies when possible. Although he harbored doubts about
Zionism toward the end of his life, there is a small lane in Jerusalem named
for Angelo Levi Bianchini.

While the "Big Five" reached a consensus over Zionism's future in Palestine, the possibility of a British mandate had yet to be guaranteed. Britain's next approach to securing international support for that mandate occurred when a US delegation from the Paris Peace Conference, led by Henry
Churchill King and Charles Crane, toured Palestine and Syria in June 1919
to investigate the wishes of the people regarding the future of their country.
The King-Crane Commission concluded, rightly, that Britain would confront
conflict if it went ahead with the Zionist policy, and that French rule in Syria
would face similar opposition. Its report, which emphasized Arab preference for independence or a US mandate above British or French rule, was
suppressed by the State Department. The mandate was supposed to support
independent government, not substitute for it. The report's findings were
ignored by the newly founded League of Nations, especially as the US Congress resisted Wilson's international entanglements.[35]

Britain had US support for the Balfour Declaration but not for a British
mandate. Censorship helped to convince the commission that British rule in
Palestine was preferable to French rule, and that the region was not ready for

absolute independence, but provisional independence with mandatory support was possible. British officers stage-managed much of the tour. Before and during the commission's visit, British intelligence suppressed the Nadi and Muntada—the leading groups agitating for nationalist representation. Since November 1918, these clubs had exercised their right to free speech, calling for independence, but had also mobilized armed resistance from affiliated secret societies. After the first PAC petitioned the Paris Peace Conference, British delegates downplayed the representativeness of quarrelsome Arab notables. Future administrators would continue this tactic to ignore Palestinian demands.

Immediately following that petition, in February 1919, the military government suspended the rights of the Arab clubs to operate and publish pan-Arab propaganda, which undermined Britain's sherifian policy. Britain and France already had determined that the region would fall under European control, even if Feisal retained his throne in Damascus. Intelligence did not have to work hard to expose differences in the national movement: clan competition obscured the common aims of its factions and provided a pretext for British intervention. The al-Husseini family led the Nadi, while the Nashashibis and Khalidis led the Muntada. After its members stormed an MCS meeting, the Muntada was closed by the OETS. Intercepted mail revealed that the Nashashibis had spied on the al-Husseinis; both plotted to dominate the MCS.[36] This clan competition had a lasting legacy in Palestinian politics.

In May 1919, the military administration consulted intelligence on whether to allow the Muntada and other clubs to reopen. Authorities wanted to allow open discussion, but also to ensure that the clubs did not oppose a British mandate in Palestine or even the mandatory system, which the peace conference had already decided to apply to the whole of the former Ottoman territory. With the King-Crane Commission soon to arrive in Palestine, the military decided to use its leverage over the clubs.

Upon reopening the Muntada, the intelligence officer forced the removal of the sherif's flag (the basis of today's Palestinian and Jordanian flags). Palestinians and Syrians were using it, and Feisal's titular leadership, to promote the independence movement. The military governor of Jaffa reasoned, "Freedom of speech is not understood in this country and the privilege is invariably abused." In another letter he wrote, "Freedom of speech, so innocuous in Europe, is impossible in Eastern countries, and we are only asking for trouble by allowing it."[37] Other clubs were subject to similar draconian, if temporary, measures. Britain suppressed proindependence voices and emphasized divisions in Arab politics that only European supervision could manage fairly. Zionist pronouncements were also suppressed, so as not to affect the US commission or peace conference.[38] These moves were successful.

In August the commission report was issued in secret. It voiced cautious support for a British mandate if a US mandate was impossible. It warned against allowing the Zionist policy to lead to a Jewish state. The US delegation approved the League of Nations' mandate scheme, and Britain planned to limit its military presence in the Middle East and to introduce a civil government. Confident in the outcome of the commission and league discussion, the FO clarified its policy to the OETA on 4 August: there would be a British mandate over Palestine, including the Balfour Declaration, but Arabs would "not be despoiled of their land" and "there is no question of majority being subjected to the rule of minority, nor does Zionist programme contemplate this."[39] The OETA eased censorship restrictions. Intelligence had successfully suppressed opposition that might have inhibited Britain's plans for a mandate in Palestine, and for the implementation of the Zionist policy there. It also had maintained security and paved the way for Britain's strategic aims.

Security Intelligence and the Prospect of Revolution

Britain cautiously tolerated open political societies, but suppressed independence propaganda and monitored secret societies that planned violence. In an August 1919 memo, Camp defined the makeup of the Palestinian national movement, naming the organizations and men, and detailing their backgrounds and aims. He characterized the Muntada as predominantly Muslim and a powerful propaganda society in Jerusalem, connected to the center of Arab propaganda at Damascus.[40] The Jerusalem branch of the Nadi mainly comprised al-Husseinis. Camp wrote that its aim "is about the same as that of the Muntada, but the members of the Nadi are not so radical. That is, they are not so strong on Arab independence, but are just as much opposed to Zionism and Jewish immigration." Important members included Amin al-Husseini, brother to the contemporaneous mufti of Jerusalem, Kamil. "Hajj Amin al-Husseini might be added to the list [of most dangerous members]," Camp noted, "but is by no means so violent and dangerous as the others."[41] In 1919, the al-Husseinis appeared more moderate and less violent than any other leading Palestinians. They also worked closely with Feisal's Damascus government. Seemingly only interested in the power of their clan, from an early stage the al-Husseinis appeared to be the most likely group for collaboration with Britain.

Camp's report also described secret societies such as Ikha wal-'Afaf, which was "composed of the more violent propagandists as leaders of a host of ordinary ruffians and cut-throats. These latter members are expected to do the dirty work for the Muntada and Nadi if and when any needs to be done." Ikha had attempted to stir up trouble among Indian troops, and some of its members had penetrated the army, police, and gendarmerie in Palestine. Parallel to Ikha was Feda'iyeh, formerly known as al-Yad al-Sawda, or the Black Hand, a group of fighters that Camp said were "ready to sacrifice themselves." The Muntada and Nadi had encouraged Ikha and Feda'iyeh to arm themselves. The radicals prepared lists of prominent Jews and pro-Zionist non-Jews, and spread propaganda among Bedouin in Transjordan—"the prospect of Jewish women and loot being held out before them," according to Camp. The societies' agents learned Hebrew in order to monitor Zionists and their press. They had been trying to persuade members of the police and gendarmerie to hand over arms or not to obstruct their efforts in case a revolt occurred.[42] The government closely monitored dangerous persons and interned some of them. The gendarmerie was purged under the guise of reorganization. Since political membership was forbidden to police, many Arab members quit the force, and were replaced with very limited numbers of Jewish police.[43] These measures against the police and gendarmerie, however, did not go far enough to suppress the potential for violence completely.

British officers were aware of the paradox of dealing with subversive nationalists. The army could arrest organizers of the Nadi and Muntada, but this would raise their popularity and damage Britain's. Most importantly, intelligence understood that Clayton's Weizmann-Feisal designs were dead. Camp wrote, "If we mean to carry out any sort of Zionist policy we must do so with military force and adopt a strong policy against all the agitators in the country."[44] Camp thought the Feisal-Weizmann agreement worthless. If the Arab movements discovered it, they would see Feisal as a traitor.

Presciently defining one of Britain's great dilemmas throughout the mandate, Camp believed that open societies would work clandestinely through armed organizations to resist Zionist immigration. This intelligence was passed to the FO, as Camp's commander, Col. C. French, emphasized that "there is every reason to believe that the facts as stated therein are accurate and unexaggerated and they may be taken as indicative of the widespread antagonism and organisation against the Zionist programme."[45] Intelligence had acknowledged the emerging conflict, and anticipated violence. Arab nationalists never would accept Zionism, and failed to reshape pro-Zionist policies emerging at the league. The Feisal-Weizmann agreement had not been designed to pacify nationalists, but just to persuade the peace conference to approve of a British mandate in Palestine. Britain would have to forcefully impose its policy against the will of Arab nationalists.

Zionist cooperation contributed to Camp's report, which aligns closely with material found in the Alex Aaronsohn and Zionist intelligence papers.[46] Yet British officers had begun to see the contradiction between the Zionist policy and their aim to hold Palestine. During the autumn of 1919, British intelligence cooperation with Zionists declined. OETA officers such as Col. M. Watts Taylor, assistant adjutant and quartermaster general to army headquarters in Haifa, expressed worry about Arab-Zionist conflict, pointing to Weizmann's "miscalculation" of Arab tolerance for the Zionist policy. The general staff also worried about declining intelligence cooperation, saying, "The Zionist Commission have in Jerusalem a very efficient contre-espionnage service and I suggest that their reports have either not been sent home or ignored as alarmist."[47] Zionist intelligence continued to warn about the activities of Ikha wal-'Afaf and Feda'iyeh, and the roles played by the Arab clubs, Feisal, and the Turkish nationalist leader Mustafa Kemal in supporting them. British intelligence also monitored these activities, but focused instead on the regional picture and how those activities might impact emerging conflict in Syria, Cilicia, and Anatolia.

British security intelligence needed to address issues across the entire region. For example, naval intelligence reported on relations between nationalists in Syria and Palestine, who were thought to be organizing simultaneous disturbances along the lines of the Wafdist independence revolt in Egypt. Naval intelligence reported on a Muslim-Christian rapprochement underway in Jaffa, with anti-Zionism forming the "bond of union."[48] Such reports were meant for consumption by the Foreign and War Offices, as well as officers in Constantinople, Baghdad, and Cairo. The reports affected the OETA's cooling attitude toward the Zionists, but largely were seen as indications of a broader regional trend of transnational anti-imperial violence. British officers saw this Muslim-Christian rapprochement in Jaffa as part of pan-Arab propaganda that sought to bolster Feisal's leadership. They did not consider that it could lead to armed resistance in Palestine, as intelligence officers were more concerned with Feisal's ability to prevent open conflict between his movement and France, or Mustafa Kemal's influence over the Arab movements.

British intelligence and policymakers began to conceive of this transnational underground activity as a Syrian, anti-French movement. Anti-British propaganda was blamed on French intrigue rather than on any genuine anti-imperialist feeling among Arab nationalists. Intelligence focused on questions of Britain's future policy, the form of government to be established in Baghdad, and the growing chaos in Syria. The issue of Arab opinion on Zionism returned when on 8 March 1920 the PAC and MCS joined the Syrian

Arab Congress in proclaiming Feisal the king of Syria and Palestine. Peaceful demonstrations were held across Syria and Palestine in support of Feisal and against the Jewish national home. This "recrudescence in anti-Zionism," according to a memo, had been attributed to "outside intrigues." French propaganda, it was suspected, was attempting to co-opt Feisal's role as titular Arab or Muslim ruler in order to exert French influence in Mesopotamia and Palestine and to undermine Britain's standing.[49]

Naturally, the WO found the rapidly evolving situation difficult to appreciate, and with troops withdrawn from Syria, the most important source of intelligence was lost. It asked headquarters, recently established in Constantinople with Britain's largest intelligence station on Islamic matters, to investigate events in Turkey, Cilicia, and Syria and to submit weekly reports.[50] Meanwhile intelligence, probably sigint, confirmed suspicions about French propaganda: "[The French] state the only reason they remain [in Syria] is because British do so [in Palestine] and that they recognize they are not wanted by the people. They will, whilst recognizing Feisul, claim their zone if British remain."[51] Other officers such as Meinertzhagen blamed France for anti-British propaganda.[52] All ignored the nationalists' motivations for resisting British and French imperialism.

Feisal's weak control over the parties, and his inability to prevent French encroachment from Lebanon, led to war in 1920. The political divisions in Damascus spilled into Palestine, where clan competition further obscured the picture for intelligence officers. Palestinian members of the Nadi were alienated from the pan-Syrian Hizb al-Watani (National Party; also appears as Difa'a al-Watani, or National Defense), which wavered between support for Feisal and desire for revolution. The Nadi, especially the al-Husseini family, expected independence and confrontation with the great powers and so continued to organize for revolution.[53]

British assessments also were prejudiced by their tendency to focus on notables and other literate activists, while only vaguely mentioning the roles of peasants or workers. In 1918, Clayton had assumed the Zionist policy would be embraced by peasants for the economic improvement they could enjoy, and rejected by the educated classes who feared progress. By 1919, his tone had changed. He warned after the first PAC that all classes were anti-Zionist, but added that elites and especially landholders should be considered the representative leadership.[54] Ironically, he and British policymakers told Palestinians and the League of Nations the exact opposite. The next chapter shows how this aimed to limit Palestinian claims for self-government.

Palestinians had their own solutions to class division and representation. For example, Amin al-Husseini and his cousin Jamal were active propagandists among villagers. They read the news aloud in public spaces and discussed politics. This was an important means for political communication until radio became more widely available during the 1930s. Through print and broadcast, the literate wielded authority and influence over peasants who depended on them for news, and often their livelihoods.[55] The peasants, in turn, provided mass support for notable politicians and their politics.

The Zionist Information Bureau observed this kind of activity, noting that in their news reports, notables focused on the simmering rebellion in Syria, politics in Damascus, and the conflicts in Cilicia, Iraq, the Caucasus, and Syria against Western empires. Their news concluded, "These are good tidings and may God give victory to the heroes, and we will know what we must do to the Jews and British."[56] Such evidence likely was interpreted as reflecting a widespread conspiracy for revolution. While it specifically pointed to Palestine's connection to the wider conflict, it was not likely seen as a direct warning of events to come. Intelligence monitored this form of mass mobilization and communication in a largely illiterate society, but did not credit peasants with political agency.

The OETA overlooked the potential for explosion in Palestine. Anti-imperialism appeared to be targeting France in Syria, and any Christian power in Anatolia and Cilicia. In Syria, nationalists had made gains against France's initially weak positions. At Tel Hai, close to the Lebanese border with Palestine, Lebanese Mutawalli Shia fighters engaged the Jewish settlers while looking for French soldiers. The skirmish produced one of Zionism's early martyrs, Joseph Trumpeldor. In the aftermath, the British consul concluded, "There seems to have been nothing political in this affair which was an act of pure brigandage."[57] Even if Tel Hai was as apolitical as reported, this comment illustrates how British officers believed Palestine was isolated from nationalist revolution elsewhere.

British decision makers had access to good intelligence on the Arab and Turkish movements, but these assessments differed from those of Alex Aaronsohn. He thought that resurgent nationalist propaganda, Feisal's coronation, and the organization of armed groups in Syria would spark an outbreak in Palestine. British observers, focused on great but distant problems in Cilicia and Anatolia, overlooked local dangers. Intelligence centered on how this violence might affect France's position, or Mustafa Kemal's growing power. It was difficult to see how events in Turkey, Syria, and Iraq would affect Palestine, or how France's weakness in Cilicia and the Levant would encourage revolutionaries in Palestine. Confusion also stemmed from the fact that, as Aaronsohn wrote, "during [the past] two years there was no proper organisation in the Arab movement. Though there have been some centers . . . the entire movement is internal and that of Palestine in particular received the shape of an intrigue conducted by single individuals for their own benefit."[58] Violence exploded in Jerusalem against the background of competition between clans, class, and party. These divisions masked true cooperation under the Arab nationalist banner.

The Nabi Musa Riots, 4–7 April 1920

Yehoshua Porath argues that Feisal's coronation and the associated nationalist activity started the path to violent conflict.[59] Between 4 and 8 April, the Nabi Musa riots took five Jewish and four Muslim lives, and left 251 injured.[60] The OETS lost control over Jerusalem, as it did not deploy enough force to manage the crowds. Some policemen joined the violence. Others were left impotent as the mob looted their barracks and stores. Troops were not deployed until thirty-six hours after the situation had spun out of control.

British military intelligence possessed the necessary evidence to predict the danger, but it only put the pieces together after the riots, when the role of the Nadi became clear. On 15 April, SIS—the British foreign intelligence service—reported on a captured letter written by Mustafa Kemal during March 1920 that firmly established the role of the Nadi, "a club of Damascene and Palestinian nationalists which plays the same role in Arabia as the committee of union and progress does in Turkey." The memo noted that Kemal had subsidized Arab nationalist newspapers, and coordinated propaganda with 'Izzat Darwaza and the Nadi. Kemal allegedly reported that "the operations undertaken at several points by the French military commanders, although they have acted with prudence and moderation compared with the British in the occupied territories, have been the cause of preparations for an Arab revolt, which is already feared." He described the allegiance of tribal chiefs to nationalist forces as proof that "the movement carried out in the name of Islam finds sympathy in the Arab countries which are under foreign rule. The task of the Nationalists is greatly eased thereby."[61] While Kemal would become an enemy of pan-Islam by 1924, in 1920 he exploited it to strengthen Turkish and Arab nationalists fighting foreign occupation. His views illustrate the mutable and confusing relationship between pan-Islam and pan-nationalism.

Hajj Amin al-Husseini would eventually become a central node in both pan-Islamic and Arab nationalist networks. In late March 1920, he returned to Jerusalem from a mission to Damascus on behalf of the Nadi and reported optimism in that city. He believed Britain favored handing Syria to Feisal, which would happen without war: "The Damascus government receives large sums of money and starts to organise the whole of United Syria. In case the French refuse to leave the Lebanon, then Feisal is going to send a strong Army, guns and new aeroplanes which arrived lately; then no French soldier will remain within 24 hours on the soil of Syria."[62] At Nabi Musa, al-Husseini electrified the crowd, holding Feisal's portrait from the balcony of the Nadi and exclaiming, "This is your king!"[63] Al-Husseini was joined by many notables who also gave incendiary speeches. Their expectations were reasonable, given that even the Paris Peace Conference had reinforced faith in the Arab kingdom.

Zionist intelligence records contain a verbatim account of a meeting held before Nabi Musa between Ronald Storrs, Jamal al-Husseini, 'Aref al-'Aref, Fakhri Nashashibi, and others. It illuminates Storrs's trust in the notables' ability and willingness to control their followers. Meanwhile, 'Aref al-'Aref, editor of the Nadi mouthpiece, *Suriyya al-Janubiyya* (Southern Syria, or Palestine), had returned to Palestine from Damascus. His newspaper was receiving paper supplies from Syria, perhaps funded by Kemal. However, al-'Aref opposed violent revolution. Seemingly aware of what was to come, he attended an all-party meeting hosted by the Muntada and demanded steps to ensure that British and Zionists were neither attacked nor even insulted. No arms should be carried in the Nabi Musa procession.[64] On the eve of Nabi Musa, he warned that disturbances, especially anti-Jewish violence, would bring disaster. "We shall ruin our future by our own hands," he said.[65]

On 2 April 1920, Jerusalem celebrated Good Friday, Passover eve, and the beginning of the Nabi Musa festival. Storrs had requested that the notables prevent the religious procession from becoming a political demonstration. However, that is precisely what happened, as nationalist hymns were sung and flags were flown. Some sixty to seventy thousand people participated in the procession. 'Aref al-'Aref implored leaders of the other Arab clubs, "My Brethren, we are exposed to a danger if anyone of us ventures to cause disorder or exclamations, and I therefore ask you to safeguard order."[66] It was too late. Tensions boiled over on Sunday, 4 April.

Administrators possessed contradictory assessments, from a variety of their own and Zionist sources, suggesting that nationalist violence would be aimed at France in Syria, and that secret societies were planning simultaneous revolts in Palestine, Egypt, Iraq, and Syria. These assessments also assumed that the national movements in Palestine, Syria, and Iraq were unrelated. Few observers considered the coordination of various Nadi branches in advance of Nabi Musa as evidence of a widespread threat against all armies occupying the Middle East. What unfolded was a loosely organized attempt to coordinate revolution simultaneously against all colonial powers. Arab attacks against French forces had occurred sporadically for months, organized in November 1919 and early 1920 by the Nadi, seemingly with Mustafa Kemal's encouragement. 'Izzat Darwaza later confirmed that Nadi branches in Syria coordinated this attempt.[67]

The failure of this anticolonial revolution only became clear to the Nadi and the Muntada at the end of April 1920, after a skirmish at Semakh, on the Haifa–Dera'a rail link, near the southern tip of the Sea of Galilee. Bedouin attacked British troops and the train and telegraph lines. Indian cavalry and RAF aircraft retaliated, defeating a much larger attacking Arab force. Arab propaganda about this campaign caused inflated expectations in Jerusalem. Aaronsohn's intelligence reports reveal that the Nadi and the Muntada in Jerusalem and Haifa heard rumors of an Arab victory at Semakh, where Indians allegedly joined Bedouin against the British, causing two thousand deaths and thousands more injuries. At the Jerusalem Nadi, it was believed that Arabs fighting at Semakh were supported by the sherif with money, arms, and officers. Some thought it might be British policy to allow a sherifian victory. Such disinformation sought to encourage wider participation in the anticolonial revolution. Zionist intelligence soon reported on plans for revolution, directed from Damascus. When British forces secured the Semakh area, which had been under French administration, the pan-Syrian revolution was over.[68] Feisal disavowed knowledge of it, and promised to punish the offenders, including two of his officers and local governors in Quneitra and Ajlun.[69] Later that summer, a force authorized by Feisal was defeated by the French at Maysalun, ending the Franco-Syrian War and Feisal's government.

After Semakh, Zionist and British intelligence highlighted the connections between the Bedouin who had campaigned in Palestine, and Damascus-based plans for a general revolt, inspired by the Nadi.[70] 'Auni 'Abdul Hadi, a Nablus-born and Paris-educated lawyer, was a founding member of al-Fatat and Feisal's adviser. He rejected any colonial rule. Uncharacteristically, he boasted to a Zionist informant that he and the Nadi inspired the revolution against France, and had mobilized the Bedouin in Palestine. He warned that foreign Zionists risked the lives of Palestine's Jews.[71]

In response to the Bedouin threat, the IB sent officers to Transjordan. They discovered that Bedouin political feeling was mixed and fickle. Joseph Davidescu, disguised as a Bedouin but known to his host, met an amir who had participated in a raid on Givat Ada. He heard Bedouin discussing British military movements in Palestine. The amir had invited Davidescu because he needed help: after the Semakh battle, he had been fined by Feisal and a relative was expelled to Egypt. He sought financial assistance, and asked

Davidescu to repair his relationship with Feisal and Britain. Realizing the benefit the Yishuv could accrue from this sheikh, Davidescu and Shneerson helped him. He only paid half his fine.[72] This action became the seed for future secret diplomacy between Bedouin, Britons, and Zionists, which sought to provide security on both sides of the Jordan River.

The collapse of revolutionary plans exposed the lack of unity among Palestinians. The Nadi plotted to assassinate Fakhri Nashashibi, a leading Muntada member, because of his alleged collaboration with France.[73] (Al-Husseini agents would finally kill him in Baghdad in 1941.) During May 1920, tensions between al-Husseini and Nashashibi were exacerbated when Ragheb Bey Nashashibi was appointed mayor of Jerusalem by the military government. He replaced Musa Kazim, patriarch of the al-Husseini clan. Meanwhile Hajj Amin and 'Aref al-'Aref were now fugitives living in exile in Damascus.

Suspicious of the notables, 'Aref began to organize a labor party made up of Jerusalem merchants, who were irritated that they were forced by organizers of the demonstration to close their shops during Nabi Musa—an unusual step with so many visitors in town. The organizers hoped to swell the number of demonstrators. Resentful, 'Aref promised to organize a countrywide labor movement that would deprive the notables of their power over the merchant class.[74] He was held responsible for the Nabi Musa riots, although all evidence showed that he tried to prevent them. After being pardoned, 'Aref joined the civil service.

Emerging Anglo-Zionist Cooperation and Competition

After the 1920 riots, Aaronsohn prepared a paper that described the administration's responsibility for failing to prevent the strife. He appended the evidence that had been provided to the OETA about Arab secret societies and their penetration of police and gendarmerie, and concluded, "We have given sufficient evidence time and again to cause the arrest of at least half of the local Arab police but the intelligence and the police ignored the evidence."[75] The crackdown on nationalists during the previous summer had not gone far enough to guarantee security. The Nabi Musa riots convinced Aaronsohn and the Zionists that Britain, having achieved its political aims in the region, must reaffirm its commitment to Jews in Palestine.

Zionist relations with the OETA broke down over the Nabi Musa riots. Claims by Aaronsohn and Zionists about British maladministration are hard to confirm. Repeating statements from Richard Meinertzhagen's diary, published in 1959, Isaiah Friedman argues that Bertie Harry Waters-Taylor, chief

of staff of the OETS, deliberately allowed the riots to occur.[76] The Meinertzhagen diary, however, is a demonstrably unreliable source.[77] No docu-
mentary evidence supports this simplistic explanation. In fact, Allenby fired
Meinertzhagen for insubordination, and Waters-Taylor used the documen-
tary record to defend his actions. Recognizing that Feisal was being pulled
between commitments to his family, the nationalists, and the peace conference, Waters-Taylor (perhaps uselessly) warned Feisal that he should keep
some distance from the revolutionaries, whose violence would threaten the
Syrian throne.[78]

Zionists were frustrated with the OETA for not fulfilling the Balfour Declaration, for preventing a nascent Jewish militia from acting during the violence, and for arresting its leader, Jabotinsky. They accused British officials
of allowing a pogrom against the Yishuv. The OETA responded that the civil
administration must fulfill the Balfour Declaration, and admitted its shortcomings during the riots. Privately, however, the chief administrator of the
OETS, Maj. Gen. Louis Bols, previously a supporter of Weizmann's policy,
expressed his misgivings about the ZC, which he thought should be abolished. He described its large parallel administration, about the same size as
his own, which he said made his job "impossible." Jews ignored his regime
in favor of the ZC, he said, while Muslims and Christians "can only see that
privileges and liberties are allowed to the Jews which are denied to them."
The ZC, Bols continued, was disobedient, "hostile, critical and abusive." It
could not be convinced of "British good faith and ordinary honesty," and
sought preferential treatment under the law. Bols complained that where it
was the majority, the ZC wanted to take over the law, but elsewhere it sought
government protection.[79]

While the OETA called for the disbandment of the ZC and the Jewish battalions that composed the new defensive militia, Zionists, including former
home secretary Herbert Samuel, advocated an end to military administration.[80] The latter won; at the San Remo conference in April 1920, which finalized plans for the mandatory division of the Middle East under the League
of Nations and incorporated the text of the Balfour Declaration into the
Palestine Mandate, the failure of the OETA was evident. The San Remo conference created two pressures on Britain: to establish a civil government in
order to promote stability in Palestine, and to make good on the Balfour
Declaration. These pressures explain the hasty appointment of a Zionist
Jew as the first high commissioner (HC) in Palestine.[81] Lloyd George tapped
Samuel, an old friend, for the post, starting on 30 June.

His appointment caused great change. Meinertzhagen told Weizmann that
military administration was in an uproar, and that he considered "Samuel's

appointment the culminating victory of a series which started really with the sad events of April 4th."[82] He overstated British trust in the Zionists. Intercepted Zionist cables throughout June 1920 revealed their activities to raise funds, to convince the British government to retain the Jewish battalions, and to secure the freedom of Jabotinsky, imprisoned for preparing an armed defense of the Jewish quarter in Jerusalem during Nabi Musa. Weizmann asked the ZC to maintain discipline in Palestine and to prevent demonstrations during the final hours of the handover to Samuel's administration. As growing Franco-Syrian violence threatened security in Galilee, the army promised to deploy troops and even to arm Jewish colonists with two hundred rifles. Weizmann guided the Yishuv through a very tense month and proved his influence over the population, which had been in a rebellious mood. The intercepts confirmed the Zionists' reliability as partners who did not seek to undermine British rule. Yet the cables misinterpreted an important development. They took the Hebrew word *gedud*, meaning battalion, to mean the "Central Zionist Committee," when it probably referred, in code, to Jabotinsky's defense committee, composed of soldiers of the Jewish battalions. The British missed the fact that these cables revealed preparations and fundraising for the defense of outlying settlements, especially in Galilee.[83]

Measured confidence returned to Anglo-Zionist relations, despite disagreements over how to interpret the Balfour Declaration. Zionist intelligence cooperation had helped to create the mandate. The Feisal-Weizmann agreement, orchestrated by Clayton, convinced the peace conference that a British mandate was possible and that Arab and Zionist interests were reconcilable, especially with British guidance. Britain censored the Nadi and the Muntada to prevent them from undermining Britain's claim over Palestine. From then until the Nabi Musa riots, intelligence missed key signals warning of danger. Even though British and Zionist intelligence held mostly the same data about Arab politics in the region, they looked at events differently. Neither predicted that Nabi Musa would be a forum for nationalist activity that might become violent. Only Alex Aaronsohn foresaw how events in Syria could inspire a revolution in Palestine. Zionist intelligence was concerned mainly with Yishuv security, while British intelligence focused on Feisal, and France. After Nabi Musa, the Yishuv demanded independent security and distrusted British officers. This trust was restored with the appointment of Samuel and the San Remo announcement. What emerged was a cyclical pattern in which intelligence cooperation was always conditioned by, and always influenced, the Anglo-Zionist partnership. Despite the mutual mistrust that emerged during the military administration, this partnership remained at the heart of British policy until 1939. The same cannot be said for Anglo-Arab relations.

CHAPTER 3

Cause for Peace

The Establishment of a Civil Government

Tensions in the region never were far from the surface. The violence that unfolded in Jaffa during May 1921, taking forty-seven Jewish and forty-eight Arab lives and wounding hundreds more, resulted from a May Day parade originally led by Zionist Socialists. Communist counterdemonstrators forced the assembly out of the Jewish suburb of Tel Aviv toward Jaffa. The police attempted to disperse the crowd, and Muslims and Christians from Jaffa "rushed to help the police against the Jews," according to the Information Bureau.[1] Violence became deadlier, escalating with revolvers and dynamite; funerals during subsequent days became scenes for renewed clashes. The Haganah, founded by the Labor Federation (the Histadrut) in December 1920 to organize the Yishuv's defensive militias, called the remnant of the wartime "First Judeans" battalion to Jaffa. About thirty soldiers arrived on the second day of the riots, further exciting tensions. On the third day, martial law was declared and the Arab police who had participated in the violence were disarmed, as were Jewish soldiers.

This was not a localized urban disturbance. Troops, police, and aircraft had their hands full fighting violence that expanded to other Jewish settlements such as Petah Tikva, Kfar Saba, and Rehovot, and then on to Arab villages, especially Ramleh and Tulkarm, where false rumors of atrocities brought tensions out into the open. According to General Staff Intelligence (GSI), at the beginning of the disturbance, the Palestine administration "did not take the matter seriously, and Zionists have always pretended that the [Bolshevik] movement was of no importance."[2] The administration was indeed surprised, although the response was far swifter and decidedly harsher than during the disturbances of 1920.

There were significant, long-term implications to Britain's military and political responses to the violence. The Communist and Arab nationalist threats that caught British security short came into focus. The Bolshevik threat was annihilated with Zionist help. Anglo-Zionist intelligence cooperation strengthened as the CID relied on Zionist staff for the Communist section. Zionist and British officers conducted a psychological warfare campaign that aimed to undermine the Executive Committee of the Palestine Arab Congress (ECPAC) by funding its opponents. This was less successful than the anti-Bolshevik campaign, but still strengthened the pattern of cooperation and dependency that had developed since the war.

Whereas Bolshevism was treated as a political crime, nationalism was considered a force to be wielded or manipulated. After May 1921, Palestinian leaders ceased violent resistance and instead pursued negotiations. British officers exploited the peace and lengthened those negotiations. Unable to reconcile Palestinians to the Zionist policy, policymakers turned to communal self-government as an alternative to national self-determination. Aiming to neutralize the nationalists, Samuel had appointed Amin al-Husseini as mufti of Jerusalem just before the riots. By the end of 1921, al-Husseini had been granted even more powers as president of the newly created Supreme Muslim Council (SMC). British policymakers in Palestine, London, and Geneva sheltered the Zionist policy from international scrutiny. British authorities pursued constitutional negotiations with Palestinians knowing they had no intention of ever meeting the Arabs' demands. Britain's psychological warfare and empowerment of the mufti divided Palestinian nationalists and capitalized on the peace that prevailed as a result.

The 1921 riots occurred during a process of transformation of intelligence and governance systems as Palestine stabilized following the introduction of civil government. The Zionist policy became enshrined in international law and the text of the mandate, while Palestinian resistance to those developments was—unsuccessfully—pursuing its goals through diplomacy.

In the absence of a strategy to address Britain's contradictory policies, improvised decisions made from 1921 to 1924 had dramatic consequences. Zionist intelligence provided new forms of partnership to the British Mandate, and although immigration faced its first limits, new intelligence capabilities contributed to the increased power of the Labor Zionist parties. Anglo-Zionist codependency increased as well. On the other hand, the new

powers concentrated in the person of Amin al-Husseini made him partner
to British policy. His government authority and popular influence may have
been tied to his partnership with government, but they never displaced his
nationalist ambitions. In the aftermath of the latest round of Jewish-Arab
violence, a zero-sum conflict had emerged, which would have to be managed by the high commissioner and district governors through improvisation. British decision makers in Palestine believed they traded some authority for peace; in reality, they purchased time. Meanwhile, Palestinians resisted
by other means.

British Response to Bolshevism

British perceptions of a Bolshevist threat in Palestine must be seen in the
broader context of that threat from around the world. Threats to democracy were real, but the capabilities and intentions of Bolsheviks were poorly
understood until the mid-1920s. Britain shared concern over Bolshevik agitation with the leading parties of the Zionist movement. Weizmann had long
encouraged British policymakers to think of Zionism as a means to win over
Jewry from the Bolsheviks, as did Jabotinsky, who was the first to suggest so
in 1917 when he advocated for the formation of the Jewish Legion.[3]

The international Zionist Socialist party, Poale Zion (Workers of Zion),
split between Bolsheviks and Social Democrats in 1919. Bolsheviks orga-
nized themselves as Miflaget HaPoalim HaSotsialistim (Socialist Workers
Party, henceforth MPS). The MPS was a constituent member of the Third
International (or Comintern, est. March 1919) and supported the Bolshevik
Revolution. The social-democratic and Zionistic faction, led by David Ben-
Gurion and Yitzhak Ben-Zvi, took the name Achdut Ha'avoda (Labor Unity),
and dominated Zionist politics in Palestine. Using a broad brush to paint all
Jews as Communists, British observers often misunderstood this split, and
overlooked the social-democratic nature of Achdut Ha'Avoda. Yet Zionists
proved reliable opponents to Communists. Socialist Zionist activity in Europe and Palestine became an important source for SIS in its investigations
of the Comintern. Communist parties threatened Achdut's dominance at
the congress of the Histadrut (the trade union federation) in December of
1920. Partnership between Britain, Achdut, and other social-democratic parties revolved around their shared perception of a Communist threat. More
broadly, the Comintern threatened the Zionist objective to found a Jewish
state as it sought to convert Zionists into internationalists.[4]

Britain was less concerned about Communism in Palestine than in Europe or the United Kingdom. Since demobilization began, MI5, fearing

revolutions that rocked Europe, had defended against Communist infiltra-tion in the armed forces, in the workforce, and in British domestic politics.[5] Alarm about Communism in Palestine was first raised in November 1920 by Robert Vansittart, permanent undersecretary to the Foreign Office, in a letter to the foreign secretary, Lord Curzon. French officials complained that Jewish immigration would create "a Bolshevik colony on their flank."[6] This issue complicated border negotiations, but also served as a reminder that Communists could join Jews fleeing Eastern Europe and reach Pales-tine. In February 1921, MI5 passed on information gathered in Cairo stating that the MPS had instigated a strike and other labor agitation in Jaffa. The accurate report described the MPS as a Communist movement that aimed to prepare Palestine for social revolution. It had branches across the coun-try, with three hundred members, although they were "chiefly inexperienced immigrants." The labor troubles had been settled by a conference: "Held at Haifa on December 4th, a 'Federation of Jewish Workmen' [the Histadrut] has been organized in which the moderate labor parties . . . are in an over-whelming majority."[7] There, Achdut and other parties had marginalized the Communists in the Yishuv. Their threat had not receded, but the rise of the Histadrut as a big-tent federation, and its inclusion of the MPS underneath, led to complacency about Communist agitation.

British and Zionist strategy treated Labor Zionism as a bulwark against Bolshevism. An FO minute observed, "The better the progress with colo-nization the less Palestine will have to fear from Bolshevism. The Zionist programme is the best counter-blast to it." Another comment stated that Bolshevism in Palestine was an exaggerated danger.[8] SIS was less complacent than Zionist and British officials in Palestine. During the months leading up to the riots, it had begun to collate data on Bolshevism in Palestine. Some assessments were contradictory, some nonsensical, but many rested on ac-curate data. Reports discussed arms imports to Palestine in preparation for a joint Arab-Jewish uprising, and also covered the propaganda aspect of this problem.[9] In April 1921, surveillance of an MPS meeting in Vienna revealed the Palestine branch's claim to influence 20 percent of Jewish workers in Palestine. SIS concluded that the MPS received constant support from the Comintern, "both in the shape of literature and money." The MPS's popu-larity had reportedly been on the rise, but SIS rightly saw it as weaker in its competition with Achdut Ha'avoda and other non-Comintern parties.[10]

Local authorities were not worried about Communist plots, and were confident that Zionists were dominating Communist influence, or so it seemed. The enmity among the parties increased and British officers saw Zionists as natural allies in the global fight against Communism. Intercepted communications proved that Bolsheviks were persecuting Zionists in Russia. Communists accused Zionists of aligning with anti-Bolshevik movements in Western Europe and Russia, and of running an espionage bureau in Russia on Britain's behalf.[11] Reports about the rise of Labor Zionism under Achdut, and the hostility Zionists showed to Communist parties, led intelligence officers to assume that Zionism was in a stronger position than was true, and to overlook the possibility for violence.

Since the MPS counterdemonstration that had sparked the violence in Jaffa in May 1921, it had become clear that Zionists alone could not suppress Communist revolutionaries. The CID began to reorganize and began to suppress Communism under the leadership of the twenty-four-year-old, Jaffa-born David Tidhar. Under Tidhar, a veteran of the Jewish battalions, the CID hired Zionists who spoke German, Russian, Arabic, and Yiddish. Tidhar's campaign lasted until 1924.

Troubled by the continuing survival of Communist parties, Chief Secretary Gilbert Clayton ordered the CID to watch them closely.[12] In response, the assistant inspector general of the CID summarized its intelligence on Communist leaders in Palestine: "I consider there is, without a doubt, an under current of Bolshevism in Palestine." Clayton admitted that no actual violence had occurred since 1921, and suggested "that the Jewish cooperative Labor Association [the Histadrut], with a vast majority of labor votes, under the leadership of [Yitzhak] Ben Zvi, is strong enough to cope with any opposition it may receive from the communist party."[13]

But it was this sort of complacency that contributed to the surprise outburst in 1921, so the CID became more aggressive. CID surveillance of Communist meetings in 1923 revealed that there was constant reference to ongoing conflict in Europe, and that Arabic Communist publications were being printed in Egypt.[14] Raids led to confiscations of literature, and to improvements in intelligence on membership in the Communist parties.[15]

Intelligence inside and outside Palestine still lacked hard evidence on Russian Bolshevik direction for Communists in Palestine. That evidence was found in May 1924, after a lengthy and careful investigation led to a police raid in Tel Aviv.[16] That in turn prompted surveillance against a suspected Comintern agent in Haifa. Documents found in the suspect's luggage revealed the extent of the involvement of Russian agents and connections to the Berlin-based International Press Bureau. The find helped the CID to uncover the names of the key paid agents of the Comintern in Palestine.[17] By the end of July 1924, after further raids, all Communist leaders were under postal censorship. In early August, the "Fractzia" Club, or workmen's faction, a constituent member of the Histadrut, was raided and closed by Tidhar, and the government considered deporting leaders by the end of the month.[18] However, only a small number of Communists ever faced deportation. The investigation of Communism opened the way to CID-SIS cooperation on Communist intelligence, shared via Clayton.[19] After 1924, Communism did not emerge as a significant problem in Palestine until recession struck in later years. Even then, the labor movement became the key tool for suppressing Communists in both the Yishuv and the Arab labor sector.[20]

By 1924, all key Communist leaders had been either imprisoned, deported, put under surveillance, or censored. The MPS evolved into the Palestine Communist Party (henceforth known by its German initialism, PKP). It was a branch of the Comintern and sought to unite Arab and Jewish workers to replace British rule with an independent Soviet government. The Palestine government reported that the Communist efforts had no "appreciable effect on the main body of Jewish Labor, at which they are mainly directed, still less amongst the Arabs. To the latter, who have not yet entirely abandoned the tribal or patriarchal system of existence, communism, as interpreted by the Russian soviet, appears to be particularly unattractive."[21]

The CID's successful war on Communism, combined with a new and improved intelligence partnership with Zionists, led policymakers to conclude that Britain now controlled the security problems that had plagued the country in May 1921. Their approach to the Arab nationalist aspect of the security problem was different.

British Response to Arab Nationalism

Intelligence was not ignorant about Arab nationalist preparations for revolution before May 1921, and did not show the same complacency that it did in its assessments about Bolshevism. By early 1921 Arab nationalist and pan-Islamic political activity had resurged. Joseph Davidescu reported that Arab armed groups were remobilizing after Churchill snubbed the Muslim-Christian Society (MCS) during his visit to Palestine and Egypt in early 1921. Realizing that its position had weakened, the MCS secretly began to prepare for renewed disturbances. Funds and arms were raised in Beirut, and over two hundred new members of Feda'iyeh were recruited. Typical for the Black Hand, Feda'iyeh began to threaten anyone who would not help, or who supported the Jews. Those under threat turned to Jews for help, to little avail. Zionists only later learned to exploit such situations.[22]

British intelligence received similar warnings in the months leading up to May 1921. A former Turkish governor of Jerusalem informed SIS that Arab nationalists were planning to attack Jews and thus embarrass the British government. He thought the scheme had been suggested by Bolsheviks, who loathed Zionists, and the Jewish section of the Ankara administration enthusiastically received the suggestion.[23] Probably referring to Dönmeler, or crypto-Jews who had converted to Islam, the informant played up notions of a Bolshevik-Jewish-CUP conspiracy with Islamists to undermine Britain, connecting events in Turkey with the Levant and elsewhere. This view fit the preconceptions of British intelligence officers whose assessments about Mustafa Kemal's pan-Islamic propaganda were alarmist but based on real data. Their mistaken views about what John Ferris refers to as a "CUP-Jew-German-Bolshevik" conspiracy, although ludicrous, were based on real evidence tainted by old prejudice.[24] British policy therefore sought to cleave local nationalist movements in Palestine from the broader pan-Islamic movement.

The Mufti

Muslims in Palestine resented Christian British authority over the *awqaf*, or Islamic trusts, so Samuel sought to offer them as much control over the lands and funds as possible. Originally Samuel was not afraid of Muslim opinion,[25] but the events culminating in the 1921 riots convinced him otherwise. By empowering the ʿUlema—Muslim scholars—and appointing an independent mufti to govern Muslim civil life in Palestine, Samuel could signal that Britain was taking steps toward communal self-government. This was not the democratic self-government prescribed by the League of Nations or demanded by Palestinians, but it was enough to mollify an influential family.

The al-Husseinis needed help recovering their social status. From 1918 to 1920, the family had been stripped of nearly all its official positions, including the mayoralty of Jerusalem, but also other posts associated with Feisal in Damascus and the previous Ottoman government. In late 1918 the al-Husseinis had pressed the Damascus government for independence. Consequently, Jevdet Pasha, chief staff officer of the Arab army, had Murad al-Husseini fired from the office of inspector of *awqaf*.[26] In the months before the death of Kamil al-Husseini, other official offices were handed to other families—for example, the Khalidis got chief qadi (judge) of the Shariʿa Court of Appeal.

In early 1921, the al-Husseinis bargained hard with Samuel to reclaim their status. They were the obvious target for co-option. They had aristocratic and Islamic pedigrees, and during the Ottoman period had often held similar high appointments. They did not participate in the Arab delegation to the Cairo conference, which ignored Palestinian lobbying, created an administrative division between Palestine and Transjordan, and cemented British rule in the Middle East. Moreover, thanks to al-Husseini influence, Jerusalem was unaffected by the May 1921 riots. Authorities such as Samuel believed the al-Husseinis could become an alternate power broker to PAC, which had convened for the third time in December 1920 in Haifa. Responding to the third PAC's demands for self-government, Samuel insisted that he could not reverse the Balfour Declaration and would not allow an elected body to do so. He was preparing for municipal elections, but the time was not ripe for a general election. Neither Samuel nor his officers believed that PAC truly represented the interests of the Palestinian public. However, Samuel and Deedes reported to the Foreign Office that they were prepared "to recognize any body of *gentlemen* [read notables] representing any *important* section of the community in the same manner as [Samuel] had already given recognition to the Jewish National Assembly" (emphasis added).[27] The al-Husseinis fit this job description.

Samuel's policy would not satisfy nationalists at PAC, who wanted legislative control, and hoped in vain to influence the 1921 Cairo conference, which determined Britain's future Middle East policy. His strategy to turn to elite families to lead communal self-government worked in the al-Husseinis' favor. They bargained with Samuel to secure the position of mufti of Jerusalem for Hajj Amin, who had only a minor background in religious education, having studied in Cairo under Rashid Rida during 1912–13 but never taken a degree. All of his rivals were qualified 'Ulema. He was not a qualified or likely candidate for the position, yet he was nominated by his family over his more qualified cousin, Tahir, who, scorned, became a Zionist informant. Religious leaders throughout Palestine supported the al-Husseinis for their reputation, their traditional influence and support, and their Arabic and Islamic pedigree, and for the possibility that they might secure Muslim interests from the ruling Christian power.

Contrary to expectations among elite families, the appointment of mufti did not follow Ottoman law. Instead, an ad hoc gathering of 'Ulema proposed four candidates for elections and elected one from among them. An election was held in April, but Hajj Amin came in fourth. In response, his family gathered petitions from throughout Palestine in support of Amin. He was young, and popular for his nationalist organization during 1918–20.[28] This posed a problem for Samuel, who needed to respond to popular demands. The results of the vote were canceled and Samuel appointed Hajj Amin. Wyndham Deedes, who had handled intelligence on Amin's role in organizing the Black Hand and Feda'iyah, resigned as chief secretary in protest of the decision.

Amin had persuaded Samuel and the administration's legal secretary, Norman Bentwich (also a Zionist), of his suitability for the position during a meeting in April 1921. He stated that his influence and that of his family would "be devoted to maintaining tranquility in Jerusalem." He publicly opposed revolt, but preferred to concentrate on fighting the Zionist policy.[29] Hajj Amin was palatable to Samuel, because his proposed authority would rival PAC and weaken that body's demands for self-governing institutions. Jamal al-Husseini, Amin's cousin and confidant, pursued the same strategy in parallel as secretary of PAC's executive committee (ECPAC). As mufti, al-Husseini wielded great influence over Muslim civil life, shaping matters of law, religion, and property. He was head of the 'Ulema, who otherwise would have outranked him. He could keep the title of grand mufti, first bestowed on his brother Kamil, which signified his authority in Palestine, not just Jerusalem.[30]

Simultaneously, Bentwich and the 'Ulema discussed the future of *awqaf* property and its governance in Palestine. In line with Samuel's policy of communal self-government, Bentwich and the government agreed to proposals from the 'Ulema and judges to form an autonomous council to govern *awqaf* and religious law. The 1921 Nabi Musa celebrations passed peacefully only days before the May Day riots. This event proved Amin's promise to Samuel and Bentwich, since Jerusalem had been peaceful while tensions exploded in Jaffa. This paved the way for his role as president of the SMC.

At the end of 1921, elections were held for the presidency of the SMC, although only Ottoman parliamentary electors were entitled to vote. Palestinian elites elected Amin, whose two roles concentrated power, influence, and finance in his official government office. The SMC had a large budget, starting at £50,000, drawn from its properties and, at times, government subsidy. This gave Amin enormous powers of patronage. Illustrating the impossibility of implementing government policy, Deedes wrote to the Colonial Office at the end of 1921 proposing to withdraw the Zionist organization from Palestine back to London, so that the Arab community would stop demanding similar forms of representation.[31] Instead, the government enhanced the authority of the mufti through his election to the SMC; his role as president became official in early 1922.

Despite the government's willingness to work with the mufti, it remained suspicious of him. In his book *The Mufti of Jerusalem*, Philip Mattar overstates the government's trust in the mufti. The British government was satisfied with Amin al-Husseini so long as he kept the peace, but it monitored his political activity. His fundraising trips abroad for the Haram al-Sharif, the Muslim holy site, added to suspicion. In 1923, the Egyptian interior ministry warned Palestine that the mufti was travelling with Mahmoud Kemal ed-Din Bey, a pan-Islamist supporter of Mustafa Kemal, so he was watched while in

Cairo. Egypt warned that his real object was to rouse Muslim opinion on the caliphate, which would be abolished by Mustafa Kemal in 1924 but at the time remained a heated issue in the Islamic world.[32]

SIS reported on the mufti's intense pan-Islamic propaganda in Palestine and elsewhere, noting especially the SMC's fundraising delegation to Hejaz. Hubert Young from the Colonial Office asked Clayton why his reports did not emphasize pan-Islamic plots, whereas SIS reports did. Was SIS exaggerating? Confused, Young pressed Clayton on whether Palestinian politics were driven by pan-Islamic, Turkish Islamic, and nationalist influence, or by Arab nationalism. Palestinian Muslims and Christians were united against Zionism, but "once they leave the common ground of opposition to the Jews does each party pursue secret and conflicting aims which relate more to international politics than to the internal politics of Palestine?"[33]

Clayton answered that SIS was exaggerating, and that "it is the local political issue which really appeals to the people of Palestine but pan-Islamic and pro-Turkish agents are doubtless quick to seize any opportunity of turning any local agitation or discontent to their own purposes." Clayton also concluded that the SMC's Hejaz delegation followed anti-British currents in Mecca, and played along. Palestinians were united against the Zionist policy, Clayton pointed out, since Palestinian movements were "distinctly pro-Arab rather than pro-Turk."[34] CO bureaucrats agreed with Clayton that local issues drove discontent in Palestine, as they had in Iraq during the revolt of 1920. Thus, it would be up to local administrators to manage the situation and keep the peace. Yet in Palestine, the government could not offer the same compromise that it had in Iraq. It had already bartered away much power to the mufti through the SMC, and neither ECPAC nor the Arab congress would agree to participate in representative government so long as the Balfour Declaration remained in force. Clayton and his colleagues could manage this situation, but they would be gone by 1928, and their successors would take a different approach.

Clayton believed the mufti was supporting peaceful conditions within Palestine, even if he agreed on the need to watch him. British authorities began to treat Palestinian nationalists in isolation from the pan-Arab movement. They knew that the mufti could cause trouble and challenge their authority, but they depended on his cooperation. For example, during the Syrian revolt against French rule during 1925–27, usually called the Druze revolt in contemporary British records, security intelligence examined the mufti's relief agency for rebels and exiles based in Transjordan. Intelligence that passed from Palestine to the Colonial Office in 1926 indicated that the mufti accepted support, via the pan-Islamic activist Shakib Arslan, from the German spymaster Max von Oppenheim, who sent medical supplies to the Druze. The Security Service reported that "Haj Amin was in charge of the fund for Druze refugees and considered to be thoroughly bad. The Palestine Authorities think he is more dangerous than Bedus in Trans-Jordan."[35]

Indeed, the mufti's cousin Jamal admitted in 1926 that "we are in direct touch with the rebel headquarters and get their informations [sic] in due time."[36] British intelligence had monitored these communications, and believed the mufti had raised £50,000 in Iraq. The former intelligence officer George Stewart Symes warned Hajj Amin against using such funds to support rebels. The mufti denied using the money for anything other than aid work and added that this figure was overestimated. British administrators could do nothing to interfere with the handling of SMC funds.[37] Regardless, the warning was received, and the crisis in Syria dwindled shortly afterward.

In 1926, the RAF reported on the mufti's involvement in pan-Islamic politics, saying that he attended a recent pan-Islamic conference in Cairo because of "his desire to acquaint himself with the Moslem leaders present; and above all his desire to draw political benefits for Palestine." The mufti saw Palestine as a distinct part of the emerging Arab world, but remained sympathetic and loyal to pan-Arab aims. He was prepared to deal with 'Abd al-'Aziz Ibn Sa'ud of Arabia, or any other Arab statesman, to secure promises for the defense of Palestine's interests. For him, Palestine must not be isolated from a future Arab federation by the Balfour Declaration.[38]

Government officials were deeply suspicious of the mufti, but saw his role as a necessary evil and a consequence of improvisation. They tolerated his international activity so long as it did not directly challenge the Zionist policy, although his views on that subject were no secret. The double-edged nature of his influence was known, but in the context of improvised attempts to balance Zionist and Arab demands, decision makers believed that their relationship with him was one of codependency. As ECPAC led negotiations, the mufti increased his own influence in the Islamic world. Periodically attacked by his rivals over his lack of academic or religious credentials for his title, the mufti improved his Islamic and nationalist standing by participating in Hashemite and Saudi Islamic conferences in Mecca and Cairo, respectively. Moreover, he restored the Haram al-Sharif and made a name for himself by supporting the Druze rebels. These were not security problems, and where the mufti did get involved in security threats, it was related to France in Syria rather than Britain in Palestine.

Psychological Warfare and Negotiations

After the May Day riots, Palestinian leaders pursued a diplomatic strategy to reverse or limit the Zionist policy. They sought greater control over Muslim affairs domestically, and the ability to influence legislation, especially if it could limit Jewish immigration. Samuel sought to address their constitutional demands through alternative means. He drew out negotiations about self-government and constitutional matters, downplayed the notables' representativeness, and raised the profile of Hajj Amin al-Husseini through his appointment as mufti. These steps contributed to divisions within PAC about how to represent Palestinian demands to government, and the extent to which cooperation should be embraced. Government policy during the early phases of civil administration, especially the appointment of al-Husseini as mufti and president of the SMC, caused rifts among the nationalists. These rifts, in turn, were used as evidence by Samuel and other officials that PAC did not represent Palestinian Arabs, and that its demands should be ignored.

Britain's partnership with Zionist intelligence solved the problem of shrinking security budgets, and helped policymakers to improvise. Before starting as high commissioner, Allenby recommended to Samuel consultation with his former military experts, now government officers in Palestine. Allenby considered Wyndham Deedes, Samuel's chief secretary until he resigned after the founding of the SMC in late 1921, to be competent and experienced in Arab matters.[39] An avowed Zionist, Deedes was central to the establishment of patterns of security and cooperation with the Yishuv. Deedes knew the value of Zionist intelligence and worked closely with Aaronsohn, Chaim Kalvarisky, and others.

The government lacked the funds to support its own centralized intelligence body. The CID should have filled that role, but it lacked trained staff, a library, laboratories, and equipment. Relationships with Zionist officers filled the gap. The Yishuv had many intelligence services, most of them ad hoc. Few had the organization, staff, or budget of the IB. Various Zionist parties and the nascent Haganah collected intelligence for their own purposes. Most Zionist intelligence work addressed the nexus of land, Arab politics, Arab attitudes toward Zionism, and paramilitary organization.[40]

Political rivalry among Zionists, especially the Zionist executive and the Va'ad Leumi, or National Council, led to the closure of the IB. The Va'ad was founded in 1920 as the executive branch to the Asefat HaNivharim, or legislative assembly, where Zionist parties voted on Yishuv policy and on the allocation of its resources. By 1921 the Va'ad was the only remaining body with a budget for intelligence work. That year, its budget for "relations with Arabs" was £50,000, a significant cut from 1920's £80,000, but still more than sixteen times the size of Britain's secret service allocation for Palestine, and the largest among Zionist institutions. Chaim Kalvarisky led the intelligence effort of the Va'ad's "Arab Secretariat," which focused on Jewish-Arab relations, the movements of leading Arab merchants, and even a telephone tap network in Jerusalem.[41]

The Arab Secretariat demonstrated a different political character than the IB, whose members were close to British officials and, like Weizmann, supported British imperialism. Alex Aaronsohn was so sympathetic to Britain that he opposed the self-governing institutions of the Yishuv. He wrote to a British contact, "I am sorry to tell you that some of our Jews here are committing a fatal mistake by convening a big congress of the Palestinian Jews [Asefat HaNivharim]. . . . This will certainly cause the Arab leaders to stir up the old political feeling, and call for an Arab congress. But, nobody has the monopoly on fools and demagogues, and we Jews have managed to secure quite a few in our midst."[42] He worried about escalating claims between Jews and Arabs, but also that socialists would dominate Yishuv politics.

As part of their tactics of improvisation, British officials turned to various intelligence bodies within the Yishuv for aid. In advance of Samuel's arrival in 1920, Storrs wrote to him about Kalvarisky, saying, "I am more than ever convinced that he is a man who will, if given the opportunity, play an effective part in the general development of the country, and also in the gradual and necessary reconciliation of the Arab; in which I find he shares my views."[43] Perhaps naive, the sentiment helped to intertwine Zionist and British interests. Years later, when British officers preferred not to depend on Zionist help, they had little choice. The violence at Jaffa in 1921, as well as budget cuts, accelerated the development of Anglo-Zionist intelligence cooperation and the resulting mutual dependence.

Aiming to persuade Muslims and Christians of Zionism's merits and benefits, Kalvarisky subsidized Muslim National Associations (MNAs) across the country as a counterbalance to the MCS's influence. Yet in the midst of public debate about representative government, the MNAs failed to convince Arabs to support elections for Samuel's legislative council. Hillel Cohen remarks that this produced no change in Zionist strategy toward Arab nationalism.[44] This may be true, but Kalvarisky's long-term aim remained fostering Arab-Jewish cooperation.

The program exploited divisions in Arab society, including competition between notable families, class divisions, and to a lesser extent, ideology.[45] Opponents of ECPAC and the mufti also served as sources for intelligence.

Kalvarisky achieved mixed success: the subsidies prolonged the lives of op-position parties and exploited preexisting differences within Arab society. British officials did not think this secret diplomacy would convince any Arab nationalists that Zionism was not a threat, but the government still enjoyed the results. A Zionist-sponsored Farmers' Party, after opening in Beisan, pro-voked the MCS to redouble its efforts in the North. Britain preferred not to stir a revival of the MCS, so one political officer wrote, "It is to be deplored that Colonel Kisch and Mr. Kalvarisky should imagine that the future of the policy lies in the hands of those who attempt to create a favourable attitude of mind through the agency of promises of financial help. The personal ac-tivities of these two gentlemen at Beisan would be amusing if they were not pitiable."[46] Opposition success consisted mainly of electoral victories in Pal-estinian cities, shutting out the al-Husseinis during the mid-1920s.[47] British policymakers regularly referred to Palestinian internal disputes as evidence that the Palestinians lacked a proper representative organization.

To encourage negotiations, British policy signaled limits to Zionism. After the riots of May 1921, the Middle East department of the CO composed a memo, with Churchill's support, that redefined Britain's position. This policy aimed to uphold Zionist development, and to limit the effect of Jewish immi-gration on Arab opinion. Knowing that the disturbances were premeditated and organized, the policy also sought to prevent Bolsheviks from immigrat-ing.[48] Britain's new policy tied Jewish immigration to the absorptive capacity of the country, and reinterpreted the Balfour Declaration accordingly. Pal-estinians saw this policy as a victory, as Zionists complained about the new limitations, which, they argued, defied the spirit of the Balfour Declaration.

Optimistic, and wishing to follow up on the cold treatment they had re-ceived at the Cairo conference of 1921, the Palestinians formed a delegation (PAD) to travel to London to negotiate a reversal of the Zionist policy. Yet British policymakers, especially Churchill, remained firmly committed to Zionism's aim of creating, through immigration and development, a Jewish national home in Palestine. The alteration in immigration policy was a mi-nor issue to British authorities, and resulted from a problem of "tactics, not strategy, the general strategic idea being the gradual immigration of Jews into Palestine to the extent to which they can be absorbed into the economic life of the country without detriment to the rights and privileges of the non-Jewish majority," as Churchill explained to the cabinet.[49] Anti-Zionist govern-ment officials were stripped of their positions to support this strategy.

One of PAD's main obstacles was that British officials rejected the no-tion that it represented PAC, nor was PAC seen to represent Palestinians. As in most colonies after 1918, British policymakers questioned the motives of local elites and doubted the survival of democracy in their hands.[50] Administrators exploited social and political differences between elite families in Palestine as evidence of this. This pattern began during the Paris Peace Conference, but became a staple of British improvisation during negotiations with Palestinians.

PAD resulted from months of frustration, and the fallout from the Jaffa riots. Senior leaders understood that policy change would come from London rather than local officials. Musa Kazim, elder statesman and leader of the delegation, understood that Herbert Samuel's "scheme of popular representation" was merely an attempt to mollify Arabs and the League of Nations. He left for London resolved to achieve a change in policy that would affect Jewish immigration. Musa Kazim told Churchill about Palestinian grievances related to the Zionist policy and the lack of representative government. The Balfour Declaration, Churchill said, was binding, but was open to some interpretation. He said to Musa Kazim, "I do hope that what you are going to do over here is to find some satisfactory way of carrying out the policy of the British government, and not merely a way of bringing it to an end."[51] Churchill and Musa Kazim could not agree on self-government, which, according to the CO, never was promised.

Frances Newton, an English missionary in Haifa, and daughter of Britain's former consul at Beirut, served as aid to Musa Kazim. Newton debated with Churchill's undersecretary, Maj. Hubert Young, about the meaning of "national home." In Arabic, two terms for "national" gave very different impressions of British aims for that policy. Major Young exclaimed, "You cannot imagine they want all the Jews in the world to go and live in Palestine. Nobody could ever imagine that. They cannot mean that—all of the Jews in the world—that Palestine should be to them what England is to us."[52] Yet precisely this end is what many Zionists imagined, and what Arab nationalists feared.

The talks failed because of this and other misunderstandings. Churchill insisted that Musa Kazim negotiate directly with Weizmann. Yet Weizmann and his associates set as a condition for talks that PAD accept the Balfour Declaration. Musa Kazim thought this meant acceptance of moving all Jews in the world to Palestine, and refused. Churchill ended the meeting with a lengthy lecture about Britain's commitments to Zionists and Arabs. He conceded nothing to PAD, believing it should negotiate directly with the Zionists.[53]

PAD sought autonomy guaranteed under the mandate, but acknowledged Britain's benevolent intentions and emphasized the wrongdoing of the Zionist policy. PAD proposed representative government, with Britain as suzerain, and an organic constitution that guaranteed religious freedom and equality and that could "make impossible state aid to any religion." This clause is particularly interesting, since it challenged Samuel's approach to communal self-government as a substitute for representative institutions. It also challenged the authority that was being concentrated in the al-Husseini family during 1921. PAD offered Britain military rights to the territory and offered to guarantee "some small area in Palestine which should be, in regard to the Palestine National Movement, extra territorial."[54] This was a remarkable and surprising concession. Hoping to at least set legal limits on Zionist power, and to align more closely to the British point of view, Musa Kazim proposed a vision for Palestine to become some sort of religious center for world Jewry.

Churchill referred Musa Kazim to Weizmann, and effectively killed any possibility for a representative legislative council. Frustrated, PAD ordered a boycott of Samuel's attempts to form a representative or consultative council, since participation would have amounted to Arab surrender to the Zionist policy. Wyndham Deedes reported on the quiet in Palestine produced by PAD's absence, and the anticipation of good results.[55] The quiet reinforced his tactic, shared by Clayton, Storrs, Symes, and other intelligence-officers-cum-administrators, to keep alive Arab hopes for change by prolonging negotiations. This set a pattern in which British officers and administrators would play for time and downplay the credentials of Palestinian leaders. In doing so, they continued to enforce the Zionist policy, allowing Jewish immigration against Palestinian demands for self-government or legislative control over immigration.

Although talks in London had failed, Jewish-Arab discussions about representative institutions continued. Jamal al-Husseini negotiated with Chaim Kalvarisky, who was in charge of Arab-Jewish cooperation for the Va'ad, among other roles. The pair were neighbors and met socially. Jamal used those encounters to complain about Zionist support for Arab opposition parties, but offered a tantalizing proposal: PAC and the Arab executive could change their policy from one of a "national government" to a bicameral legislature. The lower chamber would be proportional, while the upper chamber would be formed on the same basis as Samuel's executive council—communal representation. This system could thus safeguard Zionist interests. He also proposed an immigration commission with an English chair, two Jews, one Muslim, and one Christian. This was the most significant concession offer by any Palestinian party, and would remain so until 1939. If it had been accepted, it easily could have led to self-government. Yet neither the Zionist institutions nor the British government were willing to concede this much democracy to Palestine by 1922. Col. Frederick Kisch, a senior official with the Palestine Zionist Executive, remarked that ECPAC's change of stance came "no doubt as a consequence of the realisation of the hopelessness of the attitude hitherto adopted." He worried that if the proposed upper house consistently vetoed immigration legislation, world opinion would turn against Zionism. He warned that the Zionists would have to move in some measure toward democratizing the government.[56] Britain considered such an option impossible by this point. Satisfied with the negotiations themselves, and the discord caused by Kalvarisky's program, all of which produced peace on the ground, Britain had little reason to risk changing governance.

The British government was outwardly sympathetic to Arab nationalists, but according to Yehoshua Porath, prevented any significant limit to the Zionist policy through democratic self-government. A new condition became attached to any proposal to create a new consultative or legislative body: the high commissioner must consider the proposals to come from an "effective body" representing the population. That term was easy to dispute, especially since ECPAC's influence had greatly declined in favor of the opposition.[57] British policy could not afford to be tied down to a constitution as it had in Iraq, which is what Palestinians desired. Palestine's political problems already had proven to be irreconcilable, and representative government would endanger Britain's basic interest in remaining in Palestine and protecting the Zionist policy.

Policymakers used the promise of negotiations to coax Palestinian politicians toward collaboration. Samuel concluded that "nothing could be more desirable than a détente, as Sir Gilbert Clayton urges. . . . The difficulty is to find any solution which the Arabs will accept short of the transfer of the government to their own hands." Britain would not accept proposals that would destroy the Zionist enterprise. Opposition parties including the Farmers' Party and the MNAs, sponsored by Britain and Zionists, had thrived on the existing uncertainty. According to Samuel, "The possibility that power may after all be transferred to their hands has given them adherents and increases greatly the difficulties of the government [to reach a constitutional agreement]."[58] Unwittingly, the Palestinians' main ally in Britain contributed to this effect.

The NPL and Resistance by Other Means

Frances Newton accompanied PAD to London via Geneva, where they had attended the Syrian Congress.[59] In London she joined the National Political League (NPL), a group of mainly conservative ex-suffragettes who had become sympathetic to Arab complaints against Zionism.[60] Aiming to facilitate negotiations, Newton, Mary Adelaide Broadhurst, Margaret Milne Farquharson, and others wrote letters to the *Times*, Parliament, the House of Lords, and ministries in support of Palestinian demands. It is possible that the NPL influenced a 1922 motion in the House of Lords against the Zionist policy; the motion urged the League of Nations Council to delay acceptance of the British Mandate, on the grounds that it violated pledges to Husayn. This was the first such public claim about the secret wartime agreement. The result was that Churchill rushed confirmation through the House, and then the League of Nations.[61]

The NPL gained the support of Col. Stewart Francis Newcombe, formerly of the Arab Bureau, as well as a few other soldiers and intelligence figures. This group maintained varied influence throughout the mandate years. During the 1930s, the NPL organized a pro-mufti propaganda service called the Palestine Information Centre (PIC). It attracted the support of British Nazi sympathizers such as Robert Gordon-Canning and Barry Domvile, and the attention of MI5.[62] The members of the NPL were neither fascists nor Nazis, although some had reactionary tendencies. They objected to foreign socialist influence in the Labour Party and feared social revolution in the United Kingdom. Their statements about Communist influence in the Labour Party or the threat to British jobs by allegedly Soviet-controlled foreigners edged toward antisemitic paranoia, although they did not explicitly name Jews as the enemy. Mary Broadhurst wrote to the *Times* in 1922 urging that both women and men use their right to vote to protect British jobs from foreigners, to fight Communism, and to support the Arab cause in order to engender Muslim loyalty to the British Empire.[63]

Broadhurst's criticisms of the League of Nations mandate and British policy were reasonable, but were premised on wishes for the continuity of empire and her class. Lewis Namier, a senior British Zionist, met with Broadhurst in 1922. Their discussion turned into a debate, and Namier concluded that she was ignorant about matters of trade and the economic threats to empire. He dismissed her concern for empire altogether, telling her that she was naive to think that Arabs would ever support it. He did learn, however, that Broadhurst was most concerned about Bolshevism. He thought she regarded Jews as bound up with it—not an uncommon view in the early 1920s. Misreading the NPL's interests, Namier concluded that the NPL had taken up the Arab cause not for its love of Arabs, but for its suspicion of Jews.[64]

During the 1920s the NPL played an important but accidental role in supporting the efforts of British administrators to foster peaceful conditions through negotiations with ECPAC. While its members successfully raised support for the Palestinian Arab cause in middle- and upper-class circles in London, they unwittingly produced an adverse effect because their advice played into the improvised tactics of British authorities in Palestine. In 1923, the NPL attempted to make the Arab cause an issue in the UK general election, with little success. With NPL encouragement, the Sixth PAC left Herbert Samuel's experimental "advisory" council in protest of unfair taxation, an unwanted public loan, troop reductions while the roads remained unsafe, and Britain's enforcement of the Zionist policy.[65] At the same time, the NPL stepped up its efforts at the League of Nations as Shakib Arslan, who headed the Syro-Palestinian congress in Geneva, began to petition members of the Permanent Mandates Commission (PMC). These steps reinforced claims by the Palestine government that ECPAC was not a representative body.

The league mandate came into effect in September 1923, and the PMC only began to discuss Palestine in 1924. By then, some PMC members had been influenced by PAC. William Ormsby-Gore, formerly of the Arab Bureau and the Zionist Commission, became colonial undersecretary, and traveled to Geneva to represent Britain's case. He argued that the development of self-governing institutions had been made impossible by PAC, which aimed to use such institutions to prevent Jewish immigration, which was legally enshrined in the mandate. At Weizmann's prompting, Ormsby-Gore reminded the league that it had sanctioned and guaranteed the Zionist policy. The PMC ceased to question the Zionist policy, and a Zionist delegation was posted to Geneva to continue to lobby.[66]

The government, through communications intercepted by its censorship office, was aware of Palestinian efforts abroad to reverse the Zionist policy, and it used this knowledge to influence the PMC. Samuel reported on these communications to the Colonial Office. In 1921, he wrote that PAC had sent telegrams to European governments, the Vatican, and the League of Nations. However, he downplayed the representativeness of the congress, saying that the "vast majority of [the] population take no overt part either for or against [PAC], and degree of support accorded to it is far from indicating anything in the nature of a national movement. This information is sent in case the attention of Mandates Commission of League of Nations is drawn to the resolutions of the Congress."[67] PMC members met privately with Arab delegates, and normally included Shakib Arslan on the agenda, likely as a result of his petitioning. Yet they never considered a revision of the text of the mandate between 1924 and 1929, due to the quick reaction of Zionist diplomacy to early attempts at revision. Only the 1929 riots would raise new serious discussion.[68]

These hard limits were unknown to Palestinian nationalist leaders. In 1926 Mary Broadhurst, on behalf of the NPL, advised PAC on how to address the league: "The Legality of the terms of the Mandate should be called in question and judicially considered by an impartial tribunal. If the League Council refuses to face the point there should be an appeal to the judicial commission. It is a point not only affecting the Arabs but of international importance. Your case should be drawn up by an experienced international lawyer, and I will try to get help in this respect also."[69] Broadhurst reminded Jamal al-Husseini to send money, since "we should like to be able to tell your supporters that you are helping yourselves in this way. They think you are not sufficiently in earnest if you do not show a proof that you can sacrifice a little in money for keeping alive your great cause. We are finding it harder to make excuses for you." The next year, the NPL again asked for money to support their efforts to block the Jewish acquisition of rights to mine the Dead Sea salts.[70]

The NPL also promoted PAC's strategy of a tax boycott and supported demands for self-government. "You will see that members of the House of Commons are being organised for a push on as regards a representative government in Palestine," Broadhurst told al-Husseini. "This question was for the purpose of eliciting and giving publicity to the weakness of the position from a constitutional point of view—one that will appeal to the British people. You have a cry that can be accepted by all—'no taxation without representation' and now that a heavy burden is being imposed [at home], that attitude will have a very strong influence and should unanimously be taken up."[71] The group also encouraged ECPAC to fight British economic policies, especially when it granted monopolies over electric power and potash mining to Jewish industries.

The NPL's efforts saw little success, other than persuading the *Encyclopedia Britannica* to remove the Zionist flag from its entry on Palestine.[72] The group continued to ask for financial support from PAC on a periodic basis, despite providing no tangible result. ECPAC did not understand that the NPL had failed to move British opinion at Whitehall. In contrast, British intelligence observed ECPAC's weakness, its belief in the NPL, and the lack of results from either body. This intelligence enabled policymakers to comfortably maintain the status quo. Intercepted letters revealed the Palestinians' shift in focus from revolt to negotiation, as well as their financial struggles. In September 1923, an intelligence summary referred to PAD's abrupt decision to cancel the US leg of its trip, and Musa Kazim's sudden return to Palestine. One member, Amin Tamimi, stayed in London to keep contact with the NPL. These messages follow the exact contents of the telegraphic correspondence between Jerusalem and London found in ECPAC's records.[73] Another intelligence summary referred to a police report that discussed the contents of the NPL's letters in which it referred to its propaganda work.[74]

ECPAC was led by the NPL in a fruitless exercise. The true result was that the status quo prevailed at home in Palestine while they negotiated abroad. British administrators were aware of this effect and enjoyed its results. Chief among them was Clayton, although he knew the situation was not sustainable. He reportedly told the French consul in Jerusalem about Britain's "web of complications." Britain was not playing a Machiavellian game. Rather, its rule in Palestine was directionless. It had no policy options and was limited in means, especially money. "I am therefore convinced," Clayton reportedly told the consul, "that we should abandon Palestine and its stony grounds and leave its starving and quarrelsome population to themselves, if we could. We are however the prisoners of our Balfour Declaration. The Jews seized our government by the throat and do not let go."[75]

If Clayton was quoted accurately, it was hypocritical of him to blame "the Jews" for Britain's policy problem, when he had become an enthusiastic champion of Zionism in 1918 and had enjoyed partnership with the Zionists' intelligence services since. Britain's unusual inflexibility in Palestine frustrated strategic thinkers like Clayton, but simplified policymaking for successive high commissioners and the governments at Whitehall. A dangerous situation had emerged: British decision makers in Palestine were forced to improvise since there was no policy on the future of the country. Nor was there a plan to simultaneously fulfill Britain's commitment to the League of Nations to guide the country to self-government while upholding its league commitment to the Jewish national home.

The need to improvise caused decision makers to welcome any development that promoted stability. This included the appointment of the mufti, prolonged negotiations with ECPAC, and the fostering of opposition to ECPAC. On the other hand, British officials no longer paid attention to the pan-Islamic and pan-Arab connections of the Palestinian political elite. They took comfort as the mufti swore off nationalist politics during his journeys abroad to Hejaz and elsewhere. They watched key players, intervening at times, but they never calculated that the same clique of nationalists supporting revolt in Syria might turn their guns on Britain in Palestine.

Hillel Cohen and Yehoshua Porath have argued that the years 1924–28 were, as Porath originally put it, a "nadir for the Palestinian national movement." ECPAC nearly disappeared, leaving "no more than an office run by Jamal al-Husseini."[76] Porath attributes the relative peace of the 1920s to the

Yishuv's economic and morale crises, and to declining Zionist immigration after 1925, which resulted in net emigration in 1927.[77] These views under-state Palestinian resistance to British policy. Palestinians focused on negotia-tions with the government at Whitehall and Jerusalem, and with the League of Nations. There was more to Arab nationalism than the mufti, riots, and re-bellion. Educational, cultural, and athletic organizations took shape, and pro-duced the next generation of nationalists. In particular, the Najah and Rawdat al-Ma'arif schools, the former subsidized by the SMC and the latter con-trolled by it, fostered a national spirit and a broad base of support for Amin al-Husseini.[78] Organized resistance to Zionism took place abroad, with a dip-lomatic character, in London and Geneva.

Palestinian nationalist leaders attempted negotiations, but had very lit-tle chance of achieving their aims. Both the mufti and the PAC Executive bolstered their international connections and ensured that the Palestinian movement remained part of the reconfigurations taking place in both the pan-Arab and pan-Islamic theaters. British officials in Palestine exploited negotiations to maintain peace. Improvisation came with a price, trading power for time.

Zero-Sum Conflict

The civil administration depended heavily on intelligence for solutions to the policy problems that emerged in Palestine after the 1921 riots. This intel-ligence state was not organized in formal institutions, but was embodied in the expertise of former soldiers and their relationships. Britain could depend on Zionist intelligence for support in suppressing Communism and Arab demands. Policymakers believed they could manage Palestinian demands through Amin al-Husseini in his new role as mufti. They were not naive about his influence or his ability to arouse trouble, and they watched him closely. The government officers who first managed these issues were all experienced intelligence hands. Their successors were not.

So long as intelligence had a grip on the situation, policymakers could im-provise their treatment of conflicting Arab and Zionist demands. Samuel, his successor as high commissioner, Sir Herbert Plumer, and many former intel-ligence hands agreed that representative government was needed to solve the political deadlock between Arab nationalism and Zionism. Yet this never became a priority, and most doubted this would be possible since PAC re-jected imposed solutions. Nonetheless, throughout the 1920s, British policy maintained the status quo without much security risk. Intelligence played an important role in that outcome.

Britain's realization that it was managing irreconcilable claims marked the diplomatic point of no return for the Arab-Zionist conflict. It is no coincidence that the RAF, army, and government had come to the same conclusion in the summer of 1921 when they determined that it would be impossible for Jews and Arabs to serve together in a locally raised self-defense force (see chapter 4). The zero-sum nature of the conflict emerged because British authorities made acceptance of the Zionist policy by the Arab delegation a condition for self-government. When discussions over governance failed in 1922, Palestinian nationalists also saw the conflict as zero-sum, and recognized their woeful lack of preparation to confront the problem. In his 1923 essay, "The Iron Wall," Jabotinsky acknowledged that Arabs never would be reconciled to the Zionist policy.[79] He thought the Zionist Left was foolish for believing that reconciliation was possible. The socialist parties never admitted that a zero-sum conflict that existed with Arabs over the land had reached a watershed. The conflict could not be solved without defying or damaging the interests of at least one side. With Britain enforcing the Zionist policy, there was no way back.

CHAPTER 4

Security, Air Control, and the 1929 (Attempted) Revolt

In August 1929 in Jerusalem, demonstrations quickly turned into riots and extensive violence between Arabs and Jews, which spread to other towns, ultimately causing hundreds of deaths. The relative peace of the 1920s was broken as Palestinian resistance returned to armed struggle. British security was unprepared to handle the situation. This resulted from failures of intelligence, force, and policy. Britain's response initially was slow and weak, but gradually escalated toward full-blown counterinsurgency. The core problem was eight years of policy-strategy mismatch. At no point during that time was the strength or organization of British forces, intelligence, or policy appropriate to Britain's aims or challenges. The government attempted to manage a state of heightened intercommunal tension with little force, focusing on the imperial defense scheme known as "Air Control."

Strategists saw Palestine as a deep base for the defense of the Suez Canal, for air links to the Far East, and as a point of control for a future air or naval war in the eastern Mediterranean. As a base, Palestine would keep enemy air forces a safe distance from Suez.[1] In 1923 strategists and the chief of Imperial General Staff appended imperial ambition to British strategy. "So long as British influence is supreme in Palestine in Transjordan, so long we control Arabia," read one comment. The mandatory regime was to create internal peace that would favorably affect Egypt, Syria, and Iraq. Future rail and oil communications were to be protected.[2] Britain aimed to have a supportive Middle East behind the empire in any future war. This strategy, developed in 1923, remained at the center of British planning in the Middle East until Britain's 1939 decision to abandon its Zionist policy.

It was clear to seasoned officials that British policy in Palestine was not engendering the desired support. During the 1920s, British forces globally were at minimal strength, given the unlikelihood of a major war. Furthermore, financial limitations had caused a gradual withdrawal of military force from the Middle East. This lack of force weakened internal security. Britain tended toward the relinquishment of control to local powers and locally raised forces in Iraq, Transjordan, and Egypt. But in Palestine, because of its unpopular policies of promoting Jewish immigration and denying self-government, Britain could not raise a local defense force. As a result, the government depended on a divided Palestinian nationalist leadership, and on the mufti's goodwill and influence, to keep the peace. This was not enough to prevent the violence of 1929. Britain's weak response to escalating violence had important consequences for Arab and Jewish politics, but also for British policy, including security.

Since 1920, no formal mechanism for handling politico-security intelligence had existed in Palestine. By 1921 centralized intelligence had been removed from the mandated territories. By 1923, the last center of military intelligence in the region, based in Istanbul, had been withdrawn. Thus, Britain was so unprepared in 1929 that reserves were only called up after violence had broken out.

Although they lacked centralized intelligence, British decision makers were not ignorant about Arab politics. However, by 1928 most of the governors and secretaries who understood these issues, and had been members of Allenby's GSI or Arab Bureau, had left Palestine. In 1926 G. S. Symes, who had managed security as district governor in northern Palestine and Samaria, left for Aden. In 1928, Clayton was made high commissioner in Iraq, and Albert Abramson, district governor of southern Palestine, became a special service officer (SSO) in Transjordan. With their departures, the quality of intelligence declined in ways that mandate authorities could not appreciate. As Arab politicians began positioning themselves in 1928 to regain control over their movement, British intelligence was inadequate to the coming challenge. No British official in Palestine could have interpreted events during that year as precursors to riot or attempted revolt.

Administrators such as Plumer, Clayton, Deedes, and Storrs could manage simmering conflict. They knew where to pay attention and when to intervene. The fragile quiet shattered soon after the departure of those experienced intelligence hands and the replacement of the firm Plumer, a general, with John Chancellor, a professional colonial administrator. Chancellor had less experience with intelligence, and exhibited a doctrinaire approach to colonial government. He took Clayton's stalemate for granted, and instead of trying to restart constitutional negotiations he worked through the SMC and liberal-internationalist institutions in a drive for good government. A situation that Clayton found unworkable was perceived as normal and static by Chancellor and successive administrators. This sense of normalcy proved dangerous.

Religious-Nationalist Politics and the Riots

During the 1920s, the mufti allowed ECPAC to challenge British policy, while he built a reputation as a pan-Islamist and national leader. He sought to raise his prestige among Palestinians, and to raise the profile of the Palestinian cause in the Arab and Islamic worlds. At the same time. opposition parties, supported in the North by Zionist and British subsidy and in the center by his Nashashibi rivals, began to challenge his domination of the SMC. His activity outside Palestine was one response to that contest. He maintained his role as a nationalist anticolonial figure through his support for the Druze rebellion in Syria, and through pan-Islamic propaganda. As a government officer, however, he did not formally lead any political movement, although his SMC fostered anticolonial nationalism and pan-Islamism through its school system, the funding of clubs, and other branches of civil government. Beginning in 1928, the mufti used a religious dispute over an ancient holy site to mobilize Islamic sentiment for national purposes, and thus revived public opposition to Zionism, which had been weakened by internal Palestinian political divisions. Though his campaign was ostensibly directed against Jews, his real target was Arabs.

His campaign focused on the Western, or Wailing, Wall of Jerusalem, known in Arabic as al-Buraq. This site was holy to Jews, since it was believed to be the outer retaining wall, and the last remaining part, of Herod's Temple, destroyed by the Romans in 70 CE. Muslims, too, valued the site, believing it to be the place where Muhammad had tied his steed, Buraq, and then prayed at al-Aqsa before ascending to heaven. There are records of Jewish-Muslim disputes over the site from at least 1840. A stream of Zionist immigration to Palestine since the late nineteenth century added to Muslim fears that they might lose their holy site. Under the Ottomans, the site was ruled to be the property of the Waqf, the Muslim religious trust. Britain's first and most important commitment regarding the holy sites of Jerusalem was to maintain the status quo, which governed decisions throughout the 1920s. For both nationalistic reasons and because of their experience with Christian holy sites, Muslims opposed any deviation from the status quo.[3] Despite failed Jewish attempts to legally purchase the site, Jews maintained the right to worship there, often by bribing Ottoman officials. Devout Jews sought to repair the narrow alley along the wall. It was a small and crowded area. They wanted to pray there, to bring chairs, and to set up a dividing screen between the sexes. The obstructions had not been permitted in the past, and therefore aggravated residents of the adjacent Mughrabi Quarter (demolished after the 1967 Israel-Arab War).

In the early 1920s, the SMC and ECPAC disseminated examples of Jewish religious art or posters depicting the Haram al-Sharif (Noble Sanctuary or Temple Mount), which they wrongly interpreted as proof of Jewish designs to demolish the Muslim holy site and replace it with a third temple. Such images had been the basis of anti-Zionist propaganda in their delegations to Hejaz, Egypt, Iraq, and India from 1922 to 1928.[4] On Yom Kippur 1928, at the urging of Jerusalem's Arabs, police forcibly removed the dividing curtain from the Jewish prayer service. The British saw the curtain as a deviation from the status quo, but this caused a scuffle with the Jews who were defending their right to pray as they pleased. The SMC and the mufti began a propaganda campaign in defense of al-Aqsa and the Wailing Wall, and persuaded the British government to support their position. The Jews interpreted this step as an extension of Ottoman oppression and a departure from British religious freedom. The action enabled Jabotinsky's Revisionists, like the SMC, to exploit the Wailing Wall issue for its national and religious importance. Not wishing to be upstaged, the new Jewish Agency for Palestine, the reorganized remnants of the ZO that now represented all parties, including non-Zionists, also took up the campaign for Jewish rights at the wall.[5]

The government sided with the mufti and sought to prevent future provocations. As Zionists attempted to negotiate the issue in London and Geneva, SMC propaganda pressed the matter in Palestine. Meanwhile restrictions on Jews at the site gave momentum to the Revisionist youth movement, Brit Trumpeldore, or Betar, named for the Jewish legionnaire killed at Tel Hai in March 1920. Betar aimed to provoke the British government to reconsider Jewish rights at the Wailing Wall. On August 15, 1929, ten months after the Yom Kippur incident, they held a demonstration at the wall on Tisha B'Av, a fast day that commemorates the destruction of the Temple in 70 CE. Jerusalem's Muslims held a counterdemonstration there the next day. Yehoshua Porath attributes responsibility for that, and culpability for the ensuing violence, to the mufti, who knew that the Wailing Wall was an issue that could unite Muslims throughout Palestine and that did not affect his relations with the government. Porath remarked that "'Izzat Darwaza . . . stated that the national movement was overcome by weakness but it renewed its activity for some time after the *al-Buraq* uprising, and it was this [reactivation of the movement] that *those who caused the uprising from behind the scenes* had hoped for" (italics in the original).[6]

'Izzat Darwaza's reflection is important, since it better aligns with the other original evidence than do most narrative histories of the 1929 disturbances. Military and police evidence agrees that considerable forethought went into the propaganda and even military preparations on the Arab side. Historians tend to characterize the events of 1929 as "riots" that lasted from 23 to 29 August, even though fighting lasted until 11 September, but the brutal skirmishes were anything but spontaneous disturbances. The violence took the form of insurgency in the countryside, which was organized in its inspiration but not in its operation. The mufti had sufficient power that his intervention helped to end violence in the cities, but the events already had inspired Bedouin and other armed groups to pitch battles against British forces and Jewish settlements in the countryside. The available evidence is not clear as to whether this was part of the plan, or whether events slipped out of control. 'Izzat Darwaza's statement, as well as British and Zionist sources, lend weight to Porath's argument that the disturbances were planned.[7]

The mufti biographer Philip Mattar offers an alternate view, suggesting that historians such as Porath have "ignored or assume too much in an effort to tailor the facts to fit their theses. They ignored the sequence and sources of provocation on both sides, and assumed that the Mufti had the intention and ability to orchestrate events and to sustain them for eleven months."[8] Rather, says Mattar, the mufti intervened after a week of Jewish protests in Palestine and London and at the League of Nations. As president of the SMC, the mufti had to defend Waqf property. Mattar underemphasizes evidence presented both by himself and by Porath, which demonstrates the mufti's role in organizing the "Committee for the Defense of the Buraq" and other such groups. In fact, in Palestinian memoirs and other written evidence, the 1929 riots are known as *thawrat al-buraq*, or the Buraq revolution.[9] In retrospect, "revolution" seems like an exaggeration. However, it captures the Palestinian hopes of the moment, for the first British restrictions on Zionist claims. The events provoked a course correction for Palestinian nationalists seeking to oppose British support for the Zionist policy. But although it came close, it did not provoke change in British policy.

Evidence surrounding the committee's propaganda and its intended target suggests that the mufti did guide events to a considerable extent. His decade of experience in both nationalist/anticolonial and pan-Islamic politics eventually led to a blended political stance not unlike that of Shakib Arslan. One cannot prove that he planned an uprising. However, he did seek to use Muslim sentiment to raise as much attention as possible to the anti-Zionist cause, with violent results. Moreover, his tactics, public statements, and propaganda activity align with a pattern that he had established as early as 1919–20, and periodically refined through 1938. Finally, it was an opportune moment for the mufti to turn his hybrid political warfare toward Palestine. The Syrian revolt had ended, and candidates backed by the mufti and ECPAC lost to opposition parties in Palestinian municipal elections during 1927–28. Their movement required new energy. As discussed in the previous chapter, British administrators had divided Palestinian elites and left room for opposition parties to make gains. The Pan-Arab leaders Nabih al-ʿAzmeh, ʿAdel Arslan, and Shukri Quwatli facilitated restored communication and cooperation between the mufti and a faction of ECPAC from Nablus led by Amin Tamimi. Tamimi, previously ECPAC's liaison in London, disliked the mufti's role in colonial government.[10]

After the violence, the Vaʿad reminded the British government of the precedent for religiously inspired resistance: "For some considerable time there has been conducted in the country a systematic propaganda, both secret and open, for an attack on Jews who are engaged in a work of peace and reconstruction." The memo noted that this had happened before, in 1921, although the Vaʿad probably meant 1920, when Amin al-Husseini led the Nabi Musa disturbances.[11] The Vaʿad's mistake in dating the mufti's role in the 1920 riots may be a symptom of its lacking intelligence agencies and the forgotten archives and expertise of those that had closed in the early 1920s. The Yishuv was unprepared for a violent outbreak in 1929; as Yoav Gelber remarks, "In the summer of 1929, not a person remembered the Information Bureau [of 1920] or the information accumulated there."[12] After 1929, Zionist intelligence was rebuilt from scratch.

Attempted or Failed Revolt

The Buraq revolt had no central command; it lacked organization and leadership. Almost no Arabic evidence from the rebels survives. It was inspired by the mufti's campaign to protect Muslim holy sites, but was not necessarily planned by him. This was the mufti's way of handling politics: a hybrid approach toward domestic, nationalist, and religious politics that sought to inspire and unite the devout, illiterate peasant population, the urban literate classes, and the notable families under a common banner. This method offered unity of purpose to diverse, often competitive, parts of society. As a result of this mass mobilization, a broader segment of the public embraced the mufti's cause and discipline. The mufti could deny accusations that he was a nationalist agitator while upholding his responsibility as spiritual defender.

In 1929, the reorganization of the Palestine Zionist Executive (PZE), which was renamed the Jewish Agency (JA) and given expanded powers, contributed to Muslim fears about holy sites.[13] The JA was formed to represent all of world Jewry instead of just Zionists. Thereby, the religious demands of Jews and the nationalist demands of Zionists to the British government regarding the Western Wall were now represented by one officially recognized international organization. Following the Tisha B'Av demonstrations on 15 August, led by Betar and Jabotinsky, two thousand Muslims marched to the wall, desecrated a Torah scroll, and destroyed other property. On 17 August, a Jewish boy was stabbed after startling an Arab woman while trying to retrieve his ball from her garden. He died on the twentieth, and his funeral was the scene of further demonstrations. An Arab youth was killed in retaliation. Aharon Cohen, disguised as an Arab on behalf of the Haganah, entered al-Aqsa sometime shortly after 17 August and witnessed the stockpiling of pistols.[14] Rumors emerged from Hebron that the Jews aimed to attack al-Aqsa on Friday, 23 August. Armed men, inspired by the call to defend the site, began to pour into Jerusalem. After a week of incitement and propaganda, violence exploded on 23 August 1929.

Police monitored the tension, but it being August, many officials were away on holiday, including the HC, John Chancellor, and the police commandant, Arthur Mavrogordato. The acting commandant, Alan Saunders, did not attempt to disarm the peasants from the countryside for fear of provoking them. In any case, he only had a small reserve to call up, so he took the chance of allowing the leadership at the mosque to defuse the situation. The acting governor, Harry Luke, believed that leaders at al-Aqsa had complied with his plea that they should appeal for calm, yet certain sheikhs in its courtyard in fact delivered inflammatory Friday sermons. The mufti personally assured Saunders that the crowd would not act unless provoked. Saunders trusted al-Husseini's good faith, having worked with him for many years. However, the mufti did not control the mob that his propaganda had helped to create. By midday, Saunders had ordered the preparation of rifles for the British police, in anticipation of violence, but it was already too late—rioters had begun to rampage in the old city.[15]

By the end of 23 August, Luke had cabled Malta, requesting reinforcements, including one warship each to arrive at Jaffa and Haifa, and had asked London for a battalion of troops. On the twenty-fourth, he was informed that the battleship *Barham*, the cruiser *Sussex*, and the carrier *Courageous* would be dispatched. Egypt made available one composite battalion (typically eight hundred soldiers) and one section of engineers, who were to be dispatched by train on the night of the twenty-fourth. On the same day, the air officer commanding (AOC), Group Capt. Patrick Playfair, was ordered to arrange air transport for two officers and fifty soldiers, to be flown directly from Egypt to Jerusalem.[16] On the twenty-sixth, after several days of violence, a naval landing party took control of Jaffa, and various detachments dominated major cities. Brig. William Dobbie, who commanded troops from Egypt, reported that the situation in Jerusalem, Haifa, and Jaffa was "now well in hand. . . . But country outside these immediate centers [remains] unsettled."[17] Unprotected Jewish settlements were under constant attack, and Dobbie worried that assailants might began to attack British establishments. The settlements were widespread over rough terrain, which frustrated British movements to protect them. Dobbie called for an offensive policy to put an end to the attacks, since there were still not enough defensive troops available.

The Palestine government lacked the force to contain violence quickly. The British section of the police was too small, and unprepared to confront violence of this scale. To make matters worse, the Palestinian section of the police proved unreliable. Some Arab policemen refused orders, or withheld intelligence; others even participated in the violence on the side of the rioters.[18] Table 4.1 demonstrates how the trickling of reinforcements to Palestine was insufficient to secure the country.[19] It took a week for British forces to secure Palestine's urban centers and borders. Violence simmered in the countryside.

The violence caused the deaths of 133 Jews and 110 Arabs. Most Jews were killed by rioters, most Arabs by British police and military. Hillel Cohen's research shows how the events transformed the Yishuv by creating newfound solidarity between Arabic-speaking Palestinian Jews and the Zionist colonists.[20]

Two cases particularly scarred the Yishuv. On 24 August, fifty-nine religious Jews in Hebron were massacred, and the surviving residents of that centuries-old community were displaced by the violence. On 29 August in Safad, another ancient Jewish holy city, twenty Jews were killed.[21] And the violence continued beyond that date. During the first week of September, British troops and the RAF battled large bands of infiltrators from Transjordan and Syria who had come to attack Jewish settlements as the revolt spread. Dobbie reported on 5 September that "internally, the arrests which resulted from the numerous raids have had a good effect and disorder appears to

Table 4.1 Trickling of reinforcements to Palestine, 1929

DAY	MAJOR INCIDENTS	POLICE	TJFF	ARMY	RAF	NAVY
Fri., 23 Aug.	• Midday violence in Jerusalem • Reserves called	~1,375 local and ~250 British		none	• 1 sqn bombers • 1 section ACC arrived J'lem midday, another at night	none
Sat., 24 Aug.	• Overnight sniping in Jerusalem • AOC Playfair assumes command • Hebron massacre • Mufti disavows attributed call for defense, rumors of Jewish attack • Partial control of J'lem by nightfall • Colonies in North attacked • Decision against martial law • Decision against arming Jews • Press suspended	Volunteer special constables	• One coy in North • One coy near Jericho	Evening arrival by air of two pltns, 1/SWB	80 armed airmen arrive from Amman	
Sun., 25 Aug.	• Ongoing battles in Jerusalem • More reinforcements requested • 1 coy 1/SWB to Jaffa prevents worsening of situation • Police and SCs in J'lem exhausted, relieved by 2 coys 1/SWB • Bn HQ personnel armed and deployed		North: Detachment at area of Beisan and Beit Alfa, another at Safad	Arrival by train of remainder of 1/SWB, one coy 2/GH, and 1 sec RE.		
Mon., 26 Aug.	• 1 coy 2/GH to Haifa • Bedouin from Gaza move north, turned back by political officer • Persistent reports about incursions from Syria and TJ	Tel Aviv special police disbanded		Arrival remainder of 2/GH, 1 coy 1/Kings and 1 MT coy		*Sussex*, 270 Marines in Jaffa

(Continued)

Table 4.1 (Continued)

DAY	MAJOR INCIDENTS	POLICE	TJFF	ARMY	RAF	NAVY
Tues., 27 Aug.	• Dobbie assumes command of all forces in Palestine • 100 British constables requested from England • Attacks at Beit Alfa	Jewish special constables disarmed		One coy 2/GH moved to Afula, remainder of 2/GH to Jenin and Nablus		*Barham* to Haifa
Wed., 28 Aug.	• Calm in Jerusalem • Riots in Haifa, Acre • French intelligence and border cooperation			2/S.Staffs from Malta via *Courageous*		*Courageous* + six flights, + *Wanderer* and *Veteran*
Thurs., 29 Aug.	• Safad massacre • Chancellor returns • Battle at Hittin (vs. 1,000 underarmed Arabs)			One coy 2/GH arrives late to Safad		

Notes:

Squadron (sqn): 12 aircraft, or 3 flights. Naming convention: 2/S.Staffs—2nd Battalion, South Staffordshire Regiment.

Flight: 4 aircraft. Regiments: SWB—South Wales Borderers; GH—Green Howards; S.Staffs—South Staffordshire; RE—Royal Corps of Engineers; Kings—Kings Regiment (Liverpool).

Platoon (pltn): typically 30–50 troops.

Company (coy): typically 3 platoons.

Battalion (Bn): typically 800 troops, or 4 companies plus an HQ coy.

MT: Motor Transport.

have generally stopped."[22] He added that Bedouin from the South and cross-border raiders had been excited by false rumors about Jewish atrocities. In the countryside, he said, "the attitude of the Moslems [was] by no means settled," and propaganda for the defense of Buraq still inspired resistance. Yet even the previous day, the Transjordan Frontier Force (TJFF) and a company of Green Howards fought battles at the border near Jisr-Majmie' and Beisan.[23] The situation was precarious but the army had prevented outright rebellion. Operations lasted until 11 September 1929. For neither the first nor the last time, pan-Islamic propaganda had influenced the violence that unfolded outside Jerusalem, in the countryside, led by foreign fighters.

After suppressing rioters in the major cities until 29 August, police worked with troops to arrest offenders and to collect evidence that might lead to criminal convictions for rebels and rioters. Through "punitive actions," troops raided "offending villages." Then forces concentrated on border defense, which was secured by cooperation with the RAF and French authorities in Syria. Dobbie attributed the success of the operations to the mobility of his battalions. He thought the quick restoration of order had prevented a wider disturbance in Syria, Transjordan, Sinai, and Iraq.[24]

Dobbie aimed to "deal with this menace as far from the Palestine frontier as possible, and in any case, to get timely warning of any such hostile movement."[25] Although sometimes aircraft confronted attackers at Jewish settlements alone, RAF reconnaissance was coordinated with ground forces, including British troops and the TJFF. The TJFF was a mounted border force founded in 1926 to substitute for the disbanded Palestine gendarmerie (discussed below). Its praised performance paved the way for its expansion. Palestine's defense plan worked the way it was designed to—reserve troops responded to aid the civil power in an emergency. Yet the response was slow, and British decision makers were surprised by the outbreak. Rapid reaction depended on intelligence forewarning. The system obviously could not cope with the enormity of the problem: the complexity of the politics, the mechanics of deterrence, or the security of cities.

Violence had not completely ended in September 1929. Between October 1929 and March 1930, the army confronted an armed group called the Green Hand. According to Chancellor, the Green Hand was formed "of absconded offenders and other bad characters, inhabitants of Palestine and the neighboring territories, who for a considerable period after the disturbances of August last terrorized the more inaccessible parts of upper Galilee. . . . The question of organizing such bands has been discussed by disaffected politicians in both Palestine and Trans-Jordan."[26] Chancellor emphasized that these were not highway robbers, which had been a problem in Palestine until the early 1920s: "They are mainly escaped criminals, fugitives from justice and desperados from Syria. They have nothing to hope for and little to lose and they have been used as tools by disaffected politicians in order to create a state of anarchy in the belief that any change which might arise out of it would be better than the existing state of affairs in Palestine."[27]

The Green Hand exposed one of the country's essential policing problems—the challenging topography. The North had rough terrain ("broken and rocky," noted Chancellor), which favored the movements and concealment of brigands. To ameliorate this situation, Chancellor called for the construction of roads from Acre to Safad and improvements in other village tracks in the Golan and Sea of Galilee areas. In October 1929, while the army and police were still processing detainees from the riots, the gangs began to coalesce around Safad and attack police. On 1 November, the band was reinforced by Syrian Druze, experienced from their anti-French rebellion and connected to the mufti, who had previously supplied them through his aid agency in Transjordan. After numerous skirmishes, on 19 December 1929, the gang captured four policemen at the small village of Suhmata. There, the captive police learned that the band had adopted the name "Green Hand."[28] The group did some damage to police and troops, who responded forcefully. By the new year, substantial reinforcements had arrived in the region, and French troops had closed off the Syrian border. Secret agents supplied information to the police, suggesting the population's acceptance of government, although locals were sympathetic to the pious mujahideen, or holy warriors. At no point was the gang stronger than twenty-five armed men. By February, sixteen members had been caught, and by mid-March, the gang was broken: the ringleader, Ahmed Tafish, and several of his followers were arrested.[29]

The HC had expected other armed groups to form around Nablus, Hebron, and the Jerusalem–Jaffa corridor. However, combined operations by troops, the RAF, and police over the space of six weeks had "so harassed" combatants that the movement had been stunted. He warned, "It may, however, be anticipated that in the event of a recrudescence of disturbances in Palestine this method of embarrassing the government would be resorted to on a considerable scale."[30]

Telephone taps found in Jewish Agency records from October to November 1929 suggest that the mufti was connected to ongoing violence. (In 1938 the CID noted that the nationalist and religious supporters under the patronage of the mufti had backed the Green Hand.[31]) Jamal al-Husseini asked the mufti about preparations for a demonstration to coincide with the Shaw Commission of Enquiry, sent to investigate after the riots. Amin and Jamal debated whether to act immediately, or to wait until after the commission, when the movement would be better prepared. Impatient, the mufti said that to depend on the opinion of the Shaw Commission was "impossible, as the Jews are flowing into Palestine and the government is allowing them to come in. We must look for a way to frighten local and foreign Jews so that nobody should arrive here and that is the best means. Listen, Jamal, the matter must be examined thoroughly and we cannot do it by telephone."[32] What they were planning is unclear, but within weeks the mufti ordered arms to be distributed from a cache in David's tomb in Jerusalem to the youth in villages around Jerusalem. Curiously, like the Haganah, the mufti's supporters used euphemisms such as "bananas," "cucumbers," and "feathers" for arms.[33]

The end of the Green Hand was not the end of violent resistance in Palestine. Another group, called al-Kaf al-Aswad, or the Black Hand, emerged in Haifa in late 1929, and threatened to murder anyone who stood in the way of the Palestinian boycott of the Yishuv and British goods. The boycott was a youth-led response to the crushing of the Buraq revolt. A note in Haganah intelligence records from September 1930 described another Black Hand group centered in Tel Aviv, with some three thousand followers armed with wartime-era rifles and pistols.[34] It is unlikely that these various secret Black Hand societies were connected structurally. Rather, they adopted the intimidating motif of the Black Hand for the same reasons: to enforce secrecy and coerce conformity. The term "Black Hand" was ubiquitous, but groups with this name all had the common aim to kill any collaborator, or anyone who hampered the national movement, especially boycott efforts.

Air Control, Gendarmerie, and Palestine Security

The Israeli historian Eldad Harouvi eloquently characterizes the problem in Britain's response to the upset: "This was both a political and intelligence failure alike. It is possible that the army possessed the force to prevent the events, if only force had arrived in time."[35] Yet for intelligence to have failed, it would have had to exist. In this case, Britain's security failed as the result of a basic design flaw in its defense policy for Palestine.

The origins of the problem lay in the concurrence of the establishment of the British Mandate over Palestine and the slashing of security budgets at home. A colonial security policy known as "Air Control" sought to economically provide enough security that British policy could be enforced. The newly created RAF was granted responsibility for Middle East security. Championed by Churchill, the RAF had bested the army in a struggle for scant financial resources after proving its value in suppressing insurgencies in Afghanistan in 1919, and Somaliland, Palestine, and Iraq during 1920. Air

Control sought to substitute air forces for ground forces. The RAF had lower administrative and maintenance costs, as aircraft could patrol a wider range and respond more quickly than troops or cavalry. Air Control aimed for efficient and cheap imperial policing.[36]

Air Control was a key aspect of British strategic policy after 1918, as money was stripped from the armed services and Whitehall pressed its colonies to become self-sufficient in defense. Under the "ten-year rule," the treasury's guideline for defense estimates, military spending was limited by the expectation that no great war could occur within a decade. One cost-saving solution was the replacement of manpower with mechanical devices, especially in imperial policing. Indian cavalry was replaced with RAF armored car sections. But such measures were not enough. As the 1920s advanced, Britain's services became, according to John Ferris, "too weak to support its foreign policy yet too expensive to suit its financial one."[37] Nowhere were these problems more apparent than with Air Control in Palestine.

The main driver for Air Control in 1919–22 was Churchill, first as secretary for war and air, and then as colonial secretary, with power over Palestine and Iraq. In May 1920, he cautioned the cabinet that commanders in these locales were attempting to occupy huge territories: "Thus are they led under the pressure of local policy to wide dispersions of force and to consequent enormous increase in numbers and expense." Churchill instead argued for

> one single concentrated force at some convenient center point . . . and that from this base gradually in the process of years, ten or fifteen years if necessary, our influence should gradually be spread throughout the country. This process may be greatly assisted and accelerated by the use of air forces. It is, after all, the same process which we have hitherto always followed in the development of our great Asiatic and African possessions. Never have we attempted to settle down all over the country at once with a large proportion of the army used for the purposes of conquest.[38]

Air chief marshal Hugh Trenchard likewise thought that Air Control would enable political officers, who managed relations with tribes on the frontiers of colonial states, to quickly back up their threats with force, and so hold a country with small forces. He stressed the need for intelligence, gathered on the ground and by air reconnaissance, that could provide early warning of disturbances.[39] Some political officers had parallel views. Deedes, for example, warned that the presence of troops in Transjordan "might be regarded in some quarters as provocative rather than a means of pacification."[40] He believed that political officers could work better without a garrison, not by administering Transjordan directly, but rather by advising the local population in the conduct of their government. Though Transjordan was a unique example, the British also hoped to govern Palestine with a tiny administrative capability, and consent from the population.

Neither Churchill nor Trenchard envisioned the complete replacement of ground forces; both accepted the need for a small, preferably local, garrison and gendarmerie. In Transjordan, this vision was realized with the creation of the Arab Legion for local security and, in 1926, the TJFF for border security. In Palestine, after 1929 the TJFF replaced the gendarmerie's function in the North of the country. Local policing and paramilitary forces remained weak, and British policy toward arming Jewish settlements was inconsistent.

The role of the RAF, intelligence, and military forces in British imperialism within the Middle East has been a source of controversy in recent scholarly works. In *Spies in Arabia*, a study of the culture of British intelligence and imperialism in the Middle East, Priya Satia has characterized Air Control as "terror" stemming from the imagination of paranoid officials.[41] This postcolonialist interpretation neglects the breadth of evidence on this issue. For instance, it overlooks the fact that economy in administration was the main motivation for Air Control. Nor does "terror" explain why officials feared the moral repercussions of using tear gas against rioters, but not aircraft and demolition.[42] These norms were in flux, and a source of tension among British officials after the First World War. In Satia's words, *Spies in Arabia* is not about policy, but "is essentially about the realm of *practice*—military diplomatic intelligence. It does not dispute the historiography on policy so much as provide a cultural-historical explanation for the particular institutional environment in which it was formed."[43] Satia's work aids our understanding of colonialist attitudes in the intelligence realm, giving shape to an important missing dimension in the relationship between colonizer and colonized. Yet *Spies in Arabia* offers skewed assessments of how policy was made and executed, and on those issues, rests on assertion over evidence. Satia overemphasizes racism and orientalist imagination; while these are important issues, they must be taken together with the broad base of multinational and multilingual evidence about intelligence and policy.

Air Control was an administrative arrangement, first and foremost. It aimed to save money, to maintain British force abroad, and to assert British security interests. This arrangement helped persuade conservative skeptics to agree to allow self-government in Transjordan and Iraq, since it left the empire with the means to influence local authorities and to strike in case of emergency. Air Control promised to limit the recurrence of bloody and lengthy "small wars." As Churchill wrote in 1922, "This does not imply that

Palestine is to be controlled from the air, but merely that as a convenience the administrative channel through which the military affairs of the country will be conducted will be the Air Ministry and not the War Office."[44]

Air Control worked as it was designed, but this was not enough to secure Palestine, since the policy exacerbated the basic contradictions of the mandate. It was better suited to frontier security than to an urban and settled country such as Palestine. So long as the Balfour Declaration had to be imposed against the will of the Arab population, Air Control's aim to minimize forces and costs was especially ill advised. The proposed system would depend on early-warning intelligence, a garrison, and the raising of local security forces: police, gendarmes, frontier forces, and defense forces. This vision never came to fruition, blocked by a series of uncoordinated actions. A gendarmerie comprising mainly ex–Black and Tans from Ireland was raised in Palestine, and then disbanded. By the end of the 1920s, only Arab local forces—that is, the Arab Legion and TJFF—existed. The police force lacked personnel, especially British officers. Table 4.2 illustrates how

Table 4.2   British forces in Palestine and Transjordan, 1921–29

YEAR	ARMY GARRISON	RAF	POLICE[a]	GENDARMES	TJFF
1921	4,400 British, 10,800 Indian	1 sqn	~1,300 local, ~200 British	—	—
1922	4,879 British, 1,763 Indian, 875 Egyptian	1 sqn	~1,300 local, ~200 British	762 British, 533 local	—
1923	1 British company	1 sqn, 3 AC (armored car) sections	~1,300 local, ~200 British	762 British, 462 local	—
1924	1 British cavalry regiment	1 sqn, 3 AC sections	~1,300 local, ~200 British	462 British, 482 local	—
1925	Jan.–Aug. none / From Aug. 1, British cav reg	1 sqn, 3 AC sections	~1,300 local, ~200 British	462 British, 475 local	—
1926	1 British cav reg departed February	1 sqn, 3 AC sections	~1,375 local, ~250 British	Disbanded	787
1927	—	1 sqn, 3 AC sections	~1,375 local, ~250 British	—	675
1928	—	1 sqn, 3 AC sections	~1,375 local, ~250 British	—	628
Jan.–Aug. 1929	—	1 sqn, 3 AC sections	~1,375 local, ~250 British	—	506
Aug.–Oct. 1929	3 bns, 1 AC section, ancillaries	2 sqns, 5 AC sections	+100–170 special constables	—	536
Dec. 1929	2 bns	2 sqns, 4 AC sections	~1,300 local, 378 British	—	593

Source: Kolinsky, "Reorganization of the Palestine Police," 158.

a The sources have major discrepancies for this. For instance, in 1928 the police force may have been as strong as 2,100 total.

the strength of the British garrison in Palestine declined throughout this decade. Security was vulnerable to sudden crises and was left dependent on reinforcements from Egypt.[45]

Compounding the problem, the end of the military regime also meant the end of centralized intelligence, which was seen as an expensive wartime mechanism and redundant in peacetime, along with the general staff. RAF staff handled maps and statistics, and only scant political intelligence from Transjordan. In fact, in 1927, RAF intelligence officers were explicit in their need to focus on tribal events in Transjordan and were not disposed to watching Palestine. The high commissioner told Air headquarters that "Palestine is a settled country and that we may expect no trouble there beyond that well within the capabilities of the police." He even went so far as to say that he was "not justified in keeping Imperial troops in Palestine merely to cope with the Palestine situation."[46] Indeed, those troops left the next month. RAF intelligence only handled tribal politics between Transjordan, Syria, Iraq, Hejaz, and Nejd. Adding to the challenges was a shortage of Arabic-speaking intelligence officers throughout most of the 1920s.[47]

Colonial governors and district governors handled political intelligence, as did the CID, but no single staff ever saw all the material. This situation transpired because of improvised decisions made at Whitehall and Jerusalem that lost focus on the vision for Middle East security, outlined in 1920, while no strategic policy for Palestine ever truly materialized. In other words, a patchy security and intelligence regime was meant to enforce Britain's ill-defined Palestine policy. As Gilbert Clayton reportedly told the French consul in 1924, "You cannot explain a policy, if you do not have one. We live for the moment without any foresight, only maneuvering between the cliffs, as soon as they appear. Where the journey goes, nobody knows."[48]

The Yishuv played a part in security strategy. Britain could not raise a mixed local defense force, and it could not deploy enough troops to cover all of Palestine, so it armed Jewish settlements. The Yishuv would have to defend itself in an emergency. Richard Meinertzhagen, still a political officer, proposed that Jewish militiamen should be "embodied in an official reserve to the existing police, and it should be explained to the Arabs that they will not be called out except in the event of unprovoked aggression, in which case the whole force of the Government will be behind them."[49] Samuel approved. He told Sir John Shuckburgh of the CO that economy prevented the establishment of an imperial garrison while intercommunal tension prevented the formation of a mixed Jewish-Arab force, or all-Arab or all-Jewish forces. Arming the Jews to defend themselves could ease this burden. T. E. Lawrence thought that a serious rising against Jewish colonists was a real danger, which should be prevented by Samuel's proposed legislative council or some kind of representative government. He also thought that arming Jewish colonists would allow the Yishuv "to resist in case of local trouble until the British troops can be moved to its support."[50] Without representative government, Britain must arm the Yishuv.

Yishuv settlements were given locked armories containing shotguns, to be used in emergency. The Jewish and Arab sections of the gendarmerie remained segregated. Samuel accepted both Meinertzhagen's proposal and Air Control, but the two policies were in direct contradiction. Air Control, which aimed for cheap imperial security, required locally raised forces, which proved politically impossible in Palestine. Deedes concluded that a mixed force could only work if it was led by British officers and had equal numbers of Jewish, Arab, and foreign recruits.[51] These plans were scrapped and the government promoted local settlement defense instead of expanding the Jewish section of the gendarmerie or desegregating it. The arming of Jewish settlements later would become one of Britain's more controversial policies, but Samuel and others understood that mixed security forces would be unreliable and could not protect the Yishuv.[52] Their security policy, which armed Jewish settlements and required the importation of British officers, undermined the need for economy. The contradictions between representative government and locally raised defense forces showed that British policy was unworkable—a term used by officials only in 1937—but British decision makers improvised, as if tightrope-walking on a tug-of-war rope.

The British gendarmerie consisted of ex–Black and Tans from the Royal Ulster Constabulary, a large Arab section, and a smaller Jewish section. It was a paramilitary force meant to police northern Palestine, which featured rough terrain, bad roads, porous borders, and brigandage. Until 1922, this area was managed by Indian cavalry, expensive to maintain abroad. That year, Maj. Gen. Henry Hugh Tudor, who was appointed AOC in Palestine and director of public safety (police and prisons department), negotiated with Whitehall for financial support to improve the gendarmerie, but was limited by budget cuts.[53] The Air Ministry approved other cost-saving measures, such as limits on the RAF squadron's flying duties, and planned to withdraw British cavalry by 1925.[54] Whitehall was pleased with the savings realized from replacing Indian troops with local gendarmes, whom Tudor and Deedes attempted to professionalize.[55] Clayton had feared the loss of mounted troops and so tied reductions in imperial forces to increases in gendarmerie. The presence of imperial troops, he said, had "a strong moral effect" and deterred violence.[56]

In 1926, Whitehall supplied a grant-in-aid to the Palestine government to pay for the gendarmerie, and enacted loan guarantees for the development of the country.[57] These loans, however, were for economic development, not security. In order to further the aims and efficiencies of substitution, the Air Ministry sought to foster self-sufficiency for Palestine's defense, and to eliminate imperial forces save for those needed to protect air bases.[58] As HC, Lord Plumer adapted to limited means with cuts. His plan to disband the gendarmerie was driven by the notion that "Palestine is a police country only."[59] He assumed that imperial help would be able to react in time to a major disturbance.

The CO and Air Ministry argued over whether the gendarmerie should be incorporated into the police, or the defense force under the RAF. Under financial pressure, the Air Ministry aimed to cut the proportion of British gendarmes. The force was more expensive than had been imagined in 1921, even more so than the cavalry and regular garrison, which was due to be permanently withdrawn.[60] Since Palestine bore the cost, Plumer's decision to disband the gendarmerie in 1926 and allow the withdrawal of cavalry was sensible. Palestine maintained those expenses during economic recession in 1926 without financial assistance, and began to borrow. As forces in Palestine were cut, Plumer assumed that in an emergency he could depend on reserves in Transjordan and Egypt. Plumer alerted Egypt and the CO that he might need emergency reserves from Egypt in the event of disturbances.[61] The high commissioner in Egypt rejected this idea, which might have set a precedent and cause the War Office to impose military reductions on Egypt. He wrote, "Plumer only a few weeks ago decided he could not only do without British troops, but also, I believe, that he could afford to dispense with the British personnel in the Palestine Gendarmerie. That was his risk. I propose it should remain his."[62] Such limitations shaped the unfolding of violence in 1929, since Egypt was expected to be a base for an imperial reserve force, but the politics of austerity prevented the commitment of such forces. Nevertheless, British troops based in Egypt formed the main response to contain violence in 1929.

With the gendarmerie disbanded, the newly formed TJFF secured the rough terrain in the North, but only in Transjordan. It deployed to northern Palestine after the 1929 outbreak. Papers included in a report by the Palestine Garrison Subcommittee of the Committee of Imperial Defense reveal the discrepancy. In 1925, the gendarmerie could control the main strategic centers of Palestine. By 1929, the police had no paramilitary support and no reserve force. There were only 140 British officers out of a force of 1,300.[63] In addition to the police, there was one company of armored cars, and one RAF squadron.

Another decision by Plumer that damaged security was to disarm the Yishuv in 1928. Understandably, Jewish arms worried Arabs. Plumer replaced the sealed armories in the Yishuv with village watchmen, known to the British as *ghaffirs*, or *notarim* in Hebrew. They fell under the command of the Palestine Police and received salaries, but were only placed in villages that could pay those salaries. When the decision came in early 1928 to disarm the Yishuv, Achdut leader Yitzhak Ben-Zvi highlighted the risk that this could pose to the Jewish settlements.[64] It also contradicted earlier promises. After much negotiation, Colonel Kisch only achieved a partial cancellation of the disarmament. Older settlements could keep their arms, but new ones would have to pay for *notarim*. Kisch warned the government that guns that had been smuggled to the anti-French rebels in Syria could easily flow in the opposite direction.[65]

Decisions made between 1922 and 1929 in Whitehall and Jerusalem left Palestine unprepared for disturbances. Mismatched policies emerged due to financial restrictions in London and Jerusalem, and differing views among the Air Ministry, the Colonial Office, and the Palestine government about the role of security forces. These issues overrode the strategy that had been envisioned for Palestine, which necessitated the raising of local security. Air Control never could have managed Palestine, which was urban, settled, and volatile, and lacked local defense forces. However, this strategy was not comprehensive enough to address the main shortcoming in security—the lack of a force to manage the irreconcilable politics of the country. The resources Britain cobbled together were designed to provide cheap security. The revolt of 1929 proved that there could be no cheap security so long as Britain enforced the Zionist policy.

The Evaporation of Security Intelligence

During the First World War, military and political intelligence was coordinated under Allenby's General Staff, based in Cairo. Political intelligence from the Arab Bureau, sigint, and other sources could be coordinated with General Staff Intelligence (GSI) for war planning. Allenby's coordination of political and military intelligence was cutting-edge practice in the British system. The system continued under the military government in Palestine until Herbert Samuel's takeover as high commissioner in July 1920. It dissolved when security control was handed to the RAF in the spring of 1921. From then on, British security became increasingly dependent on Zionist partnership.

During 1919–20, many officials proposed establishing a permanent combined intelligence service for the Middle East on the model of the Arab Bureau. Deedes, then chief secretary for the civil government of Palestine, argued that Britain was not fully exploiting its occupation of Turkey and Syria, and that the work of the Arab Bureau should expand to include all of the Islamic world.[66] In the name of austerity, Deedes's suggestions were rejected and the GSI system was abandoned, as Whitehall aimed to cut budgets and decentralize control. Consequently, intelligence bureaucracy, well developed in 1919, declined during the 1920s.

Security was one of Samuel's main concerns during his first month as HC. The Franco-Syrian War raged, as did the war in Anatolia, while London began pressure to reduce military forces and slash intelligence budgets. This affected intelligence expenditures in Palestine, and forced Samuel to ask the Foreign and India Offices for expertise and finance.[67] The Palestinian government had access to the scant secret service funds allocated by secret vote in London, which could be used to pay agents. Other ministries, usually the Foreign Office, could provide funding for intelligence work, but the secret vote allocated resources for SIS. In 1922, after the army command was replaced with RAF administration, the FO authorized a mere £40 (no more than two months' salary for one low-level official) for Palestine from its own budget to pay for agents.[68] The War Office had received part of the secret service budget because it occupied Istanbul and the Rhine. Its allocation for Palestine was £3,000 in 1922.[69] However, this money was designated for intelligence on Bolshevism and pan-Islam, issues related to security in Istanbul and elsewhere. For local intelligence targets Samuel needed another solution, and turned to Zionist partnership.

Zionist institutions also fell victim to budget cuts, albeit to a lesser extent. A sudden shortage of cash led to one curious spectacle in August 1920, when Arab informants began to line up outside ZC offices asking for their payment. That year the IB spent £2,000 on bribes for Nablus notables—a fraction of its intelligence budget. But that resource was quickly depleted.[70] Intelligence officers such as Davidescu complained of lack of resources. Agents were not paid.[71] Bribes for Bedouin sheikhs, notables, and newspapermen had exhausted financial resources.

For most of the 1920s, Kalvarisky's Arab-Jewish cooperation program was the sole surviving intelligence office under the umbrella of the PZE. Kalvarisky reported to Colonel Kisch, chair of the PZE; the Va'ad Leumi; and Edmund de Rothschild of the Palestine Jewish Colonization Association (PICA).[72] The PZE used Kalvarisky for political and economic intelligence, while the Va'ad authorized budgets for his Arab Secretariat. Kalvarisky had worked for Rothschild and PICA's predecessor, the Jewish Colonization Association, since around 1900. PICA required intelligence that would facilitate land acquisition and settlement. During the war, Kalvarisky proved his worth as he managed to secure land through loans while cut off from France and Rothschild's funds.[73] In 1928 the PZE dropped Kalvarisky's Arab-Jewish cooperation program to save its cost, which had always been controversial as the various Yishuv institutions never agreed about Arab policy.

The lack of organized intelligence work left the Yishuv unprepared for the 1929 riots.[74] So did the lack of expertise on the British side. Martin Thomas argues that in Palestine an "intelligence state" was "elusive."[75] Indeed, no central machinery could process the various sources of intelligence available to the police, the RAF, the high commissioner, or district governors. All of these bodies used intelligence of different sorts, and not one grasped the entire picture. The problem was not so much one of incompetency as one of ignorance, derived from a lack of experienced staff and inadequate organization. From 1920 to 1927, Clayton, Deedes, Symes, and others managed an informal "intelligence state," which departed the country with them. A community of colonial officials experienced in intelligence and familiar with local problems was replaced by inexperienced ones who lacked their predecessors' habits for handling intelligence. They did not know each other or the country.

In 1927, the Palestine authorities and SIS characterized the mufti as being "thoroughly bad."[76] The next year, the close watch on the mufti, which lasted from 1921 to 1927 and raised many suspicions, simply vanished. Suspicions were based on access to secret intelligence, and the colonial relationship was guided by that knowledge. This careful handling of a core problem in Palestine evaporated from the regular practice of the police, the high commissioner, John Chancellor, and his deputies. No single arm of government saw the dangers associated with the mufti's Wailing Wall campaign, or how his machinations might cause disturbances. Police assumed the mufti's plea for calm would have more effect than what materialized.

British Security Reforms

Security reforms after the riots created two parallel "intelligence states." One took civilian form: close collaboration with the chief secretary by the police and the CID. The other was embodied by RAF Air Staff Intelligence (ASI). HC Chancellor sought to reorganize the CID and make it the main source of political and security intelligence, on which all arms of government and the military could depend. His emphasis on the civilian CID was part of a philosophy of good government, never explicitly articulated but evident nonetheless. A short time after the riots, he met with Air vice marshal Hugh Dowding, the district commissioners, and the commanders of the police,

TJFF, and Arab Legion to discuss the recently stabilized situation. Chancellor insisted that they "must rely on the reorganised Criminal Investigation Department for information." Saunders, still acting commandant of the police, said that they were "experiencing difficulty in getting information as their sources were weaker now than they had ever known before."[77]

Dowding, who had just taken command of the RAF, reported on the situation before the meeting with Chancellor. He blamed the "melting away" of the Palestinian police while under stress, combined with a lack of intelligence. He maintained that the CID must be drastically reformed, and include a liaison between civil and military intelligence. He recommended that a small intelligence staff be attached to Air headquarters in Palestine, to control four special service officers (SSOs), modeled after the system the RAF was using in Iraq.[78] Chancellor did not wish to install SSOs, which he thought were better suited for tribal warfare on the frontiers of empire.[79] They were also controversial, as many Iraqis interpreted "SSO" to mean "secret" service officer, which in a sense they were. A hybrid system was put in place, which included a new and improved police and CID, embodying a "civil" intelligence state, and staff intelligence coordinating SSO and other sources, embodying a "military" intelligence state. SSOs were recruited and given authority to run agents and handle military and political intelligence across the Middle East.[80] Within a few years, SSOs in Palestine took on the roles of both intelligence liaison between civil and military authorities, and assessors of multiple sources of intelligence. They would become the main coordinators of military and political intelligence.[81]

In 1930, the policing expert Herbert Dowbiggin was brought in to examine and reform the regime in Palestine. His secret and harshly critical report drew many conclusions about the form and organization of police, of which he determined intelligence was the weakest branch. Officers and men needed more training and supervision, he said, and the whole organization lacked vision, initiative, and leadership. Dowbiggin criticized police commandant Mavrogordato in particular.[82] He called for a new commandant—brighter and with vision. Dowbiggin insisted, "The days of the illiterate constable are over." Mavrogordato, to his credit, at least understood the role of police, and its limitations. He lacked British policemen and, as of November 1929, could only effectively cover the three main towns of Palestine. He thought troops were necessary to come to the aid of the civil power after disturbances had occurred, and also as a deterrent.[83]

Dowbiggin also called for the coordination of military and police intelligence. He prescribed a formula for a binational, federalist police force that would not discriminate by race or religion. While his report was not entirely implemented, it did influence the reshaping of the Palestine Police and its organization, staffing, and use of intelligence.[84] One reform that could not be implemented was the mixing of Arab, Jewish, and British police. Instead, by the 1936 rebellion some three thousand Jews had been drafted as supernumerary police for settlement defense.[85]

Police reforms accompanied broader security reforms. The RAF helped to suppress disturbances, which otherwise might have become a revolt. The chiefs of staff focused on the role of police in suppressing riots, and on the need for intelligence to anticipate them. The lack of reserves and the disbandment of the gendarmerie were seen as mistakes. Dowding believed that a mobile battalion was necessary to fill this role—perhaps the TJFF, but a British battalion might be more reliable (but expensive). The cabinet considered recruiting Assyrian Christians from Iraq, but this would introduce political problems to both countries.[86] Dobbie, however, insisted on a permanent garrison of two British battalions, preferably under a Palestine command, separate from Egypt. Air policing would continue in the deserts of southern Palestine and eastern Jordan, but Palestine was different. By the summer of 1930, the cabinet had agreed that two battalions would remain in Palestine, and that the entire security regime would be reevaluated annually.[87] The CID became a political police, investigating Communists, the pan-Arab and pan-Islamic movements, local Jewish and Arab politics, and immigration and naturalization.[88]

This system still restrained security policy. Military forces, as during the 1929 riots, could only serve "in aid to the civil power" and never take over a policing function, or adopt a war footing. The air minister emphasized the bad optics of maintaining order in a mandate through military force.[89] This attitude defined government thinking until 1938. From these reforms in 1930 until 1936, an air officer remained in command of British forces in Palestine. As a consequence of this hybrid arrangement, an informal process of interservice coordination of operations and intelligence developed.

The formulation of the ASI in Palestine, which coordinated military and political intelligence and produced periodic reports, was an important step forward for security. The ASI was the first return to staff intelligence since the military regime ended in 1920. Its relationship with government was difficult.[90] Its activity was distinct from and often competed with the CID. SSOs were installed in Palestine by the end of 1930, and became active in 1931. They employed office staff, paid informers, and Jewish and Arab liaison officers. They served as liaison officers between the army and police, but SSOs and the CID competed over agents.[91] SSOs functioned as a security service for the country, coordinating military and political intelligence.

Intelligence assessments also were produced by the army's "I" Branch, which informally cooperated with the ASI. A position/individual designated X2, which first appears in documents around 1935, worked with the CID and military intelligence. X2 played a coordinating role with SIS intelligence from abroad, and may have been an SIS representative in Palestine. According to the official historian Keith Jeffrey, the SIS office in Palestine was opened in 1933.[92] X2 may also have been the cipher officer at staff headquarters, or perhaps those roles overlapped. Since that officer shared intelligence from outside Palestine with local officers, he may also have handled top-secret material from the listening station in Britain's large military base at the village of Sarafand, which monitored wireless communications in the Mediterranean, the Red Sea, the Black Sea, Arabia, and Central Asia. Sarafand intercepts were passed to the Government Code and Cypher School (GC&CS, today's GCHQ).

The reformed security regime was only loosely coordinated—mainly by the chief secretary and high commissioner, who consulted each intelligence service but worked most closely with the CID, and tended to exclude the ASI from decision making. This new security regime faced several tests during 1931–36. One of its biggest weaknesses was the coordination of policy with intelligence. The effectiveness of the police and CID was the acid test of the viability of the mandatory system, and of Britain's stewardship of Palestine in the eyes of the League of Nations. The league pressured Britain to perform, since it overwhelmingly supported Zionist claims that Britain had failed to protect the Yishuv in 1929, and that the Shaw Commission inquiry into the riots had whitewashed the mufti. The PMC reaffirmed its view that the development of democracy and the Jewish national home were the priorities of the mandate. However, the former project was vaguely defined, and contradicted the latter so long as the majority of the population opposed Jewish immigration. Such objections, and consequent delays toward democracy, were justified by the immediate obligation of the mandatory power: to protect the inhabitants.[93]

The reform of the CID was approved in August 1930. By February 1931, it began production of at least two political summaries per month, which were submitted to the chief secretary.[94] Fresh faces were brought into the police leadership, along with a clearer command hierarchy, professional record keeping, modern fingerprinting, and other reforms.[95] Dowbiggin reshaped the police on a civil model (later criticized by Charles Tegart[96]).

Britain had been embarrassed at the league for its failure to protect Jews; the Yishuv had demanded the restoration of sealed armories, and Arab politicians increasingly expressed their dismay that Britain had acquiesced to that demand. Both Arabs and Jews were arming themselves. In a strange incident, Joseph Davidescu, long inactive in the realm of intelligence, was arrested in Beirut in early October 1929 with five others in possession of rifles, pistols, grenades, and a machine gun. He was sentenced to six months' imprisonment. Palestinian leaders worried that compatriots had helped Jews purchase arms. Subhi al-Khadra, a member of the 1919 Istiqlal Party and graduate of the Ottoman Military Academy, phoned Ahmed al-Imam, a mufti supporter based in Haifa, to discuss such activities.[97] Al-Imam, in turn, asked the future first prime minister of Lebanon, Riad al-Sulh, who said, "Many Moslems were buying arms in Beirut for Arabs. We helped them to buy. They have purchased a large quantity of rifles and revolvers, and a small quantity of machine guns. All this was purchased for Arabs and it is possible that part of it was sold to Jews."[98] They did not realize that the buyer was indeed a Jew from Palestine. Curiously, Arabs referred to Davidescu as Joseph Daood (David).

The Arabs arrested with Davidescu included Khayr al-Din al-Ahdab, who became an agent of the JA's newly created intelligence arm, the Joint Bureau (JB), in 1930. Hajj Khalil Taha and one of his brothers were also arrested. They had Jewish contacts, but never were Zionists. In fact, the testimony of Hussein Effendi Taha, a Haifa landowner of the same family, led to Davidescu's conviction.[99] The French authorities sent his arrest and conviction records to the British, who considered revoking the OBE that Davidescu had earned in 1919. He could keep his award, forgiven, just as Churchill forgave his conviction for perjury in 1922—an affair for which Davidescu had resigned from the Haifa police.[100] After he was released from the Beirut prison, he returned to Palestine and began official work for the newly installed SSO in Haifa. Here began a new pattern, as Davidescu only worked on matters "which would not harm Jews." Davidescu reported that the SSO and CID were in competition.[101] Other sources also reported that the two services often competed for and manipulated each other's agents.[102]

Zionists also cooperated with the Jerusalem SSO, Patrick Domvile, the "best Zionist informer on the English," according to the historian Tuva Friling.[103] Domvile hired Reuven Zaslani, then a protégé of Dov Hoz of the Histadrut and Labor Party, Moshe Shertok of the Jewish Agency Political Department (JAPD), and the Haganah's de facto commander, Eliyahu Golomb. Golomb, Hoz, and Shertok were brothers-in-law, and among the first graduating class of the high school Gymnasia Hertzliya in Tel Aviv. Zaslani, born in 1909 in Jerusalem, was an Arabist trained at Hebrew University, although he never graduated. He later changed his name to Shiloah, and became the founding chief of Israel's Mossad. Still very junior in 1931, he was hired as Domvile's translator, personal secretary, and liaison to the

Haganah's Jerusalem commander, Yacov Pat. As Domvile's secretary and head agent, Zaslani visited the headquarters of RAF and army intelligence, and the CID. This experience played an important part in the relationships that he cultivated during later years, and in his "hospitality policy," which fostered friendly relations with British military, intelligence, and political figures while they were stationed in Palestine.[104] Anglo-Zionist cooperation reached new heights, even as the government grew more suspicious of Yishuv hostility, arms smuggling, and illegal immigration. Zaslani's work was the foundation of Israeli intelligence. It was also the beginning of what would become Zionism's most important weapon against Britain in the 1940s, as JA and Haganah intelligence penetrated British government and mastered intelligence work during a secret war against the mandate.[105]

The 1929 riots were a watershed for politics and security in Palestine. Uncoordinated government decisions between Jerusalem and London had left Palestine defenseless, and without an effective body to handle politico-security intelligence. The Wailing Wall dispute and ensuing violence exposed all the security weaknesses that had developed since 1920. An intelligence state had not materialized, and security forces were, for all intents and purposes, nonexistent. In the aftermath, two intelligence states were created, one civil and one military. Liberal values embodied by the league and the mandatory system pushed policy toward making government as civilian as possible, so the CID became the main source for security. Whitehall and Jerusalem both strived for liberal solutions, hoping in vain to resolve Arab demands for self-government and to limit the Zionist policy. Meanwhile, security was enhanced at considerable cost. A garrison was introduced to Palestine, as well as a military intelligence staff who began to work on political matters and to cooperate with Zionists. Reforms addressed many of the security flaws that had led to the 1929 disturbances, but none of the underlying political problems. Palestine's security reforms were the price Britain paid for not reconciling its conflicting commitments as the mandatory power.

CHAPTER 5

British Intelligence, the Mufti, and Nationalist Youth

During 1930–35, a number of changes in Arab politics occurred that affected relations with Britain and the Palestine government. Youth leadership came to prominence as the older guard, who had founded the first Istiqlal Party after the First World War, sought to inject new energy and drive to their movement. Palestinian nationalism, formerly an elite domain, became a mass movement. This youth-led cause adopted the objective of full independence in response to a decade of British intransigence around the Zionist policy, and because of Palestinian alarm about the Yishuv's growing foothold in Palestine. The new nationalists no longer wanted to reform the constitution or reverse the Zionist policy: Britain had become the enemy. Arab notables, having achieved little, saw the need for a course correction and counted on youth leadership to achieve that. Ambitious younger leaders sought more—at times highlighting the shortcomings of ECPAC and accusing notables such as the mufti of working too closely with government. And yet these were the years when the mufti climbed toward peak influence, when he and his inner circle inspired and initiated the growth of mass movements through the youth. Newly available evidence from intelligence records highlights his complex role as a popular leader and government officer. He had to balance those interests, but clandestinely supported mass movements through his official offices. With other pan-Arab leaders, the mufti intended to use mass movements to pressure British poli-cymakers. That strategy paved the road to the 1936 revolt.

It began with the optimistic outcome of a visit to Britain. The 1929 distur-bances forced a review of policy. After receiving a delegation including the mufti but led by Musa Kazim, Lord Passfield of the Colonial Office issued a White Paper revising the terms of immigration policy for the first time since 1922, when Churchill had tied it to Palestine's "absorptive capacity." Passfield's new policy interpreted that capacity using stricter metrics. Arab unemployment would have been an obstacle to Jewish immigration, and land transfers would be subject to British approval.

These diplomatic gains were soon scuttled by Chaim Weizmann and Prime Minister Ramsay MacDonald. In early 1931, Weizmann's intervention into parliamentary and cabinet affairs secured MacDonald's reversal of Pass-field's restrictions. Land transfers remained open to Zionist agencies, and absorptive capacity was measured within the Yishuv alone.[1] To Arab elites and youth alike, it was a gauntlet thrown down.

British and Zionist intelligence developed what they believed were good assessments of increasingly complex Palestinian politics. They understood the need to look beyond Palestine's borders to appreciate events in that coun-try, as well as the importance of rising mass political movements, especially the new Palestine Istiqlal Party, founded in 1932. As their grasp of these is-sues improved, the government obliviously and confidently maintained a sense of control, when in fact Palestinian nationalists were increasingly en-raged by, and prepared to attack, British rule. Both the government and the CID failed to understand the mufti's relationships with movements and indi-viduals across borders and time, or how these relationships shaped Palestine.

It is not surprising that the CID and the government overlooked the mufti's influence over the youth movements and the Palestine Istiqlal Party. These groups were some of the mufti's main critics, especially as they sought to wrest the national movement from elites. Although some historians ar-gued otherwise, new intelligence evidence demonstrates that the mufti and his close circle were instrumental in the rise of the nationalist youth, who actually worked symbiotically with elites. The contradictions in the body of evidence explain why policymakers did not grasp the symbiosis between the main Palestinian auxiliary to British power and the parties hostile to it.

The mufti was a consummate manager of relationships: in pan-Arab and local nationalist networks, with youth movements, and as president of the SMC. His skill is revealed in the British intelligence assessments covering the mufti and youth movements, and explains why the government believed it could depend on the mufti despite evidence of his subversive activity. The government believed it could exploit the vicious competition between the al-Husseini and Nashashibi families in order to maintain its supremacy in Arab politics. The high commissioner, Arthur Wauchope, felt he had maintained his predecessors' well-established codependency with the mufti, and believed that the mufti would not dare risk government financial or moral support for his official status as president of the SMC.

Nepotism determined SMC committee and employee appointments. Leading politicians, including 'Ajaj Nuwayhid, 'Auni 'Abdul Hadi, 'Izzat Darwaza, Ya'aqub al-Ghussein, Rashid al-Hajj Ibrahim, Subhi al-Khadra, and others, were all members of ECPAC or the SMC; all benefited from SMC funding, and therefore the mufti's patronage. They were all delegates to the mufti's 1931 pan-Islamic congress in Jerusalem, and many were party to the pan-Arab program that developed on the sidelines. They all became members of Istiqlal and its affiliated youth parties, which, historians agree, led Palestinian resistance from its founding until the revolt.[2] The mufti and his inner circle deserve partial credit for the rise of Istiqlal and the youth parties.

The intricacies of Palestinian and pan-Arab politics were studied intensely by the military and civil intelligence states. Their evidence reveals the inner workings of those states, and the government's relationship with Palestinian leaders. Wauchope enabled the mufti to improve his status in the Islamic world, believing this was a check on Palestinian nationalists, when in fact it was another avenue to mobilize Palestinians against the Zionist policy. Beginning in 1931, the mufti used the pan-Islamic congress to improve his own prestige while the British used it to secure his cooperation. The mufti and the government struck a bargain: the SMC would receive a subsidy and the mufti would stay out of nationalist politics. In line with the government's cooperative approach to the most influential Palestinian, the CID ceased to provide assessments that attributed nationalist violence to the mufti's influence. To do so made government policy look impotent, and left it without a Palestinian partner. Military intelligence, however, remained suspicious.

Younger nationalists began to perceive the mufti as part and parcel of British imperialism. Yet many of them were also sympathetic to pan-Islam and the mufti's leadership, and they certainly benefited from his allocation of funds to regional officers of the SMC. The mufti shaped the nationalists, including their ideas about resistance. His pan-Islamic activity served to reinvigorate higher-level pan-Arab activity, and to increase the influence of the Geneva-based Syro-Palestinian congress under Shakib Arslan and Rashid Rida. Arslan and Rida were always admired by the youth, who gobbled up their writings. They remained close to the mufti throughout, despite differences over strategy. It was on the sidelines of the 1931 pan-Islamic congress that a new pan-Arab strategy took shape. Characteristically, the mufti took the spotlight at the conference and maintained comfortable distance from his compatriots, who formed a pact to exploit European crises to pressure Britain and France for independence. That strategy evolved and escalated from 1932 to 1936.

On the Mufti and the Politics of Notables

Historians discussing these issues have been limited not only by lack of access to records now available, but also by the way in which the debates have evolved. The first histories of Palestinian leaders emphasized the "politics of notables"—the leadership of elite families such as the al-Husseinis, Khalidis, and Nashashibis—in shaping the national movement. Albert Hourani, C. E. Dawn, and Philip Khoury examined the evolving relationship between local elites and the Ottoman Empire during its twilight years, and how that relationship changed under the mandatory powers.[3]

Other interpretations, which place less emphasis on elites, have since dominated the field. Rashid Khalidi and Hasan Kayali examine the younger, newer intelligentsia in Arab nationalism.[4] Weldon Matthews's study, relied on heavily in this and the following chapter, brings to light the role of the youth movements and the Istiqlal Party in leading the way to revolt.[5] Matthews emphasizes the oppositional force of the youth parties vis-à-vis the mufti. Similarly, Sherene Seikaly's history of the Palestinian capital class during this period shows their very mixed responses. Some financed the revolt, while others saw economic growth as the way to build the nation.[6] Studies such as Ted Swedenburg's oral history of the revolt from the peasants' perspective shed important light on the grassroots nature of the revolt. Issa Khalaf's study of Palestinian politics, focusing mainly on the period after 1939, uses empirical evidence to support the argument that the revolt was not led from above, but rather was peasant led. This book takes the perspective that the mufti's powers of patronage were central to his power and influence in Palestinian politics, and that radicals in his party and in Istiqlal dominated the national movement and led public opinion toward revolt.[7] Nonetheless, most of these studies have embraced the view that the mufti had little responsibility for instigating the revolt. While not denying the views of other well-argued studies, this book shows that the mufti was instrumental to the revolt, even if it was not the result he desired.

The story of Palestinian leadership is further obscured by the tendency of the mufti's biographers to focus on his inclusion on the United Nations War

Crimes Commission list in 1945. His association with the Nazis, especially with the creation of Bosnian SS battalions, has meant that biographies of the mufti are skewed toward those issues over his political aims and strategies in Palestine before his exile in 1937. His record before the war has been eclipsed by his deeds during and after. Furthermore, most of his biographies are not scholarly, and associate Palestinians or Islam with fascism in a bald attempt to influence contemporary opinion, unfortunately with some success.[8]

Zvi Elpeleg's biography offers the fairest treatment of the mufti, parsing his various roles as nationalist leader, government officer, and Nazi collaborator. He supports the widespread view that the mufti was surprised by the outbreak of the general strike and revolt in April 1936 and tried to stem it.[9] Philip Mattar takes this a step further, arguing that that mufti had little control over the national movement during 1930–36 and tried to preserve his roles as government officer and national leader. He contends that the mufti never tried to inspire radicalism, and that the youth and Istiqlal pushed the movement in that direction. Like Mattar, other historians have also overemphasized the competition and underrated the cooperation between the mufti and the youthful nationalists, or with Islamists under 'Izz al-Din al-Qassam.[10] While such groups pressured the mufti, and affected his balance of interests among his family, his politics, and those of his Palestinian followers, such pressure went both ways. Those groups owed the SMC considerable credit for their rapid development. They also enjoyed outside support, especially from the Syro-Palestinian congress. Ilan Pappé's biography of the al-Husseini dynasty downplays the significance of the mufti's pan-Islamic and pan-Arab activity, while emphasizing his personal ambitions.[11]

Histories that have rejected the focus on elites, and a top-down approach, have shed important light on youth and mass movements, labor, education, women, and other aspects, and have affected the way historians have written about the mufti. Even Israeli scholars such as Michael Cohen have concluded that the mufti "refrained from any anti-British activity" until 1936.[12] Yet he was linked to the Palestinian struggle for independence from an early stage. A bright and canny operator, he reshaped his role, to simultaneously build the movement and his own place as its leader. The symbiotic relationships between notables, the middle and working classes, capitalists, Islamists, soldiers, and peasants on the road to revolt have been compartmentally described in the scholarly literature. The following is an attempt, using intelligence records, to tell a more comprehensive version. With more evidence available today than ever, it must be acknowledged that this story also is complicated by the mufti's indirect methods. The mufti was a central node in pan-Arab, pan-Islamic, and domestic nationalist networks as they intersected in Palestine. He encouraged the growth of Istiqlal and youth movements, including radicals, through his financial and networked, semiorganized means.[13]

The mufti's communications with Syrian parties, the Syro-Palestinian congress in Geneva, and his supporters in London and in Arabia demonstrate his instrumental role in shaping the pan-Arab national pact, which sought to coordinate efforts to achieve independence in Syria and Palestine using the influence of the independent Arab kingdoms, and hoping to exploit the looming possibility of European conflict. It is not clear that the mufti designed this strategy, or that he ever articulated it. But if not for him, its authors would never have convened, or reconvened, in order to develop their plans for independence.

The evidence also shows the mufti's role as organizer, inspiration, and accelerant for resistance in Palestine. To these ends, he mainly worked through his closest associates—especially Jamal. The mufti aimed to keep and improve his official position as mufti and president of the SMC. That body's finances were instrumental to the organization of youth movements throughout the country, which, most scholars agree, were the key drivers toward revolt. Islamists such as 'Izz al-Din al-Qassam were on the SMC payroll, as were senior leaders of Istiqlal and youth movement leaders. Most youth movements were led by beneficiaries of SMC funds or graduates of SMC-funded schools. Youth movement and sport club branches were the main connection between the peasantry and the rest of the national movement.

Notables and nationalist youth were interdependent. After a decade of failed negotiations for constitutional protection from Zionist immigration, the elites needed the pressure of mass movements to achieve their shared aims, whether reversal of the Zionist policy or independence from colonial rule. This required the landholding and moneyed classes to cooperate in unprecedented ways, through the structure of new parties. Istiqlal and youth movements depended on the moral and material support of elites. They could not have grown so quickly between 1930 and 1933 without the financial support of the Supreme Muslim Council, or the energetic leadership of Palestinian entrepreneurs.

Again, the mufti did not directly control these elements, but he certainly unleashed them. He easily managed their opposition to his collaboration with Britain and his ever-increasing authority at the SMC. His main Palestinian threat was from the Opposition (Mu'arada) faction, led by the Nashashibi family, which sought to roll back the al-Husseinis' rising influence in local government, the SMC, and pan-Islamic and pan-Arab affairs. Their efforts to contain the mufti's Majlisi, or "Council," faction failed miserably during the 1930s. Other opponents of the mufti were murdered, at increasing rates, throughout the decade.

As the center of a complex social and political network, the mufti was positioned to be able to maintain a facade of collaboration with Britain, and to maintain his powerful government offices and the privileges they brought, but also to fuel a reinvigorated, youth-led national movement. He inspired its activism, but also its militancy. He likely hoped this would provide leverage in direct negotiations with Britain on behalf of his people. The Buraq revolt followed a year of the mufti's propaganda. It tied down two British battalions in Palestine after a decade of reductions to the garrison. He had the government's attention, and the 1929 revolt sparked new interest from the Palestinian people themselves.

The Evolution of Pan-Arab Strategy

In June 1923, the Sixth PAC appointed Shakib Arslan as head of the Syro-Palestinian congress, which represented the pan-Arab movement at the League of Nations in Geneva. Arslan also proliferated Islamic-nationalist ideas, and criticized imperialism.[14] He sent regular reports to Jamal al-Husseini about league proceedings.[15] The mufti's support for the Syrian revolt reinforced his ties with Arslan and his Syro-Palestinian congress—the face of the Arab cause in Geneva.[16] Meanwhile, Arslan's support for Palestinians, according to William Cleveland, put him "at the forefront of the Arab cause in the minds of his compatriots and of European leaders."[17] He supported both the Syrian and Moroccan revolts, mobilizing the support of sympathetic English men and women, and coordinating these actions with his program. Arslan and Rida were involved in the short-lived unity scheme that sought to install Feisal as king of Syria and Iraq in 1931. His element of the pan-Arab movement was pan-Islamic at its heart, even though it cooperated with more secular Syrians and Palestinians.

By 1930, members of the original Istiqlal Party of 1919 (henceforth "Old Istiqlal") were eager to mobilize the younger generation with a similar spirit to their own. Pan-Islam was an important means for elites to mobilize the peasant and working populations. The mufti likely first identified with the politics of Islamic and Arab revival as a student of Rashid Rida during 1912–13. At that time, Rida had traveled to India for propaganda work—a pattern that Hajj Amin emulated as mufti.[18] His views on Islam and Arab nationalism crystallized while he was a young man in the Ottoman system; he was influenced by the power of pan-Islam, which he had witnessed during the war. He could not have overlooked the influence of the kaiser's propaganda promoting anti-British jihad in Jerusalem during 1915.[19] Hajj Amin had been a member of Arab decentralization societies. After joining the Ottoman army in 1916, he was influenced by nationalist Arab officers, and had a tense relationship with his Turkish commander.[20] He served as an officer until Britain's conquest of Jerusalem, and then assisted Britain's Arab propaganda program for the duration of the war. Afterward he began his activism in the Nadi al-'Arabi.

A former student of Rashid Rida, influenced by Arab nationalism and Islamic modernism, he was appointed mufti in 1921. He was only twenty-four years old when charged with such enormous authority. He was a privileged young man; at the center of his experience were the mobilizing forces of nation and religion. During 1919–20, he experimented with those forces. Disappointed by the Hashemites' failures during 1920–24, and in need of outside support to reverse the Zionist policy, he drew closer to Shakib Arslan's Islamist anticolonialism, through his connection to Rida.[21] During visits to conferences in Mecca and Cairo in the mid-1920s, he used his religious connections to gain international attention and raise funds for the restoration of the Dome of the Rock.

Negotiations

During March–May 1930, ECPAC sent a senior delegation to London to represent its interests to the government. It included Musa Kazim, the mufti (technically not on ECPAC), Ragheb Nashashibi, Jamal, 'Auni 'Abdul Hadi, Alfred Rock, and others. Files declassified in 2004 reveal the heavy police surveillance of the delegation, with special interest in their relations with Margaret Farquharson of the NPL, as well as Robert Gordon Canning, who visited Palestine in the aftermath of the 1929 revolt. In addition to his later membership in the British Union of Fascists, Canning was notorious for supporting militant anticolonial movements elsewhere, beginning with the 'Abd al-Krim revolt in Morocco.[22] Surveillance reports of the delegation provide some insight into Britain's attitude toward Palestinian demands, but also toward security more generally.

The mufti was worried about his personal security, after hearing rumors of threats against his life; these fears were supported by the Palestine Police, which notified London in advance of the mufti's arrival. The Metropolitan Police responded positively to the mufti's request for personal protection during his stay in London, although upon his arrival, the police told him they had no indication of threats against him. Then, J. F. C. Carter of Special Branch reported, "His Eminence stated he had been the recipient of threats of personal violence from Jewish enemies and feared that, should an opportunity occur, the threats would be put into effect, and that he was followed as far as Paris on his journey from Palestine by two such enemies."[23] The mufti was not lying, although perhaps he exaggerated. He had, in fact, been followed by agents of the Joint Bureau—the Jewish Agency's new centralized intelligence service. Their intentions were not to harm the Palestinian leader, but to observe. This produced fruitful results. David Tidhar, now a private investigator, reported to Colonel Kisch that at the train station in Qantara on the Suez Canal, the mufti met with ʿAdel Arslan and at least ten others. The mufti was protected by armed bodyguards throughout. Tidhar had been tracking the mufti's financial resources in Egypt around the same time.[24] The mufti's fears may have been well founded, if based on mistaken assumptions. While he was indeed under surveillance by the Jewish Agency, his request for protection may have been manipulative, perhaps aiming to amplify the gravity of the situation, or to gain sympathy.

Although Lord Passfield was sympathetic, the delegation did not consider his 1930 White Paper a major achievement. Voices in support of limiting the Zionist policy during negotiations in March–May 1930 were vastly outnumbered. The Palestinians returned home with limited satisfaction: at least they could begin serious constitutional negotiations having achieved their first concession from British policymakers. When Ramsay MacDonald repealed Passfield's immigration restrictions a few months later, Palestinian leaders, mainly from the youth movements, looked to the Indian example of boycott and civil disobedience movements. While the Palestinian delegation achieved little in London, Gandhi's "Salt March" demonstrated the power of mass movements. Gandhi had Britain's attention, and came to London in 1931 for round-table talks. This thinking affected Palestinian elites as well as the youth movements. The mufti, the Syro-Palestinian congress, and other pan-Arab parties began to coordinate their strategy, beginning around New Year's 1932 at the Jerusalem Pan-Islamic congress. While the mufti consolidated his domestic power and foreign connections, he fueled the youth movements, allowing them to form popular opposition to British policy.

The 1931 Pan-Islamic Congress

In February 1931, the CID began to monitor proposals for a pan-Islamic congress. It focused on the visit to Palestine of Shawkat ʿAli, an Indian pan-Islamist and leader of the defunct Khilafat movement. Palestine was a key stop on his tour of Arab countries. Hosted by the mufti, ʿAli was in Palestine to discuss the revival of the pan-Islamic movement and to support the growing anti-British boycott. The CID doubted whether Palestinians could take concrete steps toward a complete boycott of European goods. However, the movement had derived its momentum from regional Arab unity efforts. The CID warned that "the struggle against Zionism and for national independence will leave its limited circle to merge into the whole Arab and Islamic world movement. The money which may be raised will enable Haj Amin to surmount one of the main difficulties of political activity in this country and to remove one of the causes of friction with the opposition and other political workers."[25]

'Ali praised the mufti and urged Palestinians to unite under his leadership. The opposition faced difficulty competing with the mufti's prestige, which steadily improved both locally and internationally. The CID presented this information as an avenue through which the government could exploit the mufti's core need to secure 'Ali's cooperation. Later in 1931, the government reached a financial understanding with the mufti in support of his congress plans. By 1932, after Harry Patrick Rice took over the CID, this level of insight by the CID had disappeared.

The government believed in the mufti's role as a Muslim leader. It monitored his pan-Islamic activities, and used his desire to hold a pan-Islamic conference in Jerusalem as an opportunity to bargain. Weldon Matthews has argued that the mufti depended on the British to underwrite his status, and in exchange for financial support, he influenced the Islamic congress and the nationalist youth not to advance an anti-imperialist agenda. In the context of reforms introduced after the 1929 disturbances, the SMC faced a decline in tithe revenue. The mufti's negotiations with Britain brought a larger subsidy to the SMC, which in turn increased his ability to generate patronage.[26]

Until Rice's takeover, the CID was not naive about the mufti's methods and motives. The government also negotiated during 1931 with ECPAC over a proposed legislative council, which, it was hoped, would mollify the demands of nationalists. A report from March 1931 said that "the cause of the extremist section led by Haj Amin (who from the beginning was in favour of boycotting the Legislative Council) has accordingly been strengthened."[27] Understandably, Arabs had lacked confidence in government since MacDonald's "Black Letter," which repealed the 1930 Passfield White Paper.

The mufti used the upcoming Islamic congress as a vehicle to expand and transform his movement. By elevating his own status as a pan-Islamic, pan-Arab, and domestic unifier, he would reduce his local rivalry with the Nashashibis to a petty local matter. Meanwhile, all classes of society would begin to reject British policy and consider ways to strengthen the national movement. The Islamic congress of December 1931 was an important victory for the mufti, who was elected president of its executive, to which nine of his supporters were elected. The congress aimed to raise enough funds for its plans, including the founding of an Islamic university in Jerusalem to rival Hebrew University (although Egyptians worried it would compete with al-Azhar).[28] The congress led to the expansion of nationalist parties and youth movements, which fostered public discourse about resisting British policy and national development.

The National Pact

The Islamic congress also served as the birthplace of the pan-Arab movement's new strategy, which would guide nationalists in the region, especially Syria and Palestine, for a decade. The congress's pan-Islamic program provided the pretext for a gathering in Jerusalem of pan-Arab leaders from across Palestine, but also from the Syrian National Bloc. At Shakib Arslan's request, a large group including Rashid Rida, 'Izzat Darwaza, 'Ajaj Nuwayhid, Subhi al-Khadra, and many others met at the home of 'Auni 'Abdul Hadi. According to the CID, the group conspired to threaten another anti-French rebellion to force more concessions. For the first time since the end of the First World War, the pan-Arab movement had reorganized and developed a new strategy and objective. Their Mithaq al-Watani, or "National Pact," opposed colonization and now promoted complete independence. They would apply pressure in Syria and Palestine in the form of strikes and boycotts, timed to exploit European tensions. From 1932 to 1936 this strategy evolved with an eye on the European situation, but, as will be seen, it worked more effectively in Syria than in Palestine.

The CID noticed influence from abroad, saying that Shakib Arslan was preparing a "revolutionary campaign" that aimed "to arouse other Islamic countries, which are under foreign rule. The campaign is expected to take the form of armed attacks along the lines of those made in 1925 [in the Syrian revolt]." That violence, it said, "may extend to Palestine, where operations will be directed both against government and the Jewish Colonization."[29] The CID connected Arslan and his "high diplomacy" in Europe with the Old Istiqlalist leaders, who held meetings in Syria and Palestine from May through July 1931.[30] The CID, however, did not understand the mufti's support for Arslan's aims.

The National Pact meeting was preceded by months of preparations, orchestrated by Arslan from Geneva. Connections between signatories to the pact and Syrian ex-rebels living as political refugees in Transjordan worried the CID, which thought their strategy could escalate into revolt.[31] Perhaps

the government's support for the Islamic congress also aimed to neutralize that possibility. The creators of the National Pact looked to the youth
movements—a new generation, not unlike theirs when they began Arab
national activity during the Ottoman period—as the driving force for their
platform. The CID reported that Jamal al-Husseini worked in the South, and
Subhi al-Khadra in the North, to organize Young Men's Muslim Association
(YMMA) branches.[32] This became a standard example of the mufti's influencing younger nationalists through his closest supporters.

Youth and Mass Mobilization

Between 1928 and 1935, a younger generation of nationalists rose to prominence, but not dominance, in Palestinian politics. After the 1929 riots,
ECPAC organized countrywide strikes against the government's heavy-
handed crackdown, which killed 116 Arabs and led to the detainment or
arrest of some 1,300 more. Some twenty-five death sentences were passed,
but only three people were executed. The government pressured ECPAC to
cancel the strike, and it complied.[33] According to Weldon Matthews, the initiative then passed to the YMMA.[34] Of Egyptian origin, the YMMA sought to
preserve Islamic values and counter the Young Men's Christian Association's
(YMCA's) proselytizing work and association with colonial government. It
became the incubator for the Muslim Brotherhood. The Palestinian YMMA
was founded in 1928 with a pan-Islamic modernist orientation, but it was
also an important tool for nationalist organization. Certain branches had
Christian membership.

Each major city in Palestine had its own YMMA branch. They each had
their own characteristics, but were often led by individuals loyal to the
mufti. The Haifa YMMA, mostly influenced by Syrian Islamic modernism
and Arab nationalism, was founded by Rashid al-Hajj Ibrahim and 'Izz al-
Din al-Qassam, both SMC employees and thus on the mufti's payroll. The
Nablus branch had the strongest connections to Old Istiqlal, mainly through
ex-members of Feisal's Damascus government such as Darwaza. He directed
the al-Najah schools, whose graduates led Istiqlal and the Youngmen Congress movement.

The Gaza YMMA had Communist connections, as it was founded by
Hamdi al-Husayni, who was an agent of the Comintern in Palestine and
worked with the PKP to, as Matthews puts it, "Arabize the party."[35] The mufti's influence extended to Arab Communists as well. MI5 documents contain a cross-reference from June 1930 that states that "Jamal Husseini and
'Ajaj Nweihed [sic; Nuwayhid], the right-hand men of the Haj Amin, were

associated with Hamdi Husseini, the local secretary of the anti-Imperialist league."[36] Shakib Arslan was on the board of that Berlin-based Communist organization.[37] Thus the mufti had sway over them through both local and international channels. Neither Arslan nor the mufti was a Communist, but they shared anti-imperialist objectives with the Comintern. As Arab frustration about Britain's support for the Zionist policy grew in the early 1930s, Hamdi al-Husayni's partnership with the YMMAs and the mufti emerged on the basis of these shared objectives.

In August 1931, the Youngmen Congress first convened at Nablus to protest the government's arming of Jewish settlements, with the guidance and direction of the mufti, mainly through Darwaza. Confusingly, the CID said that after the congress it did not know whether the movement still followed the mufti's direction. The misunderstanding emerged from the mufti's opposition to the Youngmen's call for a strike or civil disobedience campaign. He still needed British support for his forthcoming pan-Islamic congress, eventually held in Jerusalem in December 1931. The CID understood that both the mufti's faction and the Youngmen were meeting with each other and with Syrian nationalist leaders. The CID mistakenly assumed that the Communists under Hamdi al-Husayni had penetrated the Youngmen, and were competing with the mufti for influence.[38] Yet these groups all cooperated along anti-imperialist lines.

Having received agents' reports from the first Youngmen Congress, the CID reported on the Palestinians' "increasingly prevalent belief that protests and political action on constitutional lines are of no avail and that the Arabs should resort to revolutionary activity." Hamdi al-Husayni was seen throughout the 1931 Youngmen Congress to have been passing directions to Akram Zu'ayter. "A purely militarist spirit was in evidence throughout the proceedings," read another comment.[39] The CID emphasized that youth, not the veteran politicians, were leading the way. It rightly anticipated that the nationalist youth would eventually form a new party to contend with the notable factions.

The mufti's connections were indirect, but still powerful. Increasingly, Palestinian parties adopted anti-imperialist resolutions, forcing the mufti to distance himself from them. Jamal al-Husseini helped resolve the friction—at times he tried to rein in youth leaders such as Akram Zu'ayter. After the 1931 Islamic congress, Jamal was reported to be "unusually active" in organizing a new Nablus youth conference for the sake of dominating the Opposition faction.[40] Influence went both ways, and as quickly as Jamal scrambled to control the Youngmen, they lobbied the mufti to support civil disobedience

and oppose the government. While historians tend to emphasize the oppositional relationship, current evidence illustrates its symbiotic nature.

The CID reported in 1932 that Jamal al-Husseini organized the Youngmen Congress aiming to provoke a civil disobedience campaign on an Indian
model. He did not hide that aim.[41] Weldon Matthews argues that the youth
movements modeled themselves on Gandhi's example following the frustra-
tions of 1929–30. Yet this evidence shows that, while inspired by the Indian
spiritual leader's ability to unite different religions against colonialism, Palestinian Istiqlal and Youngmen leaders were radicals who preferred militarism
over nonviolence.[42]

The Youngmen Congress attempted to govern the YMMA and coordinate
its branches. In reality they were parallel, often overlapping movements. The
Youngmen sought to mobilize the educated youth, and to promote alternate
leadership to the notables through an all-party coalition. It was hoped that
this unity would advance the movement's independence agenda. Elite control over national politics had become an object of youth frustration. The
Youngmen achieved limited success as a unifying body and rarely exercised
control over all the YMMAs. More generally, though, both the YMMA and
the Youngmen were effective vehicles for recruitment and mass mobilization. By 1932, those younger members founded the Palestine Istiqlal Party,
and the Youngmen Congress became its own political party. The Youngmen
were more loyal to the mufti, but were disappointed by his erstwhile opposition to civil disobedience.[43] In 1933, the YMMAs were subsumed by the
Istiqlal Party. Ya'aqub al-Ghussein, a Cambridge law graduate and leader of
the Youngmen Congress, maintained his chair, and grew closer to the mufti
over the years.[44]

The meeting of the National Pact, and the SMC's extra funding from the
government and the Islamic congress, helped to revitalize the Palestinian
national movement. These resources and Jamal's organizational skill helped
to let loose youth leadership to influence public opinion and government
policy. A good illustration of this influence can be found in plans in the summer of 1932 to commemorate the battle of Hittin of 1187, when Saladin's
army defeated the crusaders at the Horns of Hattin. This event symbolized
Muslim victory over Christian invaders, but also came after a press campaign
against the predominance of Christians in government posts. The battlefield
had been the scene of skirmishes between police, army, and Arab fighters
during 1929.[45] Before the commemoration, in order to exert more control
over the Youngmen, Ya'aqub al-Ghussein was installed as chair of the Youngmen Congress.[46]

The Palestine Istiqlal Party planned the Hittin proceedings. Its organizers were all mufti supporters, and the party was formed with his approval, the CID noted. The mufti, it reported, had been anxious to "extricate himself from the present party conflict, and to unite both factions." Istiqlal was to address Palestinians' distrust of the notable elite, and its internal conflicts. Rashid al-Hajj Ibrahim appealed to his Haifa branch of the YMMA for cooperation with Istiqlal's plans for the commemoration. The CID reported that 'Izz al-Din al-Qassam and other sheikhs spread pan-Islamic propaganda through lectures and sermons in the North, and had been actively preparing for the commemoration of the battle of Hittin.[47] Haganah intelligence records contain a Hebrew handwritten transcription of a CID report, elaborating on the event. Jamal al-Husseini and Hamdi al-Husayni (no relation) were among the leaders of a procession through the Jewish neighborhood of Hadar in Haifa.[48] The event was a success, as it galvanized public opinion against both Britain and the Yishuv.

Afterward, the CID reported that the event had a positive effect on Istiqlal, and more generally the nationalists. The mufti's attitude toward the demonstration could not be ascertained, despite all prior evidence the CID had found, which suggested his guidance of the movement. Conflicting reliable reports varyingly suggested that the mufti had influenced the rise of Istiqlal, but also that it was related to the "general pan-Arab movement" beyond Palestinian borders.[49] Both assertions were true, as the CID soon realized: the pan-Arab congress movement and Istiqlal were "one and the same party."[50] It was an intergenerational coalition of parties, from the Syro-Palestinian congress under Arslan in Geneva to the youth-led Istiqlal Party in Palestine.

Istiqlal, which often criticized the mufti for not openly opposing the government, still was subject to his influence. Its leaders came from a similar pan-Islamic modernist environment as the mufti, and saw the world in a similar light. Ibrahim al-Shanti and Akram Zu'ayter, leaders of Istiqlal in 1932, had been members of al-'Urwa al-Wuthqa while students at the American University of Beirut.[51] 'Ajaj Nuwayhid, a member of Old Istiqlal, taught al-Afghani's principles to the YMMAs during the late 1920s.[52] Leaders from the older generation, such as 'Izzat Darwaza and 'Auni 'Abdul Hadi, held diverse views about religion and politics, but having done this before as founding members of al-Fatat and Old Istiqlal, were experienced at accommodating heterogeneous sets of individuals and ideas.

Other clubs were involved in propaganda. Very often, they seemed innocuous, like the Moslem Sports Club. In the wake of the 1929 riots, the CID requested further intelligence on the club's connection to Communist or Arab nationalist political agitators.[53] At the time, evidence of such connections was lacking—but that soon changed. Even during 1930, while the YMMA suffered from British censorship, it proposed unification with the sports club, and later gave institutional cover to the Islamic Rover Boy Scouts.[54] This organization became an important vehicle for youth mobilization and paramilitary training. Arab Boy Scouts and sports clubs modeled themselves after Betar, the revisionist youth movement. The CID remarked, "Secret defensive organisations such as Hagana is not a new idea; it is only a continuation of efforts started by the young extremist faction several months ago."[55]

Younger nationalists changed the face of Palestinian politics, and caused new trouble for the mufti. They were their own agents with their own interests, and not pawns of the mufti or the SMC. However, Amin al-Husseini had connections and influence with each political community, including the young and Old Istiqlalists, the pan-Islamists, the Communists, and others. Moreover, many Istiqlalists shared the mufti's Islamist modernist outlook. They were not part of a conspiracy, but shared a worldview and similarly approached nation and religion.

Relations between Istiqlal, al-Qassam, and the mufti's faction were closer than has been appreciated. Pan-Islam and Arab nationalism were linked because Islamic modernist reform shaped Arab movements before the First World War, and the way those ideas were disseminated afterward. The two shared anti-imperialist objectives. The mufti, by both fate and design, became a nexus in these social, religious, and political networks. If we accept that al-Qassam and the nationalist youth most directly spurred rebellion, and the mufti closely influenced these movements, then his leadership and responsibility for the Arab rebellion must also be recognized.

The Mufti Consolidates His Power

The mufti was a central node in nationalist networks and was the principal leader of and driving force behind the rapid political transformation in Palestine between 1929 and 1932, and beyond. Historians tend to emphasize the mufti's conflicts with the youth and Istiqlal as evidence of his weakening leadership and lack of control. Yet even when Darwaza and 'Auni 'Abdul Hadi defected from the mufti's faction to join and lead Istiqlal, he still dominated Palestinian nationalists. 'Abdul Hadi, Darwaza, and other employees of the SMC were frustrated that the mufti was moving closer to the British in the early 1930s, and had difficulty reconciling their official positions with their anticolonial views.[56] They had long felt the need to form a new party to oppose the mandate and Zionism. Whereas the mufti previously rejected such action, he now welcomed efforts to coordinate the Old Istiqlalists with the new party, so long as he had no direct hand.

CID evidence explains the mufti's growing hostility to Istiqlal, which accused him of self-interested policies and government collaboration. The new CID chief, Harry Patrick Rice, said, "These leaders are actively engaged in the organisation of the movement in Palestine and other countries, and the revival of Arab parties which had been working under the Turkish regime, before the Great War, such as 'al Ahd', 'Al Fatah' [sic; al-Fatat], is much spoken of in nationalist circles."[57] Notably, this is the only evidence that the CID or any agency identified the importance of prewar movements such as al-Fatat in shaping the present political landscape. It is to Rice's credit that it was raised, although he and the CID thereafter refrained from connecting the mufti to the nationalists. It is clear, in hindsight, that this issue should have caused further investigation.

There was more here than meets the eye. The mufti welcomed the division, and used it to his own benefit and that of the movement. He preserved his relations with the government while simultaneously expanding the reach of the national movement and mobilizing more youth. His open dispute with Istiqlal coincided with efforts by Jamal to organize scout and YMMA branches, which, being the local centers for nationalist youth organization, actually formed the Istiqlal Party's base. Meanwhile in Nablus, the political base for 'Abdul Hadi and Darwaza, the SMC used its resources to appoint mufti supporters and influence Istiqlal politics in that city.[58] The movement nonetheless grew. Scout groups cooperated with Istiqlal to protest the eviction of Bedouin from the Wadi Hawareth lands, today known as Hefer Valley, which had been sold to Jews. The mufti's faction alleged that 'Abdul Hadi was involved in the sale in order to isolate him from Istiqlal.[59] Yet, ironically, 'Abdul Hadi and Darwaza had defected to Istiqlal in the first place when the mufti refused to protest land sales to the government.[60]

So while relations appeared hostile in the partisan press, the conflict was not so serious. The mufti, 'Abdul Hadi, Darwaza, and others likely agreed that Istiqlal was a vital organ of national revival. 'Abdul Hadi's alienation was only temporary. The spat risked his reputation, but ultimately proved harmless. Subsequently, a chain of public disputes propelled the national movement toward its larger goal of youth mobilization without damaging the mufti's status as a government official. Meanwhile, the Hawareth protests featured cooperation between Istiqlalist youth, the Youngmen Congress, and pro-mufti youth groups. Their leaders were clearly not so divided as to prevent public demonstration over land transfers. This was a circle of negative blows, each canceling the last, which caused little damage to 'Abdul

Hadi, the mufti, or Istiqlal. ʿAbdul Hadi played the villain for a moment, and his embarrassment might deter others from selling land to Jews. These disputes mobilized the population against the greater threat—the Zionists and the British Empire. This must have been the main objective: the unity of the youth across classes under a common banner. The CID either did not understand, or was unwilling to describe, these cynical maneuvers for what they were.

The conflict with the Nashashibi clan was more significant to the mufti than that with the youth, who would not exist without his support. The opposing faction maintained much influence at grassroots levels—holding mayoralties and civil service jobs. Opposition propaganda illustrated the mufti's misdeeds, or those of his supporters, in order to embarrass him. This situation supported Wauchope's complacency—he tempered political surveys with evidence that the mufti was restrained by Nashashibi politics. In response to the mufti's Islamic congress, the Nashashibis organized a formal opposition party, with its own congress, which sought to reform the SMC and challenge the mufti's wide reach.[61] The mufti then changed tactics, and launched a press campaign against Ragheb Nashashibi, highlighting his weak support of the national movement. The move satisfied the mufti's extreme supporters but alienated his senior partners such as Jamal, who warned of the harm that personal attacks would cause to the national movement. The mufti then suspended the newspaper, and gained some popularity by appearing to offer an olive branch.[62] Small steps temporarily upset his base of support but dealt long-term blows to his opponents.

The SMC was the main instrument of the mufti's influence. For instance, in 1932, the mufti asked Abdul Rahman al-Taji, who managed the *awqaf* for the SMC, to resign. The CID reported that al-Taji was forced to admit maladministration, when in fact the mufti's faction wished to replace him with a younger, more active nominee. They threatened to expose al-Taji's land transactions with Jews were he to object. Al-Taji had backed the mufti on the SMC during the previous year, but now the mufti saw fit to be rid of him.[63] Exposure of land transactions was initially an important means to coerce other notables. However, most families had sold or brokered land to Jews, and by the Second World War, almost all leading figures had been accused of that sin.[64] The mufti exercised political options according to immediate need—in this case, a more energetic manager of the *awqaf* who could direct money toward the youth movement. Al-Husseini lost very little by alienating notables when it furthered the national cause. Preachers, teachers, and other civil servants working through the SMC—all of whom were government employees—played their part in the mufti's vision. They were not robots, but benefited personally from cooperating with him and shared most of his political objectives—especially ending the Zionist policy and increasing self-government.

When the opposition struck at the mufti's prestige on certain fronts, he was able to improve it elsewhere. The CID reported on the mufti-maneuvered appointments at the SMC, where he isolated his opposition from official government positions. The opposition parties had accused the mufti of misappropriating funds. In response, the mufti muscled them out of office with the same accusations, and sought to replace them with loyal employees such as Subhi al-Khadra.[65] CID assessments reported these facts, but rarely commented on their implications. That is, they did not draw attention to the mufti's unusual power in Palestinian political theater, or connect these maneuvers to his relationship with radical youth movements. Yet it was in this way that he controlled the SMC executive, shut out opposition, and garnered support from the youth.

The mufti could also resort to violence. From 1929, various groups loyal to the mufti threatened Palestinian collaborators with death. Beginning in October 1929, with the murder of Musa Hadeib, Palestinians feared assassination on the mufti's orders or influence. Hadeib, a source of firm opposition to the mufti in Hebron, was friendly with Zionists, and had sold land to them. He was the first of many examples to be made.[66] These attacks, and those committed by the Black Hand and Green Hand—both led by al-Qassam—typified extremist aims and means. As a tool, assassination was supposed to be a deterrent to collaborators, although it was ineffective, as both British and Zionist intelligence rarely had a problem finding informants. More importantly, assassination and intimidation were a means to coerce opponents of the mufti or the boycott movement. Notably, the CID political survey rarely commented on political murder by such groups, unless Jews were their target. The new CID chief, Eugene Patrick Quigley, related in a memoir that the CID focused heavily on Arab murders of Jews, but not Arab family feuds or other murders.[67] The police and government perceived the need to prove their legitimacy to the League of Nations and the Yishuv following the security reforms in 1930–31. By ignoring political murder within Arab society, Britain allowed the mufti and others to use assassination as a form of politics by other means.

Murder of opposition members was rare during the early 1930s, and would have been looked on scandalously, whereas during the later 1930s it became increasingly common. Until 1936, the mufti dealt with opposition through maneuver and propaganda. The opposition was a player in nationalist politics in the early 1930s, and could interfere with the mufti's influence over the youth. For example, the CID warned in 1931 that unless the opposition faction defeated the mufti's supporters at the forthcoming youth assembly, the government could expect mufti supporters to lead a boycott against the proposed Legislative Council and Jewish and foreign goods.[68]

The mufti's faction slowly eroded opposition connections to government positions, especially on regional and municipal councils. Istiqlal and other new parties now dominated. This disparity became more pronounced during the 1934 municipal elections, when Ragheb Bey Nashashibi, the incumbent mayor of Jerusalem, was defeated by Hussein Khalidi. The CID summarized the cause of this turnover, as well as two other pro-Majlisi decisions in other cities. Although the Khalidis and Nashashibis were erstwhile allies in the Muntada al-Adabi, Haj Amin persuaded the Khalidis to leave the opposition faction. They formed an independent "Reform" party that aimed to replace the Nashashibis as leaders of the Opposition, according to the CID, "in a liberal, but a true national spirit. They will not hesitate in cooperating with the pro-Mufti factions . . . but will not allow themselves to be assimilated into or subordinated to, the Husseini family." During the mayoralty contest, the mufti's faction relied on persuasive propaganda, whereas the Nashashibis resorted to accusing Khalidi of collaboration with the government. The mufti personally led a propaganda campaign that focused on Ragheb's pro-Jewish and pro-government inclinations. Ragheb vocally opposed Jewish immigration in response to this propaganda, which, ironically, alienated Jewish voters, who largely supported Khalidi.

The CID was impressed by the mufti's political skill and use of his religious offices. The downfall of Ragheb, it reported, "has been described by many Arabs as a master stroke." Moreover, the result was that the al-Husseinis lacked any obstruction, and could "now proceed with their national and family advancement unhampered."[69] The CID seldom discussed the consequences of al-Husseini control over every important civil and political office, either directly or through patronage, family connection, or party. As its later reportage about splits between the Histadrut and revisionist organizations shows, the CID could offer penetrating political analyses, when the government wanted to receive them. Its silence regarding the mufti speaks volumes.

With the Nashashibis isolated from the national leadership, the mufti improved relations with Istiqlal, using his influence through the SMC. By supporting the election of Rashid Hajj Ibrahim to the Haifa municipal council, he brought in Istiqlal, including 'Auni 'Abdul Hadi, Nuwayhid, and al-Qassam. This is key to understanding how the mufti exercised his influence over other Arab parties, and expanded his own power in the process. On the advice of Ihsan Jabri, partner to Shakib Arslan and brother in-law of Jamal, Istiqlal now fully cooperated with the mufti.[70]

The parties reconfigured, and Istiqlal was eclipsed by the mufti's faction, since their independence platforms had closely aligned with the National Pact, especially its subsequent iterations. ECPAC no longer mattered to the mufti's strategy, and so in April 1935 Jamal founded the Palestine Arab Party (PAP). The CID reported that the al-Husseinis intended to ignore ECPAC or any future congress, and "allow it to die a natural death, and then proceed with their own programme to lead the national movement in the country."[71] There seemed to be no obstacle in the mufti's path, until the Nashashibis mysteriously came into possession of the mufti's correspondence with Italian agents.

The Nashashibis were down but not out, or so they thought. In January 1935, they and other opposition elements formed Hizb al-Difa'a al-Watani, the National Defense Party, also known as al-Difa'a. Al-Difa'a used its journalistic connections to publish copies of correspondence between the mufti and Shakib Arslan, revealing that Arslan and Ihsan Jabri were Italian agents—support welcomed by the mufti.[72] By April, these accusations had become the subject of a press war between the factions. Controversy was rooted in the fact that Italy had for decades been the most hated of imperial powers. Ironically, at the pan-Islamic congress in Jerusalem in 1931, Britain had tried to suppress criticism of Italy as the two sought cordiality.[73] The mufti's organ, al-Jami'a al-'Arabia, praised Italy and its Abyssinian policy, whereas Al-Difa'a and Filastin both criticized the mufti's pro-Italy inclinations and highlighted Italian persecution of Muslims, especially in Tripoli.

Air Staff Intelligence (ASI) concluded that Arslan had influenced the Old Istiqlalists' move toward a pro-Italian stance, with the mufti's collusion, since the latter was fully informed of Arslan's contact with Mussolini. ASI considered Arab acceptance of Italian support to be cynical. Al-Husseini and Arslan were "not at all fond of Italy, but hope[d] to obtain financial assistance for their own schemes by playing up to her."[74] ASI reports reflect the mufti's deep worry that this scandal might impact his influence in Palestine.

The historian William Cleveland accepts claims by Arslan, Rida, and others that the letters were forgeries, although he admits that Arslan's policy aligned closely with their content. Moreover, he notes, Rashid Rida warned Arslan "that he was carrying his self-defense to extremes." Arslan denied being an Italian propagandist, and insisted that his rapprochement with Italy was sensible under the circumstances.[75] Massimiliano Fiore, in his study of Anglo-Italian relations in the Middle East, offers evidence of the direct support that Italy provided to the mufti personally. The Italian propaganda officer in charge of this liaison went so far as to warn the mufti in 1936 that future contact would have to take place outside Palestine, because Italian military intelligence was under close observation by British security. Fiore's evidence shows that this close cooperation began only in 1936. Both Fiore and Nir Arielli demonstrate that Italy's support of Arslan was a quid pro quo: Arslan stopped criticizing Italy in his publications in exchange for an easement of pressure on Muslims in Libya, to advance the pan-Arab cause—and, of course, considerable funds.[76]

Without further evidence, it is difficult to know the entire truth of the matter. It was a good case of black propaganda, possibly guided by the ASI, whether the letters were forgeries or bona fide. The ASI's assessment of Italy's connection to the mufti's party certainly was accurate. In the end, the Nashashibis achieved little in publishing the letters. The embarrassment failed to harm the mufti's ever-growing influence. Radicals were pleased that he turned to Britain's enemies for support.

By August 1935, Palestinian politics had overcome the press scandal, which Istiqlalists, also in receipt of Italian funds, helped to defuse. Jamal visited branches of PAP, recently established throughout Palestine, and found broad popular support, owing to the public view that PAP represented the mufti. Through PAP, Jamal organized youth along what the CID described as "Fascist-Nazi lines," calling them "Dawsarieh," to serve as a strike force.[77] Boy Scout and Youngmen activity was on the rise as well. The mufti led agitation against land sales and brokerage, and instructed SMC employees and sheikhs to do the same.[78] Yet contrary to the common misconception about German support for the mufti, the opposition was the first Palestinian party to align with Nazi Germany, probably in response to the mufti's relations with Italy. In 1934, the opposition newspapers al-Difa'a and al-Jami'a al-Islamiya printed Nazi propaganda.[79] The mufti's people did not seriously communicate with the Nazis until 1938, when the latter began to reach out across the Middle East.[80]

The mufti's prestige could be rescued by the role he played in the pan-Arab theater. In 1934, he and Arslan led a delegation of the Islamic congress to Mecca, where they played up their facilitation of the treaty between 'Abd al-'Aziz Ibn Sa'ud of Saudi Arabia and Imam Yahya of Yemen. Their war, between two of only three sovereign Arab states, was thought of as an obstacle for pan-Arab unity schemes. For his part, Ibn Sa'ud saw little value in uniting the region, and preferred partnership with Britain. He was reportedly irritated by the mufti and Arslan for their exaggerations about their role in the peace treaty. According to the Jewish Agency official Eliyahu Sasson's source, Farid al-Shanti—an Opposition journalist from Jaffa—this irritation led Ibn Saʿud to welcome a Nashashibi propaganda delegation to Hejaz in 1935.[81] Regardless, Arslan and the mufti placed themselves at the center of a peace treaty hailed as vital to the pan-Arab movement. Arslan returned to Palestine after the delegation—his first steps in the Levant since 1917. He was sent back into exile after France pressured Wauchope.[82]

By August 1934, Old Istiqlalist plans for Arab confederacy felt within reach. A European war seemed increasingly likely, and the situation presented new opportunities for the independence movement to pressure Britain and France. The National Pact movement had first articulated this strategy in 1933, but division between the Arab kings made the prospect improbable.[83] In February of 1935 Arslan urged the mufti to cease cooperation with Britain, saying, "No friendship, no bribery, and no policy is of avail with the British as nobody can play any tricks with them, because they are the most cunning people and can not be taken by sympathy, evidence or leniency. The Englishman has a special language that cannot be understood and the only language he can understand is resistance."[84]

By September the mufti was fully committed to the independence movement. He made a visit to Syria, where, the ASI reported, his "real intention" was to meet the Syrian National Bloc, and then he planned to proceed to Geneva to attend the European Islamic congress. "More probably," noted the ASI, "the intention is to consult with Amir Shekib Arslan and his associates." Italy was still believed to be supporting Arslan and the mufti.[85] Arslan corresponded with Akram Zuʿayter, urging him to, according to the ASI, "maintain his anti-British activity," and asking him "if he were willing to support Italy by direct Italian propaganda." The ASI concluded that Zuʿayter had accepted Italian financial support, as had PAP, for running the al-Liwa newspaper (the same title as Arslan's German pan-Islamic project fifteen years prior).[86]

The ASI justifiably connected the mufti's visit to Syria in 1935 with the broader campaign that he had organized in Palestine to mobilize and unite the youth movements and parties. He was laying the groundwork for resistance to Jewish immigration, alleged Jewish ambitions to control Islamic sites, and British policy. The ASI studied the mufti's role in this campaign closely because, in March 1935, it had discovered a memo in Haj Amin's handwriting, which outlined his Islamic propaganda designed to arouse religious-nationalist sentiment. The CID reported that the propaganda was distributed during the pilgrimage to Mecca, but also to "prominent persons in all Moslem countries and to certain royal personages." The CID, upon seeing the material, confirmed its authenticity, but downplayed its significance. The chief secretary, John Hathorn Hall, forwarded translations of the material to the Colonial Office, saying it was "allegedly" authored by the mufti—despite confirmation by the CID's handwriting expert. Hall shared his concern that the mufti's call to the Muslim world for assistance played up fears that Jews coveted the Muslim holy places on al-Aqsa in order to rebuild Solomon's temple. The material also included a manifesto by the Jerusalem Islamic congress meeting of January 1935, which was intended to be spread during the Hajj pilgrimage.[87]

The mufti aimed to use Islamic propaganda to contribute to popular mobilization. A CID memo noted that "a pamphlet containing the speeches delivered by Haj Amin Husseini at the Ulemas Conference and at the Villages assembly has been printed in the Moslem Orphanage for distribution during the forthcoming Feast. It is expected that further copies of the fatwa of Sheikh Rashid Rida and of the statement by the Society for the Protection of the Haram will also be distributed."[88] The CID may have reported on this global and local mobilization, but it did little to handle it, downplaying its significance for local security. This is in stark contrast to its occasional censorship of the Arabic press for seditious language.

In contrast, the ASI was unequivocal: PAP was positioning itself to be the "main spring of Arab resistance to the further Judaizing of the country." Jamal al-Husseini's campaign had mobilized the youth movements, Boy Scouts, and athletic clubs—all militant movements "of a fascist or Nazi complexion"— in preparation for demonstrations, when the time was ripe. Religious propaganda was on the rise, exploiting a dispute between non-Zionist Orthodox Jews and Muslims at the Cave of the Patriarchs in Hebron. The ASI warned that "it is considered that no incident could be better calculated to arouse intense resentment. . . . The inference is made that Jews of all persuasions, militant and otherwise, have a common object in view."[89] In fact, these kinds of conflicts and anti-Jewish positions served to further unify Zionist and non-Zionist elements of the Yishuv. Clearly the Palestinian revolt was not spontaneous. It depended on preparation.

The CID and the government believed they could manage nationalist groups via the mufti. The ASI, on the other hand, saw a recipe for disaster, although it expected religious-inspired outbreaks. The spark that ignited the fires of violent resistance was, surprisingly, not a violent incident itself, but an apparently harmless accident at a Jaffa pier—the "cement incident" of October 1935. As a consignment of cement barrels was being unloaded at the port, one fell off a crane and cracked open, revealing concealed arms, obviously destined for the Haganah. The result was widespread public outrage. Arms smuggling came into focus for the work of the CID, ASI, and SIS alike. Britain was thought to be turning a blind eye to this activity, and quickly took

Italy's place as the European power most hated by Arab nationalists. The Youngmen organized an all-party meeting, and with the mufti's guidance, it was convened on 21 October 1935. They led the first completely observed nationwide strike.[90]

The CID downplayed the al-Husseinis' relationship with the youth movements and their persuasive and mobilizing power. The ASI, conversely, reported that Palestinian leaders had become more antimandate than before, and that the

> activities of the agitators of the Husseini faction point to the preparation of unrest at no distant date. . . . Over and above the "scout" groups organised by Jamal Husseini there are in existence more especially in the Tulkarm area, gangs of young men who give themselves high-sounding titles such as "The Terrorist Youth" etc. . . . Heretofore, the activities of these gangs have been confined to talk but it is probable that if any disturbances break out as a result of political agitation, they would attempt to carry into effect their threats against the coastal Jewish settlements.[91]

Rice, of the CID, was invited to comment on this report. He agreed that the al-Husseini faction had intended to create unrest through this agitation, but did not expect much trouble since they lacked a concrete plan. Rice was unimpressed by radical activity, probably believing that its divisions were more debilitating than was true. He gave no comment about PAP's behind-the-scenes activity. He doubted that gangs truly threatened Jewish settlements, and minimized the importance of the Boy Scouts, although he promised to follow up with the Tulkarm groups.[92] Subsequent events proved Rice wrong.

From the ASI's perspective, evidence of illicit arms traffic was even more foreboding. Italian vessels brought arms to Haifa, and other deliveries occurred via the Syrian frontier. "An official of the Arab Bank in Haifa," an ASI summary noted, "is reported to have stated to an informant 'The Arabs of Palestine are supplying themselves with arms which reach them from places no one is aware of.'"[93] One cannot be sure, but the source was probably citing Rashid al-Hajj Ibrahim—director of the Haifa branch of the Arab bank, which was founded to finance the Sunduq al-Umma (Arab National Fund). Ibrahim was close with 'Izz al-Din al-Qassam, the likely recipient of these arms. In November, the ASI reported on the weak coalition of parties, which had submitted demands to the government. Yet behind the scenes, the ASI emphasized, PAP was destabilizing the country.[94] Sure enough, the armed groups turned their guns on Britain at that moment. Al-Qassam launched his campaign, and his martyrdom at the hands of the British led to the 1936 general strike and revolt.

The mufti became instrumental in leading the public toward confrontation with the British government. This situation resulted from the government's own policy, especially its misplaced faith in the mufti, as well as its constitutional proposals, all of which included compromise with Zionism. Around the time of the pan-Islamic congress of 1931, the high commissioner and the Colonial Office reaffirmed the policy of co-optation of the mufti, which had originated with Herbert Samuel. They did so before a security-intelligence regime existed to assess the wisdom of the policy, believing that the normal colonial politics of cultivating elites would preserve British interests in Palestine. In 1932, the high commissioner in Egypt, Percy Loraine, wrote to the Colonial Office, warning against the "danger in allowing so much power to be concentrated in one Moslem personage in Palestine."[95] Loraine argued that Britain should not fear offending the mufti; instead, he warned, it should fear the consequences of allowing him to consolidate so much power.

This advice went unheeded. British policy thereafter was based on the presumption that the mufti was a willing and able partner, because his status depended on British concessions, for which he had to bargain. While he was a government officer, willing to work with British administrators, he simultaneously fostered anticolonial nationalism through intermediaries. His official position contributed value to the mass movements, which could protest in ways that he could not. Fundamentally, it was Shakib Arslan who convinced the mufti to risk his official status by openly promoting activism.

The British, for their part, lacked alternatives. The mufti had a rare degree of freedom of action compared to other British-sponsored elites in the empire. According to the historian Rob Johnson, elsewhere, especially in India, "neotraditionalist elites" sought to damage collaboration through the organization of modern political parties that forced elites to side with mass movements.[96] In Palestine, the mufti was viewed as essential to British governance despite his deleterious influence. Elsewhere in the empire, Britain usually could rely on alternate collaborative elites. As Percy Loraine indicated in 1932, British policy endangered itself by not creating such options. Moreover, the case of Palestine and the mufti is unique, since as a leader, the mufti was part of the old and new elites: a wealthy landowner, a populist leader of the nationalist movement, and a government officer. His actions gave the appearance of normalcy when, as in India, nationalists attacked his collaboration with the government. Yet these attacks ultimately served the common aims of the notables and the masses.

Once the opposition of the Nashashibis had been crushed in 1934, Wauchope lost leverage over the mufti, but continued to believe in his good faith until 1936. The government failed to see the connection between the mufti's creeping domination of Palestinian politics and the violent extremism that his faction and his religious officers were promoting for the sake of the national movement. The difference in ASI and CID reportage during 1935–36 clearly demonstrates how the government and the CID lost control of this process. According to the liberal-imperialist philosophy that had prevailed since Dowbiggen's reforms, good government had to provide security via the police and the CID—the only appropriate source for security intelligence and enforcement. The successful standoff by police and the CID against disturbances in 1933, discussed in the next chapter, likely reinforced this view. Yet this attitude politicized CID reportage in favor of Wauchope's accommodating attitude toward the mufti, and obscured the mufti's leadership over the national movement, its adoption of independence as an aim, and its embrace of violence as a means. The CID provided lots of valuable data and political news, but little intelligence.

The ASI was more critical than the CID, and skeptical that the mufti could maintain his distance from the nationalists for much longer. The ASI also likely had access to top-secret sigint, which would not have been shared with the civilian CID. In fact, after years of wrangling, high-grade sigint was only shared with the CID on specific Jewish underground matters in 1945.[97]

The CID and the government both clung to the civilian-oriented system of good government, knowing that real democracy could never be implemented, but hoping that a legislative council could change the political course. As much as Wauchope wanted to achieve some form of democratic self-government through a legislative council, he and his staff were loath to admit that this would require either enforcing the Zionist policy against the Arabs' wishes or sacrificing the Yishuv. CID reports fed the complacency of Wauchope and the chief secretary, and also masked the possibility that the most powerful Arab officer of government might need to become a police target. The government tended to ignore ASI political assessments because they contradicted the fundamental assumption of Wauchope and other civil servants, who were best suited to handle matters of politics and civil security. Thus, the mufti seized leadership of the Palestinian national movement and succeeded in obscuring the reach of his power from government until the Arab rebellion broke out in 1936.

The mufti's actions to this point were rational, and his expectations were reasonable. His growth in strength was unparalleled among nationalist leaders in the British Empire between the wars, because he did not openly oppose Britain, which patronized him and, in any case, lacked alternatives. Under al-Husseini's leadership, Palestinian nationalist politics had become sophisticated by the 1930s, trailing only Egypt and India, whose bureaucracies had expanded to include a "native" civil service aimed at paving the way to self-government. The mufti's secret violent campaign contributed to his growth in power. Had he died in 1936, he would be remembered as a hero. Not one volume would have taken interest in his nonexistent Nazi connections, and fewer would focus on his violence against Palestinians. He might even have been commemorated on Palestinian postage stamps. But he did not die; he continued his manipulations on a risky path. His missteps proved fatal to the national movement.

CHAPTER 6

Intelligence, Security, and the Road to Rebellion

Britain's parallel intelligence states in Palestine faced numerous tests in addition to normal monitoring of the political landscape during the early to mid 1930s. The civil intelligence state offered reasonable security assessments, and was able to interdict organized Palestinian resistance from 1933. The military intelligence state could not influence policymakers, but still acted in support of the civil power, as prescribed by the reformed law. It prepared for the possibility of revolt, and strengthened its links with Zionist intelligence. These competing systems faced certain limits in enforcing security, but largely were successful. Despite a lack of agreement on Palestine's constitutional future, the government focused on introducing some form of constitutional self-government.

Britain improved its ability to impose law and order, but mistook this form of strength for power, though it lacked popular support. However, Arab nationalists, mistrusting Britain's good faith in negotiations, were increasingly committed to achieving independence. In pursuit of liberal solutions to governance, Wauchope encouraged police to focus on political murders of Jews, rather than Arab assassinations or blood feuds. This deepened Arab grievances, and fueled the radical youth. The high commissioner was blind to evidence that the mufti was preparing the ground for rebellion, and instead believed that the mufti could and would reign in radical nationalist parties. He also thought that a constitution could solve the country's problems. In

light of such misunderstandings, policymakers failed to address the fundamental issues. Britain's grasp on good government eroded. The government
enabled the concentration of power in the mufti's hands. Crucially, the drive
for both Arab nationalists and Zionists to arm and organize themselves demonstrated Britain's loss of control. Intelligence observed these developments,
but the government and security forces could do little to stop them.

After the 1929 riots, rebellious groups immediately began to form in the
North. In particular, Green Hand, based in Safed, endangered British security. Murders of Jews at Yagur and Nahalal, inspired by al-Qassam and the
Black Hand, challenged British police and Britain's competency to provide
good government. The League of Nations criticized the British administration in Palestine and reaffirmed its expectation of Britain to protect the
population. Britain's reformed security regime succeeded in most cases, and
was ready to confront open rebellion early on. The civil intelligence state did
not expect widespread problems, whereas the military one organized drills
and improved conflict readiness. Britain had to prove to the Yishuv and the
League of Nations that the government could competently police the country. Distrustful, the Yishuv had already taken steps to improve its security
and the organization of the Haganah. The police struggled to control arms
smuggling in the Yishuv.

Britain's cooperation with the Zionist Histadrut and intelligence services
comes into focus here. Although the government feared the alienation of
Arab workers, as the number of vital infrastructure projects grew, it had to
depend on the Histadrut's ability to break strikes and constrain Revisionists
and Communists. Intelligence monitored the Yishuv's self-armament and
defiance of immigration rules, but could not yet enforce the law as British
forces were being reorganized. Meanwhile, the potential for an explosion
of Arab nationalist violence was the main focus of both Britain and the Yishuv. Security reforms, initiated by Dowbiggen and continued by the RAF
and army garrison, were successful. Between 1930 and 1935 British security,
while imperfect, had vastly improved its competency. Intelligence also improved, even though the ASI and the CID differed in their analyses of Arab
matters. The competence of policymakers was the root problem as the Arab
national movement marched toward revolt.

Anglo-Zionist Relations: Cooperation and Competition

One of the most reliable forms of control available to the Palestine government was the Labor Zionist movement. Economic woes normally plagued
the country, and the inquiries following the 1929 disturbances focused on

landless and unemployed Arab peasants as a key target for development. Competition between the Histadrut and various Arab parties for influence over a growing Arab working class was intense.

In his book *Comrades and Enemies*, Zachary Lockman assesses the interaction between government, the Labor Zionist movement and the Histadrut, the various Arab labor unions and parties, and the Communist Party. He explains that the Histadrut tended to pursue its own interests regarding Arab labor, at first attempting to co-opt this powerful force, to monopolize the labor supply. It then shifted to confrontation with Arab labor as part of a movement to promote "Hebrew Labor." This was a means for the Labor Zionist movement to create and lead a Jewish working class. Histadrut propaganda appealed to Jewish workers not on national, ethnic, or religious lines, but rather as a Jewish proletariat that had been boycotted by Jewish employers in favor of cheaper, unionized Arab workers.[1]

Unlike most of the world during the Depression, Palestine's economy boomed during the early 1930s, largely because of the influx of capital from Central European immigrants fleeing persecution. The shift in balance made "Hebrew Labor" difficult to maintain. In Haifa, where the port development and the Iraq Petroleum Company (IPC) pipeline attracted many workers, the Histadrut competed with the Palestine Arab Workers Society (PAWS), the labor union comprising Arab workers who had abandoned a short-lived binational railway workers' union during the 1920s. Histadrut-PAWS competition was nationalistic, but both strove to meet the needs of workers, and those of the government. By the 1930s, PAWS was hostile to the Histadrut for replacing Arab workers in Haifa with Jews. Arab workers also often collaborated with the Histadrut out of choice or need, and not because they were, in Lockman's words, "gullible dupes."[2]

The Histadrut formed the Palestine Labor League (PLL), which sought to organize Arab workers in competition with PAWS, and later with Fakhri Nashashibi's Arab Workers' Society (AWS). The role of the Histadrut and the Mapai labor party was no secret. Palestinian and Zionist labor shared the common aim of excluding immigrant Arab labor, which drove down wages for all. Although "Haurani" refers to people from Hauran in Syria, the term came to apply to unskilled migrant workers from all neighboring countries. They lived in slums, faced blame for crime, and played a role in the Arab rebellion. The police in 1934 estimated that fifteen thousand to twenty thousand Hauranis lived in Palestine illegally.[3] Action to deport them was discussed in 1935–36, but none was taken.

The Histadrut served and shared many interests of the Arab workers. To attract workers, the PLL offered health care, a loan fund, legal services, and other benefits to its workers in Jaffa. Histadrut lawyers sued Arab employers on behalf of Arab workers, making a strong impression. PAWS and the AWS could use nationalist pressure on PLL members in Jaffa to defect or at least participate in national strikes.[4]

The government benefited from the Histadrut's role in bringing strike breakers to important industries such as the Nesher cement factory and Public Works Department projects, especially strategic infrastructure such as ports and the IPC pipeline.[5] During the Arab general strike and revolt from April through October 1936, the Histadrut organized strike breakers while the British Army supplied military force to protect them. These men were motivated by poverty and a desperate need to work.[6] Haifa-based David HaCohen, a senior manager in the Histadrut and director of its subsidiary building contractors, Solel-Boneh, played a key liaison role with British military during the Arab revolt and secured supplies for the construction of new security infrastructure. During the Second World War, he personally financed a volunteer engineer company to the British Army from among Histadrut workers.[7] The Histadrut and Mapai also were the backbone of intelligence collaboration. Yitzhak Ben-Zvi, Moshe Shertok, and Reuven Zaslani coordinated their intelligence on Communists and labor unions with the British, thereby promoting confidence in the Histadrut.[8]

British reports on the boycott movement from 1929 to 1935 consistently doubted the viability of a complete boycott of Jewish or European goods. During the IPC strike in February 1931, the CID reported that the Histadrut and PAWS cooperated to defend their common interests, demonstrating the results of the Histadrut's efforts in previous years to reach cooperation, despite anti-Histadrut propaganda. Communist influence, despite PKP efforts, was negligible thanks to labor organization.[9] In 1932 the CID credited the Histadrut and Jewish socialist parties with a successful anti-Communist campaign; both sides battled over the hearts and minds of Arab workers. The CID reported, "By organizing Arab workers the Jews would establish good relations with them, would secure their help in case of disturbances, would ensure an increase of wages for both working communities and would be able, with a united front, to demand an increase of wages of workers employed by the government."[10] On the eve of rebellion in early 1936, the Histadrut countered Arab attempts to boycott the employment of Jews and succeeded in replacing Arabs with Jewish skilled workers in Jaffa. No violence was used, and the contractor retained unskilled Arab workers.[11] The government and the CID knew that the Histadrut dominated the labor market. The message even reached the Security Service in London. GSI Palestine explained to MI5, "The main reason for the lull in communist activity can be ascribed to the opposition of the Jewish Labour Party [Mapai] and the Histadruth . . . as the organisations are *national* whilst communism is *international* [italics in the original]. It is true that the Labour Party incorporates many ideas which may be similar to those of communists but, as previously stated, the organisation of Jewish labour is, in the main, national."[12]

This accurately reflects the way the movement saw itself, and demonstrates the close working relations among Labor Zionist–controlled intelligence bodies, and between them and British intelligence. Curiously, during and after the Second World War, Jews would find it increasingly difficult to cooperate with their British counterparts, partly because the Jews came to be seen as "bloody bolshies."[13] This view emerged in the context of Anglo-Zionist competition and the Jewish insurgency. The competition became intense as Zionists disputed British limitations on their right to immigrate and to defend themselves.

The Haganah had thus far been a group of lightly armed and loosely coordinated militias, concentrated in Jewish settlements. It had contributed to the defense of Jerusalem, but was outperformed even by Oxford theology students who served as special constables.[14] The 1929 disturbances prompted a deeper investment by the Haganah in armament and training, but also exposed the three main ideological divisions in thinking on defense. David Ben-Gurion's Mapai party sought to improve investment in defense and to fight the legitimacy of Arab nationalism's claims. This position closely aligned with British policy. The left-wing movement, led mainly by HaShomer HaTzair, sought to invest more deeply in its chances of reconciliation with Arabs.[15] Jabotinsky's Revisionist Party stood apart. During the later 1920s, Jabotinsky and the parliamentarian Josiah Wedgewood lobbied for Palestine to become the seventh dominion of the British Empire. After 1929, Jabotinsky called for the establishment of a Jewish state rather than a "national home," and he began on the path toward uncompromising political and defensive stances, modeled partly on the Irish Republican Army.[16]

The Left and center found common ground, and each believed that the other's program would suit its interests. In 1930, when the Jewish Agency founded the Joint Bureau (JB), it was a cooperative effort with the Left, especially HaShomer, which still sought reconciliation with Arabs. A. H. Cohen, from HaShomer, took on the dual role of gathering intelligence for the Jewish Agency while promoting peace and cooperation. His work was based on contact with Arab figures throughout the country, and a general effort to reach compromise. Cohen had emerged from the 1929 riots as a superstar of intelligence—providing crucial defense information at the last minute that saved many lives in Jerusalem.[17] The JB officially sponsored the activities of the left wing to reach reconciliation, believing that it could reduce anti-Jewish agitation and would strip power from the mufti.[18] This renewal and expansion of Kalvarisky's defunct program would be coordinated with the Jewish Agency's overall policy and strategy. Zionist intelligence gathering now featured an increased degree of central organization and systematic direction that crossed party lines.

Although Zionists had worried about British policy since the cancellation of the Passfield White Paper, the policies of the Jewish Agency and the British government were closely aligned, facilitating intelligence cooperation. Jewish staff were employed by SSOs, and Zaslani even undertook missions to Iraq on behalf of the Jerusalem SSO Pat Domvile, which addressed one of SIS's major concerns. SIS had discovered evidence from a "well placed Moscow source" or "a Moscow source which has proved reliable in the past," which indicated Soviet intentions to use the Iranian Communist Party to attack Britain's main interest in Iran, the Anglo-Persian Oil Company.[19] In 1929 SIS sent Lt. Col. Geoffrey Wheeler to Iraq to create a network to monitor that threat. Sometime later, Wheeler wrote, "By far the most important object of my enquiries was to be the activities of Soviet propaganda and intelligence agencies" against British interests in Persia. Over the next two years, after some effort, he concluded there was no threat. Whitehall had been misled by refugees, forgeries, and its tendency to credit the Soviets "with superhuman skill in manipulating Eastern governments and peoples according to the requirements of Soviet policy." He believed that many documents about a Soviet attack on Britain were forgeries. Wheeler's memoir emphasizes his reliance in reaching these conclusions on the help of a Jewish employee, obviously Zaslani.[20]

Although cooperation was the rule for British and Zionist intelligence, there remained a secretive, competitive aspect to that relationship. The armament of the Yishuv was a core Palestinian grievance against British policy, and naturally created tension. The Jewish Agency executed a dual strategy of advocating for the return of officially sanctioned sealed armories at Jewish settlements, while simultaneously turning a blind eye as the Haganah illegally procured arms. The Haganah's aims were defensive, although Revisionists sought to change its policy of restraint. In 1931, this and other issues led the right wing of the Haganah, known as "Haganah B," to evolve into the militant group Irgun Zva'i Leumi (National Military Organization, henceforth known as the Irgun). The question of Jewish arms, from the arrest of Davidescu in November 1929 to the cement incident in Jaffa in October 1935, is key to understanding how British intelligence and policy treated its relations with the Yishuv. It is also important to compare that treatment with the government's attitude toward Arab arms.

Arabs responded with reasonable hostility to the government's decision in 1931 to bolster the policy of police-administered sealed armories in Jewish settlements. There were reports that Arabs from Nablus had been raising funds and arms in response, and that the Youngmen had organized demonstrations against the decision.[21] A hand-copied CID note from July 1931, found in Haganah intelligence files, records a meeting in Safad of about thirty men and some village Mukhtars ("chosen" village heads), where it was decided to purchase arms via agents in Syria.[22] The First World War had left large stockpiles in Palestine, particularly among the Bedouin. Many of these had been sold to Druze rebels in Syria during 1925–26. A police report from October 1931 outlined the situation: "It was obvious during the 1929 riots that there was not a great number of arms in the country because they were not extensively used or carried, but after the riots, both the Arabs and the Jews decided that they must arm themselves." Jews were thought to have purchased more than Arabs, and apparently, Arabs had assisted Jews in their purchasing and smuggling of arms into Palestine. Arms that had left Palestine in 1925–26 had now returned, in addition to deliveries from Europe. The police could not guess as to numbers of illegal arms, but showed statistics of seizures, and concluded that "it is safe to say that the country is, simply, an armed camp." The border control force was still small, so the flow of arms could not be prevented. The law prevented police from searching for arms indiscriminately. As one solution, they proposed monetary rewards for the recovery of illegal arms.[23]

This allowed Yishuv intelligence to disarm its Arab opponents and reap financial compensation. In one instance, Lulick Bercovitch, an agent of the police and of Joseph Davidescu, provided information leading to the capture of arms from an Arab family, for which he received government payment.[24] Undoubtedly, that money went to Haganah coffers. Zionists' close relations with the police and arms smugglers suddenly paid dividends. Equally, however, the Haganah was concerned with the armament and organization of Revisionist youth groups. It reported on Brit HaBiryonim (the Ruffians' Alliance) and its activity, as well as arms smuggling by Arabs and Jews from Transjordan. It also highlighted that soldiers from the garrison near Rosh Pina, in the North, had been training Arab youth in military drills. The police were informed and Maj. Gerald Foley, the district superintendent, investigated.[25] Thus Haganah maintained its advantage. Later reports showed that British soldiers had been assisting smugglers bringing arms in from Syria and from Transjordan: "Their names are known to us. 'Z' investigated and handed a report, but they did not believe him. The police sent a senior officer to investigate, and found more than what Z had indicated."[26] Tellingly, these issues never appeared in CID summaries to the government.

In contrast, reports on Jewish attempts to bribe British officials or pur-chase arms directly from them were handed directly to the Air Ministry. In 1932 a Haganah representative asked a British policeman for help, saying he had collected £4,000 from the United States and Europe to purchase arms. He and a few others were arrested, as the police carefully controlled the case until the moment before arms were transferred.[27] In 1934, a large consign-ment was intercepted during offloading at Haifa, leading to the arrest of the ship's crew and a few Haganah members.[28] Attempts by Zionists to buy arms from the RAF led Palestinians to public demonstrations.[29] Arab and Jewish self-armament embarrassed Britain and its claim to good government. When the government intercepted illegal Jewish arms and offered the seizure as evidence to Palestinians and the League of Nations that it upheld the law, it failed to ease fears. After all, why were sealed armories not enough for the Yishuv? Until the revolt, government confiscations of Jewish arms caused Palestinian uproar rather than relief. The ASI reported such an event in Janu-ary 1935, when the government censor suspended two Arabic newspapers for publishing "violent articles" after police seized Jewish arms. Palestinians saw this as evidence of a threat beyond the government's control.[30]

Despite all this, the defense of Jewish settlements was still a key part of British security planning. An unpublished memoir by the spymaster Dudley Clarke illustrates how British soldiers saw the illegal arms issue and their role in the security of the country. Clarke, then an officer in the TJFF, described a 1931 visit to Beit Alfa, where he organized a joint training drill to test the de-fenses of the colony. It went well, but he knew they were hiding their arsenal "for reasons which I well understood, and I left with the firm impression that they would be well able to hold their own until I could bring the squadron to their aid in an emergency."[31]

Official sealed armories were only part of the debate. Britain's inability to control illegal arms imports to the Yishuv, and its unwillingness to acknowl-edge the problem, was a root source of insecurity in Palestine. The cement incident of October 1935 was but one of a series that left little doubt among Palestinians that British policy sheltered the Yishuv's illegal activity and posed a threat. The incident sparked a mass strike movement and the country spi-raled toward violence. In a panicked response to Palestinian agitation and queries from London, the government began to collate data about Yishuv armaments that it had collected since 1930. The CID discussed likely storage sites, as the government asked the Jewish Agency to dissociate itself from the Haganah and the illegal arms. It was too little, too late. Characteristically, the JA maintained silent ambiguity on the matter. X2, compiling all-source intelligence on the Haganah with its own top-secret material, asked the CID about the size of that force. The CID said that the size was difficult to pinpoint, and that reports varied between seven thousand and fifteen thousand. News reports suggesting a size of sixty thousand were exaggerated.[32] The true number was likely between twenty and twenty-five thousand.[33]

Intelligence also collected statistics on the confiscation of arms in neighboring countries. The British liaison officer periodically met with the French sûreté générale in Beirut, which had been interested in the arms question since the cement incident. Tribes in Lebanon had been stockpiling arms and the French authorities sought to warn their British counterparts. Arms seizures rose dramatically between 1934 and 1935.[34] Surprisingly, intelligence on arms stockpiling did not lead the British to conclude that a rebellion was imminent.

Over time, intelligence on the Haganah was improving, and becoming more useful. After the cement incident, Harry Patrick Rice, commander of the CID, summarized previous reports on the Haganah. The first, from 1930, illustrated the division between the Revisionist and Histadrut sections of the Haganah. It named some but not all key members and organizers. Rice admitted that it was impossible to confirm details about the Haganah, whose existence was an open secret, yet which still maintained secrecy about its arms, organization, and size. He assessed the organization's size, which he broke down as four hundred to five hundred first-line members working as storm troops (which in fact the Haganah did not yet have) and instructors, about seven thousand second-line members capable of bearing arms for settlement and town defense, and unknown numbers of third-line reserves able to serve in transport, works, and supplies. Arms were thought to number seven thousand of various sorts, mostly pistols. The CID warned that every Jewish immigrant or visitor to Palestine "should be looked upon as a possible arms smuggler." Finally, the CID referenced a report on the Haganah from 1933 that commented on its intelligence section, including its mapping, planning, and signaling capabilities.[35]

The CID also gathered intelligence on Revisionist activities, including intelligence gathered in Poland. It monitored the effects of the maximalist faction on Jabotinsky and the Revisionist movement overall. In November 1935, the consul in Warsaw passed unverified intelligence that discussed Betar and the radical leadership of the Revisionist movement in Poland. It also outlined (with some mistakes) the Hebrew terms used in military organization.[36]

Investigations revealed the large amounts of arms smuggled during 1929 alone. One report described the surveillance of a man known to be smuggling arms for the Haganah via Syria, and the means he used.[37] Arab intelligence work also attempted to understand Haganah arms smuggling, as Jamal al-Husseini prepared such a report for the police.[38] This appears to have been an ad hoc effort, rather than a systematic approach to intelligence gathering. Little else is known about Arab intelligence work, although it is safe to say that preserving the secrecy of their own activities was far more important to Arab nationalist leaders than was breaking British or Zionist secrets.

By the end of 1935, the illegal arms situation was out of control. Roy Spicer, the inspector general of police, remarked that the Jewish Agency, for about one year, had not complained about the sealed armories in settlements, and one could therefore infer that they possessed clandestine supplies.[39] The officer administering the government (OAG) during Wauchope's temporary absence, Chief Secretary John Hathorn Hall, passed a telegram to Jamal al-Husseini, Ragheb Nashashibi, and a member of the Budeiri family, insisting that the government was investigating the cement arms incident and that the culprits would be brought to justice. A note at the bottom of the document suggests that this was an attempt to induce Arab leaders to abandon their plans for a general strike.[40] It was too late.

The mass influx of Jews from Central Europe was a main source of tension, and illegal Jewish immigration became the most serious dispute between Britain, Jews, and Arabs. Britain was determined to prove to Arab politicians that it controlled the situation. The Jewish Agency and the government disagreed over the number of immigration certificates that should be allotted. This number was still fixed to the "absorptive capacity" of the country, for which both sides used different metrics. British decision makers had been influenced by the reasoning in the 1930 white paper that sought political limits to Jewish immigration. The Jewish Agency, on the other hand, sought to expand immigration so as to absorb rising numbers of Jews fleeing Europe. While the official limit was economic, all sides assigned political meaning to immigration figures.

In the early 1930s, Arab leaders organized the youth to form vigilante coast guard and shore patrols. Fearing a setback in law and order, the CID improved its efforts to prevent Jews from entering Palestine illegally. Organized illegal immigration, known in Hebrew as Aliyah Bet, began in 1934 with the Zionist youth movements: the left-wing, labor-affiliated HeChalutz, and the Revisionist Betar.

Meanwhile, antisemitic laws in Germany and violence in Poland led to calls in the Zionist movement for mass immigration as a moral response to the rising oppression of Jews. HeChalutz worked in both Poland and Palestine to prepare potential migrants for arrival, and to increase the number of legal certificates issued. It organized the first illegal sailing in mid-1934, which brought some 340 passengers to Palestine without detection. Subsequent attempts were blocked, and HeChalutz faced financial disaster in maintaining its ship. Betar initiated its first attempt at Aliyah Bet in part because it felt discriminated against by the majority Labor Zionists who secured legal certificates for their followers in Poland. In 1934 it began to bring in immigrants under the guise of tourist groups, especially during the Maccabiah sports tournament. This "adventurism" was better suited to the Revisionist ideology, and had official sanction. Betar also purchased ships, holding one successful sailing in September 1934. A second ship sank in harbor in Danzig. These setbacks caused both groups to hold off on Aliyah Bet until 1937.[41]

Good Government and the Rule of Law

Jews were not the only ones to take the law into their own hands. Vigilantism among Arab youth, which aimed to stop illegal immigrants and was officially encouraged by Palestinian leaders, added fuel to the smoldering dissidence. Moreover, the issue created tension between Revisionists and the Histadrut. A CID report from 1933 indicated earlier attempts at illegal immigration. Informers had warned police about attempts by HaPoel Hatzair, the Mapai youth movement, and the Revisionist Brit HaBiryonim to conduct illegal immigration. Public opinion had turned against the police, and informants faced intimidation by Jewish youth movements. A demonstration on 9 December 1933 led to a clash with police.[42]

By mid-1934, the Youngmen Congress had begun to organize volunteers for its vigilante force. Little had materialized so far except for a watch network. Jewish newspapers described Jewish youth efforts to counteract such a movement and to prevent Arabs from interfering, reporting that "this may mean clashes between both parties." Border security and patrols had been increased, but were not thought to be effective. One Jacob Gordon had been arrested bringing tourists in from Warsaw via Syria. His coconspirators had fled to Italy.[43] By August the youth activity had led to clashes between Arab Boy Scouts and Jewish youth, presumably from Brit HaBiryonim or Betar (the former was fascist and more radical than the latter). In one instance, the scouts, acting as a volunteer coast guard, had marched through the town of Netanya on their way to the beach but were forced to retreat by a Jewish group, despite police patrols in the area. The incident led the government to clarify that volunteer coast guards were illegal and would be prosecuted. The government also stepped up its patrols, and employed TJFF units and RAF aircraft in search and patrol functions. The show of force, it hoped, would calm Arab sentiment.[44] The CID knew that Jamal al-Husseini and Ya'aqub al-Ghussein, the chair of the Youngmen executive, had led the committee that organized the coast guards. Downplaying the matter, the CID noted, "It should be stated that no such committee in the proper sense exists. It is merely a group of persons who are intent on agitation."[45] It is not clear what the CID's idea of a "proper committee" might have been. Here was a clear example of the mufti's party directly encouraging youth militancy and confrontation with police and Jewish armed groups. Nevertheless, no action was taken against them or their organizations. The incident was not reported in CID summaries to the secretariat, and thus encouraged the militant youth to continue. Good government and the security structure had both failed.

Palestinian nationalists were not satisfied with measures against illegal immigration—they desired an end to Jewish immigration altogether. Nor was Arab opinion affected by efforts to stop Haganah arms traffic. The CID and the ASI seemed to realize this, but the government still attempted to placate nationalist leaders.

The root problem was a failure of good government: Britain treated Arabs and Jews unequally under the law and failed to manage Palestine's security problems. Arabs complained that Jews were not treated as harshly when caught with arms. Jews complained that the government dared not confront Haurani illegal immigrants, who outnumbered Jewish illegals by a large factor. British coercive power was small, while that of both the Arab and Jewish communities was rising. Illegal arms, illegal immigration, vigilantism, and the general rise to prominence of Jewish and Arab youth gangs eroded Britain's grasp on law and order. Britain could not enforce the law, or instill public confidence in its ability to govern. Its reliance on the Histadrut was part of this problem, as was its growing dependence on the Yishuv's self-defense and intelligence cooperation. Yet Wauchope continued to feel that he could rely on the mufti's influence and that of the Labor Zionist movement. Wauchope rarely consulted intelligence opinion, even when the CID and the ASI agreed about the gravity of the political problems.

Security Reforms on Trial

The security system that had evolved since 1930 was put to many tests before the revolt. While the reforms achieved significant improvements in policing, they never addressed the fundamental policy and legal problems facing the government. Political murder between the Arab and Jewish communities was given far more attention than that which took place within those communities. Police reports from this period often comment on *fasad*, or blood feuds, within Palestinian communities. This was considered a police matter rather than a political one, and so CID reports rarely cover it. Police, however, rarely intervened. The investigative resources of the police were dedicated to managing the Arab-Jewish conflict, but neglected to solve thousands of crimes within the Palestinian community. This was a significant failure of civil government. The law also failed to bring justice to one of the most famous cases of political murder within the Jewish community.

One of the first improvements in policing was that of censorship. During most of the 1920s the Palestinian government was reluctant to conduct political censorship, except against Communists. Although it monitored the press to gauge public opinion, it tended not to interfere, except in the case of "immoral literature." Yet even the thought police had their weaknesses. The postmaster general once requested that confiscated French magazines such as *Lingeries libertines*, *Sex Appeal*, and *Froufrou* be forwarded to his office.[46] Even at the height of the Arab rebellion, moral censorship was given relative priority. As a result, it was the army rather than civil government, with the help of Ezra Danin, a Haganah intelligence officer, and other JA Arabists, that intercepted and translated Arabic mail and other captured documents during that time.

After the 1929 disturbances, the government began to enforce the registration of societies and their publications. This measure existed before the 1929 disturbances, but CID records on registered societies seem to concentrate on Arab, Communist, and Revisionist Zionist movements. These records demonstrate the government's increased concern with monitoring youth groups; any youth movement or sports club drew interest, since these were perfect sources for political movements to raise paramilitary forces. This attention gave the CID a window into the mindset of the youth. For instance, one report about a meeting led by Akram Zu'ayter and more senior nationalists at the Moslem Sports Club in Jaffa noted that leaders suggested "introducing among the young adult students some form of military training similar to that shown by the Jews." During the previous year, the Arab journalist 'Ajaj Nuwayhid called on the youth at the sports club to "be brave like the Europeans, devote their lives towards their country."[47]

Press control also became an important part of the government toolkit for security and control; however, censorship rarely silenced publications. After the controversial eviction of Bedouin from the Wadi Hawareth/Emeq Hefer lands, Musa al-Husseini, a relative of the mufti, published an article in *al-Jami'a al-'Arabia* of "a seditious character," according to the CID, which asked the chief secretary whether the writer and editor of the paper should be prosecuted under laws enacted in 1929.[48] It does not appear that any action was taken in that case. The government generally was hesitant to close a newspaper or journal, although it would fine them. Emergencies increased the incidence of penalties and closures of news media following the 1933 disturbances.

Thought policing aside, the reformed security regime had to prove to the Yishuv, the League of Nations, and itself that it could protect the citizens of Palestine. A series of murders, especially the major incidents at Yagur and Nahalal, served as the main test case for that particular objective, as did the murder of the Yishuv labor leader Chaim Arlosoroff.

The challenge to police became more serious when 'Izz al-Din al-Qassam's followers murdered three Jews in an ambush at the gates of the Yagur (Yajur in Arabic) farm on 4 April 1931.[49] This launched a series of anti-Jewish murders, which caused the Yishuv to demand that Britain provide better security and law enforcement. Simultaneously, the Haganah improved its own capabilities. Police pointed to al-Qassam as head of the organizing group, which included the Istiqlal leader Subhi al-Khadra.[50]

Haifa became a center for counterterrorist activity, under the guise of the investigation of the Yagur murders. Yishuv intelligence worked with the CID, with figures such as Davidescu coordinating intelligence from multiple sources. The first CID summary to attribute any political activity to al-Qassam was from February 1932, when it highlighted the role of "marriage registrars, preachers, and other officials" of the SMC who had been "instructed to enlist support for the Husseini party in the course of their visits to villages."[51] Clearly, the SMC's role as medium between the mufti and resistance was known. Yet it was underemphasized throughout the CID reports of the early 1930s, and did not affect the views of Wauchope or the chief secretary. For some unknown reason, perhaps a lack of trust, or even the security of ongoing investigations, the CID never reported al-Qassam's connection to violent groups, or even to Subhi al-Khadra, despite the reportage of the Haifa police and the SSO.

Regardless, the CID never caught the Yagur perpetrators. The Yishuv increased its efforts to arm itself and improve its own defensive capabilities. The next major incident was the murder of Joseph Yacoubi and his nine-year-old son on 22 December 1932, when their home in Moshav Nahalal was firebombed. Five arrests were made during subsequent months, and one interrogation led a suspect to name al-Qassam as having instructed the YMMA branch in Saffuriyya (today's Tzipori), which called itself Black Hand, to commit the act. Rashid al-Hajj Ibrahim, in his memoir, considered the bombing to be the first "revolutionary experience" during that period, and discussed the requirements for recruitment to al-Qassam's gang.[52]

In February 1933, the CID attributed the energy of the YMMAs in the North to Ibrahim and al-Khadra. Likely competing with the SMC and the mufti, Istiqlal aimed to control these groups. It warned of a "dangerous element who hold revolutionary views and are intent on militant activity."[53] Ibrahim and al-Khadra were inspired and encouraged by the mufti in this work. Both SMC employees, they depended on the mufti's patronage, and supported his leadership. To further illustrate the point, months before the Nahalal murder, the CID reported on the role played by al-Khadra and Ibrahim in reviving YMMAs and improving the popularity of the mufti in the North.[54]

Despite all this, the CID summaries to the government never reported such connections. The CID barely acknowledged political murder as a topic, although Arlosoroff's killing was an important exception. The CID and the government worried about Jewish perceptions of their competency. CID reports did not emphasize the politics behind the Nahalal murder, but instead focused on the political fallout. It reported on Revisionist demonstrations and resolutions that criticized the police and security forces, which were financed by Jewish taxes but which failed to protect Jews.[55] Revisionist agitation caused greater worry than the unsolved crime. When it was solved, the government noted the Yishuv's satisfaction. Police interest in the assassination of Chaim Arlosoroff was limited to the problem of increased Revisionist militancy.[56]

Chaim Arlosoroff was head of the Jewish Agency's political department and had, with Ben-Gurion, founded the Mapai labor party. He clashed with Ben-Gurion over certain matters of strategy, and was a fierce critic of the Revisionists. The Revisionists' hatred for Arlosoroff boiled over after the signing of the 1933 Ha'avara (Transfer) Agreement with Nazi Germany. The deal allowed the immigration of German Jews to Palestine with most of their property, but helped Germany avoid a growing boycott movement. Jews consigned deposits to the Nazi state in order to finance German exports to Palestine and elsewhere.[57] Arlosoroff aimed to rescue German Jews from persecution and to accelerate Jewish immigration to Palestine. After returning from negotiations, Arlosoroff was murdered while walking on the beach in Tel Aviv. The Zionist Left expressed unprecedented outrage, and some seventy to one hundred thousand people attended his funeral. One of two accused assassins was acquitted. The other, Avraham Stavsky, first was convicted and then was acquitted on appeal. Court proceedings lasted months and caused a public sensation. Abba Ahimeir, the fascist leader of Brit HaBiryonim, was cleared of ordering the murder before the trial began.[58]

Patrick Domvile wrote to Zaslani about the case, sharing the glee of the Labor Zionists about the conviction of one of the perpetrators and about the government's measures to prevent disturbances with Revisionists. He attributed peace between the parties to the good behavior of Mapai.[59] Stavsky's acquittal on appeal outraged Mapai and the Histadrut. The CID reported on the gravity of the case, describing the unprecedented confrontational behavior of the Revisionists, their success at stripping the Histadrut of its middle-class followers, and the possibility that this might set back the Zionist project—or even destroy it.[60] Surrounding the Arlosoroff trial were many violent clashes between right- and left-wing street gangs. The CID worried about civil war between Histadrut members and the Revisionists. Assessment of the incidence of armed conflict and the probability of its escalation stands out in CID reportage. The Histadrut was an important supporter of the government, and Jabotinsky was seen to subvert Chaim Weizmann's influence, which Britain still believed in. Adding to the sense of injustice, the security agencies tended to tolerate far-left antifa (antifascist) gangs that stood against Brit HaBiryonim demonstrations.

Yet unlike Arab factions, Revisionists and Mapai members shared a common political goal, which was paramount. A paradoxical phenomenon emerged in the Yishuv where rival ideologies curbed action against each other and shaped a common social framework. The voluntary nature of the Yishuv and its political system also curbed extremism.[61] At first the Histadrut rejected attempts to reach détente, over bitterness at the loss of Arlosoroff and because of its opposition to fascism, represented by Brit HaBiryonim at that time. CID records also detail the herculean efforts of Ben-Gurion and Jabotinsky to negotiate solutions to their differences, against the wills of their respective parties. Tenuous peace was reached between Ben-Gurion and Jabotinsky in 1935.[62]

Wauchope was satisfied with the results of police reforms. He praised Spicer for his leadership of the police and its newfound efficiency. Crime rates between 1931 and 1934 were reported to have fallen. The police performance during October 1933 was a source of specific praise, especially for the Palestinian section of the police. Wauchope wholeheartedly backed Spicer's defense of the quality of the police force.[63] This reflected the fact that the force was a civil police force and did not account for the performance of the CID, which was practically a political police. It also whitewashed certain problems, not all of which were caused by politics. Britain also had to prove that it could prevent major disturbances—which it did successfully in autumn 1933. A countrywide drill in 1934 served as proof that if matters spun out of control, the army was prepared. The biggest and most important test of this security regime was its ability to translate intelligence into wise policy decisions. It was also its biggest weakness, resulting from the government's belief that it could manipulate the mufti, and its faith in the liberal-constitutional solution for Palestine. It also resulted from the politicization of CID intelligence, and the lack of influence by the ASI outside of military matters.

The 1933 Disturbances and the 1934 Security Exercise

During 1933, 30,327 Jews legally entered Palestine—about three times as many as the previous year. Nazi Germany was now a factor in Palestine politics, as more and more Jews fled persecution and opted for a new homeland. In 1935 alone, 61,854 Jews legally entered the country.[64] The rising rate of immigration was the principle source of fear for Palestinians. The disturbances in Jaffa in October 1933 resulted from the encouragement of all Palestinian leadership to resist British policy.

The CID's successes culminated in its preparation of the police for confrontation with demonstrators during the 1933 disturbances. CID summaries leading up to the disturbances described the activists' motivations: "The Arabs believe that immigration has exceeded all bounds, that they are destined to extermination and expulsion, that Government has disregarded Arab interests and representations and its own expert opinions, that protests and words are of no avail and that nothing but action can save them."[65]

In early October, the press and youth organizations became especially active and vocal, while the mufti's faction and Istiqlal quietly considered next steps. The CID concluded that the party conflict caused leaders to realize that "general action is not possible without centralized control."[66] Yet the parties achieved some form of unity. Musa Kazim, despite his advanced age (eighty) and alleged favoritism of the opposition, led a strike in Jerusalem on 13 October 1933, and received widespread admiration for his stance. His actions probably rescued ECPAC, which had become unpopular in the eyes of the youth for its ineffectual approach and its elitism. ECPAC appealed for a national strike; the CID believed it was forced to do so, lest the more extreme youth replace its leadership of the national movement. Istiqlal hosted lectures intending to "strengthen the spirit of resistance, hatred and revenge." Jamal al-Husseini received particular attention for having supervised the closure of shops in Jerusalem. The CID noted that this "calls to mind the influence which he exerted on political agitation during the earlier years of government."[67]

The strike leaders, especially Jamal al-Husseini, were disillusioned with government, and believed that Britain would "not yield except to force . . . that riots are the only means of delivering them and that a European war is the only chance for the Arabs to rid themselves of foreign rule." The CID did not forecast how antigovernment sentiment might affect public security. It knew the facts surrounding these events, and focused on Jamal's organizing role. A memo noted that "the decision of the executive marks the beginning of the resumption of the Arab political campaign and the revival of agitation on the lines of that pursued in the years 1920–23, although with some different objectives."[68] Whereas in 1920–23 the mandate without the Zionist policy might have been accepted, the movement now aimed for more. The Arab executive and the leading parties—Istiqlal and the Youngmen—were satisfied that the population was rallied around the goal of independence. Without this newfound unity, the executive might have collapsed.[69] The anti-British aspect of the national movement became more pronounced and more determined, and it led to reconciliation between the Old Istiqlalists and the mufti's faction.

When, on 13 October, Musa Kazim led a procession from al-Aqsa, the group was intercepted outside the old city by police, who dispersed them by means of baton charges. British authorities downplayed the violence that occurred and even covered up their excesses, saying that the police caused some injuries and that Musa Kazim was allowed to pass through the British line on account of his advanced age. He was not so fortunate the next week in Jaffa: photographic evidence emerged showing that British police beat the elderly and widely admired leader during those demonstrations, adding to the list of failures of law and order.[70] He died on 27 March 1934 at age eighty-one, likely as a result of his injuries. His death left the mufti and Jamal free to dominate the opposition faction.

Authorities in Egypt were kept up to date about intelligence in Palestine, in case of the "un-anticipated event of reinforcements being required." After the demonstrations, AOC Palestine asked Egypt for a signal detachment—perhaps to manage the unfolding of potential disturbances. Egypt had complained that intelligence was arriving slowly.[71] Either way, on 27 October in Jaffa, riots broke out when a procession in that city was dispersed. This time the crowd fired on the police, who shot back. One policeman and ten rioters were reported killed. Within two hours, the scene had calmed down. The high commissioner proudly reported that no troops were called on for support.

This outcome was possible because of police preparation. The district superintendent of police at Jaffa prepared a briefing about the event, which survives in the papers of J. A. M. Faraday, a senior police officer and ex-gendarme. The plan that was outlined two days before the riots exhibits a precise knowledge of how the procession was to unfold, the armament of the demonstrators, and their objectives.[72] Only the date was a surprise: the

FIGURE 6.1.   Musa Kazim al-Husseini struck by a policeman, Jaffa, 27 October 1933. Institute of Palestine Studies, Photograph Collection 81/144. Wikimedia Commons.

government had expected demonstrations to coincide with Balfour Day on 2 November.

Similar warnings came from the SSO in Haifa. Police benefited from Zionist intelligence cooperation, although the Haganah learned of the demonstrations through its observation of police preparations in Jaffa during the weeks leading up to the events. This calmed nerves within the Haganah and enabled restraint. The JA Arab Department learned firsthand from the source "Ne'eman" that concerted trouble was to be expected. Schools ordered youth to stay home. The source was one Abu-Na'ema of the village Battir, a contact of Ben-Zvi and A. H. Cohen who was motivated by his friendship with local Jews. He was in touch with Musa Darwish, the mufti's right-hand man during the 1929 disturbances. Other Arab informants confirmed that youth were being summoned for demonstrations, and that medical facilities were being prepared. Another source was a Jew working in the electric company, who happened to be connecting the home of Musa Kazim and reported to the Haganah on the senior leader's visitors. This gave forewarning of the demonstrations in Jerusalem, so the police intervened.[73]

Informants told the Jewish Agency that the Jaffa disturbances would be even larger during the coming week. Throughout the month of November, the Haganah and the JA cooperated with the CID and SSOs on the deteriorating security situation. The Haganah maintained constant telephone taps in Jerusalem and Jaffa, since at that time, both phone networks depended on a central exchange that was not automated. Shertok, now head of the JAPD, shared the Haganah's intelligence directly with the chief secretary. This source, along with reports from Eliyahu Epstein (Eilat) of the Arab Bureau of the Jewish Agency, who was in Beirut, also highlighted the role played by the Syrian Istiqlalists in preparing for general demonstrations in Palestine. The British consul in Damascus, Gilbert MacKereth, reached the same conclusion.[74] Italian financial and propaganda support was discovered thanks to surveillance of Mohammad Ali al-Taher, based in Cairo, who worked closely with Shakib Arslan and the Italians.[75]

British security managed the increasing tension in a number of ways. On Balfour Day there was some "slight desultory sniping" near Jerusalem and some cutting of telephone wires, but the situation was otherwise quiet.[76] Security also took steps to manage the press and refute allegations printed in Arabic papers.[77] The Palestine Police corresponded with MI5 to suppress allegedly false news and rumors being spread to Arab communities around the world. One telegram in particular sought to encourage Syrian nationalists in Brazil to protest to the League of Nations. MI5 did not see the need to suppress this particular message, but sought clarity from the government on MI5's power to suppress international cables, for future reference. Valentine Vivian of SIS believed they did have the legal power to do so.[78] Communist attempts to monopolize the Jaffa disturbances were suppressed by the police and army through successive raids over the two days preceding 27 October.[79] In all, British security measures worked.

Certain leaders had been held accountable for the disturbances: Jamal al-Husseini and 'Izzat Darwaza stood in front of a judge, but refused to recognize the court. Their party reiterated its demands for the stoppage of Jewish immigration, and planned further demonstrations. Meanwhile the mufti visited India to raise funds in his capacity as president of the pan-Islamic congress. Certain Istiqlal leaders were reported to have been dissatisfied with the quiet, and with the mufti's apparent control "from behind the scenes."[80] This had now become a consistent pattern—every time actual tension rose in Palestine, the mufti reached out to the Islamic congress. By doing so he dissociated himself from nationalists, while conferring with senior pan-Arab leaders.

The NPL became more active in London as a result of these events. Margaret Farquharson wrote to Musa Kazim, reporting on a meeting she had hosted at the Hyde Park Hotel on 12 December 1933. She promised that the majority of British people supported the Arabs, adding that she was pursuing the matter of immigration in the House of Lords. NPL allies in the House of Commons were asking questions about Arab compromises.[81] One cannot be sure, but this political pressure in London may well have helped to secure the lenient treatment of the strike and riot leaders, many of whom accepted bonds for "good behavior" instead of sentences for prison or hard labor.

The CID attributed the government decision to forgive the other strike leaders to "farsightedness," believing that it weakened their influence.[82] The government and the CID believed they were manipulating competing forces: the mufti's faction, Istiqlal, and the opposition. In reality, the former two were more related than the CID admitted. Wauchope obviously saw the promotion of notable politics through ECPAC as an antidote to the rising influence of younger nationalists. These actions concentrated influence in the mufti's hands, and undermined the opposition.

The army, while not called on during the October riots, was deployed around the country to enable a swift response—just in case.[83] This was the first major test for British security since 1929, and it was a success. Reports summarized lessons learned, which were then applied to military and police policy and procedure throughout 1934 and 1935. Plans for defense against external threats were well established, but in 1934, the army and the RAF drilled a simulated rebellion. Tony Simonds, then commander of battalion intelligence in the Royal Berkshire Regiment, remarked that battalion/regimental intelligence was rated of such low importance by the system that it was combined with the role of railway transport officer, and twelve members of the intelligence section were also the drummers in the regimental band.[84] As head of battalion intelligence, Simonds saw much of the country and learned its terrain and people. Senior army commander Col. Jack Evetts, who had observed what Simonds described as his own "enthusiasm for mixing with Arabs and the country side, ordained that there would be an exercise by the Royal Berkshire Regiment against a guerilla band, (incidentally, far ahead of its time in military thinking)."[85] Simonds's section was dressed in Arab clothes and planned an ambush of the rest of his regiment. The drill was a success, although he broke his ankle. Simonds's remark that the drill was ahead of its time was indeed true. It was only at this time in the UK that the army even began to revise its thinking for war preparation and revision of field service regulations under Archibald Wavell, another Palestine "graduate" of the First World War who would return as general officer, commanding (GOC) in 1937.[86]

The countrywide drill was held in June 1934. Army, RAF, police, and civil departments participated, making up the entire garrison: two infantry battalions (1,600 troops), two TJFF cavalry squadrons, a half company of mechanized TJFF, three armored car sections, and a signals detachment, as well as one and a half squadrons of aircraft. The drill, according to one report, "envisaged a state of unrest throughout the country on the first day" and sought to achieve a high degree of realism. The second day simulated the dying-down phase of disturbances and was more of a test for senior command and control, and the army's communication with the government. The drill even simulated the deliberate distraction of SSOs, who would normally supply warning in emergencies—but often were prevented from doing so. It simulated situations such as Labor-Revisionist disturbances, Arab-Jewish disturbances, a plot to murder a senior police officer, a Bedouin incursion from Transjordan, the widespread cutting of telephone lines, and other events typical of emergencies and disturbances in Palestine.[87] Wauchope was most satisfied with the exercise, remarking that difficulties experienced in communications were normal. He also expressed concern about poor civil-military liaison. In fact, many records from the ASI and the government that survive in the Central Zionist Archives show consistent concern with these issues as the politico-security situation developed during 1935.[88] Thus, as the situation spun out of control between November 1935 and April 1936, the government was continually revising its security procedures and ensuring that infrastructure, especially signals and telegraph, was in place to enable a military response.

Road to Rebellion

Security preparations and reforms proved themselves in the defeat of 'Izz al-Din al-Qassam's Black Hand gang in November 1935. Pan-Arab meetings attended by the mufti, along with illicit arms imports and a complex propaganda campaign, had laid the groundwork for resistance. The cement incident kicked off the first strike in October. On 7 November, while investigating a theft in the settlement of Ein Harod, the Jewish police sergeant Moshe Rosenfeld was shot while tracking the suspects near Mount Gilboa. Police backup found Rosenfeld dead, as well as the remnants of a rebel camp. According to an ASI summary, "Subsequent investigation . . . identified his murderers with the gang reported to have been formed by Sheikh Essedin el

Qassam." Intelligence about al-Qassam's movements in the Nablus-Jenin area led police to close in on the region. Skirmishes broke out in the countryside near Jenin during police searches. Al-Qassam's rebels fired on police again on 20 November, engaging them in direct combat lasting from 6:45 to 10:00 a.m. Four or five gang members were reported killed, and five captured. Al-Qassam was among the dead. Police hoped that their success would have a deterrent effect; however, information obtained after al-Qassam's death gave evidence of the contrary.[89]

From a security point of view, this was the peak of success—proof that British rule could stand up to serious disturbances, despite all the failures of 1929–32. After much preparation and training, the police had led the murder investigation, and then discovered and defeated the dissidents believed responsible. Aircraft had passed reconnaissance information to the CID, and intelligence had been coordinated between civil and military sources to support a police operation. The intelligence state had taken a sophisticated shape in its role as enforcer. Yet the government, the CID, and to some extent the ASI failed to appreciate the political significance of al-Qassam's death. The CID and the ASI agreed that new gang formation was mostly talk and little action, and that nothing in the immediate future could be expected. They also believed the action against al-Qassam had had a deterrent effect against "unorganised banditry."[90] The ASI was more apprehensive than the CID about the potential for future violence organized in response to al-Qassam's defeat and concluded with a severe warning that the gang was connected by family and other lines to national leaders such as 'Auni 'Abdul Hadi.

In the wake of al-Qassam's death, the ASI reported that the peasants were "entirely in sympathy" with the gangs. The Palestine Arab Party had encouraged the formation of gangs, with the aim of arousing hostility to the government. Extremists such as Zu'ayter attacked leaders like the mufti "to remove the restraining influences which impede the adoption of militant action as a means of coercing the government."[91]

The mood in the country certainly had changed. Hamdi al-Husayni told the Jaffa branch of Youngmen that now was the time for confrontation with England. "Bad leadership changed the course of our struggle," he said. "If we fought the English face to face we should not be as we are now. We fought in 1921, 1929, and 1933 and our blood was lost because of the leaders. We are not succeeding because we do not fight the right way, that is, face to face with England."[92]

Britain, not the Yishuv, was the main obstacle to Palestinian national aims. The youth movements now sought unity in their struggle against the mandate. The youth and peasants could not have been successful in their drive toward the general strike without the preparations of the previous five years by the mufti and his party. At the same time, the mufti was making efforts to consolidate support from outside Palestine. While many historians have preferred to attribute the strike and revolt to the youth rather than the mufti, we must account for the words of those who organized the movement in the first place. It was no coincidence that mujahideen in the North began to mobilize at the same time.

Fawzi al-Qawuqji, who led foreign volunteers and mobilized local rebels beginning in August 1936, wrote in his memoir that the revolt had been planned since 1935. Al-Qawuqji had long pondered the Palestine problem, and since 1929 had considered how to prepare a platform for the armed defense of Palestine. In 1934, as an authorized army officer for Iraq, he went to Palestine, but met with the nationalists in addition to his official business. Tellingly, his memoir does not specify with which Palestinians he coordinated military preparations. "I suggested a broad plan which we seek for preparation, to be implemented when needed," he recalls. "Every detail of the plan was agreed upon. Regretfully, one of the means which we agreed upon was not fulfilled."[93] He traveled again to Jerusalem in 1935, as the Syrian crisis was simmering. If he was planning in Jerusalem, it is almost certain that he was working with PAP on military preparations, and possibly with Istiqlal.

Al-Qawuqji states explicitly that the revolt was preplanned, especially with the Syrian crisis in mind. He recruited volunteers from Iraq and Syria to join his campaign. Under the guise of official work for Transjordan, he reconnoitered the border areas and prepared maps for the forthcoming campaign. He believed he was under investigation by British intelligence, and began to spread a mix of false and true rumors about volunteer groups from the Iraqi Army wishing to volunteer to fight in Palestine. He became friendly with British intelligence officers, and "began pretending to be shameless and drunk." This he used as an excuse to resign and pilfer or purchase arms from Indian army bases.[94]

Al-Qawuqji's story aligns closely with other evidence about the National Pact's ambitions to exploit a European crisis. His description of plans for Palestine is similar to plans developed in Syria to confront French policy with a general strike and the threat of escalation. The French, caught between the Rhineland crisis, the Abyssinian crisis, and the prospect of revolution in Syria, were forced into negotiations after a fifty-four-day strike. The same action was intended for Palestine, where nationalists were cognizant of their compatriots' success in Syria. A deputation of Arab notables from Jaffa told the district commissioner there that "following the example of Syria, strikes and

agitation would continue until their national demands had been granted."
A similar public declaration was made by notables of Nablus, and PAP, according to Wauchope, published an appeal to "all Arabs to continue to strike
until 'the atmosphere is clarified and calamity removed.'" He added, "To
ensure that continuance of strikes and agitation is being actively encouraged
committees of action are being formed throughout Palestine," and reported
that "the present situation appears to be developing on lines of the recent
situation in Syria."[95]

Nabih and 'Adel al-'Azmeh's memoir, based on their papers held at Ex-
eter, records that Nabih and Akram Zu'ayter played the role of coordinators
between Iraq, Syria, and Palestine during the Syrian general strike. Fighters
were prepared to escalate the strike in Syria, but were not needed in the end.
Pan-Arab parties were limited in how they could support the strike and revolt in Palestine. Only during the Syrian strike did the Syrian National Bloc
begin to seriously collect financial resources in Palestine and Iraq. Only by
June 1936 did they start to seriously discuss Iraqi support for the revolt.[96]
Arabic evidence is clear that armed resistance was anything but spontaneous, although events unfolded in unexpected ways. Read alongside British
intelligence records, the body of evidence shows that Palestinian parties coordinated with other pan-Arab parties in Syria and Iraq in a premeditated
attempt to escalate pressure against Britain. It is curious how historians have
ignored the words of the men who planned it.

The new Palestine National Bloc's platform demanded complete independence, but it was a smaller party composed mainly of professionals
and merchants from Nablus and Jaffa. The CID observed that most Palestine "National Bloc" or "National Party" members were prepared to accept
Wauchope's legislative solutions.[97] In response to growing tension during
April 1936, the colonial secretary invited an Arab delegation to London to
meet with them. The invitation created some discord, as certain parties were
more willing to accept than others. The five main parties—PAP, Istiqlal, the
Bloc, the Youngmen Congress, and Defense—met to elect representatives.
The Arab parties also wished to discuss British policy in Syria, where France
had recently conceded to strikers and begun negotiations. Jamal al-Husseini
aimed to dominate the delegation with his own party members. The Bloc's
leader, 'Abdul Latif Salah, responded furiously, almost coming to blows with
the mufti's cousin.[98] When the delegation finally went to London during the
summer of 1936, the Colonial Office refused to discuss constitutional solutions, and so the group instead organized a propaganda office, the Palestine
Information Centre (PIC), in conjunction with the NPL.

Akram Zu'ayter's memoir shows that Istiqlal and the youth had revolt
in mind long before April 1936. In it he writes about the coincident deaths

of al-Qassam and Ibrahim Hananu, who had led Syrian revolutionaries and published a related article about the role of leadership and self-sacrifice. Zuʻayter had recorded in his diary in early 1936, "The revolution is our path until the end. Propaganda and preparation for revolution are the most important duties. Public opinion has incessantly been injected with the spirit of revolution, and it is necessary to transition to the phase of action."[99] Sure enough, Hamdi al-Husayni began a renewed program of activism and demonstrations at that time. Zuʻayter's memoir describes his correspondence with al-Qawuqji in April 1936. Al-Qawuqji had recently visited Jerusalem, and Zuʻayter wrote that he regretted that they had not met. He updated al-Qawuqji on the revolutionary excitement in the country, the efforts to organize a movement, and the hopes that he had tied to al-Qawuqji in the revolutionary movement about to explode.[100] No doubt al-Qawuqji's visit in April was intended to coordinate military preparations. Al-Qawuqji's volunteer force only arrived in August 1936 and was the only force of an organized, militarily capable character.

The historian Mark Sanagan demonstrates clearly how nationalist youth and Istiqlal co-opted the martyrdom of al-Qassam to increase the spirit of rebellion. Al-Qassam was eulogized by many. Youth demonstrations focused frustration against the mufti and senior leaders. Sanagan describes this as "rhetorical posturing," arguing that the leadership feared a loss of power to a populist revolt.[101] Yet the mufti played a role in preparing the ground for these events. Sanagan cites Jamal's statement to the government that perhaps "one day it might be that every Palestinian would become as one of those [al-Qassamites] who were killed a few days ago near Jenin."[102] This statement has been mischaracterized as an expression of fear. Perhaps it should be understood as an implicit threat.

Gilbert MacKereth, while visiting Jerusalem during the escalating crisis, shared with the government an intercepted letter from Jamal, in his capacity as head of PAP, to the Syrian nationalists. The letter used typical Islamist language to arouse fear of Jewish aims to take over Muslim holy sites at al-Aqsa and Hebron. According to MacKereth, in the letter PAP urged "their brethren in race and religion to unite to bring such tyranny and injustice to an end so that Palestine may remain an opulent Arab country with its sacred shrines."[103] Meanwhile CID intelligence reported on Istiqlal's push for noncooperation.[104] The CID also discussed the efforts of those connected to SMC sheikhs to increase membership in YMMA branches in the North, and spread propaganda.[105]

The mufti and Jamal wielded strong influence despite frustration from below about their lack of support. It was nearly time to pull the trigger. The outbreak of the general strike in 1936 was a way for PAP to take concrete action while still restraining revolt, which was premature, since foreign fighters were not yet organized. In March 1936, France bowed to the strikers and launched negotiations. It was now the Palestinians' turn. The pan-Arab strategy was to force Britain to concede as France had. This was the reasonable next step in a strategy that had developed since about 1932. By 1935–36 this strategy had taken a mature shape.

Typically, the mufti's campaign centered on raising alarm in religious and nationalist circles separately, while maintaining personal distance from the nationalists' dirty work. The mufti likely wished to be the man who negotiated independence with the British government, which was expected to cave under pressure. He underestimated Britain's refusal to negotiate under armed threat and its preparedness to push back forcefully, and could not have anticipated that by April 1936, the British Army would have begun rearmament and would be relieved of the preoccupying crises in Europe and the Red Sea.

The intelligence states, both military and civil, survived their trials of the 1930s: the steady escalation of public disturbances that were intended to pressure British policymakers to address the mandate's basic contradictions. The implication was that if the government would not address Palestinian grievances, including the Yishuv's arms, legal and illegal immigration, constitutional self-government, and their equal treatment under the law, it could face further escalation. Britain would not satisfy these demands. The intelligence state in Palestine was prepared for revolt and had proved its ability to deal with mass movements. These pressure tactics would not work against the civil or military intelligence states, now more confident than ever. Yet more security led to more resentment, as did Britain's protection of the Zionist policy and its armament of the Yishuv. Democratic self-government remained elusive so long as these conflicts raged, while Britain refused to impose a different solution. The result was rebellion, which came at a regrettable cost to all.

CHAPTER 7

The Arab Revolt

Intelligence and Politics

The government gave increasing authority to the military to escalate its response to the general strike as it slid toward revolt. Intelligence reports illustrate how the government managed these escalations, but also its hope for diplomatic intervention by the independent Arab states to restore order by autumn 1936. Signals intelligence records are crucial to that story. Wauchope corresponded in secret with the Colonial Office, seeking approval to approach Saudi Arabia, Iraq, and Yemen for their intervention with the mufti on Britain's behalf. He believed this would allow the mufti and his allies to save face, enjoy the attention of the independent states, and return to negotiations. The three independent Arab kings—'Abd al-'Aziz Ibn Sa'ud, Imam Yahya of Yemen, and Ghazi of Iraq (represented by Foreign Minister Nuri Sa'id)—called on the Palestinians to end the strike, but not before military reinforcements arrived. Wauchope's scheme was a temporary and limited success. It exposed a key vulnerability in pan-Arab plans for independence: the National Pact expected partnership with the independent Arab kings, whose stately interests aligned more with Britain than with the nationalists.

As tensions escalated, Wauchope believed that internal Palestinian conflicts could be exploited to help Britain maintain control. He thought the mufti was primarily interested in his own power, and so overlooked his increasingly obvious association with the pan-Arab plan to exploit the global crises of 1936 and secure concessions from Britain. When that failed, he and Whitehall turned to the Arab kings to spare Palestine from Britain's military might. When the royal commission headed by Lord Peel recommended the partition of Palestine as a solution, intelligence anticipated the explosion that followed, but could do little to stop it.

The General Strike and Creeping Violence

The government hoped that constitutional negotiations would prevent an outburst. Both the ASI and the CID anticipated that outcome should talks fail. In March 1936, the CID remarked on the concessions granted by France to the Syrian nationalists: "The concessions which are regarded as the result of the strike and demonstrations have inevitably led to the suggestion of similar activity in Palestine."[1] Although the treaty was eventually signed in September, France never ratified it. But in March–April 1936, pan-Arabists believed Syrian independence was at hand. PAP, Istiqlal, and most of the Youngmen executive favored bringing the strike to Palestine. Old Istiqlalists such as Nabih al-'Azmeh thought such action should be delayed until details with the French were finalized. Palestine erupted before that time, when both the senior political and the paramilitary leadership were unprepared. PAP held an executive meeting on 28 February 1936, where a "negative" policy of civil disobedience, strike, and demonstration was adopted. Tellingly, Jamal al-Husseini added that "before anything effective could be done, the 'Futuwah' [militant youth] groups must be formed."[2] If the establishment of a legislative council and limits on Jewish immigration and land transfers were delayed, the CID said, "methods adopted in Syria and Egypt are bound to appeal with greater force to the Arabs in Palestine." In fact, the mufti's propaganda had already led Palestinians on this course. Palestinian Futuwwah were being mobilized. Their induction oath for new members declared, "Liberty is my right—Independence my hope—my language Arabic—Palestine is mine and mine only. This I attest and God is my witness to my loyalty."[3]

Back in Britain, Parliament debated Wauchope's proposed legislative council. It would give legislative powers to Jews and Arabs, but still shelter the Zionist policy from voters. The Lords attacked the proposal, while the Commons proposed a royal commission of inquiry. Jews and Arabs watched these debates closely. Meanwhile, tensions on the ground had been palpable since the death of al-Qassam. Palestinian Arabs had been encouraged by the progress made by the Syrian general strike, but were disappointed that British lawmakers always sheltered the Zionist policy.

The CID reported on the changed atmosphere in the government of Stanley Baldwin: "Following so closely after the debate in the House of Lords, where a formerly friendly atmosphere has now become definitely hostile to them, it has made them [the Arabs] realize more than ever the strength of Jewish influence in England, and they are now definitely suspicious as to Government's intentions in regard to the establishment of the Council." The CID concluded that Palestinians now doubted that they would get any concession from Britain, and believed that British members of Parliament had been corrupted. From the Palestinians' point of view, the deals offered by Churchill and Leo Amery in the 1920s outweighed the present offers. The CID warned on the eve of revolt that any delay in implementation of legislative reform would lead to disorder.[4] The stakes were clear, but the negotiations for a Palestine legislative council collapsed. Palestinians demanded that Jews surrender control over immigration. Jews demanded more immigration, given the increasingly dire situation in Europe.

Between 15 and 19 April 1936, against a background of political tension, violence gradually escalated to the point where riots broke out in Jaffa on the nineteenth. It began with a highway robbery on the fifteenth in which three Jews were shot, followed by reprisal attacks. Funerals were the scenes of mass demonstrations and confrontations between crowds and police. By the nineteenth, all major parties—PAP, al-Difaʻa (Defense; Nashashibi's party), Istiqlal, the National Bloc (Nablus), Reform (Hussein Khalidi's liberal party), and the Youngmen Congress—had coalesced to form the Arab Supreme Committee (ASC; also called "Higher Committee," but "Supreme" is a better translation). With apparent reluctance the mufti accepted calls to head the ASC, which then led the general strike and articulated three familiar demands: prohibition of Jewish immigration, prohibition of transfer of Arab land to Jews, and the establishment of a national government responsible to a representative council. The general strike was said to have been observed nationwide, at first. The CID suggested that disunity within the ASC could be exploited, as it was not "entirely free from party interests."[5] The CID and Wauchope tended to emphasize these differences, ignoring evidence that the mufti was pulling the strings.

In May 1936, five weeks into the Palestinian strike, Whitehall proposed sending a royal commission to investigate the disturbances and propose solutions. At the top of the list was the problem of governance, which was connected to each Palestinian grievance. The ASC rejected this proposal, but nonetheless a commission headed by Lord Peel was imposed by Britain the next week. However, the Peel Commission would only begin its investigations once Palestine had returned to peace conditions.[6] This was the "carrot and stick"—the Palestinians could have a say at the royal commission or face even worse consequences. Britain's aim now was to force an end to the strike and disturbances, and cause Palestinian leaders to participate in the royal commission. To meet the objective, eventually the military escalated. One way or the other, Britain had begun the road to an imposed solution.

The government could not force the ASC or the Jewish Agency to agree on a council.[7] Some officials now saw the danger of the government's relations with the mufti and his party. These conflicting views reflect the dissonance between Wauchope's conciliatory approach to PAP and the ASC, and the latter's role in driving escalating violence in Palestine. Zionist intelligence saw the role played by this leadership in fomenting disturbances, but had been surprised by the outbreak on 19 April.[8] So too were RAF and army intelligence officers. They all quickly adjusted their perspectives.

The Haganah coordinated information with Davidescu and shared news with the Arab Bureau of the Jewish Agency Political Department. Their evidence reveals a scramble among senior Palestinian leaders, who were unprepared for what was unfolding. Davidescu reported that Rashid al-Hajj Ibrahim and others were waiting for a coordinated violent outbreak, so their calls for calm in Haifa were intended to prevent the youth from starting prematurely. Bedouin strike leaders asked the mufti by telephone for his views on next steps. He replied evasively, saying that each action was uncoordinated, and so it was "every man for himself." Clearly, chaos reigned at the top. Haganah agents followed the prominent journalist, lawyer, al-Difa'a activist, and strike leader Hasan Sidqi Dajani in Jerusalem during the last two days of April. They observed his visit to Barclays Bank, and his meetings with Ahmad Hilmi Pasha, director of the Arab Bank. He also met Ya'aqub al-Ghussein and several Bedouin sheikhs.[9] No doubt he was trying to distribute funds to strike committees, which had been formed throughout the country. Simultaneously the Palestinian parties convened in Jerusalem and formed the ASC.

Weldon Matthews writes that the ASC, composed of factional leaders, "ostensibly took up leadership of a movement that was in fact leading them."[10] Indeed, the leadership was unprepared for the events as they unfolded. They had laid groundwork for a strike, not armed revolt. The youth and peasantry demanded and took action before organized armed forces became available. They had been led and encouraged by the Youngmen, SMC sheikhs, YM-MAs, and sport and youth clubs. The mufti did not control everything that happened, and like all actors in this drama did not always get the results he hoped for; yet he was a player—the key one on the Arab side.

Evidence on these issues was available to British decision makers and intelligence services, although perhaps not all at once. It did not take Zionist intelligence long to understand what was happening. Davidescu was the first to raise the possibility of holding the mufti responsible for disturbances. He dragged Alex Aaronsohn back into the intelligence business, using his London contacts since the JAPD's exhortations fell on deaf ears in Jerusalem.[11]

Discussions between government and members of the ASC occurred against the backdrop of a persistent cycle of violence, a steadfast strike movement, and increasing anxiety toward the Yishuv. Wauchope's first move was to check whether 'Abdullah bin Husayn of Transjordan could influence an end to the strike. It was pointless. 'Abdullah was deeply unpopular among most Istiqlalist, Islamist, and other nationalist leaders. However, it was a convenient way to reinforce Wauchope's refusal to suspend Jewish immigration, or to entertain negotiations outside the royal commission. Wauchope regretted that Arab leaders made "no strong pronouncement against murder and acts of violence." He thanked 'Abdullah for keeping Transjordan quiet at this time, and mentioned the negative effect that Palestinian violence was having on English public opinion.[12]

The Palestinian leaders who met 'Abdullah told him they did not control the movement, and complained of other difficulties, which they asked 'Abdullah to convey to the British.[13] They did not treat 'Abdullah as an Arab leader, but rather as a British official. In June, 'Abdullah tried again, but was told that violence was a response to harsh measures imposed by the British Army and police, such as searches, destruction of property, shooting Arabs, and emergency laws that allowed detainment in prison camps.[14] 'Abdullah's influence would not alter the situation. Instead his attempts to intervene put him in the rebels' crosshairs.

In mid-May, Wauchope met face to face with the ASC. They must have noticed his overly cordial tone. After telling them that the royal commission would not come to investigate political grievances until violence stopped, Wauchope asked them to publicly use their influence to restore calm and to denounce "lawless acts." He emphasized that the royal commission would not "recommend any alteration of the terms of the Mandate."[15] The next year it did just that, but in the meantime his pleas fell on deaf ears. The ASC had no reason to cooperate unless British policy might change. Wauchope could not provide the opening they needed, and so the conflict continued. The incoherence and weakness of his policy prolonged the crisis.

Shertok added to the mounting pressure on Wauchope. After the HC complained that his staff were ill and tired, Shertok asked who would be going to Geneva to report on disturbances in Palestine. Wauchope did not respond well to the unsubtle threat. According to Shertok, the HC "looked a little roguish and replied that he was not at liberty to tell me that. I said that

I had put up the question on the supposition that Geneva still existed which seemed now rather doubtful, after it had been flouted so openly by Italy in addition to its having been deserted by Germany and Japan. The High Commissioner thought it was yet too early to despair of the League of Nations altogether."[16]

Shertok exposed Wauchope's sensitivity to league criticism. Wauchope emphasized division among ASC leaders regarding the strike, but Shertok did not believe that ASC leaders such as 'Auni 'Abdul Hadi could be manipulated, since, he said, Hadi "had always struck me as a type of doctrinaire revolutionary, very rigid and dogmatic, with little sense of realities. The High Commissioner remarked that I would be surprised if I knew how many times 'Auni Bey had changed his mind in the last few weeks." Shertok was baffled by the HC's inability to see the situation as he did: so-called "moderates" had rejected invitations to London, and prevented the royal commission from launching. Wauchope interjected, saying that the ASC would not budge unless Jewish immigration could be stopped.[17] There was no basis for negotiation.

This exchange is telling. Wauchope was unwilling to treat the ASC as insurrectionist because he hoped their internal disagreements would produce compromise with Britain. Yet they demonstrated remarkable solidarity. Lacking alternatives, he thought he could continue his older patterns of influence and control. Shertok, the next day, pleaded with Wauchope to take tough measures against strike leaders in Haifa. They had so far failed to persuade most workers to join, but the workers could not hold out much longer under the pressure of the strike committee.[18] As military, police, and civil servants steadily realized the gravity of the crisis, Wauchope began to make excuses. He admitted to a government executive council (exco) meeting that stronger action must be taken against the organizers of the strike and disorder. He suddenly considered action against ASC, but according to the minutes of the meeting, "It was clear that no useful purpose would be served at present by proceeding against individuals for civil disobedience; . . . it was [also] necessary that he should have some responsible body with which to continue negotiations." The ASC twice had publicly dissociated itself from violent methods, and its unity was expected to collapse.[19]

The government ignored evidence that connected the ASC to violence, because it needed a power broker to control the movement. Wauchope was not alone in this view. The CID also overemphasized political divisions in its reportage—focusing exclusively on the Nashashibi-al-Husseini conflict, and the youth-driven extremism. It believed the ASC's claim that any capitulation before an immigration stoppage would lead to a loss of its control over the strike.[20] In fact, this was an indirect threat: if the ASC did not get what it wanted, it would not be responsible for the dire consequences. Even so, it admitted influence, not control, over the strike. Still hoping to exploit disunity within the ASC, Wauchope nonetheless authorized the police to prepare lists of agitators and political suspects who could be arrested for provocations. The situation escalated even further—Jaffa essentially had become a war zone between 23 May and 9 June, and the government asked Whitehall for permission to use tear gas, an "effective and merciful weapon," for riot control.[21]

The CS concluded that "'moderate' Arabs do exist, but they have no influence in a situation like this one simply because they are moderate."[22] The situation in Jaffa became so grave that Wauchope relented and allowed the AOC, Air Vice Marshal Richard Peirse, to escalate the government's response. Peirse organized a combined service command comprising the RAF, army, and intelligence staff, an important innovation to be discussed in the next chapter. Its first major operation was the pacification of Jaffa, where it destroyed houses in the old port city, leaving room for a promenade. The tightly packed and impoverished neighborhood, a symbol of Palestinian resistance, was no longer the source of persistent gunfire and harassment of British troops and police.[23]

The situation worsened. With a clear objective of restoring peace and allowing the royal commission to proceed, the AOC was given more power to arrest strikers and riot leaders, and to search villages. Detention camps were opened and police blacklists were used to round up Palestinian leaders. Peirse warned that he would need reinforcements. He believed that the ASC had "made retreat impossible for themselves but hoped the government could find some face saver." The options were carrot and stick: military escalation, or a face-saving gesture to provide for cooperation. No doubt Peirse and Wauchope also hoped to save face for allowing the situation to boil. Peirse reported that Wauchope refused to escalate the military response or to request reinforcements until "this last card . . . had been played." By mid-May, "the outlook was one of continued civil disobedience, e.g., arson, destruction of telegraph and telephone wires, interference with rail and road communications; minor disturbances and isolated attacks on individuals." On 16 May Peirse told the GOC Egypt that he would probably require an extra battalion.[24]

The escalation of the military campaign continued, especially in response to the arrival in August of foreign volunteers under Fawzi al-Qawuqji's command. Al-Qawuqji, a former Ottoman soldier who had fought in the Syrian revolt in 1925–26, had long prepared for the campaign in Palestine. A fugitive from French Syria, he had been living in Iraq, where he trained army officers. There, British surveillance observed his movements. One intelligence officer reportedly warned him against leading the Palestine campaign. In late August, he entered Palestine with some three hundred volunteers and began to reshape the rebellion into an organized paramilitary campaign.[25] The government possessed intelligence that should have forewarned of this problem, as Mu'in al-Madi, an Istiqlalist and secretary on the SMC, was seen in Baghdad spreading propaganda for the Palestinian cause, and was promoting anti-British and anti-Jewish propaganda in nationalist clubs.[26] The mufti's people were recruiting volunteer fighters.

Escalation in Palestine was a reciprocal problem, as Britain's heavy-handedness mobilized further Palestinian resistance, which deepened lawlessness, hunger, and dislocation.[27] This would be a more pronounced problem in 1938 than it was in 1936, but claims against Britain's treatment of Palestinians fueled potent propaganda. This news was spread not just in the Arab world. In June 1936, Jamal al-Husseini traveled to London with a few other leaders in an unofficial delegation. The CID reported that "they received a sympathetic hearing from many people in England, including a number of Members of Parliament, and they have enlisted a great deal of support for the Arab cause."[28]

The true purpose of Jamal's mission was to fund and organize a propaganda office in London, and to secure a concession from Britain. For years Jamal and the mufti wanted a stronger campaign in Britain, so now was the time to reinvigorate their propaganda strategy. They contacted the NPL, which had been an important source of support after the October 1935 cement incident.[29] Together they formed the Palestine Information Centre (PIC). The prime minister was advised not to pay too much attention to their efforts.[30] Key figures were now organized to lobby parliamentarians and other officials in favor of the Arab case. They produced pamphlets and hosted lecture series and social functions to promote the cause.[31]

Escalations on the ground in Palestine led Wauchope to hand increasing authority to Peirse, whose combined staff centralized intelligence and improved its role in decision making. As the government began to militarize, military intelligence increasingly affected policy. Tellingly, the CID did not offer intelligence summaries between 23 May and 23 June—the period during which urban violence spilled into revolt. Yet its report in June recorded that the movement lacked any organization or control. It claimed that the extremist 'Ulema were asking the mufti and the SMC to declare jihad.[32]

British intelligence revealed foreign support for the revolt. In June 1936, it discovered clear proof that Italy was supporting the revolt. Italian clergy were smuggling money into Palestine, and Jewish Agency intelligence was cited as saying that Banco di Roma was distributing funds to support the strike and resistance. The ASI believed the mufti was pooling cash along with contributions received from India and other Muslim countries in his SMC treasury.[33] There was little to be done about Italian support. British forces could try to interdict deliveries within Palestine's borders, but such instances were rare in 1936. The funds were more serious, but the government still lacked the political will to prosecute the SMC or seize its assets. It feared the repercussions of interfering in Muslim affairs.

In late June, the next important step on the path to revolt took place as the strike focused on Arab officials in government positions. The CID reported that Arab policemen and government officers had come under pressure to leave their jobs. The less cooperative received threats from the Black Hand society.[34] Each month from May until October, the CID reported that the strike would be called off "in the near future." Its assessments were weak, and reflected the wishful thinking of the civil government. Nonetheless, the CID still reported important facts. For instance, in August 1936 it reported that the mufti completely controlled fundraising in Palestine and abroad as well as the disbursement of funds, including those received by armed bands. 'Abdullah had again tried to mediate between the mufti and the government, but his attempt to corner the mufti with Nashashibi supporters at the meeting annoyed the Palestinian leader. When those talks broke down, "an immediate breaking out of disorders throughout the country" resulted.[35] Unable to crush the movement and unwilling to admit defeat, the government sought to rely on the influence of Arab statesmen instead of attacking the mufti or his official position. Wauchope reasoned that without the mufti, there would be nobody with whom to negotiate or who might control the violence.

In September Air Control ended, and Gen. John Dill came to Palestine to lead military operations as GOC. For the first time in months, Wauchope met the mufti, and he expressed his regrets that despite his "true feeling of friendship," his advice had not been followed. Dill would take over next week. "I shall have no influence over General Dill's actions," Wauchope said, "and His Eminence [the mufti] must be sure that His Majesty's Government will continue military action until all resistance has ended. As a friend of the Arabs I would say that it is clearly in their interest to end resistance and violence now rather than be forced to do so later . . ."[36] Wauchope finally had resorted to threats, although he had one more trick up his sleeve.

The Arab Kings Scheme

Seeking a way to avoid further escalation, Wauchope attempted a diplomatic pathway in concert with Whitehall. He did so in secret, and excluded every other authority in Palestine. In mid-July 1936, Whitehall asked Wauchope to arrest the mufti. They were frustrated that he had not used his influence to end the strike, and so he should be held to account. Wauchope refused, fearing the "religious cry in Palestine and other countries." In an unusual step, Wauchope ordered a cipher officer to send his reply from the chief secretary's house. He wanted to hide the correspondence from other members of the exco. According to a handwritten note by a Jewish Agency mole, Wauchope and the colonial secretary, William Ormsby-Gore, thus corresponded in secret. Wauchope brought the results of those month-long exchanges to the exco on 15 July.[37] What he proposed was a compromise, and a gamble: Britain would invite the independent Arab kings to use their influence to induce the mufti to call off the strike.

Anglo-Saudi relations were at the heart of this move. That relationship will be elaborated on in chapter 9, although it is important here to cover the evidence about the Arab kings scheme. Ibn Saʿud had an important connection to the pan-Arab movement, and his influence therein was noted by British diplomats. They had access to his communications with his own ministers, elaborating on their talks with pan-Arab parties. Ibn Saʿud's key ministers were Syrian admirers who joined him during his expansions of 1918–25. They had been in the original Istiqlal or similar parties. Intelligence also showed that Ibn Saʿud was sympathetic to British interests and sought a closer partnership, while members of the National Pact believed Ibn Saʿud would use his influence in favor of Arab independence.

The CID reported on a pan-Arab conference in Syria that laid the groundwork for the strikes of 1936. The mufti attended, as did Ibn Saʿud's minister Fuad Hamza, who was "well connected with certain members of the Istiqlal party in Palestine." Hamza discussed the conference's deliberations about strategy. Istiqlal "endeavored to obtain a decision in favour of Ibn Saʿud to speak in the name of Syria and Palestine, leaving the question of other territories to their respective rulers."[38] The nationalists had long hoped for this level of representation. However, they did not realize that Ibn Saʿud's stance was pragmatic. He only addressed territories whose future remained uncertain. He had to balance his relations with Britain and other great powers, especially Italy, now on his doorstep in the Red Sea.[39]

Ibn Saʿud was genuinely sympathetic to the Palestinians, and hostile to unlimited Jewish immigration. As the crisis in Palestine began in April 1936, the diplomat in Jeddah, Sir Andrew Ryan, told Wauchope and the FO of his discussions with Sheikh Yusuf Yasin, Ibn Saʿud's private secretary. Yasin presented a telegram he received from the mufti: a plea for assistance. Ibn Saʿud politely declined. He told Ryan that he did not want to harm British interests, yet this issue affected his "prestige in the Arab world," which was experiencing unprecedented unity. Palestine should not be left behind.[40]

British sigint confirmed that Ibn Saʿud had rebuffed the mufti's plea for help.[41] Through Yasin, Ibn Saʿud told Ryan that he had no interest in interfering against Britain's interests. Ryan discouraged any hope of Ibn Saʿud's future involvement in Palestine. Yasin assured Ryan that Ibn Saʿud did not wish to interfere.[42] Yet by summer 1936, much had changed. Wauchope was desperate to end the rising violence as the strike drifted toward revolt. Whereas Ryan had discouraged Ibn Saʿud from any involvement in the mandate, authorities in Palestine and Whitehall soon saw it as essential to ending the strike and the violence and moving toward a political settlement.

During 1935–36, FO Arabists such as George W. Rendel believed they could exploit pan-Arab aspirations to leverage Saudi leadership. For that and other good reasons, Britain drew closer to ʿAbd al-ʿAziz. The CID report concluded that the National Pact sought to exploit a European emergency such as the Rhineland crisis. They saw it as "the only opportunity for them to force the British government to grant their aspirations and they are careful not to forego the opportunities afforded in the last world war or to repeat the mistakes of the late King Hussein. It is alleged that this was hinted to Emir Saoud [sic] at private conversations."[43] Foreign Office undersecretaries with access to sigint knew that Ibn Saʿud disliked the mufti, that he prioritized British interests, that the nationalists admired him, and that he could sway them.

In June, Ibn Saʿud instructed Hafez Wahba to approach the British government regarding Palestine, saying that he preferred not to interfere but was under pressure from Muslim and Arab opinion. He emphasized Saudi friendship, and noted that he had suppressed anti-British demonstrations in his country: "My instructions are that you should explore suitable means, without causing misgivings, to sound the British government regarding the Palestine question, and in particular how we are to make excuses for ourselves in any action we might eventually have to take concerning the Arabs. You should insist that our sole object in this is to guard against our own people disapproving of our policy."[44]

Saudi prestige was at risk since Ibn Saʿud had not taken a position on Palestine, and he feared being branded a coward or traitor. He sought guidance as to how to approach the other Arab kings.[45] He anxiously awaited Britain's reply, and revealed that he knew of Britain's attempt to settle the

Palestine question with 'Abdullah, whom he did not trust. His approach was well timed, as it solved many problems for policymakers. It spurred Wauchope's approach to Whitehall for permission to approach the Arab kings in mid-July.

Wauchope received approval from the Foreign and Colonial Offices, the main "customers" of Sarafand's intercepted Saudi communications. British officials responded to Ibn Sa'ud "that if he was able to use his influence to persuade the Arabs to abandon the campaign of violence he would be doing a service not only to HMG but to the Arabs themselves." Ibn Sa'ud suggested coordinating his action with the kings of Iraq and Yemen. He did not want to approach Baghdad or Sana'a without British approval. On 3 July, Britain "gladly accepted" the Saudi proposal.[46]

The move paid dividends. The king restrained Bedouin who wished to fight in Palestine, and told the British government that anyone who slipped through would be arrested. He used bluntly pro-British language with Palestinians, and rejected their stated aims: namely, that they were only quarreling with Jews and wished simply for the release of all prisoners, remission of collective fines, and cessation of Jewish immigration. Ibn Sa'ud told the Palestinians that before they proceeded, "the first thing necessary was submission," since Britain would not negotiate under fire.[47]

When Ibn Sa'ud realized that Iraq and Yemen both insisted on suspension of immigration as a precondition for ending the strikes, he immediately so told the British. Britain quickly dismissed Ibn Sa'ud's suggestion that Britain meet some Palestinian demands. The king was unequivocal, saying, "I preferred to follow the advice of the British government and sent the required counsels to the people of Palestine." He believed Britain was suspicious of his motives, so he secretly communicated everything to them in order to demonstrate that he had "taken no steps in the Palestine affair except to offer counsel and reply."[48] British authorities could confirm many of his reports through their own secret sources. The Foreign Office reassured Ibn Sa'ud, and promised to keep him informed of developments.[49] Britain could verify his honesty with sigint, and so Ibn Sa'ud earned the trust of the Foreign Office.

In fact, the Arab king told the Palestinians that Britain had left the future of Palestine to the royal commission. Palestinians might get some concession, but should give up fighting and turn to talk.[50] Ibn Sa'ud presented the Palestinians with the dilemma designed by Britain: die fighting and get nothing, or give up and perhaps get something. No guarantees. This careful approach to the problem was foiled by Nuri Sa 'id, the Iraqi foreign minister (and Old Istiqlalist). He visited Palestine on behalf of King Ghazi in order to win British favor, and that of Palestinian "moderates." By acting out of step with Ibn Saʿud and British policymakers, he irritated both of them. His visit also contradicted his prime minister, Yasin al-Hashimi, who, with his brother and chief of the army Taha, espoused a militant policy and supported al-Qawuqji's campaign.[51] They were deposed in a coup later that year. By trying to mediate an end to the revolt independently, Nuri sought to boost his reputation through the Palestine question, and possibly to situate Iraq at the center of a unity scheme. He told the Palestinians he represented the three independent kings, when in fact he did not coordinate his moves with them, or with Britain. He promised limits to Jewish immigration during the royal commission, if only the Palestinians would end the strike and revolt. This was not a promise he could keep.

Group Capt. Kenneth Caron Buss, of military intelligence, visited Shertok with another intelligence hand, Flt. Lt. V. J. Sofiano, to gauge the Zionist reaction to the pan-Arab kings scheme. Shertok worried that Nuri ignored Jewish interests while overemphasizing those of the Arabs: "This shifting of the emphasis was definitely contrary to the whole spirit of the Mandate. Buss remarked that he had been surprised to learn that Nuri claims to represent also Ibn Saud and Imam Yahia. I said that this only added weight to my argument." Shertok detailed a rumor about Arab plans to establish a joint Iraqi-Saudi-Yemeni embassy in Palestine to represent Arab interests in Palestine vis-à-vis the British government. Buss and Sofiano discouraged Shertok from attributing any credence to the rumor. Shertok replied, "To me the rumor was in any case an indication of the impression produced on the Arab mind by Nuri Pasha's intervention and of the expectations which it aroused for the future."[52] The Jewish Agency leaked the details of Nuri's proposals to the *Palestine Post*, calculating that this would embarrass the CO and force a public denial.[53] It worked.

Meanwhile, the Iraqi prime minister attempted to deter Ibn Saʿud from intervening. Explaining to Hafez Wahba why he was being so open with the British government, Ibn Saʿud reported, "I learned from Yassin el-Hashimi that the British government suspect me and fear I am awaiting an opportunity to intervene in Palestine and that this is a practice of mine well known to the British government."[54] It was a bluff, perhaps designed to buy time for al-Qawuqji. Al-Hashimi accused Ibn Saʿud of undermining Nuri by questioning his authorization to represent the three kings. These intrigues led Ibn Saʿud to distance himself from intervening in Palestine.

Nuri's efforts failed for several reasons. His promises were impossible to fulfill. His actions likely lengthened the revolt by sowing false hopes within the ASC. Iraqi policy attempted to link the Palestinians' struggle to the pan-Arab movement, and Britain had been trying to sever that connection. Britain disavowed any official connection to Nuri's overtures toward the ASC, which was told that the "government would not yield to violence and that order must be restored before any steps could be taken."[55] As Iraqi intrigues failed, in September 1936 the British government reassured Ibn Sa'ud that, as Wahba reported, "the fact is they trust you more than any other person in Arabia."[56]

Meanwhile, the campaign escalated as Fawzi al-Qawuqji and his force entered Palestine. In response, the government boosted troop strengths.[57] Wauchope told the mufti that he could not influence Dill. With the Nuri situation neutralized, and in the interests of improved relations with Britain, Ibn Sa'ud obliged a new British request to mediate again in mid-September. The government finally considered deporting the mufti and stripping him of his offices in October 1936, but the Arab kings scheme worked.[58] According to the CID, the mufti, negotiating with the Saudi emissary to Damascus, Kamil al-Qassab, "fought until the very last minute for certain conditions" before they agreed to this mediation. Jamal "realized that it was useless to endeavor to insert any conditions whatsoever, and that the call-off [of the strike and violence] must be complete." Ibn Sa'ud demanded such assurances before proceeding. He also warned the mufti that his "struggle cannot be protracted without considerable losses finally resulting in your defeat."[59]

Al-Qassab told the ASC and the Iraqi consul that Ibn Sa'ud would not issue his call to the mufti to end the strike unless the ASC was prepared to end all violence. In essence, he guaranteed that the Arab kings scheme would help Britain, and reassured the ASC that the royal commission would treat them justly. Britain also promised Ibn Sa'ud that he could represent Arab interests only once the royal commission began.[60] On 12 October, the ASC called on its followers to pray for the martyrs who had fallen, and to return to work. Within a week, Fawzi al-Qawuqji and what remained of his forces slipped out of the country. The military escalation was abruptly halted. The royal commission arrived one month later.

By addressing the mufti directly, the kings elevated his prestige. Neither they nor Britain promised anything to the ASC beyond an audience with the royal commission. The Arab kings' intervention allowed the ASC to save face, rescued it from Nashashibi encroachment, and made the mufti an important leader among Arabs.[61] Ibn Sa'ud's prestige was so boosted that Shakib Arslan and Ihsan Jabri cabled him to enter negotiations over Syria and Alexandretta with the League of Nations, Turkey, and France.[62] This process transformed Anglo-Saudi relations, as well as the relationships between Arab statesmen and the nationalists.

In different ways, 'Abdullah's and Nuri's proposals to mediate demonstrated their inability to bring the interested stakeholders together without harming British interests. Ibn Saʿud, on the other hand, consulted British policy at every step. Nuri's failure to collaborate with the other states, or with Britain, left Ibn Saʿud in the limelight. It is impossible to know, but had the independent states acted as a bloc, they may have secured different results from Britain. Nuri's blunder divided the independent Arab states and dissociated their interests from the National Pact. It also increased British esteem for Ibn Saʿud, as he was the only statesman to work with them instead of around them; he followed their guidance while making his views plain. As a result of this process Britain conceded that the Palestine problem had become a pan-Arab one, "not peculiar to Palestine," as the CID put it.[63]

British policymakers, guided by sigint, let Saudi diplomacy end the strike without having to offer concessions to the Palestinians. By including him in this manner, Britain gave Ibn Saʿud more than was known at the time, or understood afterward: a permanent voice in Palestine policy. Very few figures in Jerusalem—perhaps only Wauchope—understood that this was happening. FO officials would soon find themselves answering to Ibn Saʿud's angry reactions to the royal commission.

Wauchope's strategy did not save his own reputation, as his relationship with the mufti was shown to be a mistake. Group Captain Buss, now in charge of staff intelligence, reported that as a result of the swift end of the revolt following the kings' communiqué to the mufti, the scheme actually confirmed the mufti's full control over the funds of the revolt. Buss emphasized that the situation was unstable, that the Arabs still held the upper hand, and that disappointment with the royal commission could lead to future rebellion.[64] The CID agreed, concluding as of late September 1936 that the violence and strike had been maintained "according to the attitude of the Supreme (Higher) Committee."[65] The ASC demonstrated its ability to end the violence and the strike very quickly, in the end.

Now British policymakers believed they had regained control over the mufti and the ASC. The Colonial Office, based on its knowledge of Ibn Saʿud's role behind the scenes, advised Wauchope, "I should certainly not wish you to deport the Mufti in the absence of further action on his part justifying this step (as to which I assume you would consult me) I hope we shall still be able to clip his wings effectively."[66] The next day, the CO ordered that any plans for deportation be abandoned entirely, unless the mufti were to take action to justify otherwise: "Question as to the best procedure for curtailing the power of the Mufti for evil and in particular to secure close control of Wakf funds by Government can be taken up separately."[67] Now seeking a new equilibrium with the mufti, Wauchope was told to raise the matter with the royal commission.

Looking Inward

During the lag time between the end of the strike and the arrival of the commission, Wauchope and Dill wrangled over policy. Dill strived to highlight the causes and consequences of revolt, and Wauchope to defend his decisions and legacy. The HC gave a line-by-line criticism of Dill's survey of the revolt from September through October. Wauchope felt that Dill was wrong to attribute the end of revolt to economic exhaustion. Rather, the Arab kings scheme offered the ASC a face-saving démarche. Of course, both generals were right. Wauchope, however, overlooked certain facts about the ASC, as there were "already signs of preparations [by the ASC] to retain present organisation and stocks of arms intact for future struggle." Dill recommended disarmament of the country, save for licensed arms at Jewish settlements, and insisted that martial law would be necessary to carry this out. Wauchope evaded the point and continued to minimize the mufti. He felt the mufti had "always to be shoved into every line of action that he reluctantly takes, and his chief fear is to be left alone in the dark." Wauchope was willing to deport him, but it would be "the height of folly to imagine that by the removal of the Mufti or this committee the danger of a fresh Arab rising will be ended or even greatly reduced." To enforce disarmament, the civil power might need military assistance. If it faced resistance, the result could be martial law.[68]

Wauchope was partially right, but also was covering the fact that the mufti had manipulated him. The ASC did not have organized or capable leadership. The mufti used this body to represent a united front—a superficial measure to mask his normal means of operation: pan-Arab and pan-Islamic propaganda, control of funds, indirect influence over radical youth and jihadi fighters, intimidation and assassination through secret societies like Black Hand, and his relations with Arab states and foreign powers such as Italy. It was through these means that pressure incrementally increased until revolt broke out, yet by September it was obvious that it would not achieve a change in British policy. The mufti's dependence on foreign statesmen was not a sign of weakness. It was his goal. Stately attention aggrandized his role and was an extension of his usual method of exercising power.

The CID reported with surprise that the strike and revolt had ended abruptly and effectively, and credited the Arab statesmen, who the population believed had secured some form of assurance from Britain. The population saw this outcome as a victory. The CID shared the same problem as Wauchope in that it had to reconcile its shortcomings with what had unfolded. Its intelligence summaries were more honest than the HC's reflections, and the police began to become more assertive in their assessments.

Unlike Wauchope, the CID saw the mufti as having emerged "as the strong man in Palestine Arab politics."[69]

Military intelligence sought perspective. Group Captain Buss met with Colonel Kisch, military liaison for the Jewish Agency. Buss, a Muslim from the Egyptian service, was head of Dill's staff intelligence. He was surprised to hear that, as former head of the JA, Kisch had experienced similar problems with the mufti as early as 1923. They agreed that it was "intolerable that one man, however sincere his convictions, should be able indefinitely to prevent any progress being made in solving a problem [the Arab-Zionist conflict] in which great and wide public issues were involved." The mufti wanted a Muslim Arab Palestine to the exclusion of Christian, Jewish, or British interests. Kisch observed, "To my remark that I was aware that it was not easy to deal with a man occupying the positions held by Haj Amin, I was surprised to hear the prompt rejoinder that 'it should not be so difficult, the Government put him there,' the implication being obvious." Looking forward to the royal commission, soon due to arrive, Buss remarked that it would be "logical for the Mufti to boycott the Commission."[70] The ASI saw the mufti as leading an ongoing threat, which had to be tolerated until government changed its policy. Military intelligence did not agree with Wauchope on these issues, and could not influence him.

The Royal Commission, Simmering Revolt, and the Future of the National Pact

PAP leaders proposed boycotting the royal commission, according to the CID, since no change to Jewish immigration schedules had taken place. The mufti's newspaper, al-Liwa, saw the unchanged immigration rate as evidence of Britain's bad faith.[71] By November 1936, the CID reported that despite efforts by Arab statesmen to change policy regarding the new boycott, the mufti and 'Auni 'Abdul Hadi were steadfast: "The belief exists in the minds of the majority of Arabs that any Arab appearing before the Commission voluntarily will be asking for ostracism and possibly assassination." Palestinians expected disappointment from the royal commission's findings. The CID, therefore, predicted further disturbances for early 1937.[72]

During the commission's investigation, violence continued, directed more at Jewish than at British targets. It was less intense than it had been previously, but was enough to spur more intelligence and defense work on the part of the Haganah and the Jewish Agency. The HC reported such acts as being nonpolitical; rather, he said, they were economic. He claimed the Jewish press was exaggerating incidents of highway robbery in order to impress the royal commission and to prevent further reduction of the garrison, or the discharge of Jewish supernumerary police. Nonetheless, he admitted that tension was high due to incitement in the Arabic press and speeches in mosques.[73] The CID reported with increasing realism about gang organization, preparing for future operations: "Sudden and simultaneous attacks will be made on Government and Jewish colonies. . . . [It is] nevertheless possible that some idea of intimidating Government more favourably to consider the Arab demands exists." The CID began to offer nuance to its assessment. It cited liaison with "Jewish intelligence sources" who were worried about outbreaks in the near future, after the departure of the commission.[74] The improvement in CID assessments derived from a combination of soul-searching toward the end of the revolt, increased military control, and liaison with Zionist intelligence.

The CID's first report for 1937 was clear that an outbreak was not necessarily imminent but that future plans were being developed, especially to assassinate British officials. The population in the North was "armed almost to a man and the surviving disciples of Sheikh Izzel Din Kassem [sic; Qassam] are said to have taken on themselves the role of assassins-to-be." The next disturbances would not be accompanied by a strike. "The proposal appears to be that terrorist activity will be carried on by special gangs now being organized," the report noted. The Palestinian boycott of the royal commission was broken after Ibn Sa'ud and King Ghazi of Iraq intervened. 'Auni 'Abdul Hadi, 'Izzat Darwaza, Mu'in al-Madi, and Kamil al-Qassab flew to Riyadh and Baghdad to consult with the kings. They explained their reasons for boycotting the commission, but also sought support for a new pan-Arab congress "to decide on a concerted programme of action for the future, for all Arab countries, particularly in the case of a European war breaking out." Neither Iraq nor Saudi Arabia consented. Ibn Sa'ud informed Britain that he had pressed for cooperation with the commission, which the Foreign Office confirmed by reading his intercepted communications. Upon returning to Palestine, Jamal al-Husseini, 'Auni 'Abdul Hadi, Darwaza, and others appeared before the commission, and so did the mufti.[75]

The royal commission returned to London. Its recommendations shocked national ambitions in Palestine. It declared the mandate "unworkable," and proposed to reestablish a permanent British mandate, restricted to the Jerusalem–Jaffa corridor, and to partition the rest into Jewish and Arab states. There would be a transfer of land and population between the two states, and a balance of revenues. The Arab state would be annexed to Transjordan, and would conclude a treaty of independence similar to that achieved by Iraq or Syria. These findings were not published until July 1937. From January until then, further security reviews took place in Palestine. Violence and intrigue persisted, but organized disturbances had not yet broken out.

Learning lessons from the revolt, the CID improved throughout the first half of 1937. In July, the CID reported on widespread anticipation of the pronouncement of the royal commission. The partition proposal was the worst-kept secret in Palestine. Rumors abounded, as Palestinians prepared to resist such a pronouncement. The CID reported that the mufti suspected that Amir ʿAbdullah would support partition. The mufti and Istiqlal were expected to "bitterly oppose" such a scheme. Following a pattern that should have been all too familiar by this time, the mufti traveled to a conference at Bludan, near Damascus. "It is reported that he discussed with Pan-Arab leaders the creation of a joint front to deal with any proposals about Palestine," noted the CID.[76]

In response to partition, the Nashashibis' al-Difaʿa party left the ASC, citing changes to that body's constitution that were made without consultation. This step may have had more to do with Ragheb Nashashibi's alignment with ʿAbdullah's pro-British stance. A plot to assassinate Amir ʿAbdullah had been uncovered and foiled in Amman. ASC politicians, meanwhile, sent delegations to London and Arab states to determine next steps. The possibility of violent outbreak was not ruled out by the CID, but it did not expect it would be organized.[77]

Through August 1937, signs of preparation for armed rebellion multiplied. Intelligence from Syria, especially from MacKereth, reported the stockpiling and smuggling of arms. British intelligence references to such matters are few. Bashir Saʿadawi was sent by Shukri al-Quwwatli of the Syrian National Bloc to Egypt with funds for arms. MacKereth supposed that ʿAbdullah's cooperation in closing the border may have forced the ASC to raise arms in Egypt. He believed that the true mission was to raise sympathy for the mufti, and observed that "there would be nothing strange in coupling this with gun-running activities. Saadawi is a very cunning old boy." Eliyahu Epstein passed intelligence to the Jewish Agency from Damascus showing that Fakhri ʿAbdul Hadi, who had served with al-Qawuqji the previous year, was now meeting rebels in Syria, and was presumed to be organizing them.[78] There is little indication of whether British sources saw such reports, although Yoav Gelber suggests that the Nashashibis were the main source for warnings to the JAPD that British officials, Nashashibi supporters, and Jewish settlements would be targets in a forthcoming wave of terrorism. The mufti was concentrating his people in Jerusalem, mainly in the Haram al-Sharif. On the mufti's instructions, thousands of weapons were concentrated in Nablus; he intended instead to use armed bands to resist partition.[79]

When the mufti had visited Damascus in June, he charged Nabih al-'Azmeh with initiating a pan-Arab gathering. The ASC members and delegations from around the Arab world convened at Bludan, on the outskirts of Damascus, in September. They aimed to raise foreign support for the forthcoming struggle in Palestine. Eliyahu Sasson, an intelligence hand of the JAPD who began his career as an Arab nationalist journalist, observed the preparations for the Bludan conference. He ran agents in Syria and Lebanon who passed reliable intelligence about it. Abba Hushi of the Histadrut also had an informant at Bludan. Gilbert MacKereth, the British consul at Damascus, also had a secret agent, "X," who attended a secret meeting after the conference where plans for jihad were arranged by Syrian nationalists. MacKereth and Sasson may have had the same agent.

MacKereth submitted a detailed report on Bludan to the FO, with agents' reports enclosed. The report and other enclosures demonstrated the mufti's intentions clearly. A "violent" anti-Jewish pamphlet that used selected hateful passages from the Qur'an to promote anti-Jewish (and anti-Christian) sentiment was distributed at Bludan. The pamphlet encouraged jihad in Palestine. The conference was rumored to have been paid for by the mufti himself, supplemented by Italian funds, distributed by Arslan, who attended. Another enclosed report was prepared by an unidentified secret informant who, by blending with the catering staff and carrying ice for the sherbet, slipped into "a secret meeting" of about a hundred Syrian and Palestinian "extremist Politicians." His report covered discussions on military leadership and tactics. These "extremists" spoke of the weakness of Bludan and the need to take further steps. Ya'aqub al-Ghussein appealed for more money to purchase weapons and described arms caches in Nablus and Tulkarm. Fawzi al-Qawuqji, long rumored to be preparing another campaign, sent a letter to al-Ghussein in which he promised to renew revolt, if invited. Al-Qawuqji's presence might have been helpful, as MacKereth's agent reported that the meeting produced few new ideas, other than means to intimidate Arabs who collaborated with Britain. In fact, al-Qawuqji would only return to Palestine in 1947. Discussions about armed tactics emphasized the difficulties in attacking well-defended Jewish settlements, but observed that police armored cars were vulnerable to mines. "The shooting of British soldiers was said to be most inaccurate, and aeroplane bombs were not to be feared," MacKereth's agent reported.[80] Preparations for a renewed campaign were underway, but there was no sense of how it would be carried out, except, like the previous time, under individual leadership of commanders over small formations.

Taher Caraman, a Haifa businessman who worked with David HaCohen, attended Bludan, and reported to HaCohen about the unprecedented erasing of borders at the conference, and the mufti's domination of the pan-Arab theater. He reportedly was more popular in Iraq than King Ghazi. Two of HaCohen's informants, Caraman and Haifa mayor Hasan Shukri, feared for their lives after Bludan. Shukri had often been threatened, and survived a number of assassination attempts. HaCohen also spoke to Rashid al-Hajj Ibrahim, who was loyal to the mufti and Istiqlal, who emphasized that Jews and Arabs could come to terms under the framework of the Bludan decisions, which sought to freeze the demographic situation in Palestine. Behind the scenes of Bludan were preparations for another revolt.[81] Joseph Davidescu gathered intelligence personally and through agents about those preparations. In one reference, he focused on the mufti's threats against the newspaper *al-Jami'a al-Islamiya*, which opposed Bludan.[82]

Terrorism quickly spread during September. Opponents of the mufti, suspected "collaborators," and land brokers were targeted for assassination. One Abdul Salam Barkawi of Jenin was assassinated for helping the police catch al-Qassam's gang in 1935.[83] These assassinations had become less frequent during February–August 1937, but al-Qassam's former disciples resumed the bloody practice. They particularly targeted the police, culminating in the murder of the Haifa CID officer Halim Basta. They even had an informant connected to RAF intelligence, according to the CID. GSI surveyed political assassinations during September.[84] The weakening of the police at this moment was critical.

The CID reported on Bludan, remarking on the mufti's disappointment at having to share control of the movement with Syrians, who would not accept his discipline. Tension in Palestine, rejection of Bludan, a pan-Arab front, and a recrudescent jihadi spirit that targeted Britons, Arabs, and Jews alike culminated in the assassination on 26 September of Lewis Andrews, the district commissioner of Galilee. This step was the last straw for the government, which immediately deported four ASC members to the Seychelles: Ahmed Hilmi Pasha, Fuad al-Saba, Ya'aqub al-Ghussein, and Hussein Khalidi. The remaining members were abroad, except for Jamal al-Husseini, who was still at large. The government decided to arrest the mufti and strip him of his offices at the SMC and *awqaf*. He holed up at the Haram al-Sharif, and the police dared not to cause an incident by storming the area. The mufti rejected the Christian government's control over Islamic affairs, and continued to organize the sheikhs in the country to support him. Government action now meant that the movement would be controlled from Syria—which posed a new and difficult intelligence and military problem.[85]

More evidence on the standoff with the mufti can be obtained from sigint intercepts of the cables of the US consul in Jerusalem to the State

Department. On 2 October 1937, the consul said that the British were apprehensive of further terrorism against them, and felt bitter resentment against Arabs after Andrews's murder. The attorney general explained their decision not to arrest the mufti, still in the Haram area. They feared the reaction of the Muslim world to any intervention in that sacred area. "It is hoped too, having clipped his wings by cutting off most important source of propaganda funds, he may be forced to retreat from his present uncompromising attitude," the consul reported.[86] Yet by 8 October, all restraints were shed. The exco concluded that "the stage in which Government sought the support of any local party has passed." Britain must assert control itself and refuse the mufti's demands.[87]

The mufti escaped arrest by fleeing the Haram in disguise, and eventually slipped away to Beirut by boat. Certain British intelligence officers, in their memoirs, claimed he had help from sympathetic government employees, and was warned before police came to arrest him. Tony Simonds, working for GSI, wrote that he thought a policeman had been bribed to extract the mufti before he could be arrested. This account may be partly true, but the details are dubious.[88] The intelligence officer Dudley Clarke regretted not having confronted the mufti sooner. Clarke had met him not long after his arrival in Palestine as brigade major in the spring of 1936, and within a few months would, along with the rest of the military, press Wauchope to arrest him. "But when we did at last gain reluctant permission," Clarke said, "he slipped away in the night and was never seen again. It was said there was some collusion in high places, for the Palestine Police made no effort to stop his flight, whereas the Lebanon authorities had ample warning to welcome him when he arrived by sea off Beirut." Clarke was satisfied by the government's prompt and vigorous action, recording, "At long last we were rid of that 'arch-scoundrel,' as General Dill once called him."[89]

Although Clarke's memoir is more reliable than Simonds's, their views on this issue reveal the centrality of the argument between the military and government over the mufti, among other matters. Both accounts reflect the deep frustration of intelligence officers that the government would not account for their product, and mismanaged Palestinian politics.

There were many rumors about the mufti's escape; one of the most persistent was that Musa 'Alami, personal secretary to the high commissioner, had provided early warning. Even the CID recorded that "a number of persons were convinced that he could not have escaped without the connivance of Government, and these persons were, therefore, confirmed in their opinion that the Mufti had throughout acted as an agent for the government." The mufti meant to reach Damascus, but was prevented by French authorities.

Authorities hoped that the mufti's temporary residence in Lebanon would limit his power. MacKereth cautioned the government, military, and intelligence authorities that the mufti had little influence in Syria, and was "weak and therefore useless in vigorous action. He must still be regarded, however, as a possible rallying point."[90] The mufti never organized the resistance that he desired, but did manage to mobilize arms and guerrillas for Palestine. As will be seen in the next chapter, armed bands never composed the cohesive force required to achieve any political or military objective.

Once in Lebanon, the mufti became openly militant. The Jewish Agency passed to its British counterparts a report from an agent who attended an ASC meeting in Beirut. Shakib Arslan, recently returned to Lebanon after some two decades of exile, had played a leading role. Ishaq Darwish (the mufti's nephew and aide), Nabih al-'Azmeh, Mu'in al-Madi, and others attended. French security did not, although it likely maintained its close surveillance of Arslan. The mufti complained that Arab states had been lukewarm in helping him to find residence within their borders. He reproached his committee for not rousing a storm in the Arab and Muslim worlds, or causing Europe to notice. England had not been deterred from enforcing its policy. Worst of all, the government's dismissal of the mufti received little reaction from the Muslim world. He was disappointed and disillusioned, and while he did not expect a reaction in Palestine because of police measures, he was dismayed by the lack of international attention. One intelligence report, prepared by the Jewish Agency Political Department and circulated in the Foreign and India Offices, noted, "The mufti was greatly exercised and irritated and allowed no one to interrupt him." This behavior reflects the general overconfidence that shaped the mufti's politics at the start of the revolt. Al-'Azmeh described his approaches to the Arab kings and committees in Egypt, Iraq, and Syria, but reported that these countries could not prioritize Palestine over their internal problems.[91]

Intelligence and Conflict

The mufti led the revolt from exile. Within two years, the Palestinian leader went from peak influence as a British government officer and nationalist organizer to a much more complicated position. He was divisive: a renegade to the British and either a threat or a hero to the Palestinians. Government deliberations about the mufti were not grounded in a reasoned discussion of the intelligence evidence. Military intelligence never persuaded the civil power that its approach to the ASC was misguided. Wauchope was reluctant to escalate and counted on Palestinian cooperation, despite all evidence that they were prepared to resist unlimited Jewish immigration. Wauchope stead-fastly told Palestinians that he did not control immigration policy, but that Palestinians might shape it after legislative reform. He possessed evidence, and access to more, that Palestinians would escalate in response to his posi-tion. He was prepared for disturbances, but was surprised by their duration and intensity.

The CID was stuck in the middle. It saw the same evidence as the ASI, but its interpretations supported the view that the mufti and his people could be managed, if only they could save face. In the end, it was signals intelligence that guided British diplomacy toward a solution. The Arab kings scheme was possible because of the evidence available about Ibn Saʿud's relationship with the pan-Arab movement and the Palestinians. The civilian intelligence state began to crack during this time. The collapse of the police would lead to military control during the height of the revolt. The CID's support for Wau-chope's compromises, despite the evidence that they still contradicted British aims to preserve the Zionist policy, was symptomatic of a bigger problem.

The mufti never achieved the main political victory he wanted—legal lim-its to Jewish immigration. In a way, the mufti won an important battle, forc-ing Britain to admit that its policy in Palestine was unworkable. The result was the partition proposal, rather than concession. Britain would not alter its Zionist policy in response to violence, but took extraordinary steps to restore order. Britain's resolve in the matter surprised the Palestinians and some Arab states, but its solutions were military. The civilian state flagged, and the mandate saw the last days of normal civil government.

CHAPTER 8

Military Intelligence and the Arab Revolt

In late 1936 or early 1937, Patrick Domvile was reassigned from Jerusalem to Baghdad. The RAF and army needed Palestine experts to monitor foreign support for the revolt. They also wished to keep him away from the Zionists as new developments were implemented in staff intelligence. Following the murder of Lewis Andrews and the mufti's subsequent escape to Lebanon, Domvile expressed relief to Reuven Zaslani that the government was taking tough action by October 1937. However, he felt that it should have come eighteen months earlier, and that most Arabs would be delighted to be rid of "a tyrant and terrorism." Domvile criticized British imperial policy, which, he thought, had regressed since Iraq's independence. The partition of Palestine, recommended by the royal commission, was a mistake in his eyes, and unnecessary now that the mufti was out of the country. Amid a serious reflection on the problems of empire, he joked, "I am not a ruthless Imperialist as I would wish my Empire built on LOVE, PEACE AND COMMON UNDERSTANDING. All in my Empire must work for these ends—anyone going against them must be ruthlessly, if humanely, exterminated."[1]

Domvile was not in charge of British policy, for good reason. He was one of many junior officers sympathetic to Zionism, probably the most so. Yet his vision was myopic. British policy could not be imposed without force—a direct contradiction of the League of Nations' aims, laws, and principles.

Those values, and nationalist opposition, led Britain to embrace home rule and types of independence elsewhere, such as Iraq and India. With the Zionist policy in force, no such solution was possible in Palestine. Partition attempted to square that circle. The mandate was unworkable. Palestinians agreed, but saw partition as a deeper legal retrenchment of the Zionist policy from which there was no escape. Their resistance to British rule had escalated under the mufti's leadership. The army aimed to restore order, in aid to the civil power. The army's measures toward that end ultimately supplanted civil government with a form of military rule, featuring emergency defense regulations, military courts, irregular warfare, arming some Jews and Arabs, and violently disarming others—in all, arbitrary justice.

Intelligence officers were at the center of three key elements of the counterrevolt. They managed police reforms under military control, and the allocation of funds toward security infrastructure and irregular warfare. Most importantly, intelligence officers played a central coordinating role in the campaign, acting as intermediaries between intelligence agencies, military and paramilitary forces, Arab and Jewish irregulars, and military and civilian decision makers. Midlevel staff officers wielded extraordinary influence.

Nevertheless, defeat of the enemy was not a victory in a Clausewitzian sense. In addition to incurring significant financial cost, Britain exposed its strategic inflexibility while trying to impose its will over the population. It caused some members of the enemy leadership to secede. Yet Britain never forced the mufti or other rebel leaders to relinquish their demand to stop Jewish immigration. Arbitrary justice and "peace bands"—the erosion of civilian rule—also cost Britain. These were important means to military victory, but never translated into political victory. As long as Palestinians could resist the Zionist policy, or British rule, Britain's twenty-year stalemate would prevail.

Other changes emerged from the revolt. Sir Charles Tegart, formerly a senior officer of the Calcutta police, arrived in Palestine with David Petrie—ex-chief of the Delhi Intelligence Bureau, who, in 1941, would be promoted to chief of MI5. Tegart and Petrie were to reform the police and apply secret service funds where they might help. From 1937 to 1939, Tegart simultaneously coordinated the construction of security infrastructure—mainly roads, a fence, and frontier posts—with the rest of the campaign. He managed that program alongside other security proposals in Palestine, coordinating the counterrebellion with police, army, and Zionists, while reforming the Palestine Police with Petrie. The historian Gad Kroizer argues that Tegart, during the process of reform, "rejected the idea of a civil police."[2] Indeed, by calling on Tegart in the first place, the government essentially admitted the impossibility of a civilian state in Palestine. Militarization of the police enabled CID intelligence to work more efficiently with the military effort.

Another important factor in the counterrebellion is the role of military organization and its incorporation of intelligence. For the first time since 1920, General Staffs used political and security intelligence to support operations in one centralized machine. In 1936, this machine existed in a very short-lived experiment of combined staffs, while Air Control was still in effect. With the arrival of General Dill in September 1936, this experiment came to an end. Dill's enlarged staff absorbed those midlevel officers who had led Peirse's Combined Staffs Intelligence. Intelligence from other sources was coordinated through GSI, but commands remained separate. When Robert Haining took command as GOC in April 1938, he operationalized plans that had been developed during Archibald Wavell's tenure since August 1937. Staff intelligence would maintain its central coordinating role in one form or another through the Second World War. It would also influence the organization of British intelligence in the Middle East during that war, as many buccaneering officers had gained experience in Palestine that they applied to their leading roles thereafter. Without centrally coordinated intelligence, it would have been very difficult for commanders to effectively apply force in the field. By 1938, this system had become so sophisticated that it incorporated deception and psychological warfare against rebels.

The cooperation of the Yishuv in both military and intelligence matters positively contributed to the counterrebellion. Matthew Hughes argues that Zionist intelligence never penetrated the core of the rebellion.[3] Yet there rarely was a true "core" to the rebellion. Its political heart was the series of conferences at Bludan. Its spiritual leadership revolved around the mufti from late 1937, but also al-Qassam's surviving disciples. Operationally, the rebellion lacked a functional high command. There was no experienced officer, such as al-Qawuqji, to manage normal military functions such as supply, logistics, morale, recruitment, planning, or intelligence. Politicians lacked military experience and struggled to manage rebel commanders. Hughes notes, "There was no Palestinian Mao Zedong able to transform peasants into a mobilized, conscious political force of guerrillas; instead there was a divisive 'Arab civil war.'"[4]

Zionist intelligence provided key support to Britain's own good sources. Although there was no core to infiltrate, Zionist intelligence got close enough to key rebel centers. The photographs and documents among Joseph Davidescu's papers reveal deep penetration of a networked but disorganized revolt. He exposed German espionage and financial aid to rebels in 1938, gave detailed reports of the Bludan conference that year, and even provided photographs of the rebel command, including Fawzi al-Qawuqji, taken in 1936.

Irregular warfare was also key to the defeat of the revolt. This consisted of Arab fighters controlled by police, peace bands under the army, and Haganah fighters under Capt. Orde Wingate's Special Night Squads. Each took guerrilla tactics to the enemy in an offensive campaign. British officers widely appreciated this cooperation, yet it never went as far as either side had hoped, and tactically speaking, Arab irregulars played a far more significant role in the field. British officials rightly feared the long-term result of arming and empowering Haganah troops, so official limits were placed on this cooperation. However, they wholeheartedly embraced intelligence sharing with Zionists.

The counterrebellion transformed the functions of General Staffs, who returned to wartime practices of centralized intelligence and joint planning. Enterprising officers from those staffs improved cooperation with the Yishuv so much that Britain lost control over the Haganah's self-armament and education. These officers led change within the British system and later shaped covert action and deception during the Second World War. They also deeply influenced developments in the Haganah. When official channels were blocked, these buccaneers circumvented formal institutions and worked with their junior Zionist partners. These officers, along with Tegart, were the core of the counterrebellion.

Military Organization and Intelligence

On 7 June 1936, Air Vice Marshal Peirse, the AOC and senior military commander in Palestine (Air Control was still in effect), reported on the formation of a combined staff and brigade under the command of Col. (soon to become Brig.) Jack Evetts.[5] This, he claimed, would be "the chance of a lifetime." With naval reinforcements imminent, it was an opportunity to experiment. Figure 8.3 illustrates the structure of this system.[6] Evetts was pleased with the results of the combined staffs.[7] It incorporated commands of RAF squadrons and armored car companies, as well as the equivalent of an army division replete with tank sections and engineers.

The experiment also incorporated intelligence into the staff and command structure. It had a lasting impact. Dudley Clarke, then a brigade major, took a leading role as a staff officer. He reorganized and expanded intelligence and planned operations. John Teague was the SIS officer at the time, and worked out of the Old Fast Hotel with GSI from at least May 1937.[8] Staff

FIGURE 8.1. Photo of rebel leaders, 1936, found in Davidescu's papers. From left to right: 'Aref 'Abd al-Razzeq, Fawzi al-Qawuqji, Fakhri 'Abd al-Hadi, and unknown. Fakhri 'Abd al-Hadi led a "peace band" against the rebels from September 1938. Courtesy of Beit Aaronsohn, Zichron Ya'akov.

FIGURE 8.2. Joseph Davidescu obtained this photostat of a check from two German templars in Haifa, Christian Kaltenbach and Charles Fisher, to their agent in the Iraqi consulate, 'Aziz Domet. Domet and his brothers were thought to be working for German propaganda and intelligence. Davidescu planned to cultivate the man as a double agent. BAZY, DP, file 1, 31.8.1938. Courtesy of Beit Aaronsohn, Zichron Ya'akov.

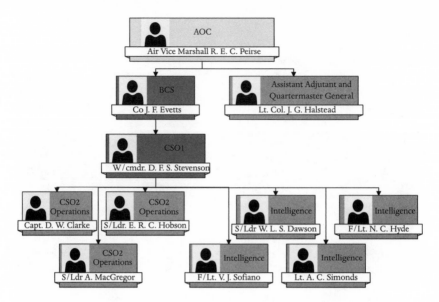

FIGURE 8.3. Partial organization chart of combined staffs, June–September 1936.

lists and distribution lists appended to intelligence reports reveal the quick expansion of intelligence personnel, and the close collaboration between GSI and other offices.[9] According to SIS's official historian, Keith Jeffery, Teague focused on the help that neighboring countries were giving to the rebellion, perhaps referring to the pan-Arab movement and foreign volunteers. He also monitored illegal Jewish immigration.[10]

Clarke discussed intelligence organization in the official report *Military Lessons of the Arab Rebellion in Palestine, 1936*. Intelligence was handled at the level of the combined staff. SSOs relied on agents, informers, and Zionist partners to complete their reports, which fed assessments at the staff level and provided important tactical intelligence to commanders. Army intelligence officers, Clarke wrote, "collected and collated the vast amount of varied information obtained by the fighting troops, and relieved the SSO of much of the routine work, particularly that concerned with topographical information. SSOs had their own wireless cars and reported direct to Force HQ, so that the value of their information was greatly enhanced by the speed with which it arrived. As officers of Force HQ, they had direct access to local commanders, and this personal contact was a valuable asset to the latter."[11]

Intelligence at GSI was coordinated with SSOs, whose branches expanded from Jerusalem and Haifa to include Jaffa, Nablus, Nazareth, and the Jordan Valley. The RAF produced new maps, and aircraft were used for reconnaissance, and for strafing and sometimes bombing of ground targets. The RAF also worked in tandem with ground forces in the "XX" and "GG" systems. In the XX system, ground forces ambushed on a road would call for air support with the map reference, road, and mile marker. Aircraft responded within minutes. The GG system was the opposite, and necessarily slower. Pilots who noticed armed bands would report it over wireless to nearby ground forces, who would attempt to search the area.[12] CID intelligence was criticized by the army for its slow reaction: SSOs used wireless sets in their cars to transmit reports. The CID was reliant on Arab personnel, many of whom faced threats to their personal and family's safety, so the organization suffered.[13]

Police intelligence was hampered by several issues. Its Arab staff were under enormous pressure to quit or to collaborate with rebels. The CID had professional shortcomings, such as a tendency to deliver urgent intelligence late, and to exaggerate the authenticity and value of intelligence. However, it was admitted that a mutual lack of collaboration and confidence were root problems. Zionist intelligence collaboration was valuable, but at times provided misleading information intended to keep troops in a vulnerable area. Nonetheless, according to Clarke, "responsible Jewish sources were however very well informed on the whole."[14]

Personal relationships between British officers mattered most. Evetts and Clarke developed a good working relationship, and remained close friends. Friendly relations between their staffs underlay the informal combined system that developed after Air Control ended. The official report remarked, "At the start [the combined staff] was frankly an experiment, but very soon it was found that the army and RAF officers had little difficulty in learning to perform. . . . Both learnt a great deal from each other and the very closest cooperation resulted."[15]

Clarke also recorded in his unpublished memoir that, while Whitehall never admitted it, "this was undoubtedly the prototype of the 'Combined Operations Headquarters' which was to set the pattern for much greater things in the years to come."[16] This system provided for the XX procedure, and led to the decision to demolish large swaths of the old city of Jaffa.[17] The combined staff found their feet early on, as they took control over matters of civil infrastructure that were crucial to the military effort.

Regular meetings were held between Evetts, the chief secretary, and Spicer (still inspector general of the Palestine Police) to coordinate the military and civil effort. A meeting on 13 June 1936 included the acting postmaster general, his chief engineer, and a representative of the Royal Corps of Signals. The three visitors planned the protection of telegraph lines, and set up measures to quickly detect interruptions and repair them. They then left, leaving Evetts, Spicer and the chief secretary to discuss questions of increasing Jewish supernumerary police, the mobilization and tactics of the TJFF, railway protection, and other matters. Evetts insisted that the general strike and all strike committees be declared illegal. This would have empowered the army to intern even more political prisoners, so more camps might have to be prepared. The discussion then turned to intelligence. The SSO in Haifa had given Evetts "a variety of information," including "a list of leaders who [the SSO] considers should be placed in detention. He reports that arms, including Italian revolvers, are being smuggled through Haifa, and states that English searchers (including women searchers) are necessary."[18] The necessity of counterpropaganda was also discussed.

The combined staff advocated martial law, which would enable seamless military planning and coordination of the intelligence system and provide a forceful deterrent against crime.[19] Dudley Clarke's "lessons" clarify this issue. He argued that the police and civil service were penetrated by Arab informants, and that sympathetic officers leaked intelligence to the rebels. Carelessness by all three bodies also caused leakage, as did loose talk at the Navy, Army, and Air Force Institutes club. Moreover, locals simply observed troop movements and would use light and smoke signals to alert their compatriots. Clarke concluded, "Without Martial Law the only legal action which could be taken to combat this extensive enemy signal organization was to arrest and hand over to the police any person caught in flagrante delicto. This was plainly very difficult to do, and more difficult still to prove afterwards, although no one . . . could have failed to observe obvious signaling in progress. Had it been possible to open fire on all signal lights, some innocent people might have been killed, but equally the lives of some British soldiers might have been saved."[20]

Wauchope argued against martial law, while Peirse and the combined staff sought to stem deterioration and to protect British soldiers. Clarke's memoir notes that all the necessary preparations for martial law had been undertaken, including court appointments, but Wauchope saw himself as destined to lead Palestine to peace, and "could not bring himself at the last moment to hand over to anybody else what had now become an almost sacred trust." Wauchope blamed the army for not having defeated armed bands, and insisted that a "happy medium" could be found that would provide the ASC with a face-saving retreat from its intransigent position and allow the government not to set "a precedent of yielding to violence."[21] Thus, in July, he persuaded Whitehall to follow the Arab kings scheme.

The British garrison spiked in response to the revolt. At first there were two battalions, or 1,600 troops, plus the TJFF, the RAF, headquarters, and ancillaries. By July there was the equivalent of a division: twelve battalions, divided into three brigades, plus support—about 12,000 troops. That number had been deployed to grapple with only a few thousand rebels, organized in bands, and fighting in units of up to seventy. Rebels usually chose the time and location for battle, and rarely were caught out. Villagers might be levied temporarily by rebel bands, shifting between their regular lives and the revolt in a single day. Military reinforcements did not have the chance to crush the revolt before being called away after the strike ended on 12 October 1936.[22] The XX system allowed the RAF to help destroy small sections, but larger formations rarely were encircled and eliminated. This required the occupation of villages and water supplies in a wide region, to deny them to the rebels and drive them into the open. Such action was not attempted during the first phase of the rebellion, but was crucial to the climactic campaigns of 1938–39. Until then, the best chance was a well-planned operation based on good intelligence, but this was rare. Al-Qawuqji's force was almost encircled on 24 September 1936 as the result of intelligence, and the ensuing battle led to forty rebel casualties. The rough terrain, however, prevented the total encirclement of the career rebel leader.[23]

In mid-September, Dill arrived with the First Division, bringing troop strengths to about twenty-five thousand, including twenty battalions, plus supports. Under his command, the combined staff experiment ended on paper, although it continued in practice. Dill's army staff officers incorporated personnel from other services, especially the RAF. Intelligence still played a central coordinating role in the General Staff work. One day before Dill took over command, Evetts, who would soon command the Sixteenth Infantry Brigade, told Clarke, "The experiment of working a combined staff was a bold one to try out, but it undoubtedly proved what can be done when all are imbued with a real team spirit. There is no doubt that the combined staff has come to stay."[24]

The War Office urged Dill to continue combined RAF and army staffs. Essential intelligence staff remained in their roles as staffs grew and reorganized.[25] Army and RAF headquarters both were located at the King David Hotel, where full collaboration was ongoing. Dill wrote, "The staff is in fact more combined than it appears on paper and on all big questions we put our heads together. At least the intelligence under Buss is really combined and functioning well under great difficulties. With every Arab to a man agin us—or rather agin our policy as represented by the Balfour Declaration—it

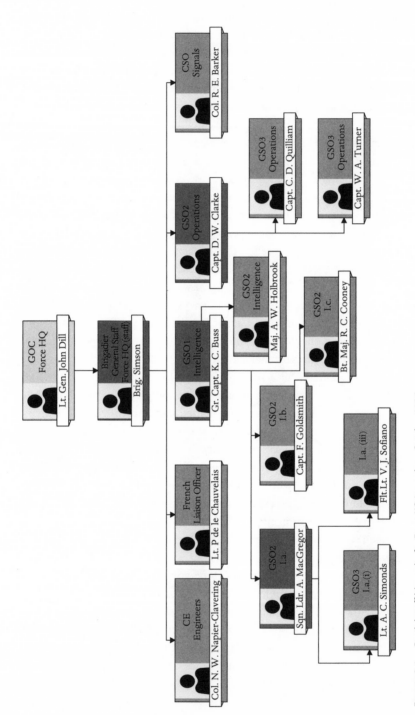

FIGURE 8.4. Partial staff hierarchy for Force HQ Jerusalem, October 1936.

is most difficult to get good information. Nevertheless some of the information Buss has got has been excellent and has led to results."[26]

Good intelligence was available on foreign support for rebels and the diplomatic efforts to have Arab statesmen induce the mufti to end the strike. It finally worked in October 1936 when the mufti accepted Ibn Saʿud's call to end the strike. Armed resistance dropped dramatically, and what remained was directed against Jews. By November the royal commission had arrived, and the garrison declined by one division—still leaving a large force. Intelligence indicated ongoing rebel preparations in Syria and Transjordan.

The chief secretary asked GSI whether intelligence on Palestinian villages could be obtained. Someone, either Buss or Flt. Lt. Walter Lloyd Dawson, chief SSO, responded that military intelligence could not achieve this aim, which was supposed to be the CID's job. The police could do nothing without money for paying agents or bribing elites.[27] The army and government were losing trust in the police. To solve the problem, intelligence officers began to work around the civil government. Buss began to improve relations with the Jewish Agency, whose sources on the Palestinian countryside proved dependable.

The rebellion caused an improvement in Anglo-Zionist intelligence cooperation. Reuven Zaslani had worked for Colonel Kisch during this time, and learned from him how to build friendly, social relationships with his British intelligence counterparts. This later evolved into policy under Zaslani as head of JAPD intelligence. His "hospitality policy," or rather doctrine, established committees of JA and Haganah intelligence officers throughout the country that managed social relations with British officers. This engendered trust and goodwill, and multiplied the JA's sources in the British government and military. Zaslani drove this kind of cooperation following the mufti's escape in July 1937.[28] Liaison continued between SSOs and various Zionist intelligence hands. British sources for cooperation included Teague and certain GSI officers. The diary kept by Teague's wife describes the close social circle of intelligence staff in Jerusalem.[29] One Maj. Frank Goldsmith handled sigint material on neighboring states and on Italian espionage, and played a key coordinating role between MI5, SIS, and the General Staffs.[30]

Allenby and later the OETA administration were the last in Palestine to use a system of centralized intelligence in staff and command. For years, many officers in the army and in the government at Cairo and Jerusalem had seen the ongoing need for some form of Arab Bureau. Problems of finance and civil versus military administration led to the rejection of that idea. It was also considered unnecessary: centralized intelligence was a novel feature of the army, a product of wartime needs.[31] The crises in Palestine proved otherwise. Certain forms of this system reappeared in the 1930s, but it was not until a few enterprising officers chose to form a combined staff command in 1936 that the road to a functioning intelligence state was paved. However, this intelligence state was militarized and at war over policy with a parallel civil intelligence state and the majority of the population.

The influence of the events and actions related to the uprising on the conduct of covert action, deception, and other intelligence operations during the Second World War cannot be overstated. By 1937–38, the army and RAF in Egypt were already planning proposals for a centralized intelligence bureau for the Middle East, to be based in Cairo. When discussions began in the wake of the Abyssinian emergency, Sudan was looked on as an example of an intelligence staff with a civilian head. General Dill was queried about his system about one year before the Joint Intelligence Committee (JIC)— the main forum at Whitehall for interdepartmental examination of open and secret intelligence—began to survey such a possibility.[32] Experience in Palestine was shaping the rest of the army.

It is no coincidence that Archibald Wavell, who witnessed the success of Allenby's GSI and that of the army in Palestine when he took command, promoted these efforts in London.[33] According to John Ferris, Wavell "disagreed with Whitehall about the organization of intelligence." Wavell had been a staff officer under Allenby during 1917. Twenty years later, he tried to re-create Allenby's staff system and his use of irregular warfare, signals intelligence, and deception. "This system was never allowed to work as he intended," notes Ferris, but Wavell's ideas about Allenby's leadership led him toward "a grander version of the 'haversack ruse.' He established [the deception organization] 'A' Force and wrote its first order."[34]

Wavell appointed Dudley Clarke to lead "A" Force, and Clarke brought in Tony Simonds. This description brings into focus the methods that had developed while Wavell was in command in Palestine, especially during his last few months. Palestine proved to be a training ground for leaders in intelligence and deception during the Second World War. The "Palestine School" of intelligence also deepened Anglo-Zionist intelligence cooperation until the end of the war. Paradoxically, this made the British state in Palestine more insecure.[35]

Intelligence officers and their systems were instrumental to the counterrevolt. Clarke was the main coordinator of intelligence with operations, while Tegart managed the entire mechanism as an outside consultant. Experienced in colonial policing, he was officially tasked with police reform. Unofficially, he managed intelligence, police, and infrastructure planning with the military campaign and was the key go-between for the various intelligence services and the general staff. Tegart's work physically reshaped the country, securitizing it with roads and fortresses, which staff officers used to take the fight to the countryside.

Collapse of Police and Civil Government

During his stay in Palestine, Tegart felt that it was time to admit that the civil state had collapsed. "Virtually all trace of civil government has been swept away by the rebellion. . . . Where might is right, blood feuds are likely to appear in nearly every village. . . . The whole police machinery has got to be overhauled and fitted for its task," he reported.[36] The campaign of intimidation by rebels and terrorists destroyed the police. This was not a sudden event, but rather a gradual process that came to a head during August–September 1938 when police stations in Palestinian towns such as Nablus, Hebron, Jenin, and Lydda were encircled and attacked. Arab police varyingly helped the rebels, suffered brutal murder, or simply stayed home. The rebels absconded with arms and ammunition at each station.[37] This period saw the capture of the old city of Jerusalem by rebels, and the declaration on 18 October 1938 of military control. New emergency regulations gave army commanders the powers previously wielded by district police commissioners, now demoted to an "advisory" role. Until then, the police had managed to survive considerable pressure. The collapse can be attributed to the especially intense campaign of intimidation and assassination from September 1937, and the uncomfortable situation that Arab civil servants found themselves in throughout most of the 1930s.

One of the most serious incidents was the murder in April 1937 of a senior figure at the Haifa CID, Halim Basta, who had been Harry Rice's personal assistant. Though suspected by A. H. Cohen of being influenced by certain Haifa notables connected to the mufti during the Qassamist murders of 1932–33, Basta generally had a good reputation. His loss cut deep, since he recorded little and did not share sources.[38] Cohen concluded that Basta was assassinated by Qassamists, encouraged by Istiqlal, in a campaign against Arab police and notables such as Haifa mayor Hasan Shukri, who maintained good relations with Jews.[39] Police noticed a methodological connection between Basta's assassination and that of Lewis Andrews. Albert John Kingsley-Heath, the deputy inspector general of the police and head of the CID, told Bernard Joseph, Shertok's deputy at the JAPD, that both Andrews and Basta, before their murders, received intelligence suggesting they could relax their personal security measures such as bodyguards, since assassins were only out to get "'Bad Arabs' like those who sold land to the Jews."[40] Deceptive tactics aside, Basta's death was part of a vicious campaign from 1937 to 1939 against anyone suspected of disloyalty to the nation.

Personal threats were but one part of this intimidation. The insecurity facing Arab policemen was well known. The CID depended on Arab staff, who, with little protection for their families, were coerced to choose sides. Nationalists aimed to destroy the police by exploiting this problem. Akram Zuʻayter described exploiting the shame expressed by an Arab CID officer who questioned him about a seditious speech.[41] Government employees went on strike during the 1936 rebellion, threatening to cripple the judicial system and rail transport during a critical period. Many services were shut down.

Consultations and Proposals

Tegart initially was called on in October 1937 to shore up crumbling security in Palestine. It was originally proposed that he take over the police entirely, perhaps a reflection on Spicer, replaced as inspector general by Alan Saunders in November. Instead, Tegart proposed that he "be deputed to go to Palestine and examine and report on the police administration as a whole. On receipt of my report, should you consider it advisable, the question of my taking charge might further be discussed."[42] Tegart's approach to security was summarized by the viceroy after Tegart's successful counterterrorist campaign in Bengal: "Tegart went on to say that the one thing he required was that he should be able to deal promptly, and before they occurred, with actual outrages. His reason, in a word, was that his counter-outrage organisation must be made to feel, in its personnel, that it was top dog. The moment outrages occurred and were not punished, his organisation began to crumble."[43]

Shortly after Tegart arrived in October 1937, he sought the Jewish Agency's assessment of the crisis. Moshe Shertok told Tegart that CID liaison with Arab sources was deficient. As head of the JAPD, Shertok received intelligence on the whereabouts of rebels and fugitives and, according to Tegart, was "often perplexed as to what to do with it." Shertok had good relations with senior British police, but did not trust the CID's ability to keep secrets. Tegart believed that intelligence leaked through the CID's Arab personnel: "An Arab may be loyal today and disloyal tomorrow either through intimidation or changes in the political atmosphere. [Shertok] thinks there should be a sort of 'Holy of Holies' in the CID where information would only be seen by British personnel." Shertok passed intelligence to Tegart, saying that he thought the "general center" of the rebellion was split between Beirut and Damascus. He believed the mufti directed policy but did not take an active hand in organizing rebel groups. The mufti could provide funds in Jerusalem, but not outside. The rebels, now deprived of access to the Waqf, resorted to extortion of Palestinian villages, donations, and foreign subsidy—especially from Italy. Shertok also gave Tegart intercepted documents relating to the mufti's contacts with assassins and rebels. He worried about reprisal attacks by Revisionists on Arabs—which he assured Tegart would be stopped by the Jewish Agency.[44] Throughout this crisis, British dependence on the JA was constant.

Tegart also met intelligence staff from Force HQ, including Goldsmith, who handled intercepted correspondence, including all telegrams and letters in and out of the country, decrypted solutions of Ibn Sa'ud's wireless messages, and those of Iraq, Egypt, and Transjordan. Goldsmith complained that in London, letter openers had been clumsy with NPL mail, compromising that source. CID intelligence was weak, and they mishandled cases involving secret intelligence: they failed to capture a courier carrying letters from the mufti to al-Qawuqji on two occasions. SSOs now collected intelligence in villages from Arab sources, which led to the arrest on 22 November 1937 of Sheikh Farhan as-Sa'adi—an octogenarian rebel leader who led the Qassamist cell that killed Andrews.[45] He was executed five days later, amid much public outrage. Later, two members of GSI and Sofiano, the SSO Haifa, agreed that CID intelligence was "almost worthless." SSOs supplanted the CID's normal role in the countryside. After a year, Sofiano had no relations with the CID whatsoever since its Haifa chief was Arab.[46] Neither the Zionists nor other British security agencies were willing to trust the CID. In retrospect, this was a sign of its impending implosion.

In December, Tegart and Petrie toured the country, observed military operations, and consulted French authorities and British liaison and diplomatic staff in Beirut and Damascus. Petrie's role, seldom discussed in the record, likely was to assign or recommend the assignment of Secret Service funds. Diary entries refer to this matter during Tegart's meetings with the CID, and with Gilbert MacKereth in Damascus. "I asked MacKereth whether in his opinion, apart from the question of recognition in other ways, Secret Service money could not be usefully expended in Damascus," Tegart recorded. "It might be taken as axiomatic that if information were wanted, it would have to be paid for. MacKereth spent very small sums (some £95 per annum)." Tegart wished to know whether an increased investment would lead to the capture of rebels and arms smugglers who regularly crossed the Syria-Palestine border, such as the Black Hand leader Sheikh Atiyyah Ahmad 'Awad. Atiyyah had led a battle, witnessed by Tegart, against British forces at Umm al-Fahm. He would be killed in battle in March 1938.[47] Whether MacKereth asked for additional funds is unclear, although his activity throughout the remainder of 1938–39 suggests that more resources were available. He had at his disposal officers seconded from the CID.[48]

In January 1938, Tegart and Petrie discussed ways to remedy the collapsing Arab section of the police. Acting police commandant Saunders felt that hiring locals was impossible, but he knew that foreigners would lack local experience. Tegart and Petrie agreed, suggesting that, based on their investigations, the government had failed to support Arab personnel who were vulnerable to intimidation. Officers with families would be spared from returning each night to potentially hostile villages or towns during a crisis if only there were enough living quarters.[49] Thus, building family quarters for Arab officers inside police barracks became part of security infrastructure planning.

Tegart understood that public insecurity reinforced British weaknesses and prolonged the rebellion. He needed to restore confidence in the police to improve civil and military intelligence, and to operationalize information that was not being shared by either side. The fundamental problem was the terrorism inflicted by rebels on Arab villages. Some sources attribute 4,500 deaths to assassinations alone—although the true number may be under 1,000.[50] If the police had been competent, reliable data might have survived for historical research. Perhaps they still disregarded political murder within Arab society. Regardless, it was dangerous for Arabs to oppose the mufti or rebel commanders. In response to this knowledge and the pleadings of the assistant district commissioner for Samaria, Tegart formed a strategy that would provide some confidence to villagers. He suggested pressuring villages to inform the government of rebel activity and to seek government protection from rebel bands. Simultaneously, he proposed, Britain should take the fight to the rebel camp.[51]

In January of 1938, Tegart and Petrie submitted their lengthy report, which contained twenty-eight recommendations. Tegart retrospectively felt that the two most important suggestions dealt with the reorganization of the CID and the creation of a Rural Mounted Police (RMP)—another gendarmerie. The CID, under the command of "an extremely able officer . . . Mr. Kingsley-Heath," was "hopelessly" understaffed and required enlargement. "Greater efficiency," Tegart wrote, "will not be secured merely by increasing the personnel. Expert control is essential and the staff must be properly trained. This applies with almost equal cogency to the other branches of the police machine which we have examined." The RMP would be used to detect and intercept the first signs of unrest at the borders, although the military would be used against large armed bands.[52] The RMP never materialized for lack of funds.[53]

Tegart also proposed a unit of "irregulars" to patrol the border. This para-military force, composed of locals, began as the main response to provide security on the vulnerable roads and rail line downhill from Jerusalem. It evolved into an offensive strategy that later embodied Arab irregulars and the SNS. Jewish and Arab irregulars were handled very differently. Arab ir-regulars under the police secured lines of communication from Jerusalem, and later part of the border. "Peace bands" were a collection of armed Arab gangs who, for different reasons, switched sides and supported the British. Jewish irregulars were Haganah members, supernumerary police trained in offensive tactics by the army. They were the backbone of Orde Wingate's SNS. Tegart's memoir makes clear his admiration for the military capabilities of Jewish colonists led by the British intelligence officer, who was an ardent Zionist.[54] Tegart wrote that the SNS "became a brave and useful force trained and commanded by that outstanding personality. . . . It is no exaggeration to say that the Jews who served under him idolized him and would have fol-lowed him to the ends of the world."[55]

Arab Irregulars

At an exco meeting that included Wauchope, Wavell, Petrie, the chief secre-tary (William Battershill), and Saunders, Tegart suggested using Secret Ser-vice funds to reward any source of good work, whether in the civil service, regular policy, or army, "but especially for irregulars." Secret Service funds could be paid quickly, were unaccounted for, and "would provide a great stimulus to persons in a position to help the Govt."[56] Tegart used his coor-dinating role to apply Secret Service funds toward the raising of irregular forces.

Tegart thought irregulars would remain a long-term feature of security in Palestine, or even could evolve into a new gendarmerie. He recommended that "enlistment of the ordinary type of policemen . . . should be stopped and a policy of concentrating more on the irregular type of men, i.e. the illiter-ated [sic] tough type capable of fighting rural lawlessness by its own meth-ods should be applied." Tegart described the two categories, by reference to uniforms, as "blue" and "buff," respectively. Tegart and Petrie also remarked that police should probably stop operating in the field in their blue uniforms during "rural operations against wrongdoers. It is conspicuous and hampers strenuous physical action on the part of the wearer."[57] The conversation il-lustrates how and why civil government disintegrated. The blue-uniformed police officer, the personified objective of the police reforms of 1930–31, was now thought impractical. The smart detective was suddenly less desirable than a brute constable; the public's right to discern a police officer was irrelevant. The pretense of liberal values was abandoned in the search for security.

Tegart's first assignment for irregular Arab troops was to patrol the Jerusalem–Jaffa road, which was constantly under sniper fire.[58] The JA wanted armed guards on buses traveling that route. With an eye to developing an effective Palestinian opposition to the rebels, Tegart began discussions with Ragheb Nashashibi. Nashashibi gave guidance as to how police and troops could cooperate with village mukhtars, who would be more helpful if they could be sure of government protection.[59] By summer, the Nashashibis had organized several small defensive militias in support of British security. In January, however, the roads remained insecure.

Aiming to improve the Arab section of the police, and to launch a campaign of irregular warfare, Tegart recruited Faiz al-Idrissi, a long-time member of the Palestine police who was considered very reliable. He was encouraged to recruit more "buffs." One such recruit was Hashim Arikat, who had been fired from the police following the Dowbiggin report, which disparaged the "illiterate constable." Tegart needed these types in his force—and told al-Idrissi to find more like Arikat, who had been recruited back into the force in late November.[60] By early January 1938, al-Idrissi's irregulars patrolled the rough terrain overlooking the vulnerable winding inclines of the Jerusalem–Jaffa road. By the end of January, al-Idrissi was included in security meetings on how to expand security in the villages west of Jerusalem.[61]

By May, the number of Arab irregulars had expanded, and Dudley Clarke incorporated the "Faiz Column"—forty Arab irregulars under police auspices—into the military campaign. Meanwhile, Palestinian rebels increased their preparations for operations against British forces. There was a rise in the plundering of Arab villages by rebels, and numerous other clashes with British troops. The rebels were believed to be in a weak position, underfinanced and outgunned. Captured rebel documents revealed that the high command in Syria had ordered groups to stop raiding Arab villages, which was harming the movement. Short on supplies, the rebels disobeyed the orders. Discipline broke down as the rebel high command struggled to feed, equip, and pay its forces. Palestinian resentment toward the rebels provided an opening for British forces to restore confidence through occupation. Those attacks increased, as did acts of murder, sniping, bombing, and sabotage. Other captured documents suggested that rebel strength had been underestimated. Rebels had been divided into at least thirteen detachments spread across Samaria and the Galilee, and were ruthless. British forces had not concentrated efforts in a similar manner, except in a few areas.[62]

Clarke coordinated intelligence with operational planning at Tegart's public security committee (pubsec); formed on 28 March 1938, it was the main body coordinating the counterrevolt between the military and the civil power. The committee also included representatives from the police and the military, as well as other government departments. At a meeting directed by Clarke, participants discussed Tegart's construction plan (examined below) and contingencies for a cordon and search operations in Hebron, should the situation there deteriorate. This was the first indication that the Faiz Column would be included in military operations to cut off and search the city with troops, the TJFF, and other police. Other security measures were discussed, as was Tegart's report.[63] This document reveals how Tegart's scheme fit into the bigger picture—which included measures for detecting railway sabotage and for secretly testing how the fence might be crossed. By July, Faiz's force was 160 strong, augmented by Bedouin, and patrolled the Jordan valley.[64]

Tegart and Petrie convinced the CS and police to introduce irregular forces for duty on border patrol and road security. Petrie's Secret Service funds would be used to pay "generous rewards for good work," Tegart said. Villages accommodating rebels would be punished, while those helping British forces would be rewarded. Tegart also proposed erecting a border fence—the beginning of a massive building program to improve security infrastructure.[65]

Security Infrastructure

Infrastructure spending was vital to the restoration of security and the success of the counterrebellion. A June 1939 report on the development of the police under military control makes special reference to the role of Tegart's fence along the northern frontier, and to the fact that many of his recommendations were not yet implemented. It also noted the importance of military control over police "as soon as rebellion has become so widespread as to need the continual presence of troops in the area, and before the disintegration of the police has set in to any great extent. This stage may be said to have been reached in Palestine at the end of 1937."[66] In other words, the situation was allowed to deteriorate, but the civil power would neither relinquish control nor prove itself "top dog." Once district police inspectors began reporting to the military, the civil state dissolved in the military solution.

Tegart's recommendations also included fences and a series of fortresses, which would both offer protection to personnel and their families and serve as bulwarks against the rebels. Although Whitehall and Jerusalem both saw the need to invest in improvement, they didn't sign a blank check.[67] Previously, the police had rented most of their infrastructure, and their families were vulnerable. In June 1938, there were only twenty "stations" in the main cities, and five "posts." In rural areas, there were thirty-seven stations and fifty-one posts. Most were small and poorly situated for tactical purposes. Importantly, they lacked accommodations for Arab police and their families. Gad Kroizer fully details the construction program: the first eleven forts were built between August 1939 and April 1940, and the remaining forty-five between then and October 1941, bringing the total to fifty-six. The HC demanded an additional seven, which were built in 1943. Altogether, the fortresses cost £4.4 million.[68]

Before the fortresses, Tegart spent at least £300,000 on roads, the renovation and militarization of police posts on the northern border, and the northern border fence.[69] This was meant to block infiltrators during the "village occupation scheme," discussed below. A full accounting of the figures is patchy, and it is unclear whether the money came from the Palestine government, the treasury, or Tegart's Secret Service allocation. In addition to capital costs, Tegart increased the annual investment in force strength, including irregular Arab forces and Jewish supernumeraries and Temporary Additional Police (TAP). The unprecedented spending demonstrates the government's commitment to restore order, even if it meant arming Jews, or that Britain would rule directly, through force, for longer than previously hoped.

As senior coordinator at pubsec, Tegart launched plans to build border defenses, roads, and police buildings, to occupy the villages of Samaria and Galilee, and to use irregulars for offensives. Pubsec coordinated the plans with military and police operations.[70] The committee handled intelligence assessments, the financing of construction, the planning of operations, and all other elements of the campaign. Dudley Clarke represented General Staff Intelligence at pubsec, and served, in effect, as its chief staff officer in charge of operations. Clarke's name appears on most of the key planning papers during the first half of 1938. He managed the funds, armaments, and manpower for projects such as Tegart's fence; coordination of security operations around the fence with French authorities; Jewish supernumerary railway police who relieved regular police and troops; and even a village register project out of Haifa that collated data on villages, perhaps in preparation for identity cards.[71] Clarke planned and executed the village occupation scheme in May 1938, and also managed the security of other infrastructure such as railways.

According to Clarke, the "village occupation scheme aimed" for "the simultaneous suppression of disorders in all parts of Palestine."[72] This led to the military occupation of villages in Galilee and Samaria, while construction began on the border installations, and irregular forces, both Arab and Jewish, took the fight to the enemy. The village occupation scheme is depicted in map 8.1 along with the construction of the border fence, frontier posts, and security roads. It was created using Geographic Information System software data compiled from multiple sources, including campaign and staff records, but also police annual reports, memoirs, and Kroizer's research.

The village occupation plan was ordered by Col. Keith Simmons, General Haining's chief of staff, and organized by Clarke.[73] The scheme went into effect on 20 May. The static occupying force was to be the main means of security. Using larger villages as bases, mobile patrols in more remote areas searched for rebels and protected construction workers. In the southern area of the scheme, run by the Fourteenth Infantry Brigade, headquartered in Nablus, road construction rapidly facilitated the movement of troops in what intelligence officers called "the triangle of terror" between Jenin, Tulkarm, and Nablus. New roads were built with gravel over smaller dirt paths and seasonal tracks and could accommodate military traffic. The building allowed troops access to remote areas for longer periods, since they could be supplied and reinforced quickly.

In the northern area, under the control of the Sixteenth Infantry Brigade, much of the western Galilee security was left to police, which took command over both supernumeraries and irregulars. Under the new chief intelligence officer, Alan Ritchie, intelligence centers were set up in Nablus, Haifa, and Nazareth, the last by Orde Wingate. These were to coordinate CID and military intelligence with police and army actions.[74]

In coordination with the Histadrut, Tegart hurried the fence and road construction programs. In early June, he submitted a secret report on the closing of the borders. He had reconnoitered the Jordan valley with Faiz al-Idrissi, and the northern border with army, police, and David HaCohen. Fords on the Jordan were to be blocked by barbed wire. Al-Idrissi was to organize the installation of these measures in the coming weeks, and to take over understrength police posts to garrison his force. The vulnerable points on the northern fence were to be rigged with electrical sensors that would set off flares and tear gas if disturbed. Tegart's report discussed other control measures, especially emphasizing the need for closer supervision of the workmen so as to keep on schedule, the installation of searchlights, and wireless telephone devices throughout the system.[75]

The combination of village occupation, the fence, and irregular forces seemed to be working, although urban terrorism posed a new problem. In mid-July Tegart wrote to Haining, describing his impressions after meeting

MAP 8.1. The Village Occupation Scheme and Security Construction, May 1938

with officials at Whitehall. The cabinet, he said, was "deeply exercised over the failure to restore public security in Palestine. They realize apart from the deplorable effect of this failure in Palestine itself, that it is having most harmful repercussions at home and abroad, alike in the political and economic sphere." Tegart told the colonial secretary of the fundamental change since Harold MacMichael, the new HC, and Haining, the new GOC, had taken over: "For the first time in many years the forces of government were being mobilised as a whole against the enemy."[76]

The infrastructure made a difference again in October 1938, at the height of the rebellion. The army faced a bigger problem than it had in 1936, with significantly less force. Understrength because of the Munich crisis and the collapse of the police, the British Army retook Jerusalem, swept other urban centers, and began to systematically isolate rebel groups in the countryside. Recently built roads hastened the army's response and enabled forces to fan out across the countryside. Thanks to security construction and other secret elements of the campaign discussed below, Britain beat back the surge in the revolt with rapid results. Although reserves were borrowed from Egypt and reinforcements were inbound by the end of October, new infrastructure helped to prevent disaster during Britain's most vulnerable moment.

Construction permanently impacted the landscape, as it reshaped the country into a security state. Map 8.2 represents the final result of all security infrastructure from 1937 to 1943. The war led to further road and fortress construction. By 1943, the final fortresses were completed and the wire fence was dismantled. This full picture of security construction offers a chilling foreboding of the 1947–49 war in Palestine, and the consequent Nakba, which saw the expulsion of some seven to nine hundred thousand Palestinian civilians. When the United Nations voted to partition Palestine in November 1947, the major concentrations of fortresses and security roads lay in the proposed Jewish state. Some of the fiercest battles, for example at Latrun, took place at forts built along key strategic British-built roads. While more elaborate study is necessary, the security road and fortress construction program of 1937–43 seems to have shaped the unfolding of the first Israeli-Arab war. Even a superficial study of the overlay of major clashes of the 1947–48 war with the infrastructure reveals a pattern, where major battles took place over British infrastructure, in areas that produced larger concentrations of refugees.

Authors such as Rashid Khalidi have discussed the origins of the Palestinians' failure to achieve independence, focusing on poor leadership as well as British repression during the revolt.[77] Britain's intelligence staff securitized Palestine's landscape so as to make any future military rebellion a certain

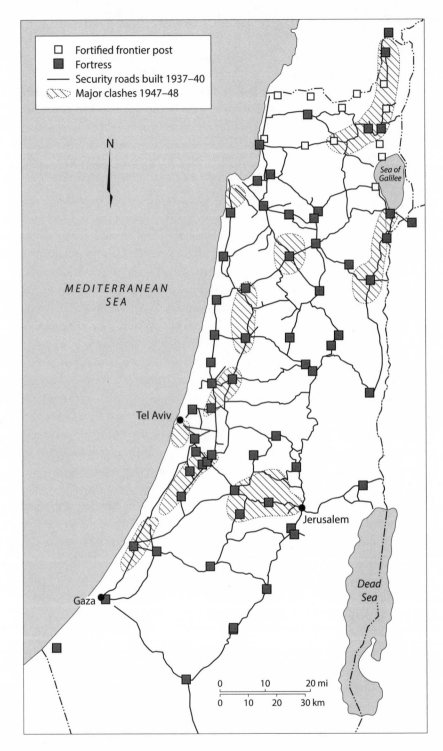

MAP 8.2. Security Infrastructure, 1937–44 and the 1948 Arab-Israeli War

disaster for the Palestinians. In the end, they created a battleground for Jews and Arabs in Palestine. Generally, with exceptions such as Latrun and Tulkarm, this development aided the Zionists. Jewish paramilitary forces, which expanded dramatically from 1936 through 1947, inherited most of these facilities and used them to fight for the roads from November 1947, and as strong frontier positions when the Arab armies invaded in 1948.

Cooperation with Zionists

Officially, the army was forbidden from using armed Jews, despite the eagerness of the Jewish Agency. This frustrated key officers such as Clarke, who, in his memoir, wondered "why, in our desperate state of manpower, we failed to make more use of the Jews. I asked this question many times myself. . . . For the Jews were on our side, and the Arabs were not—yet they were using plenty of arms against our soldiers. . . . It has long puzzled me how often, when confronted with internecine strife, the British authorities somehow managed to antagonize both sides and thus forfeited the help of either!"[78]

Misgivings about military cooperation with Zionists found justification by summer 1938. As government measures in rural areas began to pay off, urban terrorism returned with a vengeance. Reprisal and premeditated terrorist attacks by the nascent Irgun—Revisionist dissidents who broke away from the Haganah—and counterreprisals by Arabs led to mounting violence in major cities, especially Jerusalem.[79] Despairing of an end to urban terrorism, Clarke became weary of Palestine and "sickened by this almost daily toll of blood."[80] Haining sent him home, but the combined staff carried on. Tegart also returned to London in the summer of 1938. Clarke would not return to Palestine until the war, but Tegart came back in response to the collapse of the police in September. By then, largely thanks to both senior coordinators, military cooperation with the Haganah was in full swing. It was a long and gradual process.

In secret, not necessarily with official sanction from high levels, pubsec plans included the use of Jewish paramilitary forces. An important prototype developed at Hanuta, on the Lebanese border. On the night of 21 March, convoys of Jews ascended the mountain range that straddled the Palestine-Lebanon border, and founded Kibbutz Hanita in an overnight "tower and stockade" operation. Two Notarim—"watchmen" of the Haganah who were supernumerary police—were killed in defense of Hanita during its founding. The British army and the RAF played a key supporting role in the defense of this frontier settlement, even though this construction activity was technically illegal. It also was illegal to tear down settlements, so the Yishuv took to building new ones overnight, like Hanita. Turning a blind eye to government policy, the army and the RAF used the settlement as its own eyes and ears.

Monya Adam, chief engineer for the Haganah signal service, recorded in his memoir the role the RAF played in the defense of Hanita, in conjunction with the Haganah signal service. By this time, the Haganah was vigorously expanding its wireless service to cover all frontier settlements, so that the organization could be aware of attacks, border smuggling, or other dangers at the periphery of the Yishuv. The signal service had begun in the early 1930s with official police sanction, using heliographs and flag signaling to alert police of attacks on outlying settlements. Most Haganah signaling activity, however, was illegal and involved secret laboratories and smuggling of crystals for receivers. Adam and his unit built the wireless station at Hanita immediately after its founding, and returned three months later to move the station to higher ground, as the site had come under periodic attack by rebel groups. During one such attack, Haganah signalers contacted the British base at Haifa Bay. RAF aircraft appeared over the area, and Hanita's defenders indicated the direction of the rebel attackers by forming an arrow out of shovels on the roof of one of the buildings. According to Adam, "This arrangement was set by Captain Orde Wingate when he visited the place."[81]

Wingate's connection to Zionists was well established by April 1938, when he visited Hanita with a letter of introduction from Eliyau Golomb, the Haganah's informal commander. His main task was to prepare better supernumerary police defense tactics. He aimed to break the Haganah's policy of Havlagah, or "restraint," and teach the supernumeraries preemptive offensive tactics. This led to his Special Night Squads (SNS). SNS tactics were vicious and involved laying ambushes outside villages, and launching surprise incursions into them. Punitive raids sought to deter villages from harboring rebels. In June, the headmen of the Arab village neighboring Hanita asked for a truce. SNS patrols focused on the IPC pipeline, which constantly fell prey to sabotage.[82] As the wire fence in that area was completed, it improved the defense greatly.[83] Wingate had applied to Ritchie to formalize his plans to expand the SNS, but was rejected on 25 May.[84] However, Dudley Clarke approved a similar scheme the next week. In this manner, Clarke enabled Wingate and circumvented the army's wish to limit the training and armament of the Yishuv. In line with his colleagues, Ritchie granted unwritten consent, lest a paper trail attract attention from higher authorities. Clarke gave guidelines to military commanders involved in training Jewish supernumeraries, which authorized using their standard arms but also using visual signals for communications with troops and police, patrols, ambushes, and other "active measures"—an obvious euphemism.[85] According to Haganah records, with Clarke's support, Wingate negotiated with the GOC and the government to expand the SNS.[86] Nonetheless, the army preferred not to expand the scheme, and eventually disbanded the SNS in July 1939. The top brass were more interested in Arab irregulars than in further arming or training Zionists.[87]

Although Arab irregulars played a greater part in frontier security than the SNS, both were small parts of Anglo-Zionist security cooperation. Table 8.1 demonstrates the scale of improvement in the police between September 1938 and March 1939.[88] It shows the deep investment in British personnel, the weakening of Arab police, and the massive increase in the armament and training of Jews, and their incorporation into British operations. The number given for supernumeraries does not account for the approximately four thousand recruited for settlement defense in 1936. Practically all of these were Haganah members; the training and experience they had acquired from the police was transferred to the Haganah through its training and education program. The Haganah enjoyed the expansion of its capability while it

Table 8.1   Strength of Palestine Police, 31 March 1938 to 31 March 1939

TYPE	STRENGTH 31.3.1938	STRENGTH 12.9.1938	STRENGTH 31.3.1939
British			
Regulars	1,100	1,285	2,837
TOTAL	1,100	1,285	2,837
Arab			
Regulars	1,572	1,644	1,434
Temporary Additionals	302	106	—
Supernumeraries and Ghaffirs	144	115	48
TOTAL	2,018	1,865	1,482
Jewish			
Regulars	651	717	685
Temporary Regulars	37	265	1,608
Attached Police (infantry)	—	—	210
SNS Police	—	50	50
Settlement defense	1,006	931	1,282
Railway protection	—	325	434
Supernumeraries and Ghaffirs	112	449	592
TOTAL	112	449	4,861
TOTAL paid police, all classes	4,924	5,887	9,180
TOTAL specials (settlement defense)	3,853	4,430	13,650

relieved British personnel for other duties. Meanwhile, British intelligence plotted the implosion of the rebellion from within.

The Peace Bands

For some time, motivated by self-interest and survival, the Nashashibis had collaborated with JA intelligence in one form or another, out of a willingness to cooperate against common enemies.[89] Fakhri Nashashibi had also informed the CID, as Harry Rice told a New York–based Jewish Agency official. Fakhri traveled to Egypt on behalf of Rice to expose Italian financial support for the mufti.[90] Ragheb Nashashibi first proposed a deal to the Jewish Agency in December 1937, the same time that he met Tegart. The Nashashibis and the JA reached an agreement to cooperate in March 1938. They would capitalize on rebel brutality in Palestinian villages.

Short on supplies, rebels resorted to extortion in villages, where they threatened violence if tribute was not paid. In response, defensive militias sprang up throughout Palestinian villages, and even in larger centers such as Nablus. By June 1938, armed with Jewish Agency subsidy, the Nashashibis began to organize these militias. According to GSI, these initial "peace bands" actually turned back to the rebels' side.[91] Nashashibi's initial efforts were ad hoc, disorganized, even dilettante. That changed when the rebel leader Fakhri 'Abdul Hadi became a turncoat.

Unable to reach the rebels' base of support in Damascus, Britain worked to separate the rebels from the mufti's orbit. Using Secret Service funds supplied by Tegart and Petrie since January 1938, Gilbert MacKereth was also instrumental in raising peace bands among Syrian Druze, who were uniquely poised to interdict rebel bands on their way to Palestine. His other target for recruitment was 'Abdul Hadi, who was known to have fallen out with the mufti's party and the rest of the rebel leadership. In 1936, 'Abdul Hadi had served under al-Qawuqji in the rebellion. By 1938, destitute and isolated, he was the target of a bidding war between MacKereth and the mufti's people. Intelligence supplied by Yishuv and British sources since summer 1937 led to MacKereth's attempts to buy him off.[92]

According to Yoav Gelber, Nahum Wilenski, the JAPD's liaison officer in Haifa, suggested using Joseph Davidescu's connections in Syria to exploit the dispute between the mufti and 'Abdul Hadi. In March 1938, the JAPD Arab Bureau learned of Fakhri Nashashibi's first attempt to bribe 'Abdul Hadi. Nashashibi was outbid by 'Izzat Darwaza, so Gilbert MacKereth intervened with his enlarged budget. By May, the JAPD had learned of "the establishment of local armed units that would operate against the gangs."[93] 'Abdul

Hadi played both sides to get his price. In August, the Histadrut learned from one of Abba Hushi's Druze agents that 'Abdul Hadi had entered Palestine with an armed group. At first it was not clear that 'Abdul Hadi had defected. Neither the Histadrut nor JAPD intelligence knew whether his operations against rebel gangs were undertaken with British support. It was not a moment too soon. At its climax, the revolt was confronted by all the key pieces of the British counterrevolt: British troops and police and Arab and Jewish irregulars, led by a staff that planned operations based on intelligence from British and Zionist sources.

The mufti's organization and method of control from Lebanon and Syria were known to British intelligence.[94] The military structure of the rebels also was known. SIS records within the MI5 file on the mufti discuss the weak discipline of rebel leaders themselves. Fakhri 'Abdul Hadi targeted three main rebel commanders: 'Abd al-Rahim al-Hajj Mohammad, Yusuf Abu Durra, and 'Aref 'Abd al-Razeq. On 19 October 1938, the mufti's organization in Damascus struggled to prevent rebel groups from acting on their own, as they spiraled into a bloody cycle of clashes with Fakhri 'Abdul Hadi. Their jealousies and failure to follow instructions from Damascus left the revolt vulnerable to psychological disorder caused by the peace bands.

Official reportage left out details of "pseudowarfare," peace bands, and other irregular means. GSI neglected to mention Fakhri 'Abdul Hadi's role in the campaign, but emphasized the benefit accrued by the discord he sowed. An October report mentioned the competition between the rebel leaders 'Aref 'Abd al-Razeq and 'Abd al-Rahim al-Hajj Mohammad. The Damascus leadership was considering replacing Rahim as commander in chief with 'Aref. Rahim was aligned with Istiqlal, whereas 'Aref was a "whole-hearted supporter of the Mufti." Deep divisions in Damascus about the future of the pan-Arab movement prevented an effective campaign, which in any case had become impossible, given large British force. The report discussed Fakhri 'Abdul Hadi's reentry to Palestine. Ritchie noted, "The circumstances of his return about a fortnight ago are unknown, but there seems to be little doubt that it did not meet with the approval of the exiled leaders."[95]

Ritchie played coy. He knew exactly Fakhri's contribution. By the end of 1938, other officers, including police, would make use of 'Abdul Hadi's services.[96] Several accounts confirm that thorough army occupation and search operations in Fakhri's hometown of 'Arrabeh purposely skipped over his house.[97] Ritchie's report emphasized that "Fakhri's arrival has added yet another disturbing factor to the welter of personal rivalries in Samaria." The next month's report more accurately reflected his violent clashes with the other two rebel leaders, and with Abu Durra as well.[98] By the end of

November, documents captured in battle confirmed that internal bickering had caused the collapse of the organized rebel effort. The heavy military deployment enabled the temporary occupation of the area and the internment of some four thousand Palestinians over a period of two weeks in November.

Ezra Danin's annotated record of captured rebel documents considers peace band control to have occurred late, not reaching full form until December 1938, and to have mainly succeeded in ousting pro-mufti gangs from the Hebron area.[99] Matthew Hughes demonstrates convincingly that the peace bands were fundamental to British victory. They did not win the war for Britain, but helped by exploiting endemic blood feuds in rural Palestine, spreading psychological disorder. They proved to be an effective force multiplier,[100] and were part of a broader, intelligence-led campaign.

An Intelligence-Led Campaign

With the reintroduction of reserves to Palestine following the Munich crisis, the combined staffs led a vigorous campaign to restore control. It was led by intelligence, and used irregulars as part of combined operations during October–December 1938. Understrength, British commanders unleashed their hard power after the police collapsed in September. On Friday, 14 October, Hasan Sidqi Dajani was assassinated by rebels. The next day, rebels took control of Jerusalem's walled Old City, comprising an area of one square mile. Rebels took sniping positions around the city gates. Authorities imposed a twenty-four-hour curfew and prepared a response.

Within the walls, shooting and bombing attacks against trapped police and troops continued sporadically. The high commissioner introduced new emergency regulations, giving the army full control over police duties and subordinating police commissioners to brigade staffs. The recapture of Jerusalem's Old City became the highest priority. On the morning of Wednesday, 19 October, aircraft dropped leaflets warning residents to stay indoors. Using telephone lines to coordinate, authorities took care to deliver fresh bread and supplies to the besieged population. The army surrounded the walled city, while police and soldiers used underground tunnels to reconnoiter hidden entry points. Some tunnel entrances, now sealed with rebar, are visible around the outer perimeter of the walled city. In the early hours of Thursday, 20 October, British forces emerged from underground while others stormed the gates of the city in a well-timed crackdown. Searches lasted for two days. Late on Saturday the twenty-second, British forces had encircled remaining fighters in the Haram al-Sharif. The fighting claimed twenty-two dead and twenty-five wounded on the Arab side, and one killed and four wounded for the British. By Sunday, British forces had successfully reclaimed the entire Old City, including the Haram al-Sharif. Police and government officials were pleased at the lack of blowback from the Muslim world at these actions.[101]

The rapid deterioration in security was a surprise, and was badly timed with a partial withdrawal of British troops during the Munich crisis. The CID noted that "organised terrorism has now forced the fellahin [peasants] into complete subjection and various successful gang actions have raised the morale and prestige of the 'Mujahideen' to the extent of bringing about an open Arab revolt in the more distant rural areas." Jaffa, Gaza, Beersheba, and Ramallah were overrun by gangs. The same memo went on to say, "Many government supporters and moderates have been forced to seek safety by leaving the country and a number of Arab government officials have either tendered their resignations or have been given extended leave abroad for similar reasons. Those remaining are in the unenviable position of being in fear of their lives with their sympathies towards their national cause."[102] The urban campaign had quickly accomplished its objectives, but it was imperative that security extend to the countryside and its villages as well. The village occupation scheme was reintroduced with a vengeance—rebels now had to avoid British troops and peace bands.

Fakhri 'Abdul Hadi had based himself in 'Arrabeh and began to campaign against rebel leaders and grow his own force. In November, British troops concentrated in the heavily forested Carmel range to liquidate Yusuf Abu Durra's gang. Druze agents based near Haifa passed intelligence from Abu Durra's force. That, as well as other intelligence coordinated between Hushi, the JAPD, Davidescu, and the Haifa SSO, fed a well-planned and systematic campaign during November. Davidescu and the Druze agents guided two companies of the Sixteenth Infantry Brigade up Mount Carmel toward the Druze villages of Daliat al-Carmel and 'Usifiya. Abu Durra had recently angered the inhabitants by looting supplies during his brief occupation, and allegedly also desecrated Druze sacred texts. Now on the run, his group had dwindled to some forty to fifty men after numerous small clashes with troops and irregulars. Abu Durra found villages either hostile or occupied by British troops. He hoped to exploit the tree cover of the region while moving his force down the Carmel range toward Umm al-Fahm, likely a friendlier base for operations, when his force was ambushed at Umm al-Zinat, at the edge of the forest.

The army had been cordoning and searching the region when aircraft spotted the rebel force. According to GSI, a "running fight ensued" between 1:00 p.m. and dusk, when hand-to-hand combat began. Perhaps a dozen of Abu Durra's forced remained, and the commander was lucky to escape with his life. Abu Durra's band was "decisively" defeated. The cover action was sanctioned by Jack Evetts, the area brigade commander, and Bernard Montgomery, the divisional commander. Ritchie, head of intelligence, observed the whole operation. Evetts contributed by deploying an irregular force of Druze and other Arabs against the gangs.[103]

By the end of November, the situation had improved due to the presence of two divisions, and a centralized intelligence machinery able to coordinate the support of Zionists and opposition factions. With reinforcements back in Palestine, troops were free to occupy villages and deny them to rebels.[104] GSI reported that whereas Fakhri Nashashibi had previously enjoyed only secret support from the population, on 30 November "some 25 notables and Mukhtars representing 70,000 Arabs of the Ramallah, Jerusalem and Hebron districts were interviewed by representatives of the Press at Fakhri Nashashibi's house in Jerusalem. They expressed their opposition to the Mufti and his policy and their desire to assist the government in the restoration of order."[105]

GSI attributed the weakening rebel situation to an increase in intelligence due to Arabs' confidence in the government and their consequent readiness to give names and identify rebels. A large number of rebel documents captured in November also helped the troops' effort to search villages. Selective arrests in the Nazareth area had propped up the Zu'bi family, who supported the Nashashibis. GSI emphasized that "the successful arrests of the right people appears to have taken the gangsters by surprise and the constant searches by troops and the confiscation of arms, has lowered the rebel morale in the area."[106]

Intercepted rebel correspondence revealed that by the end of 1938, chaos prevailed in the rebel ranks, especially in the Jerusalem–Hebron corridor. Some commanders sought orders on what to do about Nashashibi or 'Abdul Hadi. Others began to reject orders from their headquarters in Damascus. Rebel commanders issued death sentences and expulsion orders for collaborators, which they could never enforce.[107] Psychological warfare was effective; Britain's campaign was working, but not finished. GSI warned that the rebellion was not done. Over much of the country, it reported, "the rule of terror is still supreme. . . . Any relaxation of military activity at the present time would only result in allowing the rebels once more to tighten their grip."[108] Indeed, rebel activity carried on well into the Second World War.

British authorities gradually regained control, offering symbols that order was being restored. British troops began to contain the peace bands, and to prop up the Nashashibis, the opposition, including other defectors from the mufti's camp, as the new leaders of Palestinian civil life. However, normal civil law never returned—Palestine was again occupied by British troops, and would remain so until 1948.

The End of Normal Government

For the first time since 1920, the Palestine government had available a form of centralized intelligence that was attached to both security and policymaking. This mechanism crushed the Palestinian revolt, but the campaign was not as simple as imagined during the drills of 1934. The monetary price for victory was manageable—in the millions of pounds. But there also were political costs. From 1938, civil government existed in name only. Military operations had not improved Britain's policy options; rather, the opposite had occurred. Arabs still would never accept the Zionist policy. Since 1933, Palestinian leaders had escalated their resistance to British policy, along with their demands. Military defeat did nothing to alter those demands. Democratic self-government could never be reconciled with the Zionist policy, and was doubly complicated by military control of civil institutions, internment camps, and the occupation of rural areas. Without a change in policy options, victory was incomplete. Rather than extricating British policy from these dilemmas, partition aggravated Arab demands more than ever. Importantly, partition threatened the interests of independent Arab states, chiefly Saudi Arabia. The counterrevolt led to new and improved capabilities for the Haganah and the Jewish Agency, while the political risks of the Zionist policy and partition now cast doubt over the future of Anglo-Zionist relations. From a policy perspective, "victory" was even more complicated than the status quo before the revolt.

Consequently, Britain redefined its policy. In November 1938 the Woodhead Commission—established to follow up on the recommendations of Peel's royal commission—published its report, recommending three options for implementing some form of partition. British policymakers immediately retreated from these suggestions, and pursued some way to convene Arab statesmen in London to confer on a new policy. The mufti and his clique then reconsidered their own. Shakib Arslan began to publish articles on the economic and defensive power of the Arab world. He and most others foresaw an inevitable world war, and called on members of the London conference to negotiate as a bloc—to leverage their collective power in negotiations with Britain.[109] It was a sound diplomatic strategy, but Arslan and the mufti were slow to discover that independent Arab statesmen had their own interests to preserve. When Britain invited the Arab states to London to meet with the Zionists and Palestinians, it reinterpreted the Zionist policy in favor of the interests of independent Arab states, but not to accede to Palestinian demands.

CHAPTER 9

Intelligence, Ibn Saʿud, and the White Paper Policy

The White Paper issued on 17 May 1939 ended Britain's twenty-two-year Zionist policy. The Jewish national home was declared to have been fulfilled. Jewish immigration would be limited to about 1,500 per month for a period of five years. Land purchases by Jews would be restricted. The government would rewrite the constitution within five years to prepare the country for independence within ten. The new policy, backtracking from the partition schemes of 1937–38, aimed to create an independent federal state of Palestine.

This watershed moment was the product of several factors: The revolt had tied down Britain's reserve divisions during the strategic crisis at Munich. The revolt denied Britain any normal, legal solution to its conflicting commitments to Zionists, the Palestinians, and the liberal aims of the mandate. Partition was Britain's first serious attempt to find a way out of this bind. At great cost, the Palestinian revolt forced Britain to change course. The first proposed solution, partition, angered Britain's key regional partners—the independent Arab states. Chief among them, Saudi Arabia had proved especially reliable on the Palestine question since 1936. On the eve of war, that relationship became more attractive as British strategists considered how to keep minor powers in the Middle East from siding with Germany or Italy. The White Paper was precipitated by the revolt but crafted by Anglo-Saudi diplomacy. The intelligence record reveals that the White Paper addressed not only the future of Palestine or the Jewish question, but also how Britain would hold the Middle East during a future war. The White Paper reimagined how the empire might work by stripping Britain's responsibility to rule Palestine directly while maintaining its dominance across the Middle East through the independent Arab states, and by creating more of them.

Principal among independent Arab statesmen was Ibn Sa'ud. Instead of advocating solely on behalf of the Arab movements, Ibn Sa'ud sought to secure his own interests, while emphasizing those that he shared with Britain. The White Paper was designed to give Ibn Sa'ud a political victory over the Zionists, and bring his kingdom closer to Britain on the eve of world war while boosting his prestige in the pan-Arab theater. The decision was a milestone in Anglo-Saudi relations, which had markedly improved since 1930, when Britain increasingly saw problems with both its allies: the Zionists in Palestine and the Hashemites in Transjordan and Iraq. This approach sought to secure Saudi Arabia's benevolent neutrality during the coming war, along with its pro-British leadership in the Arab world. Winning Ibn Sa'ud's partnership would foil the strategy of the National Pact by securing the support of the region's most influential ruler.

Differing Explanations for the White Paper

Historians have misconstrued these events by treating them purely as national rather than dynastic issues. In the process, they have misunderstood which Arabs mattered to British decision makers. Views about British motives for the White Paper might be divided into three overlapping schools of thought: military strategy, Arabism at the Foreign Office, and appeasement—a loaded term given the 1938–39 context. None of these views are wrong, but none tell the full story. Then again, important records now available shine new light on that era.

Preferring the military-strategic explanation, Martin Thomas demonstrates that British strategists sought alternate solutions to partition once they lacked the force needed to impose it. The JIC worried about the military commitment required for partition, especially given possible reactions in Egypt and Iraq. It discussed measures to gain the support of Arab states during a war. The military commitment involved in policing Egypt alone was cause for concern. The Palestine question would obviously have to be resolved in the Arabs' favor.[1] This argument addresses the core of the matter, but other points remain to be assessed.

The Foreign Office–Arabist explanation is exemplified mainly by those authors who discuss Britain's retreat from the partition recommendations of the Peel Commission. That process of retreat was complex and involved competing interests within the British government, and also between the government, Arab statesmen, and nationalists. Yehoshua Porath and Elie Kedourie argue that FO bureaucrats, especially George Rendel, drove this retreat, either out of empathy with Arabs or in the belief that it would help British strategy. Undersecretaries and diplomats rejected partition because it would alienate the independent and semi-independent Arab states.[2] Indeed, Rendel and others led the change from a Zionist-imperialist stance to a pan-Arab one, but for different motivations than Kedourie suggests. British observers understood the relationships between the Arab kings and the national movements: they knew that those ties were more important to the nationalists than to the kings. The kings still influenced Arab nationalists, but were more interested in improving their relations with Britain.

Yehoshua Porath writes that after the Munich crisis, Malcolm MacDonald, as colonial secretary, realized that partition was impossible, because its execution would require force that Britain did not have. He hoped for peacemaking under British guidance, but by October 1938 the government had concluded that "Arab goodwill had to be safeguarded at all costs." Britain called a Jewish-Arab conference for early 1939, at the Palace of St. James, mediated by the colonial secretary and his officers. Palestinian and Arab delegations vastly outnumbered the Jewish Agency. The mufti was excluded, but his party leadership attended. British authorities were guided by the Woodhead Commission report, which had concluded that partition was impossible without much force and suffering. Its guiding principal was to at least temporarily freeze the demographic balance, and prepare Palestine for independence and to join an Arab federation.[3] This alone should have been a victory for the ASC.

Related to this, there have also been racial-orientalist explanations for the retreat from partition. Bernard Wasserstein argues that "the retreat from the Balfour Declaration policy was also a retreat from the perception of the Jews as a nation. The Jews lacked the essential attribute of state sovereignty, and (by contrast with the position during the First World War) it was a cardinal principle of British policy that Jews should not gain state sovereignty."[4]

In fact, Britain had never considered a Jewish state until the 1937 Peel Commission. The retreat from the possibility of statehood through partition was a mere eighteen-month process—hardly traumatic for Zionist expectations. Besides, the Zionists had many reservations about the Peel report. Some felt the land allotment to the Jewish state was insufficient. Most Zionist parties still believed the time was not yet ripe for independence and the Yishuv needed British protection. Moreover, Britain's own survival was at stake, given the forthcoming struggle against Germany. Wasserstein acknowledges a "tinge of anti-Semitism in the words of some British officials and politicians" but says that "anti-Semitism does not by itself explain British conduct."[5]

Michael Cohen's 1978 study of Britain's retreat from Palestine connects the Arabist foreign policymaker and military strategy explanations. With little access to intelligence records, Cohen argues that British policymakers sought to satisfy the demands of Arab states in order to shore up Britain's regional military position. Policymakers did not expect any violent reaction from the Zionists under the circumstances. Cohen's research emphasizes Anglo-Zionist relations. Even though Arab states were the main actors in this drama, his survey of Anglo-Arab relations is light. Although he does address the Arab kings scheme of 1936, he does not discuss Saudi Arabia as a driving factor. Enter our third explanation: Cohen considers "the realpolitik of appeasement" to have driven British decisions during 1938–39, yet offers no account for why Britain considered Arab interests in its strategy.[6] He argues that on the eve of the Second World War, British strategy had never been to appease Arabs at the expense of the Jews: "But following the crises precipitated by the Italian conquest of Abyssinia, policy in Palestine had to be decided with one eye on the strategic needs of the area. Once the Arab states were brought in, or themselves took the initiative in mediation, the Palestine issue was treated as a Pan-Arab issue—at first only by the FO, but by mid 1938 by the Colonial Office as well."[7]

This assessment generally is correct. However, to be more precise, British strategists began to emphasize the value of partnership with Arab statesmen, especially Ibn Sa'ud. Cohen also argues that the Arab states, with their oil, air bases, and other assets, were vital to British defense planning against Italy. "The strategic nuisance value of the Arab states," he contends, "far outweighed any advantages the Zionists could hope to offer."[8]

Signals intelligence helped British policymakers to navigate these issues with success, and showed that at least one of these figures, Ibn Sa'ud, was influential and could be trusted. Cohen's conclusion rests on a particular reading of the diplomatic evidence, including puzzling but important evidence regarding Ibn Sa'ud. Without sigint evidence, policy change appears to have been led by activist civil servants at the Foreign Office. The sigint evidence reveals that the FO had good reason to trust Ibn Sa'ud, and reasonably involved him in Britain's Palestine policy. In December 1937, after discussions with Ibn Sa'ud, Rendel proposed freezing the demographic ratio as a concession to the Arab nationalists. Arguing that a Jewish-Arab solution would be simple if the problem of Jewish immigration could be solved, he convinced the Foreign Office to accept the proposal. This step allegedly would also ease Britain's military commitment to the region, since it was believed that a Jewish state could not survive without British troops.[9] When the Zionist policy was conceived, British strategists did not believe it would require large troop commitments in the Middle East. By 1938, that illusion had shattered. Rendel's view was influenced by Ibn Saʿud's diplomacy, and the FO's access to his decrypted communications.

The CO maintained a Zionist policy, and supported partition, but that position cracked through 1937–38, especially after the appointment of Malcolm MacDonald as colonial secretary in May 1938. In 1930, while his father was prime minister, MacDonald had championed Weizmann's cause during the controversy over the Passfield White Paper, which attempted to limit and reinterpret the Zionist policy. In a 2016 article, Cohen rightly notes that the Fabian Society, with its goal of democratic socialism, influenced Passfield's anti-imperialism and dislike of the Zionist policy. Yet Prime Minister Ramsay MacDonald also was a Fabian. His dispute with Passfield in 1930 was part of the growing rift within the Labour Party, rather than one over Zionism and empire. Zionism appealed to Britain's labor movement, but in 1938 Malcolm MacDonald had to handle Palestine policy with new urgency and practicality. Between June and September 1938, after many consultations and a two-day visit to Palestine, the Colonial Office under MacDonald opposed partition.[10]

Rosemarie Said Zahlan and Elie Kedourie are the only historians to note that Anglo-Saudi relations shaped Britain's Palestine policy during 1937–39. Said Zahlan notes the influence of Ibn Saʿud's 1937 recommendations to the Peel Commission on the White Paper.[11] As strategic issues such as the revolt and German and Italian encroachment emerged, Ibn Saʿud's goodwill became all the more important to the FO and CO.[12] Kedourie's argument, made in 1980, largely has been ignored by other historians, who, like him, lacked access to the sigint record. He emphasizes Rendel's role in Britain's retreat from partition, but his incredulity partly overshadows his scholarship. "Did Ibn Saʿud justify this blind belief [by the FO] in his absolute loyalty? Did he deserve the fond protectiveness with which Rendel and his colleagues so tenderly regarded him?" he asks.[13] Kedourie's description of Britain's about-face on the Zionist policy ignores the leverage Ibn Saʿud wielded in his negotiations with Britain. Given Britain's strategic vulnerability in the Middle East, Ibn Saʿud's prestige among his own subjects and in the Arab and Muslim worlds became increasingly dear to British policymakers. He could potentially solve the problem of Britain's overcommitment of troops.

According to Kedourie, nobody challenged Rendel's assertions that Palestine mattered to the Arab world and that Ibn Saʿud opposed partition more from jealousy of the Hashemites than fear of losing his throne.[14] Ibn Sa'ud's concern about pan-Arab perceptions of his role certainly were significant. Yet he had little reason to be envious of the "hated" Hashemites.[15] Rather, he feared their military power. Britain was not trying to solve Palestinian problems—it sought to solve the problems of Ibn Sa'ud, who, in turn, as a popular pan-Arab leader, would use his influence in Britain's favor. His independence from the great powers and his personal and military record are key to understanding his role.

Kedourie's argument is important: Ibn Sa'ud's diplomacy shaped the FO's approach to the Palestine question, and perhaps persuaded the government to change course. Nonetheless, the author's survey is flawed by a sense of injustice to Zionism. Citing discoveries by British authorities that Ibn Sa'ud was arming rebels or amassing troops on the Transjordan border, and his decision to oppose partition only once Iraq openly had done so, Kedourie argues that British support for him was not justified: "No doubt in order to protect his position, Ibn Sa'ud sent a telegram to a friend in Damascus which became known to the Palestine government. Its text is not now in the file, but it was enough for Wauchope to refer (in a letter of 14 July) to its 'unfortunate and most disappointing substance.' " Rendel continued to support Ibn Sa'ud, arguing that his message was not a sign of bad faith; Ibn Sa'ud had long warned that he might have to adopt a policy at variance with British wishes.[16]

It so happens that this telegram is available today. Ibn Sa'ud communicated with his emissary (not a friend) in Damascus, Sheikh Kamel al-Qassab. The message noted that the British diplomat at Jeddah, Reader Bullard, supplied a preview of the royal commission report to Ibn Sa'ud, but did not ask for comment. The king told al-Qassab about his discussions with Bullard where he expressed his disappointment with British policy. Partition threatened Saudi interests in three ways. First, general Arab hostility to Britain endangered Anglo-Saudi relations. Second, Ibn Sa'ud opposed a Jewish state in an Arab country. Third, and most importantly, Ibn Sa'ud feared the enlargement of 'Abdullah's territory if Transjordan annexed the Arab partition of Palestine. He feared that 'Abdullah might seek Jewish aid in asserting his dominance. In conclusion, Ibn Sa'ud instructed al-Qassab to share these discussions with the mufti.[17]

Ibn Sa'ud had previously kept the mufti at a distance, yet now shared privileged intelligence with him about the Peel report. His suspicion of 'Abdullah is understandable given his own military situation. He lacked a standing army, whereas Transjordan was protected by the Arab Legion, the TJFF, and the RAF—all formidable professional forces. Ibn Sa'ud feared an independent 'Abdullah with expansionist ambition that, given the royal commission report, could include territory in Palestine. Perhaps 'Abdullah would use his forces to retake Hejaz and Islam's holy cities, lost in the 1920s. Partition was sure to alienate Ibn Sa'ud, whose opinion mattered to both British policymakers and pan-Arabists. His message was clear and effective. In the retreat from partition, British diplomacy artfully landed Ibn Sa'ud.

The 1939 White Paper aimed to improve Anglo-Saudi relations. This aim rested on the belief, justified by the evidence available to British policymakers, that Ibn Sa'ud could influence the pan-Arab movements in Britain's favor. Britain sought to solve Ibn Sa'ud's security dilemmas, improve his prestige, and bring him closer to the empire while still maintaining his independence, which would aid British aims.

Intelligence records reveal that Anglo-Saudi relations were far more complex and important than is often portrayed. Most historians, like Kedourie, consider Ibn Sa'ud to be antagonistic to British interests. Joseph Kostiner argues that Ibn Sa'ud "was not interested in strategic cooperation with Britain."[18] Clive Leatherdale's survey of Anglo-Saudi relations, the only one that covers this period, paints a tenser picture than is warranted by the new evidence.[19] The intelligence record reveals that such characterizations are untrue. Ibn Sa'ud had moved from being an independent but minor British ally in 1915, when he gained protectorate status, to a significant regional partner by the Second World War.

Anglo-Saudi Relations

Britain's relations with Ibn Sa'ud were turbulent between 1915 and 1933, although he was generally regarded with respect. He usually was trapped in security dilemmas with at least one neighbor while Britain tried to stabilize borders in the Arabian Peninsula. Britain militarily contained Ibn Sa'ud during much of the 1920s, but also sought to ease his security dilemmas, which by the mid-1930s extended beyond containment and border treaties. Britain's main aim was to achieve stability under its Gulf treaty system. The 1915 Treaty of Darin included Ibn Sa'ud in a system of similar agreements with other Gulf rulers, responding to his expansion into the coastal Hasa territory, and also to prevent any Saudi agreement with the Ottoman Empire. Britain could not coax him to join the war effort, although he supported the landing at Basra in 1914 and never supported the Ottomans. British officials remembered Ibn Sa'ud's benevolent neutrality appreciatively, even if this was not the true spirit of his policy at the time.[20]

Britain was cool toward Ibn Saʿud during the 1920s but was always pre-pared to revise its treaties with him in response to his expanding kingdom. His Hashemite enemies also were Britain's allies, but they did not enjoy the protectorate status that Britain offered to Ibn Saʿud under the 1915 (Darin) and 1927 (Jeddah) treaties. Contrary to the way Ibn Saʿud is often character-ized in the literature, there is little evidence that he was hostile to Britain. His Wahhabi movement was more hostile to Britain than he was, but it suf-fered from the changing pan-Islamic landscape during 1924–25 as the Otto-man caliphate was abolished and the Indian Khilafat movement collapsed. The Wahhabis' international connections were severed at the same time that they conquered Hejaz during 1924–25. Ibn Saʿud and his Wahhabist Ikhwan followers deposed the Hashemites from the Muslim holy cities. Britain rec-ognized his new position by treaty, but contained the Ikhwan using aircraft and armored cars during their raids on Iraq and Transjordan in 1927–28. This proved to be a relief for Ibn Saʿud, who, while attempting to raise a new army so as to lessen his dependence on the Ikhwan, faced revolt led by a former follower and champion, Faisal al-Duwaysh, chief of the Mutayr tribe. Dur-ing 1928, British forces closed the border to protect tribes based in Iraq and Transjordan from the Ikhwan, but also to protect Saudi territory from retal-iatory raids. By early 1929, the Ikhwan revolt had been crushed. British fears of pan-Islamic revolution in the empire faded. These events caused British observers to disregard pan-Islam as a factor in their Middle Eastern empire, as compared to nationalism. Rendel observed that Islamic unity was "a fic-tion" except as a reaction against European penetration in the east.[21]

Anglo-Saudi relations improved in 1932 when Hamed Ibn Rifadah led an anti-Saudi revolt in Hejaz, seemingly with clandestine support from Hash-emites, or the pro-Hashemite faction of Istiqlal, and possibly other Arab or British sources. Ibn Rifadah was defeated with British help. The RAF, the Arab Legion, the TJFF, and police forces closed the border and disarmed rebels attempting to enter or leave Hejaz.[22] Ibn Saʿud's victory added weight to his prestige in the pan-Arab movement. The pro-Saudi faction of Istiqlal, led by Kamel al-Qassab and Nabih al-ʿAzmeh, eclipsed the pro-Hashemite faction of ʿAuni ʿAbdul Hadi.[23]

These events, as well as Ibn Saʿud's assistance in ending the revolt in 1936, were remembered during the controversy surrounding the partition propos-als of 1937. Military intelligence, with access to sigint, connected Ibn Saʿud's protests against the Peel proposals to his security dilemmas. "The key to Ibn Saʿud's attitude," one officer observed, "is to be found in his fears that parti-tion will be giving ʿAbdullah more power to damage him and that he will have to face a situation (of which the ibn Rifada incident was merely a hint) similar to that created by Feisal [bin Husayn] on the Najd-Iraq border [in 1928]." The officer added that Ibn Sa'ud's positive view of Britain depended on its control over his borders with Transjordan and Iraq.[24]

From Ibn Sa'ud's perspective, Britain proved itself a dependable partner, and Foreign Office officials felt the same way about the Saudi kingdom. Intercepted communications revealed Ibn Sa'ud's inclination to work with Britain and support its interests. But there were exceptions to this rule. British policymakers believed that good relations derived from Britain's position of strength. By 1935, the FO had concluded that its control over the region required sufficient force to contain Ibn Sa'ud. When he pressed for territorial concessions in the Persian Gulf, Britain informed Sir Andrew Ryan, the diplomat in Jeddah, that "HMG [His Majesty's Government] will not abandon their established policy in the Persian Gulf in order that Ibn Saud may play with greater effect to the pan-Arab gallery." Ryan was instructed to "disabuse" the king's representative of any notion that borders were negotiable.[25] Within months, relations were considered "extremely cordial."[26] During the 1935 Abyssinian crisis, Italy approached Saudi Arabia for partnership. Ibn Sa'ud accepted Italian gestures, including military aid, and fostered good diplomatic relations as an independent statesman and in the interests of his kingdom. However, he was suspicious of Italian intentions, and his emissaries told Britain of every step taken with Italy during 1935–36, many of which Whitehall already knew about.[27] These actions signaled to British diplomats that they were dealing with an independent entity whose interests were aligning with their own.

Ibn Sa'ud, the Arab Movements, and the Revolt

The coalition of Arab nationalist parties that established the National Pact had intended to exploit future European crises as leverage with Britain and France for independence. They believed that the independent Arab kings would be instrumental to that cause, as would the tribes. Arab nationalists spent the following four years striving for peace and unity between Ibn Sa'ud, Imam Yahya of Yemen, and Feisal of Iraq. After the 1933 death of Feisal, who was succeeded by the unpopular Ghazi, Ibn Sa'ud became the obvious standard-bearer for the movement.

By 1939, it was clear to Britain that it needed support from a popular Arab statesman. This led the government to abandon its twenty-two-year-old policy of working with Zionists and Hashemites, and to find other means to dominate national movements in the region. The latter hope was not entirely achieved, even though Britain spent considerable treasure and blood in securing the Middle East from pro-Axis sympathy and forces between 1939 and 1942. Nonetheless, that situation easily could have been far worse than it was, and policymakers never expected Ibn Saʿud to control national movements. Britain's turn to the Arab leader was rational, and perhaps worthwhile from the perspective of its interests, and even those of Zionists.

This was a cynical policy that abandoned not merely Jewish allies but Arab ones. The Hashemite card was weak. Iraq was chaotic from 1936 to 1941, as it experienced a series of coups, culminating in Britain's reoccupation of the country during the war. Between Iraq's persistent civil-military strife and King Ghazi's cool attitude toward Britain before his death in a car crash in April 1939, Iraq seemed more a pan-Arab battleground than a base of pro-British influence. Nationalist politics dominated Iraq more than the Hashemite dynasty. ʿAbdullah of Transjordan, who also sought leadership in the pan-Arab movement, had only the support of some tribes in his own territory, weak party factions, and some elements of the Nashashibi-led opposition in Palestine.

Arab movements were divided about ʿAbdullah. Most saw him as a British agent and were hostile toward him. A smaller number of pan-Arabists were Hashemite patrons.[28] ʿAbdullah had ambitions, especially for kingship over Syria, which was an open question for colonial powers, Arab statesmen, and pan-Arab parties. British support for ʿAbdullah's leadership in the pan-Arab movement was never wholehearted and was always contingent on practical and strategic issues. The British could not have supported ʿAbdullah's claims to the Syrian throne, for example, against the wishes of France, Ibn Saʿud, or other key power brokers. They knew that few pan-Islamists supported ʿAbdullah. During the Second World War, these dynamics were overshadowed by ʿAbdullah's military contributions to the British effort, which seemed to improve his chances for British support. The issue of the Syrian throne illuminates how Britain foresaw colonial control continuing as the number of independent Arab states grew.[29]

Saudi-Hashemite relations seemed to have thawed by the mid-1930s. In 1935, Saudi Arabia's Prince Faysal visited Transjordan and Palestine. The CID remarked how Faysal had captured what was left of Hashemite prestige in Palestine since the death of the king of Iraq, Feisal bin Hussein. Public excitement and enthusiasm, previously reserved for the Hashemite ruler, now was expressed for a Saudi. Faysal's visit coincided with a meeting of the National Pact. Leaders from Syria and Palestine gathered in Jerusalem to discuss what to do if war broke out in Abyssinia and other European powers became involved. The mufti, Nabih al-ʿAzmeh, and ʿAuni ʿAbdul Hadi all hosted meetings. They agreed that under these circumstances, Yemen, Saudi Arabia, and Iraq should remain neutral. Upon the declaration of war, Istiqlal delegations would visit the Arab kings to promote neutrality and build a new pan-Arab congress, which would use the crisis to leverage European governments for independence. They sought to have Ibn Sa'ud negotiate with France to appoint Amir Faysal to the Syrian throne. Istiqlal fostered Saudi-Hashemite cooperation, assuming that 'Abdullah would cooperate with other parties in the push for Arab independence.[30]

The revolt shattered these illusions. After Ibn Sa'ud's intervention to end the revolt in 1936, nationalists hoped their voices would be heard by the royal commission. They and the independent Arab states were shocked by the commission's recommendations for the partition of Palestine into Jewish and Arab states. By June 1937, when the royal commission published its report, the War Office had revised its own appreciations of Britain's strategic position in the Middle East. This review led to more support for the FO position on Palestine. The WO warned that Ibn Sa'ud might have to change his policy toward Britain if the commission findings were unfair to Arabs, and that all Arab states "welcome a firm and prompt settlement, which would remove a source of embarrassment to them in their own internal politics." Disturbances, it said, must be suppressed quickly, so a larger garrison would be needed as long as Palestine "will be a thorn in our flesh . . . until the situation there becomes stable."[31] Hoping to free reserve troops, the cabinet was attracted to Rendel's proposals to again use Ibn Sa'ud's influence to end the revolt in Palestine.

Ibn Sa'ud's London emissary, Hafez Wahba, was shown a preview of the royal commission report before it was published. The Saudis were alarmed, to say the least. Ibn Sa'ud's ministers urged him to openly support the Palestinians' rejection of partition. Al-Qassab expressed the ASC's anxiety while awaiting Ibn Sa'ud's response.[32] Ibn Sa'ud cautiously met Bullard face to face in Jeddah and bluntly asked whether partition was a closed subject, or whether "any representations concerning it were invited." Bullard replied that the subject was closed. Irritated, Ibn Sa'ud raised the stakes by tabling three matters, concerning Amir 'Abdullah, the territory around Aqaba and Ma'an in Transjordan, and the Syrian border, which collectively hinted at his ability to cause trouble for Britain. He also instructed Wahba to ask the British government whether any representations might be made in London. Realizing the risk of further alienating the king, Bullard offered an opening: "The government's decision was definite and unalterable, but . . . the nature of the partition has not yet been decided by the government."[33]

Ibn Sa'ud bolstered his bargaining position by threatening territorial claims in Transjordan and intervention in Alexandretta, then disputed by Turkey, France, and the Syrian pan-Arabists. This pressure reminded Britain of what was at stake: its reputation, its hold on the Middle East, and both Saudi and Turkish sympathy toward Britain and France in the event of European war. A Saudi victory regarding Palestine, and the consequent boost to Ibn Sa'ud's prestige, could settle these matters, so British diplomats began to reconsider partition. At the same time, Ibn Sa'ud himself was under pressure to raise jihad against Palestine. Sigint intercepts revealed that various sheikhs offered their willingness to participate.[34] Ibn Sa'ud cabled the mufti via intermediaries, asking about his plans: "We have never spared any efforts and we will never slacken in our endeavor until the end. But making a show about things which will come to nought is a mistake. They can have the utmost trust in us. . . . Our brothers in Syria and Palestine must all know that our greatest interest is that they should attain the objects which will safeguard the interests of the country and the honor of the Arabs."[35]

The mufti defined his minimum demands, as related by al-Qassab: abrogation of the mandate, Palestinian independence, and a willingness to make "adequate provision guaranteeing the rights of the Jews as a minority in the land, and to conclude a treaty on this basis with the British government on the lines of the Iraqi and Syrian treaties. They all say 'death or life with honor.'"[36] Thanks to sigint, Britain possessed the minimum bargaining position of the mufti, on the eve of the 1937 Bludan congress and renewed revolt.

Privately, the Saudis told al-Qassab their position on partition: "We replied to Sheikh Qassab that we, in accordance with our invariable policy towards HMG, have dealt with them direct and have not published anything and do not wish to make our attitude public." Despite Ibn Sa'ud's disappointment and anger, his ministers were instructed to continue cooperation with Britain on the basis of shared interests. Wahba had been recalled to Jeddah to receive further instructions on how to negotiate in London. Ibn Sa'ud asked al-Qassab to convey all information that the mufti and his associates wished to communicate to Britain or to himself. The Saudis wished to avoid Bludan altogether since it might pose more problems for Britain. The message concluded, "We wish HMG to be informed of this under the usual conditions of strict secrecy."[37] Al-Qassab even attempted to prevent the Bludan conference, but was too late.[38]

A GSI report, based on access to signals intercepts, explained that Ibn Sa'ud's opposition to partition was motivated by his fear that partition would "secure the aggrandizement [of the territory] of his hereditary foe the

Hashemite 'Abdullah." Nonetheless, the report said, Ibn Sa'ud "would endeavor to employ only constitutional means to assist the Arabs in Palestine." In the event of renewed rebellion in Palestine, Ibn Sa'ud could not control his tribes who might try to participate. Recently, rumors had swirled about the arming of tribes in Saudi Arabia, including a false one that Fawzi al-Qawuqji was there preparing a renewed rebellion. British intelligence attributed little importance to such reports, however, since it was known that the tribes feared the British forces that dominated the desert frontiers. Ibn Sa'ud was determined to avoid conflict with Britain.[39] John Glubb, commander of the Arab legion in Transjordan, agreed.[40]

Sigint records revealed that there was arms traffic through Ibn Sa'ud's territory, and that he had received weapons from Italy. Despite the claims of historians who count Ibn Sa'ud among Britain's foes, these arms were not intended to reach Palestinian rebels, but were mostly used to supply his own forces. Ibn Sa'ud instructed a local governor to tell Glubb that Saudi Arabia could not admit arms reception, but that "even if the people of Palestine are dear to us we do not wish to increase the difficulties that confront the British government." In response to intelligence about Saudi support for the revolt, Glubb's forces closed routes northward from Saudi Arabia. The rumors proved to have little foundation. The situation was resolved, and the border was reopened, after open communication with Ibn Sa'ud, his words having been verified by secretly intercepted communications.[41] Italy was looking increasingly like Britain's enemy. In Ibn Sa'ud's view, Italy was Islam's enemy.

On the basis of shared interests, Ibn Sa'ud sought to align his policy with Britain, but not at the expense of his own standing. When he handled the mufti's faction, he passed every word of those exchanges to the British, who could verify their truth. Interestingly, in September 1937, Rendel told Hafez Wahba that he did not think British policy on partition would change, given recrudescent violence in Palestine.[42] Wahba later encouraged Ibn Sa'ud to keep strategic issues in mind, saying, "Palestine is but a small section of the great Arab Fatherland."[43]

Ibn Sa'ud's response to British measures in Palestine was pragmatic, although he made no secret of his feelings. He blamed Lewis Andrews's murder on Jewish intrigue, and described Jews as "a plague in Arab lands." He defended the mufti, and the religious sensibilities that excited renewed violence. He pleaded for more talks, and for Britain to satisfy Arab demands.[44] Yet again, British policymakers worried that Ibn Sa'ud might turn against them. The FO warned the cabinet of Ibn Sa'ud's more belligerent threats of territorial expansion. On the other hand, Colonial Secretary William

Ormsby-Gore didn't think that pan-Arabism should affect British policymaking, and rejected a fixed demographic ratio proposed by the FO and Ibn Saʿud.[45] He may not have appreciated pan-Arabism, but Ormsby-Gore did accept the need to buy Ibn Saʿud's friendship.[46] Gilbert MacKereth observed that the suppression of terrorism was a condition for friendly Anglo-Arab relations.[47]

Percy Loraine, the former HC of Egypt and the only official in the Middle East to warn his superiors about concentrating too much power in the mufti's hands, also addressed Britain's policy problem. Speaking from experience, he explained that British policy toward "the Islamic Middle East" had not been coordinated between the Foreign, Colonial, and India Offices. Despite many divisions, there was "a sort of solidarity amongst Moslems, and a sort of common instinct vis-à-vis the outside." He did not want to underrate the "importance of a friendly Jewry" but said that "in the present state of effervescence of Asia . . . the goodwill of Islam must at the lowest valuation be a no less precious asset." Partition would jeopardize Britain's relations with Muslim states that had made "rapid and really astonishing progress" since the last war.[48]

Ibn Saʿud learned of these interdepartmental debates from Wahba, who told him, "High officials in the foreign office say: 'partition and the use of force will lose us the Arabs and Moslems.' The colonial office says that the Arab States are not to be feared. . . . It is believed that should the Arab States again advance towards (sic: ? confront) the British government owing to the employment of force this would strengthen the position of the Foreign Office officials here."[49] Nothing else in the record better illustrates how the FO advanced its own vision by encouraging Ibn Saʿud to continue doing what he had been all along: articulating a pro-British policy while firmly opposing partition. The king replied, "Your description of the situation at the Foreign Office and Colonial Office in regard to Palestine is useful to us. Let me know what has been verified to you." The British government had asked Ibn Saʿud to keep out, but now he wanted to see whether they would oppose a joint note from himself and other Arab kings for a second time.[50]

Bullard's discussions with Ibn Saʿud reveal the king's anxieties about the region. He could not understand how Mussolini had become so popular despite his bad treatment of Arabs in Libya. He worried about his own fate and popularity, citing the Palestine problem and his hatred for the partition proposal, and he worried that Britain might change policy without consulting him. Bullard reassured Ibn Saʿud of Britain's friendship, and of their mutual trust and openness.[51]

Intelligence and Policy: Retreat from Partition, Advance to War

Arab diplomatic protests against partition were widespread. In August 1937, the Permanent Mandates Commission discussed the royal commission report and expressed its annoyance at Iraq's attempt to intervene on behalf of Palestinians at the League of Nations. The league criticized Britain for not firmly supporting Jewish immigration. It had little faith in Jewish or Arab self-government, and castigated Ormsby-Gore for not imposing martial law. Ormsby-Gore retorted that such a step was contrary to democracy, and would worsen Arab-Jewish tensions; military force could not settle conflict between "right and right." The problem was political. He and the foreign minister, Anthony Eden, agreed that league opinion mattered, but circumstances were changing along with the attitudes of policymakers. In 1939, Britain would attempt to buy five years of peace while refusing to negotiate with the mufti, even though it had negotiated with terrorists elsewhere.[52] In reality, the government sought to supplant the mufti's influence with that of a more influential Arab—Ibn Sa'ud.

Britain was forced to reimagine its future role in the Middle East, and its relationship with local partners. Saudi Arabia had many weaknesses: it was sparsely populated, and did not begin to build a standing army until 1938, the year that oil was discovered in that country. Wahhabism was (and remains) a controversial creed. Yet Ibn Sa'ud had the power that came from being the most admired of independent Arab rulers, and the only viable standard-bearer for a future Arab confederation. His influence in the Arab world was unrivaled.

Given its growing list of strategic problems on the eve of war, Britain eventually rejected the Yishuv's demands for full control over immigration and settlement. Britain feared that militant anti-British nationalism in Palestine could spread in the Middle East and threaten Britain's secure relations with the independent Arab states, as well as its protectorates and mandates.[53] The revolt had exposed Britain's strategic vulnerabilities, so policymakers focused on keeping Palestine quiet and on keeping the region in line behind a supportive leader. This position followed a decade of attempts to find a compromise between Arabs and Jews. Out of options and time, it imposed a new policy. Britain's consultation with the Arab states was a major shift away from its tendency to negotiate the Palestine question directly with Weizmann and the Zionist Organization.

Although the revolt and looming war in Europe forced the issue, the 1939 White Paper did not attempt to appease Palestinian nationalists. British policymakers let the Arab states try to influence the mufti and his inner circle to accept the White Paper, but did not care if they failed. Convinced that the mufti would remain a problem, Britain excluded him from a constitutional solution. Officials believed Britain was just as vulnerable in the Middle East during 1939 as in 1915. During and after the First World War, the need to defeat pan-Islamic propaganda drove British policy in the Middle East. In 1939, Britain occupied even more of the Muslim world and faced far more anticolonial hostility. The pan-Arab movement had sponsored revolt, and Italy was within bombing range of the Suez Canal. These circumstances led Britain to abandon Zionism in favor of a pro-Saudi policy.

Unlike Arab statesmen, Zionist leaders had no leverage over Britain. At the 1939 St. James conference, Weizmann said that "it would be extremely unfortunate if the Jewish Agency had to break off relations with the British government." An FO official commented, "They will be fools if they do but it ~~would~~ might be a great relief to us."[54] Zionists needed Britain more than the other way around, and had ever since 1917. In 1939, for the first time, Britain demonstrated that imbalance. By turning the Palestine question into a pan-Arab one, Kedourie says, the British government did not just "surrender control and initiative in Palestine."[55] Rather, Britain readjusted its Middle Eastern partnerships.

In January 1938, Ibn Saʿud continued his efforts to coordinate his policy toward Britain and Palestine with the other Arab states. He communicated his views to Imam Yahya of Yemen. He did not want to harm Britain or to let any Arab do so. He would not object to Britain holding Palestine until it had stabilized. If partition, Jewish immigration, and land sales were stopped, Arabs could cooperate with Britain. He expressed skepticism of pan-Arabism—Egypt stood apart from Arab affairs, Iraq suffered internal troubles, and states promoted their own interests over the general good.[56] Ibn Saʿud's skepticism would grow with time. Simultaneously, SIS reported that Ibn Saʿud had angered Palestinian leaders when he told them he could only intervene in Palestine if they left the entire matter in his hands.[57]

Once policymakers decided that partition was as unworkable as the mandate, they considered Ibn Saʿud to be integral to any new solution. By the Munich crisis in September 1938, Malcolm MacDonald and the Colonial Office had finally agreed that the time had come to consider alternatives. Sigint records from that month are unavailable to researchers, but much can be gleaned from other evidence, and from the prevailing pattern of Anglo-Saudi relations. A conference at the Colonial Office on 7 September 1938 discussed reinforcements for Palestine. Given the European situation, Palestine would have to wait for these forces, although perhaps the equivalent of a division could be scraped up from Egypt and India. The partition policy was revisited in the context of the cost-balance assessment of moving units to Palestine, at the expense of deployment at home, in Europe, or elsewhere, and the blow to prestige arising from failure in Palestine. Thomas Inskip, minister for coordination of defense, felt the problem was "fundamentally political not military." MacDonald hoped that the Woodhead Commission report would find a policy to end disorder. Sir John Shuckburgh, of the FO, doubted whether abandoning partition would deliver great immediate results. Terrorists, he said, might declare victory and continue "driving the Jews into the sea." Using confident language reflecting his access to sigint, MacDonald countered that ending partition would impress the Arab states and "would definitely result in easing the situation." Similarly, deputy undersecretary of state Sir Lancelot Oliphant said that "the mere decision to give up partition would have an enormous effect upon Ibn Saʿud as well as upon Egypt and other Arab states. There would be a great détente."[58]

From the end of September, Britain's diplomatic strategy at the FO Middle East committee focused on "measures to influence minor powers and Arab states" during a future war. Some states, like Saudi Arabia, might need a bribe, nothing more. Egypt's position was more complicated.[59] By October, Whitehall had resolved to reinforce the army in Palestine and defeat the rebellion through "military control." Yet it also entertained restricting land sales and immigration. At first it resolved to avoid discussing restrictions on Jews, but then suddenly considered that topic at interdepartmental meetings.[60] In November, as middle and senior bureaucrats debated Britain's Zionist policy, the cabinet planned the St. James conference for early 1939. Arab states would be invited. Incredibly, Britain asked Ibn Saʿud whether the mufti and his party should be allowed to participate. Ibn Saʿud replied that he "had no use for the Mufti, and would not be troubled by his exclusion."[61] MacDonald held that in the long run, Ibn Saʿud's friendship would be "worth more to this country [Britain] than the friendship of the other Arab princes." Nonetheless, consultation with Iraq and Egypt would have to be part of the program.[62] The conference sought consultation and intervention from the Arab states. The Saudi delegation was the one that mattered. It led secret mediation with the other Arab states.

The JIC and chiefs of staff adopted the same view as the cabinet. They firmed up the measures required to influence Arab leaders, especially Ibn Saʿud. His support in a future war was not expected, but the JIC estimated that his "benevolent neutrality" was crucial given potentially "lavish territorial offers from the enemy." Bribery might be the only antidote—Ibn Saʿud already was inclined to support Britain, although a German legation had just arrived at Jeddah. The JIC's position on Palestine is not well recorded beyond the fear that Arab hostility could materialize if the St. James conference did not produce an acceptable policy.[63] Should it fail, Britain could face further years of revolt or lose the territory in a war. The rewards, should it succeed, included a new direction for the empire.

The Intelligence Record and the St. James Conference

Before the St. James meeting, a conference was held in Cairo between the Arab states and the Palestinians in order to obtain some support from the nationalists. The Arab delegations did not coordinate positions, but simply aimed to acquaint the delegates with one another before proceeding to London, to hear out the Palestinian delegation, and to prop up Egypt as a leading Arab state. Anglo-Saudi connivance was apparently unknown to the delegations. The first Cairo meeting agreed that "the basic point was to endeavor to separate the Palestine case from that of international Jewry."[64] This, in fact, remained Britain's aim in upholding White Paper restrictions between 1939 and 1948.[65]

At the St. James conference, British sigint observed the reports of all diplomats back to their home countries. Even Weizmann's cables were intercepted. The Foreign and Colonial Offices were the main consumers of these reports, which were considered important. During the conference, the turnaround time between interception and the final presentation of an English-language translation/interpretation fell from an average of two to three weeks to two to three days. Likewise, GC&CS aimed to improve its translations. Its civilian interpreter among the cryptanalytic staff at Sarafand, according to an unsigned memorandum, knew "Arabic and Turkish perfectly but [his] knowledge of English is poor and his translations of Arabic telegrams are now causing considerable anxiety so we have asked that the Arabic texts should also be sent back."[66] GC&CS began to centralize its Arabic translations on the eve of the St. James conference.

Probably the most important signal was a response to Faysal, Ibn Saʿud's son and delegate to the conference. When Faysal described the breakdown of the conference in March 1939, his father emphasized his desire that Jewish immigration stop: "The important matter is that of immigration, and if the British insist on continuing immigration and do not stop it this indicates a lack of good will on their part and I perceive no good in it. It also shows they are departing from the views previously held by them." At minimum, Ibn Saʿud would accept a temporary limitation on Jewish immigration, which might lead to ultimate stoppage.[67]

Two days after the conference closed in failure, Anglo-Arab talks continued. Ibn Saʿud told Faysal, "It is no secret to them [Britain] what effect this failure will have in Islamic and Arab countries; nor are they unaware of the scorn of their enemies who are exploiting the situation." The Palestine question would echo throughout the Islamic world. Propaganda was working in Egypt and Iraq against both Britain and Ibn Saʿud. His prime interest was his relationship with Britain. "This is an essential matter that may cause injury to my country," he said. "I therefore want to be quite certain regarding Britain's moral and material support to me in everything that may cause harm to my country from any direction whatever." He also wanted to preserve the status quo of borders.[68]

This position was very familiar—it followed a pattern that had emerged years earlier and served Britain since the Abyssinian crisis. The next day Faysal met MacDonald and Frederick Butler (of the FO) for two hours. The British government communicated proposals to Faysal and asked him to secretly meet each delegation to the conference. They clearly chose the Saudi delegation to lead Egypt, Iraq, and the others because of Ibn Saʿud's prestige and influence, and his place in British strategy and diplomacy. MacDonald and Butler gave Faysal an opportunity to secure a new policy from Britain, with the other Arab states behind him, and in the absence of the Zionist delegation now that the conference had failed. Faysal could not get all the delegations to agree on a proposal, but he came close. It was impossible to define a transition period for independence, or to achieve independence without Jewish-Arab cooperation, and the Jews would not cooperate without immigration guarantees from Arabs. Faysal returned the next day with the Iraqi and Egyptian delegates, who offered a new proposal—the transition period would be limited regardless of Jewish cooperation.[69] Ibn Saʿud added that the question of the period of transition to independence was secondary in importance to a stoppage of immigration and land sales.[70]

Neville Chamberlain, the prime minister, apparently accepted a counterproposal by the Saudi, Iraqi, and Egyptian delegates after they were invited to respond to his own. The Arab counterproposal was the basis for negotiation until the White Paper was issued. It set the stage for the end of the mandate, limits to Jewish immigration and land purchasing, Palestinian independence, and a plan of transition and preparation through civil service appointments for Palestinians. Chamberlain, MacDonald, and the Iraqi, Saudi, and Egyptian delegations redrafted the proposals two more times between 20 and 24 March.[71]

The exact text of Chamberlain's final letter to Ibn Saʿud is unavailable, but is believed to be the main substance of what became the 1939 White Paper policy.[72] Most importantly, Britain intended to impose the solution on the Zionists. The Iraqi delegate reported one version of the letter: that independence would be granted upon the end of the disturbances, there would be a legislative assembly, and the mandate would terminate. Immigration would continue with limits, but end after five years.[73] Jewish Agency chairman David Ben-Gurion claimed that Chamberlain told him that this policy would not outlive the war. Regardless of the truth of that claim, Ben-Gurion never believed the policy would be implemented.[74]

After the Saudi-led counterproposal was accepted as the basis for further negotiations, the Arab delegations left London and met again in Cairo. During April, the Arab delegations sifted through the various proposals and attempted to formulate a joint position, and to convince the Palestinians to approve. The postconference meetings failed to win over the Palestinian leadership for two reasons. The latter mistrusted the British government and rejected anything less than full and immediate independence. The mufti's ego played its part as well. The Palestinians steadfastly rejected any deal without the mufti's backing.

The main sticking points on the text of the White Paper were the issues of the transition period to independence and Jewish immigration. The Iraqi delegate in Cairo reported his conversation with Jerusalem mayor Hussein Khalidi, who had recently met with the Egyptian government. The Egyptians, the delegate said, "asked for information on the situation from every aspect and the meeting was closed so that the Prime Minister might try and persuade the British government to set a limit to the transition period, reduce it if possible, and include the Palestinians in the government [during] the first stage of transition. I learned that should these demands be complied with the Palestinians will facilitate the acceptance of a fixed number of Jews and likewise make concessions in the land question."[75] This outcome might have suited all parties except the Zionists—even the British government, said the Iraqi delegate, wanted Egypt to achieve such a settlement. However, the Palestinian delegation deferred to the mufti's opinion and feared they would achieve nothing if the rebellion collapsed. For his part, Chaim Weizmann simply begged the Egyptian prime minister to ask Britain to delay a new policy announcement for six months, allegedly offering him £150,000 and a promise to stop all Jewish immigration for six months. Egypt refused both offers.[76]

Meanwhile, Fuad Hamza had taken the new proposal to the exiled Palestinians in Syria. This development received particularly close attention from GC&CS, which turned over the intercept within a single day. Fuad explicitly told Ibn Sa'ud that he "explained to Palestinians latest scheme which we agreed upon with British after conference, as reported by Faysal." The Palestinians seemed inclined to accept the offer, but wanted to reduce the transition to five years from ten, to immediately be included in government in the form of a cabinet, and to wait until after a public declaration to restore calm. They would define immigration limits and refused anything higher than thirty thousand over the five-year period. A future Palestinian cabinet could be more flexible on those numbers, and on land transactions. They also offered to restore calm after amnesty from emergency regulations and punishments, and for armed men "and revolutionaries" still at large.[77]

Compromise seemed to emerge, but the mufti made more demands that Britain refused to meet. Faysal told the French foreign minister that the mufti and "the exiles had not learnt the lesson that they would expose Palestine to new dangers if they persisted in their present policy and in their well known [attitude to] the Jews."[78] Having asked the Palestinians for a response to the Arab states' proposals, Ibn Sa'ud waited for almost two weeks for the mufti's reply to Fuad Hamza. On 27 April, he sent Fuad another message: "Inform Mufti that we are prepared to assist Palestine Arabs but do not know their terms. We know British and Jews delaying settlement for their own ends, for when freed from international complications they will solve problem to suit themselves. Now is a chance not to be missed. Main problem seems to us to be immigration, land sales and general amnesty; others can be settled later. Send me precise maximum and minimum demands of Palestine Arabs."[79]

In other words, the Palestinian demand for amnesty should not obstruct the path to independence. Faysal cabled his father saying that the latest draft policy offered no guarantee about future independence. He supported his father's view that after ten years, British and Zionist interests might again dominate those of the Arabs. In mid-April, the Palestine government told the US consul that the new formula "did not constitute a specific promise for eventual independence" since the difficult questions, especially those having to do with holy places, were too complicated to be left to "necessarily inept local authorities."[80] Yet that view quickly changed because of the Arab meetings in Cairo.

The War Office's military intelligence directorate was optimistic. While many questions remained "fluid," they noted that "a great factor in our [Britain's] favour is that Arabs have achieved one of their main objects in that fear that HMG would facilitate ultimate Jewish predominance has been removed."[81] British strategists knew that policy on Jewish immigration was certain to change in the Arabs' favor, although nothing was yet decided.

Ibn Sa'ud asked Fuad Hamza for information again on 28 April, since he was about to meet Reader Bullard and had nothing to offer him. The gist of the reply exists only in part, as GC&CS reported that the original was badly mutilated (usually a consequence of mistakes by the sender, or bad weather). The mufti seemingly accepted the new draft in principle, and was ready to send a delegate to Cairo, but was waiting for a personal invitation from the Egyptians. The Palestinian leader's vanity, or even megalomania, was interfering with his people's interests.[82]

Iraq, Egypt, and Saudi Arabia found themselves caught between Palestinian and British interests. They spent the final Cairo meetings convincing the Palestinians to accept the British proposals, while at the same time pressing Britain to alter them. They achieved many concessions from Britain during this process. Jewish immigration would be limited. Transition to Palestinian independence was broken into two phases, with practical constitutional self-government in full practice within five years. Palestinians would be trained in government through civil service jobs. Amnesty would be neither general nor immediate, but gradual, and available only to cooperative leaders. The mufti refused to accept a deal that did not guarantee his amnesty.

The Egyptians implored the Palestinians to accept independence despite the limits. "How many European states, independent in principle," they said, "are now really living under the protection of the Greater Powers? Had not Great Britain herself been forced to introduce obligatory military service under French pressure? Independence is a relative word." Moreover, the Palestinians would avoid "extermination and ruin," be revived with time, and become trained in administration, preparing them for complete independence. The Egyptians highlighted the opportunity: "They are not called upon to sign any document, but simply to accept it—some of them would become ministers." The Palestinians replied, "If we accept, the revolution will end."[83]

Perhaps the mufti's series of escalating gambles had left them in a position from which they could not retreat. Or perhaps the Palestinians feared losing armed resistance as their only bargaining chip. They were warned that their revolution would be crushed anyway, and that compromise with Britain was necessary. They responded that the current Anglo-Arab proposal "proves the evil intentions of the British government." After two decades of failed negotiations and three years of armed conflict, they simply did not trust Britain's intentions. Britain's unwillingness to pardon the mufti, his closest associates, and the rebel leadership, or to immediately include them in government, demonstrated that even if Palestine became independent, the Palestinians would not run it. Warned again of the coming war, and that the Arab states could not again intervene on their behalf, the Palestinians responded, tellingly, "When the revolution was started, we had aims in view to attain. We cannot now tell our people to stop the revolution because we got some high posts."[84] Feeling committed after having risked so much at so high a price, the Palestinians were determined to see the revolution through.

The mufti wired that when his colleague, probably 'Izzat Darwaza, had returned from Cairo, they studied British government correspondence with the Arab states on the Palestine proposal. "There is nothing in them [the cables] to help understand fully intentions of Great Britain," he said. "In the same manner the modifications proposed do not contain any definite limit which will inspire tranquility."[85] Having reached some agreement, on 30 April the Egyptians communicated the latest secret proposal to Britain, but one of the delegates in Cairo had leaked it to the UK *Daily Telegraph* a few days prior. The Yishuv erupted in protest. British officials began to lose their patience. The ambassador to Egypt, Sir Miles Lampson, reported that the Egyptian prime minister responded that "it was pretty difficult for him to control all Arabs and he mentioned Hafez Wahba as being particularly indiscreet. With so many Orientals in the know it is hopeless to expect there will not be some leakages." The leaked report mentioned a federal scheme for Palestine, which had not been included in the latest draft. Arab states saw the exclusion of a specific mention of independent or autonomous government as partition in disguise. No doubt the leak and the representations of the Arab governments caused Britain to reintroduce that clause in the final text.[86]

In the first week of May, Jamal visited Ibn Sa'ud at Bahrain to go over the proposals as the Palestinian and Arab state delegations did the same in Cairo. They waited for Britain's official response to the proposal of 30 April. The British political agent at Bahrain reported on festivities that both he and Jamal attended. Ibn Sa'ud went to great lengths to demonstrate publicly his close and warm feelings toward Britain, and made several rude jokes about Hitler and Mussolini while predicting the latter's downfall for interfering in Muslim affairs. Ibn Sa'ud emphasized his intention to assist Britain on the Palestine question, offering a clear signal to Jamal.[87]

On 5 May, the FO sent Ibn Sa'ud an informal letter about his consultation with Jamal in which it offered an explanation for the delayed response. Its tone had changed. Clearly annoyed that Jamal was brought so closely, and that he was privy to HMG's secret communications with the Arab states, the FO emphasized that these consultations with the Arab governments had been informal but greatly appreciated. It did not feel bound to any proposal made during the St. James meeting, which had failed to generate any agreement. Consequently, Britain would impose its own solution on both Arabs and Jews. The Arab delegations overplayed their hand while futilely pursuing Palestinian agreement. Nevertheless, Britain's formal reply to the Arab proposals was issued on 6 May, and this ultimately formed the basis of the final text of the White Paper. It proudly read, "British proposals will entirely remove the most important grievances of the Palestine Arabs. They remove fear of political domination by the Jews."[88] There would be no Jewish state, and severe restrictions on Jewish immigration. It was worded more cautiously than prior drafts in its description of self-government. Ibn Sa'ud's base demand for limitations to Jewish immigration was clearly worded in contrast to the constitutional clauses, which, as he had said during St. James, were of secondary importance.

Although the Palestinians never supported the proposals or the final White Paper, British interests had been secured. Britain appreciated the Arab states' mediation, emphasized the importance of their joint position, and thanked each government for their assistance. The independent Arab states had eased Britain's difficulties in trying to draft a new policy. If and when peace was to be restored as a result of the conference, the FO emphasized, "a considerable part of the credit will be due to the Saudi Arabian delegates."[89] The FO then proceeded to iron out the details directly with Ibn Sa'ud. Immigration would be fixed at seventy-five thousand over five years, and there would be no clear guarantee of self-government during that period. Anglo-Saudi relations had improved dramatically because of Ibn Sa'ud's leadership on the Palestine question.

On 15 May, days before the White Paper was issued, Ibn Sa'ud cabled his minister in Baghdad, saying that he would tell Britain he could not influence the Palestinians to accept the White Paper if the text did not explain that British policy was an imposition, which resulted from lack of agreement at St. James.[90] Ibn Sa'ud wished to convey that an understanding had been reached between Britain and the Arab governments that covered items not detailed in the final text of the White Paper. Above all, the Palestinian leaders wanted Britain to address them directly, and ask them to call off the revolt and return to Palestine under amnesty. Britain would never meet this demand.[91] The Arab states still attempted to secure Palestinian agreement by finding other routes to amnesty. For example, they proposed to include Palestinian leaders other than the mufti's closest associates in government, but to bring in the latter sometime after a cabinet ministry was formed. The Arab states knew that no pardon for the mufti would be forthcoming for a few years. They assumed that British designs for a Palestinian civil service would be enough.[92] In a gamble, the Iraqi government threatened Britain by saying that if the White Paper excluded the mufti from Palestine, Iraq would call on the Palestinians to reject the new scheme.[93] Britain called Iraq's bluff. Working until the last minute, the Arab delegations achieved adjustments in the text of the

White Paper that supported Palestinian demands, especially the inclusion of a five-year schedule until the emergence of a new constitution.

The White Paper was published on 17 May, reshaping the future of Palestine. Jewish immigration and land purchases were severely restricted. The government aimed, albeit vaguely, to foster a Palestinian civil service in preparation for independence and leadership over a single, federal state of Palestine. The twenty-two-year Zionist policy was scrapped in consultation with Arab statesmen, and against the wishes of Britain's traditional negotiating partners, accustomed to influencing high-level policy decisions. This change was made to gain support from Arab statesmen, especially Ibn Saʿud. It excluded the mufti. The British attempted to foster some Jewish-Arab cooperation, but could not have hoped for much. They knew early on that the mufti had instructed his delegate, Jamal, via the Iraqis, to reject British proposals, causing the collapse of the St. James conference.[94] After the White Paper was issued, Ibn Saʿud simply told the Palestinians that if they rejected the policy, he would take no further responsibility for its future or implementation. The mufti cabled Ibn Saʿud the ASC's rejection of the White Paper, saying that it rested on the St. James proposals that it had refused, and that it did not bring into immediate force Arab demands, among other unacceptable points.[95]

Meanwhile the policy emerged as a solution imposed on both Palestinians and Zionists. It aimed to cultivate a new, more cooperative, more technocratic Palestinian leadership, and to freeze the demographic balance.

A New Narrative

Ibn Saʿud, "Bismarck of Arabia," had mastered realpolitik. British sigint confirmed his position: that he was hostile to Britain's enemies, warm to British interests, and influential in the pan-Islamic and pan-Arab worlds. The international situation forced Britain to ensure that in a future world war it would have a reliable base of support outside its own mandated territories, protectorates, and semi-independent client states. Anglo-Saudi relations became a partnership of shared interest. Ibn Saʿud's willingness to tolerate his Hashemite rivals—Britain's longstanding partners—facilitated this partnership. This was a familiar pattern: Ibn Saʿud would support British policy in exchange for British guarantees over his borders. Ibn Saʿud's importance in shaping Palestine's future cannot be overlooked. His close collaboration with Britain was fundamental to the end of the Zionist policy.

From 1937 to 1939, sigint was perhaps Britain's most important intelligence asset in the Middle East. It guided British diplomacy to a policy that maximized benefits to Britain during an expected war. The White Paper won

Ibn Saʿud's benevolent neutrality during the war, and more. The Arab leader helped extend stability across the region through pan-Arab treaty negotiations. Early in the war, Bullard concluded that "we need have no fear that Saudi Arabia may become a center for anti-British intrigue during the war." Ibn Saʿud had excluded German propagandists from his country, and ordered the censorship of public discussion of the war.[96]

Bullard was convinced that Britain could count on Ibn Saʿud's "benevolent neutrality in this war—unless, as I have frequently said, the Allies should be defeated."[97] He rejected fears that Saudi Arabia had gone pro-German after the visit of a Saudi delegation to Germany. Ibn Saʿud's word could be taken at face value since his friendship with Britain was based on shared interests. More importantly, trust was supported by sigint. Even in the wake of the military disasters of 1940, the Colonial Office concluded that "Ibn Saʿud is rendering us the best service that can be expected from him by his present attitude of benevolent neutrality."[98] Within days, sigint proved such assessments correct: Ibn Saʿud encouraged Iraq and Syria to keep the calm, maintain national unity, and not do anything that would invite aggression from any of the belligerents.[99] His advice went unheeded. He saw the fall of France as a source not of opportunity, but of danger. For the next two perilous years, Britain had three unlikely friends in the Middle East: Saudis, Turks, and Zionists.

Despite these achievements, the White Paper did not free Britain from the mandate's contradictions. As will be seen in the next chapter, it introduced further problems, and further exposed Britain's inability to enforce its policies. With war looming, the White Paper achieved its geostrategic objectives. It did not resolve competing Arab or Jewish claims over the land, nor did it satisfy Palestinian demands. The conflict between the Palestinians and Britain simmered, while the White Paper sparked a new conflict between Britain and the Zionists.

CHAPTER 10

The Consequences of the White Paper

The Zionist delegation to St. James saw the writing on the wall. Reuven Zaslani reported from London that from the moment Weizmann threatened to end negotiations in February, Lord Halifax and Malcolm MacDonald began to issue threats of their own. England was the greatest protector of Jews in these troubling times and had opened its own doors to refugees. If the Zionists issued a premature statement on the talks, Britain's relationship with the Jews might change. Zaslani concluded, "Generally, the chances are not good. . . . MacDonald has already made commitments on a few matters that we could in no way agree to."[1] With the Arab states in the spotlight, Zaslani knew that Anglo-Zionist relations would be transformed. Zaslani was a rising star in intelligence and liaison with British security; the White Paper complicated his role, but never diminished the warmth he showed his British counterparts.

The White Paper infuriated the Yishuv, and the Anglo-Zionist conflict began. Enforcing the new regulations and disarming the Yishuv were pipe dreams, as military control was applied inconsistently while Britain's attention was focused on European battlefields. Crackdowns led to further friction and popular protest during the early months of the war. The Yishuv also had its limits—exhausted by early 1940 after endless protests, and stricken by the military disasters of May–June 1940, the Yishuv eventually began to cooperate. Revisionists, however, fully cooperated once their militant leaders were imprisoned.

British intelligence was at first surprised by the terrorism aimed at them, but because of good relationships with their Zionist counterparts, they were able to limit the ability of the militant Irgun to operate under its commander in chief, David Raziel. The government also cracked down on the Haganah, and arrested forty-three officers for illegal drilling and carrying of arms—exactly what Britain had trained them to do. MacDonald pushed for disarmament from Whitehall, as he saw the Haganah as an obstacle to the implementation of the White Paper. After Germany overran France in 1940, military necessity put the conflict on pause. Haganah and Irgun members were released from prison, and began to support the British military effort.

The war made the White Paper's ultimate aims unenforceable. Britain maintained restrictions on Jewish immigration and land transfers. However, because of wartime needs, military and intelligence cooperation with the Yishuv was strengthened. If Britain were ever to create a binational Palestinian state, it would have to do so with the assent of the Yishuv's military and security institutions. Haganah and Zionist intelligence agencies were increasingly prepared to enforce Zionist interests, which, during the war, came to include statehood.

Anglo-Zionist Conflict

Conflict between the Yishuv and Britain revolved around three issues: the White Paper restricted Jewish immigration severely, and the government began deporting illegals; restrictions on land transfers for Jews became even harsher in early 1940; and the government pursued disarmament of all of Palestine, and began to target the Haganah. To manage Zionist responses to these restrictions, British intelligence and policy focused on terrorism, non-cooperation, and negotiations around disarmament. The Jewish Agency and other large Yishuv institutions lacked a coherent response to these problems, or to the war. They resorted to protest and symbols of defiance. A smaller segment of the Yishuv rejected these restrictions violently.

Terrorism

The Irgun Zva'i Leumi slowly broke from the Haganah in the early 1930s. During the 1936–37 interlude in the Arab revolt, violence against the Yishuv gradually increased. As rumors about partition emerged, the defense of the

Yishuv took on a new urgency and the old debate resurfaced between the larger left-leaning Haganah and Haganah B, which had broken away in 1931 in protest of the socialist politicization of the Haganah and control over arms stores. Haganah B commanders were persuaded to reunify with the larger left-wing body, but Revisionist political leaders refused.

Haganah B reorganized as the Irgun Zva'i Leumi in April 1937 in order to consolidate discipline within its ranks. It was also frustrated by the Haganah's policy of restraint in the face of Arab terrorism. The Irgun expelled moderates, as negotiations for reunification with the Haganah failed. Ideology, policy, territorial ambition, control of arms, and socialist politicization proved insurmountable obstacles. Jabotinsky believed, naively, that the Irgun would follow the discipline of the Revisionist Party. In fact, discipline depended on the organization's commander.

Previously, Jabotinsky had sidelined the fascistic element under Ahimeir's Biryonim. By 1937 he was struggling to reconcile his own activist message with the murder and violence of his followers. Unlike Jabotinsky, the younger radicals would not believe that Britain could safeguard Jewish interests. The royal commission proposals widened these divisions. To Revisionists, partition was a grave offense, and this was the second time that Britain had sought to shrink the future Jewish state. Jabotinsky's split with Weizmann was partly motivated by their differences in 1921 over the separation of Transjordan from Palestine. Although he was no terrorist, Jabotinsky always tailored his messaging to the audience. He told militant youth that partition could cause an uprising against Britain, but doubted that would happen. In contrast, in 1938 he told Haganah chief Eliyahu Golomb that the Yishuv might have to accept partition as a fait accompli. As the Irgun command expressed its increasing desire to prepare retaliatory attacks against Arabs, Jabotinsky distanced himself from the details of its operations.[2]

When the revolt renewed in autumn 1937, the Irgun was no longer restricted by its ties to the Haganah and its policy of restraint, or even by its connections to the New Zionist Organization. It answered terror with terror, often arbitrarily choosing Arab civilian targets in response to attacks on Jews. While the Haganah also departed from its official policy of restraint with its field companies (Plugot Sadeh, or "Fosh") and Wingate's SNS, it never sought revenge through its operations. Haganah operations usually fell within the framework of the British military effort or static defense, though it also helped create new colonies through "tower and stockade" operations— the overnight establishment of small settlements such as Hanita.

At the height of the Irgun's bloody campaign in summer 1938, three terrorists were arrested by a police patrol after a failed attack on an Arab bus, undertaken against the Irgun's orders. Britain had not yet developed an intelligence apparatus to handle Jewish terrorism—dumb luck led to the terrorists' capture. The court found one man not guilty for reasons of insanity, and sentenced the other two to hang. One was underage, so his sentence was commuted to life imprisonment. The other, Shlomo Ben-Yosef, was executed, to the horror of the Yishuv. It produced another wedge between the Left and Right, as the CID observed the failure of Jabotinsky to make political capital of the affair, while the Histadrut blasted him for not joining their policy of restraint.[3]

Jabotinsky had pleaded for Ben-Yosef's life at several levels. Most believed the execution stemmed from the desire of Harold MacMichael, recently installed as high commissioner, to demonstrate Britain's evenhandedness to the Arab states. Ben-Gurion saw the decision as an example of ineptitude, as it convinced Arabs of nothing and sparked a far more violent wave of Arab and Irgun terrorism. After the execution, Jabotinsky authorized the Irgun to prepare a new campaign. That campaign took the lives of seventy-six Arabs, forty-four Jews, and twelve members of British security forces. Irgun attacks on civilians alienated most of the Yishuv, according to the CID. They also angered British officers friendly to the Yishuv, such as Dudley Clarke, and caused others to fear that the country's problems were insoluble. Meanwhile, Jabotinsky reconsidered means to reunify the Irgun and the Haganah, but their differences blocked that end until the rise of Israel.[4] Executions such as that of Ben-Yosef eroded the Irgun's sympathy for Britain. The White Paper annihilated it.

All parties saw the White Paper as a betrayal. The Yishuv erupted. As the Labor Zionist parties organized public demonstrations and protests, the Irgun planned its first operations against British targets. From 1937 to 1939, Irgun terrorism targeted Arabs. Its Jewish and British victims were collateral damage, from the terrorists' point of view. Jabotinsky wanted a shocking demonstration of defiance—a short revolution to occupy government offices. His plan never materialized. He had little say in military matters.

SIS provided a report on the emergence of the Irgun, likely based on its relationships with the Haganah. SIS doubted the possibility of amalgamating the Haganah and the Irgun, even if the Left and Right in Zionism could reconcile their differences. The Haganah was modeled on the British Army, whereas the Irgun "had adopted a European system"—a reference to its revolutionary underground character. The report accurately described the different right-wing bodies such as Betar, and the structure of Zionism's militant Right. Jabotinsky had prepared the Irgun for a much larger immigration influx, and so the Irgun's structure was designed for a force about ten times its actual size of about 1,500 active members. The Irgun's wishful thinking inflated British estimates.[5] SIS also forwarded a CID report on the Irgun's commander, David Raziel, after his arrest in May 1939.[6]

GSI and the CID tended not to report much about Jewish terrorism until after the White Paper. British intelligence was unprepared for the phenomenon. Their only source on the subject was the Jewish Agency. In considering the Yishuv's reaction to the White Paper, the CID anticipated tax strikes and other antigovernment demonstrations. These measures did not worry the CID or the government, which assumed that they would harm only the JA and other Yishuv institutions. It also assumed that propaganda would be the Yishuv's primary weapon against the White Paper. Neither the CID or military intelligence imagined that the Irgun would attack British police and troops. The Irgun's anti-British campaign began with the sabotage of government infrastructure such as electrical stations, telephone poles, and mailboxes. It started an illegal broadcast station called "the Voice of Free Zion" where it bragged about its operations, and rapidly increased recruitment. The CID believed that this activity was aimed at drawing attention to the White Paper at the forthcoming sitting of the Permanent Mandates Commission in Geneva. It also knew that Yishuv leaders, especially the Jewish Agency, were considering whether they might need to help to combat the Irgun.[7]

In July, the Irgun attacked a public radio station and some smaller government targets. On 26 August 1939, using a remote explosive device, Irgun terrorists assassinated two senior CID officers, Ralph Cairns—head of the Jewish department of special branch—and his Arab branch counterpart, Ronald Barker. Cairns had just overseen the capture of some Irgun members. He was replaced by Tom Wilkin. Wilkin's girlfriend, Shoshana Borochov, daughter of the prominent Labor Zionist leader Dov Ber Borochov, helped him become one of the few British policemen who were fluent in Hebrew. Wilkin was well liked in Yishuv political circles, and used his charm and linguistic skill to elicit good information during interrogations. The CID responded swiftly to the Irgun attack. On 31 August, Wilkin and other officers stormed an Irgun safe house in Tel Aviv, arresting most of the Irgun leadership, including Avraham Stern, Hanoch Kalai, Aharon Heichmann, Yaacov Eliav, and Haim Lubinsky.[8] In detention they joined their commander, David Raziel, who had been held since May. With the core of the Irgun in prison, the Revisionist party adapted. It opted for respectability and cooperation instead of antagonism. In contrast, chaos dominated the Jewish Agency's response to the war.

GSI summaries from the outbreak of war through early 1940 focused on Arab rebel activity more than the Haganah or the Irgun. This situation changed after the government escalated its restrictions on land transactions on 28 February 1940. The new policy divided the country into zones—each featuring different restrictions. The regulations made it impossible for Jews to purchase land outside the coastal plain. The Yishuv responded with strikes and demonstrations that caused minor clashes with police and troops. Terrorism, however, was less of a problem with the senior Irgun leadership behind bars.

Throughout March 1940, the police increasingly relied on British troops to handle Jewish demonstrators, curfew violators, and left-right gang violence. Continuing a push for disarmament by the Colonial Office, troops and police increased their raids on Jewish arms caches. Raids that discovered illegal arms led to the arrest of the local Jewish TAP members, all of whom were Haganah members responsible for settlement security.[9]

The Jewish Agency hoped that organized demonstrations would draw Britain's and the United States' attention to their problems. However, driven by exhaustion, and assisted by more coherence from the political leadership, they reverted to cooperation by 1940. The JA began to provide notice for demonstrations and to police the crowds on its own. GSI reported that the Revisionists remained aloof during the demonstrations. They had not resorted to terrorism, but instead used the moment to score points against the JA and the Histadrut for poor leadership.[10]

Ironically, the JA and Revisionists had reversed their policies. The JA issued militant antigovernment propaganda and sought public confrontation, while the Revisionists argued that the regulations were temporary, could be reversed after the war, and were less important than fighting Hitler.[11] Public demonstrations exhausted a weary public. In late April eleven Haganah members and colony administrators received heavy sentences for an arms cache discovered at Ben Shemen. The JA and the Histadrut tried to organize a general strike in response, which failed simply because the public was tired of such futile gestures.[12]

Internal divisions within Zionist institutions frustrated the emergence of a coherent response to the war, the plight of European Jews, and restrictions in Palestine.[13] Only the German invasion of Holland, Belgium, and France shocked the Yishuv out of its divided, disorganized, and complacent state. The response was not immediately positive. In late May, GSI reported on the Yishuv's "bad attack of nerves," aggravated by "wild alarmist and defeatist rumors, e.g. that the Mufti had returned to Palestine, that pro-German demonstrations followed by mass-arrests had occurred in Jaffa, that London had been bombed, etc.'" One paper accused "the Jewish Nation of suffering from 'communal masochism'" for listening to German propaganda. GSI led a press campaign, which it believed calmed those nerves.[14]

The Revisionist Party and the World Zionist Organization both focused on the question of who would represent Zionist interests at a peace conference after the war, basing their expectations on the triumphs of 1919. Both also focused on propaganda and diplomacy for the creation of a Jewish army. They sought to replicate past success, as they believed Jewish military contributions to the First World War were foundational to the Balfour Declaration. After France fell, Zionists of both the Left and the Right, as well as the government, became less confrontational. The government canceled financial rewards for surrendered arms, and police searches became less frequent. Suddenly offenses were treated less seriously by British authorities who had bigger fish to catch, like Nazi agents in Palestine's German settlements. In one illustrative example, police ignored a small Jewish arms reserve at Tiberias and instead focused on Nazi documents discovered at Beit Lahm and Waldheim.[15] German settlements founded in the Ottoman period were converted to internment camps at the outbreak of war, and some Germans were expelled to Australia, their property confiscated.

The Irgun prisoners—thirty-eight in all—were released in June 1940 as part of a ceasefire agreement with the government, which faced new crises with the fall of France and Italy's entry into the war. One of the former prisoners, Avraham Stern, broke from the Irgun shortly after his release to found Lohmei Herut Yisrael (Freedom Fighters for Israel), known to the British as the Stern Gang. Stern rejected the Irgun's ceasefire and cooperation with Britain, and naively sought alliance with Germany and Italy. Stern was caught again in 1942 by Wilkin and, euphemistically, was "shot while trying to escape." In retaliation, the Stern Gang assassinated Wilkin in 1944.[16]

Disarmament

From the early 1920s, British agencies periodically looked into Haganah arms smuggling and illegal immigration. Officials knew that arms added to insecurity, but without another way of protecting outlying settlements, they gave the Haganah official sanction. During the Arab revolt, Haganah arms contributed to the restoration of British control. With the advent of the White Paper, British policymakers and security agencies had to consider more than public security. Haganah arms and illegal immigration still angered Arabs, but they also endangered the White Paper's prescription for Palestinian self-government. Britain depended on the Jewish Agency's cooperation in the war and in the ongoing struggle to enforce security but was threatened by the agency's increasing belligerence and self-assertive behavior as an authority independent of the government.

The White Paper also changed attitudes toward the tens of thousands of Jews serving the British police in one form or another. It was an open secret that the Haganah was expanding its military capabilities through this cooperation, which the government sought to limit. After Jewish TAP members were accused of exploding several houses during a raid on Arab villages (a normal British practice at the time), police were prohibited from using TAP, supernumeraries, or the Jewish Settlement Police in operations in Arab areas or on roads in the southern district. These personnel were to be restricted to close defense of settlements.[17] The pattern of cooperation with those groups established by Wingate, Simonds, and other officers was coming to a temporary end. However, the needs of various crises would restore and enhance this type of cooperation by 1940, and again in 1941. The fall of France drove a reversal of White Paper attitudes toward Jewish military cooperation, beginning a cyclical pattern where cooperation was conditioned by Britain's relative success or failure in the Middle Eastern theater.

Overall, army policy was not as friendly as some officers wished. By autumn 1939, the army had begun to distribute instructions for a procedure for searching Jewish villages for arms. The procedure, far less methodical than that used in Arab villages, required troops to search for arms "when there is evidence that arms have been used for illegal purposes." Such evidence included illegal military drills, and also reprisals against Arab attacks (previously sanctioned by the army, and led by Wingate). The police, not the army, were now to handle such searches. Snap army searches of Jewish villages were legal under emergency regulations, but the army wished to avoid public incidents. Troops were instructed to check with their headquarters before beginning such an operation.[18] This practice increased the chances for the Haganah to receive early warning through its agents or listening services. Even as the White Paper policy emerged, the Palestine government's security committee concluded that its response to the illegal construction of Jewish settlements should be consultation with the Jewish Agency.[19] Some officers supported the Zionist cause and felt that the White Paper wronged the Yishuv. They used war necessity as an excuse to shelter the Haganah. Reuven Zaslani's hospitality policy began to pay dividends.

Search procedures in October 1939 led to the arrest of forty-three Haganah members, including the future Israeli chief of staff Moshe Dayan and Wingate's SNS deputy, Zvi Brenner. Charged with carrying illegal arms and performing illegal military drills, most of "the forty-three," as they became known in the Jewish press, were sentenced to ten years. Brenner received a life sentence. After the incident, the Jewish Agency claimed that illegal arms had been used with the full knowledge and consent of the police and army to ward off attacks on settlements. Although true in principle, this was a slight mischaracterization. Settlement police were meant to defend settlements, and to be subordinate to the government. The Haganah's ambitions and capabilities were beginning to expand.

In response to inquiries from Whitehall about these claims, Michael Barker, the GOC in Palestine, responded, "The existence of Jewish Defense Organisations on military lines known as Haganah, one under Histadruth and the other under Revisionist auspices, has been *an open secret* for many years. The details of organisation and members were, and still are, unknown, although many agents' reports have been received." Details as to their arms varied widely—and British authorities, according to Barker, lacked "absolute proof" on the Haganah's activities. Barker emphasized the Jewish Agency's lack of faith in Britain's ability to defend Palestine, and the danger that armed Jewish organizations posed to public peace. These organizations angered the Arab community, and—although he never explicitly said so—Barker worried that such arms could be used against British troops. He asked Whitehall for support against mounting pressure from the Yishuv to reduce the sentences of the forty-three. Archibald Wavell, now commander in chief Middle East, approved of Barker's proposed course of action, but warned that demanding the surrender of illegal arms would be counterproductive, causing "serious reactions" and possibly requiring "considerable reinforcement of garrison." The search for arms, he said, should only be in response to definite information.[20]

Ben-Gurion met MacDonald in November 1939, to express his grievances about the forty-three and the government's pressure on the Yishuv. The Jewish Agency intended to stand by Britain and fight the war, but hoped that the White Paper might not be enforced during the war. Ben-Gurion expressed his desire to form Jewish units in the British Army, and his frustration at the government's refusal. "We were told first that there was no necessity" for a Jewish military contribution, he said, "since Palestine was not yet involved, and might never be; secondly that the arming of the Jews would upset the Arabs." Ben-Gurion berated HC MacMichael for rejecting Jewish military cooperation and insisting on a "fifty-fifty" contribution from Jews and Arabs. The government's policy of "complete, rule of thumb, 'equality' as between Jews and Arabs at all costs" meant that Jewish assistance was rejected for lack of equal Arab military contribution. Yet the Jews were offering military, intelligence, scientific, and industrial cooperation. "For years," Ben-Gurion protested, "the Arabs had been fighting against the British and the Jews on the British side. But here were Jews who might be accused of preparing to rebel against the British. 'Equality' can thus be preserved."[21]

MacMichael responded by saying that Arabs caught with arms had been hanged. GOC Haining had made special arrangements for sealed armories with the Jewish Agency, and authorities had so far "winked" at secret arms stores in Jewish settlements. With terrorism ongoing but the organized rebellion broken, and with the emergency of war, secret arms and military organizations could no longer be tolerated. While the Yishuv was friendly to Britain, MacMichael acknowledged, "there might all the same be some among them who would use arms to obtain possession of Palestine . . . and that the British government could not allow." Ben-Gurion accused the government of passing political sentences on the forty-three. He claimed that any attempt to disarm the Yishuv would leave them defenseless and encourage a renewal of revolt; Jewish blood would be on Britain's hands.[22]

By early 1940, Whitehall was convinced of the need to disarm the Haganah. MacDonald insisted that "the existence of an independent armed force of this nature, whatever its object, ought not to be tolerated in any country under British administration." The leniency shown toward the Haganah in comparison with Arab armed bands was unjustifiable, in his opinion. "Any suspicion of such discrimination," he said, "would arouse strong Arab feeling in Palestine with grave consequences for our relations with the Middle Eastern countries and Moslem countries further afield."[23] He had little patience for the complaints of Weizmann and Ben-Gurion. After all, the police confiscated vastly more serviceable arms from the Arabs than they did from the Jews between March and June 1940.[24]

MacDonald alerted the war cabinet of every instance of discovery of illegal Jewish arms and related arrests. He singled out the forty-three, highlighting that the Haganah was illegal and could not be ignored. He warned that efforts to form a Jewish army were "in no way an outcome of the present war, and that the object of the Jewish army would be to secure eventual Jewish military supremacy in Palestine." Now Whitehall insisted on searches for arms, based on reliable information, to be followed up with military trials. If no such information existed, the Palestine government must develop intelligence mechanisms to intensify control over arms smuggling and storage. MacDonald called for an increase in the penalties for unauthorized military drilling, and for the disbandment of the Jewish TAP.[25] Before any effective disarmament policy was achieved, Prime Minister Neville Chamberlain was replaced by the pro-Zionist Winston Churchill. Lord George Lloyd, who replaced MacDonald as colonial secretary, had been sympathetic to the Arab cause but was loyal to Churchill. This cemented the lack of any progress on Palestine policy during the war.

Things changed once the military debacle emerged during May–June 1940. The German army overran France. During the Dunkirk evacuation, Churchill feared Great Britain might be left defenseless. Amid the drama, he demanded the withdrawal home from Palestine of eight out of ten British battalions. He did not feel it would leave Palestine defenseless, and implied that the Haganah could be prepared for that job. He quashed further plans for disarming the Yishuv, adding, "You know what I think about the White Paper."[26] He could not reverse the White Paper, but the conflict with the Haganah and the Yishuv had to end.

In one of his last utterances as colonial secretary, MacDonald warned that the withdrawal of the British from Palestine could spark a renewed civil war. With stunning naiveté, he believed that "a progressive amelioration in political conditions" would free up British troops.[27] According to MacDonald, MacMichael accepted the idea of withdrawing troops only if there was no "deviation from the White Paper policy which might inflame Arab feeling; and that no steps are taken to form a Jewish military force for internal security purposes."[28] Although MacMichael remained in place, the appeasers in the war cabinet, including MacDonald, were replaced by Churchill's coalition. MacDonald's goal to disarm the Haganah was crushed by wartime necessity. The Arab-Zionist conflict was not as important as home defense, and victory. From June 1940, Anglo-Zionist intelligence cooperation became stronger than ever. So did military cooperation, both overt and covert. The stunning and successful evacuation at Dunkirk and other concerns meant that the garrison could remain in Palestine. Yet from then on, military and intelligence cooperation grew steadily.

Anglo-Zionist Cooperation and Its Limits

Before 1939, the possibility that the Yishuv might have to fight for its demands had always been in the background, but few Zionists imagined that fight would occur against Britain. From 1939, the Jewish Agency pursued a dual policy, cooperating with Britain in the war effort and on Arab issues, but simultaneously increasing its military capabilities and defying immigration restrictions. Ben-Gurion told the Mapai central committee, "We must aid the [British] army as if there were no White Paper, and fight the White Paper as if there were no war."[29] This aim proved more difficult to achieve than anyone could have expected.

Despite concern over the politics of terrorists, the Allies trusted the loyalty of the Yishuv during the war. As US intelligence noted, "The Jews won't work for the enemy naturally because of the enemy's anti-Jewish program, and any who would do would soon be caught up by the Jews themselves. The Arabs would work for the enemy for political reasons and especially for money however the chief Arab leaders are now in the enemy countries (MUFTI) so that the Arabs lack good leadership and policy. Also the Jews keep a good eye on them."[30] In other words, the Jews lacked a choice, and would seek political gain through cooperation in war. That strategy worked during the First World War and there was no harm in trying it again, especially once the mufti's loyalty had shifted firmly to the Axis.

Cooperation necessarily developed a competitive edge: both Britain and the Yishuv aimed to defeat the Nazis, but Zionists also used the opportunity to build military and technical skills for the future, to use against British interests if necessary. From the fall of France until Britain's victory at el-Alamein in November 1942, Britain and the Yishuv shared a life-or-death struggle, where competition was less important than survival. Afterward, however, all forms of wartime cooperation in intelligence and security matters became linked to developing the Haganah's capabilities as a future army. It became Ben-Gurion's insurance that the Yishuv could defend itself with or without Britain.

British policymakers knew that the Zionists could do little about the new policy and still expected them to help in an emergency. British attitudes softened as war needs increased, culminating with the new government in spring 1940, Italy's joining of the war, and the blitzkrieg. Zionists expected political reward for wartime cooperation, as in 1917. Unsurprisingly, as the St. James conference failed, Alex Aaronsohn's friends in London began to advocate for official recognition of NILI's contributions to the Palestine campaign during 1915–18. Previous approaches over the prior two decades had produced only token results. Gen. Walter Gribbon wrote the *Telegraph* as well as the Colonial Office in an attempt to achieve some recognition for the Zionist spy ring, even though "so much has been said and written about the assistance of the Arabs in Lord Allenby's campaign."[31] This was a deliberate endeavor to remind the government and the public about Britain's normally positive relationship with the Zionists after the first Arab revolt.

Weizmann also attempted to repeat his triumphs of intelligence cooperation from the First World War. Among many high-level meetings, Weizmann sat with J. H. Godfrey, who had been captain of HMS *Repulse* while it was deployed to Haifa during the rebellion. Godfrey, supposedly Ian Fleming's model for the "M" character in the James Bond novels, was director of naval intelligence. The record of their first meeting offers only a vague glimpse of how he hoped for Jewish assistance in the war effort. At the end of the meeting, Godfrey tapped Weizmann's expertise as a chemist.

He asked whether Weizmann's people in Palestine could produce a certain commodity, not specified in the record, although possibly a reference to Weizmann's process for synthetic rubber. Godfrey was impressed by the Haganah while in Palestine and paid the compliment to Weizmann.[32] However, his influence would never go as far for Zionists during the Second World War as it had during 1915–18. He met Sir Edmund Ironside, the chief of imperial general staff, about freedom for the forty-three and proposals for a new Jewish fighting force in the British Army. Ironside thought it wrong to imprison "one of Wingate's lads," adding, "He ought to have been given the DSO [Distinguished Service Order]."[33] Alas, the White Paper policy stood in the way of this kind of intelligence and military cooperation, directed from above.

Rather, the midlevel officers of the British Army who had cooperated with the Yishuv during the revolt and the early part of the war drove the Anglo-Zionist intelligence alliance. Organizational improvements and the professionalization of Zionist intelligence during 1937–40 contributed to that alliance. Haganah and Jewish Agency intelligence focused on their ability to support Britain in counterterrorism and counterespionage and against the revolt. A branch of the Haganah command, Rigul Negedi, meaning counterespionage (henceforth known by its acronym, RAN), was folded into a new intelligence service, Sherut HaYediot, or SHAY, which was founded to centralize the geographically and departmentally disparate intelligence services in receipt of Haganah funds. Haganah intelligence was developing a central bureaucracy, and became more of a national project than one that responded to local territorial needs.

In 1938 RAN began to centralize open-source material on the Irgun and Betar, and compile lists of their members. By 1941, it had produced summaries and assessments of the organizations, driven mainly by the breakaway of the Stern Gang. RAN's human sources, cultivated since 1938, later helped to prevent incidents, and by 1944 would enable the Haganah's suppression of the Irgun in support of British authorities. SHAY also had departments covering Communism, Arab issues in Palestine and abroad (working in parallel with the Jewish Agency's political department), and Britain. The latter department developed slowly and carefully as resources were cultivated throughout the war. Even during the height of wartime cooperation, Anglo-Zionist intelligence relations maintained a competitive edge. Yishuv intelligence agencies expanded their capabilities thanks to the experience of the revolt and the support of their British partners. Once the police began to renew searches for Haganah arms, Yishuv intelligence took an increasingly important early warning role.[34] However, the key to the relationship was liaison with British officers who had organized the counterrevolt during the 1930s. They intensified intelligence and paramilitary cooperation.

In 1940, Ben-Gurion and Moshe Shertok accepted an offer from George Francis Taylor, known to Zionist intelligence as codename "Khayat," to fund the expansion of the Jewish Agency's intelligence gathering in the Middle East on behalf of Section D, later the Special Operations Executive (SOE). Taylor later passed cabinet-level intelligence to Ben-Gurion.[35] Haganah members began to receive further training in wireless signaling and other technical skills. Tony Simonds trained a small number in sabotage and covert action at a new SOE base in Haifa.[36] The practical consequence of this process was that middle and senior British officers moved toward Wingate's proposal, and away from authorized policy. The British Army trained the Haganah in cutting-edge intelligence and covert action.

In 1943, John Teague, now head of SIS in the Middle East, told the Foreign Office that from their training with the SOE, especially its postoccupational schemes, prepared in case of German invasion of Palestine, "Jewish (il)legal armies are out of all measure better trained, organised and equipped than they have ever been before."[37] With the German danger pushed away from Palestine, the FO wanted to disarm the Haganah and implement the White Paper, especially to accelerate the constitutional clauses. An Arab government could not rule over a dissenting, well-armed Jewish population. Teague warned the FO against confiscation of Haganah arms for fear of provoking a conflict during the war. He felt that the SOE and SIS owed the Haganah considerable debt.

With few expressions forthcoming on high policy, middle and junior officers were free to work with Zionist intelligence officers and recruit Haganah soldiers for covert action. In contrast, generals such as Haining and Wavell quietly tolerated covert cooperation with the Yishuv, while outwardly they accepted the merits of the White Paper policy and strove to enforce and strengthen the policy prescribed by Whitehall.

The needs of the war made it impossible to disarm the Haganah or any other element of the Yishuv. The terrorists could be controlled, if Haganah intelligence supported that end. As with the question of the constitutional future of Palestine, matters of security, arms, and recruitment to the war effort were all pulled away from any high policy objective and toward improvisation. The consequences were long lasting. By 1943, British intelligence knew that it was too late to disarm the Haganah, and that attempting to do so would provoke insurrection.[38] The war limited Anglo-Zionist hostilities created by the White Paper. The war also progressively advantaged the Zionists over the British in security terms. This was especially true since contact between the intelligence and military officers of both sides reinforced the codependent relationship. If Britain would later struggle against this force, what hope did the Palestinians have?

Zionist intelligence and security institutions thrived under these conditions. During disarmament, the pressure from British security agencies drove growth in expertise in intelligence and secrecy. The need to cooperate produced the same result. Zionist agencies built their capabilities to counter terrorism and to help fight the war. Increasingly, the Jewish Agency had the power to both defy British policy and save British soldiers and policemen from terrorist attacks. Increasingly formal Zionist intelligence institutions supported Britain, but also targeted it for intelligence gathering purposes. The war and the variable pressures of the White Paper accelerated the Zionist movement's capabilities toward statehood, as these vital national institutions achieved new levels of maturity.

The future of Anglo-Zionist relations, especially the intelligence relationship, depended on policy. Would the White Paper be fully implemented? If not, would immigration restrictions continue? Would the army again try to disarm the Haganah? Would terrorism restart? The answers to these questions began to unfold during 1943–45, and presaged the Jewish insurgency against Britain. Zionist intelligence was well equipped in the confrontations of 1944–47, largely because of the relationships that had developed during the wartime liaison with British security agencies. In this way, the unfolding of the conflict during 1939–40 shaped the violent end of the mandate. Once Britain's dependence on the Yishuv was proven, its rule became conditional.

Conclusion

Britain's "Intelligence State" and the Failure of the Palestinian Independence Movement

          The countdown to the end of British rule in Palestine began once it was clear that Britain could not enforce its policy on Palestine. Either the Arab population would rebel against Britain's failure to fulfill the White Paper's goals, or the Jewish population would resist Britain's enforcement of them. The Yishuv ultimately won that struggle, but that is another story. Following this story of intelligence and policy, it is clear how intelligence paved the way to Britain's stalemate in 1940. That process began with the odd, prejudiced beliefs of officers who negotiated Britain's commitments to Arabs, France and Russia, and world Jewry during the First World War. Their views—that Jews were a powerful global ally, and that an Arab conspiracy in the Ottoman army could knock its opponent out of the war—set in stone Britain's two core contradictory commitments to the League of Nations after the war. First, Britain was to facilitate democratic self-government for the population. Simultaneously, it must create a Jewish national home through immigration and settlement. These commitments were part of Britain's legal justification for ruling. By the time intelligence officers understood the cost of these conflicting commitments, it was too late. They would have to enforce British policy against the wishes of the majority. Lacking force, Britain's intelligence state in Palestine managed the conflict, but never solved it.

Under the military administration, the first intelligence state took shape, aiming to keep the peace and to convince the League of Nations that Britain was best fit to assume the mandate over Palestine. Under these conditions, the wartime partnership between British and Zionist intelligence continued to grow and thrive. When violence broke out in 1920, the military government came to a quick end and was replaced by a civilian government led by High Commissioner Herbert Samuel. Under him, and his successor Herbert Plumer, the intelligence state remained largely intact, albeit informally. Wartime experts serving in government posts managed Arab resistance to British policy, and the burgeoning Arab-Zionist conflict.

Peace was reached in the wake of the 1921 riots, partly thanks to intelligence. Security intelligence guided policymakers in their improvised responses to Palestinian negotiations over the constitution of the mandate. Seeking to avoid contradicting the Zionist policy, Samuel, Churchill, Clayton, and other senior decision makers refused to recognize the representativeness of Palestinian political associations or parties. Intelligence, in concert with its Zionist partners, supported that tactic. In cooperation, they also crushed Bolshevik influence in Palestine. Palestinians, meanwhile, took to direct negotiations and advocacy at the League of Nations to limit the Zionist policy. They failed, but built important transnational connections to the National Political League, which unknowingly hurt the cause by extending the Palestinians' faith in negotiations. They also officially tied the Palestine Arab Congress to the Syro-Palestinian congress, based in Geneva and Cairo and led by the prominent pan-Islamist and pan-Arab propagandists Shakib Arslan and Rashid Rida.

These developments occurred abroad, after the Palestine government stopped treating Arab nationalism as a political crime and empowered Amin al-Husseini to lead the majority Muslim community. Policymakers believed they could manage their mutually dependent relationship with him. The mufti's role in governing Palestine made sense to the intelligence state. Their surveillance showed his activity outside Palestine and his connections to pan-Arab and pan-Islamic movements, but also his supportive role within Palestine's borders. Experts such as Clayton, Storrs, and Symes knew his family and believed he could be managed. Deedes thought it was a mistake. By 1928, these and other experts had left Palestine. Inexperienced government officials with little access to secret intelligence did not understand the coming danger. The mufti continued raising his own profile as before, as well as that of the Palestinian cause.

The peace of the 1920s was deceiving. Palestinians took their resistance abroad, while government security cutbacks left Palestine undefended. When disturbances broke out again in 1929, the slow pace of reinforcements and the government's surprise exposed chronic policy flaws. Weizmann neutralized British attempts to limit the Zionist policy. Security reforms invested new energy in restoring professional intelligence and police staff. The civil and military intelligence states that took shape were locked in competition for attention and influence with the government. Neither could persuade the high commissioners, Chancellor and Wauchope, to heed warnings about the mufti's transnational connections to radicals, or his role in revitalizing the Palestinian national movement's militant edge.

The real failure of the civil state was in its unequal treatment of political crime. Intelligence only noted political murder within the Arab community, but sought to prove its competence in cases where Jews were the victims, including the Qassamist campaign of the early 1930s and the assassination of Arlosoroff. British authorities feared civil war within the Yishuv in the latter case, and paid close attention to attempts to resolve the conflict between the Revisionist and leftist youth movements. They ignored the mufti's assassination campaign until after 1937, even though it began in the wake of the 1929 Buraq revolt. This blind eye was symptomatic of the basic problem of governance in Palestine. The CID's approach to political murder was as undemocratic as the mandate itself. In Palestinian eyes, that inequity compounded their other basic grievances and helped to persuade youth-led mass movements, especially Istiqlal and the Youngmen, that Britain would only respond to firm pressure. They were driven by the strategy of the National Pact, forged by Old Istiqlalists with their pan-Arab counterparts beginning in early 1932.

Both intelligence states observed these developments. The CID only considered Palestinian popular mobilization a threat when it directly affected their own work. Youth vigilantism to prevent illegal Jewish immigration was one example; the Qassamist campaign was another. Yet the organization of sports and youth clubs, and political parties, was seen as an ingredient for the self-government desired by Chancellor and then Wauchope. The military did not share their optimism.

Complacency thus prevailed in the civil intelligence state. Unlike the CID, staff intelligence and the RAF prepared for a Palestinian revolution. They reinforced their close relationships with Zionists, drilled a nationwide strike and revolt in 1934, and successfully supported the "civil power" in managing protests from 1933. As such, they performed well when the revolt broke out in 1936. The civil government did not. From the cement incident in 1935, the government's unequal attitude toward Jews and Arabs was exposed. Al-Qassam's martyrdom fueled the youth-led independence movement. Wauchope would not be able to deal only with elites anymore. His faith in a negotiated solution to constitutional reforms was proven misplaced. He believed he was guiding the country toward good government, but instead faced revolt, and reluctantly allowed the military to escalate its response. Zionist intelligence became closer than ever to its British patron through this process.

During the first phase of the revolt, the mufti was at peak influence. He organized the strike under the ASC and allowed other elements to escalate the revolt. He helped inspire and organize those other elements, and avoided taking responsibility for them. Wauchope's Arab kings scheme improved the mufti's status even more, as the kings asked him personally to call off the strike and revolt. When he did, and the country went back to work on 12 October 1936, the extent of his influence was clear. He was a force to be reckoned with, but also a loyal government officer. The royal commission was the last chance for the mufti to reach a negotiated solution, but this proved impossible after the partition proposals were announced. Palestinians faced bad alternatives: either return to war, or accept Jewish domination in part of the homeland. The former path led to destruction. It is impossible to know what the outcome would have been had Palestinian leaders sought compromise in September 1937. This approach was unlikely anyway. The pan-Arab strategy, which succeeded in Syria, sought to exploit the influence of the Arab kings and the crises in Europe to pressure colonial powers toward concessions. Britain's escalating responses in 1936 surprised Palestinians. The mufti's full embrace of radical revolution in 1937 brought further repression.

Meanwhile Zionist intelligence and military partnership with Britain became more powerful, especially during the second phase of the revolt. Zionist intelligence was involved in raising irregulars, turning rebels into peace bands, and gathering intelligence in Syria and Lebanon on the rebel leadership. These contributions fed the General Staff Intelligence that planned operations, securitized the country, and ultimately crushed the revolt. Zionist labor and supply literally paved the way toward a securitized landscape and military control. While centralized intelligence was key to military operations, it never supported civil government. The civil state resisted this centralized machinery because it defied the liberal premise of the mandate. Under normal conditions, civilian police were supposed to manage disturbances, but they were unable to do so. The CID and police, strained by the pressures of the revolt, ultimately collapsed. The military intelligence state remained in place, reorganizing and subordinating police under army commanders instead of the civil government.

Centralized intelligence was critical to the counterrebellion during its second phase, especially upon the arrival of Tegart and Petrie. They coordinated

MacKereth's work in Syria with intelligence in Palestine. The campaign organized a range of security measures, including, but not limited to, irregular forces (such as that under Faiz Idrissi), the peace bands, the SNS, and Tegart's fence and fortress construction program. Tegart integrated police and military operations, and Petrie made Secret Service funds available to useful sources such as MacKereth and Faiz Idrissi. The army could not have accommodated Tegart's reforms or operations without a combined staff intelligence. Fakhri Abdul Hadi's peace band might have been destroyed by the army had this system not accommodated that covert operation, led by MacKereth with Zionist cooperation. The irregular forces of the counter-rebellion were controversial. The peace bands posed such an ethical problem that they were never officially acknowledged. Cooperation with Jewish Agency intelligence was politically controversial, but improved coincidentally with Whitehall's abandonment of the Zionist policy. Wingate's incorporation of Haganah fighters into his SNS was acknowledged by the army as useful, but received no political attention.

In the wake of the revolt, it became clear that Britain had drifted further than ever from the mandate's liberal-democratic aims. Intelligence guided a change in policy embodied in the 1939 White Paper, which declared the Zionist policy fulfilled, limited Jewish immigration severely, and sought instead to refocus on building Arab capacity for self-government. Anglo-Saudi diplomacy drove this strategy. Anticipating a war, and in need of support from minor powers in the Middle East, Britain was relieved that sigint proved to policymakers that Ibn Sa'ud would be a reliable partner. To boost the Arab king's influence in the region, and to secure his friendship, Britain allowed the Saudi delegation to the conference at St. James to organize counterproposals after the conference failed. Zionists were excluded from this process. So was the mufti.

Although the intelligence state in Palestine thought the White Paper would free it from the contradictory commitments that had plagued it since 1920, that set of commitments never would be implemented as imagined. During the first year of the Second World War, Britain discovered that there were limits on the extent to which it could impose its will on the Yishuv. With the war on, Britain could delay facing reality: Palestine had become ungovernable except through military force. The conflict over British policy still raged, but was set aside by the Yishuv for the war, and also by the exhausted Palestinian population. Britain continued to improvise: it pardoned Irgun terrorists, but never the mufti. It fought hard to restrict Jewish immigration, and tried to expand the Arab element of the civil service. It tried to disarm the Yishuv, until it discovered that their military cooperation in the war might be vital. Britain did not yet know it, but she no longer was the sovereign power in Palestine. Sooner or later, British policy would have to favor one side, or Britain would have to leave.

Throughout these events, intelligence crafted, led, and reformed the state and its security apparatus. Intelligence molded governance and guided policymakers around constitutional obstacles. It confronted popular protests and violent resistance. Yet Britain's solution to a failure of governance—a failure of policy at heart—was to create a security state. Rather than eliminating the hypocrisy of its rule in Palestine, Britain deepened it. Such hypocrisies became increasingly common during the 1930s. Britain's original justification for taking a mandate over Palestine was to introduce democratic self-rule. After twenty-two years, Britain returned to direct military rule.

Palestine posed exceptional security and intelligence problems. Elsewhere in the empire, colonial control could play between elites. In Egypt, the Wafd party eventually agreed to the 1936 Anglo-Egyptian Treaty despite popular opposition, as Britain influenced Egypt through its king. In India a similar pattern occurred, as the Congress Party often engaged in constitutional politics and abandoned mass agitation, and was countered by other interest groups. Britain expected that Egypt and India would remain dependent, and traded autonomy for time.[1]

Britain never achieved these results in Palestine because it nurtured only one elite collaborator among Arabs, the mufti. Unlike his Indian and Egyptian counterparts, the mufti varyingly coerced or secretly encouraged the growth of competing, more radical factions. By 1935, Jamal had founded PAP and made clear its aim to abrogate the Zionist policy and achieve independence. Whereas in Egypt and India robust and stratified networks of elites competed, in Palestine the mufti was so central to such networks that Britain could only turn to the Nashashibi-led opposition as an alternative. In the years leading up to the rebellion, the government allowed the mufti's party to trounce the Nashashibis, and only sought to reverse that trend when it was too late, at the height of the rebellion. Even so, the Nashashibis never could be the viable alternative that British decision makers had hoped for. Perpetuating patterns from the Ottoman period, Herbert Samuel made the leading Jerusalem families share power and influence. When Hussein Khalidi, liberal but a mufti ally, defeated Ragheb Nashashibi in the 1934 Jerusalem mayoral elections, the latter family lost its only remaining important high office. Wauchope's administration and the CID observed these events in awe of the mufti's political skill. Wauchope and his advisers were not bothered by the outcome, even though it meant that the Nashashibis would be forced during 1935–36 to back the mufti's policy or else face social and political ostracism. Britain's lack of response to these events was a break from the norm in colonial politics. It was driven by naive faith in the mufti, and by the belief that constitutional solutions could solve Palestine's problems without compromising either the Zionist policy or democracy.

Mirroring its treatment of the mufti, the intelligence state offered extraordinary access and influence to its Zionist partners. This was yet another exceptional feature of colonial government in Palestine. Few states in history have let one element of its population establish so powerful a system of secret intelligence, so aggressively used against other elements. From the beginning of Britain's occupation, autonomous Jewish organizations were part of Britain's intelligence state. Zionist intelligence made up for Britain's shortcomings. Based on shared interest, and with the goal of maintaining British support for Zionism, the junior partners supplied staff, technical ability, translators, and agents. They served as intermediaries and analysts. When new skills were needed, British authorities provided them. The Haganah's signal service originated with the Palestine Police's need for fast communication with outlying Jewish settlements; that signal service later was used against British interests. This was the quintessential Anglo-Zionist intelligence relationship: simultaneously cooperative and competitive. Both sides believed they benefited from this relationship. Neither understood how this partnership was giving the Zionists the power tools of statehood.

This partnership was central to the survival of the Yishuv and the emergence of Israel. The skills, experiences, and connections gained during the mandate period were instrumental to the Zionists' struggle against Britain in the 1940s, but also were important components of the early state. The White Paper forced Zionist intelligence to accelerate its accumulation of these skills, including the ability to prevent Britain from enforcing its policies during 1945–47.[2] The end of the Zionist policy forced the Yishuv to prepare to defend itself from threats including the Nazis, German or Italian invaders, fifth columnists, Communists, Arab nationalists, Revisionist terrorists, and British authorities. The Yishuv learned how to fight a war, and how to win. In contrast, the Palestinians remained shattered, divided, and leaderless, ruled under the thumb of military government.

The White Paper was a response to the greatest danger Britain and Jewry had ever confronted in Palestine. Intelligence helped Britain get the best possible result from its Zionist policy until 1939, and from its White Paper policy until 1945. American Jews and the Yishuv supported Britain. Ibn Saʿud helped to stabilize the Middle East, ensuring that radicals were marginal and not leading a pro-Axis regional movement. He played the part of role model; his benevolent neutrality was the most Britain expected, and its effect was security in Arabia. In July 1942, Rommel was close to Cairo with an Einsatz-kommando in his train. Perhaps the White Paper did not prevent him from covering the seven hundred kilometers between el-Alamein and Jerusalem, but it helped to contain him. The Zionists understandably hated the White Paper, but it forced the Yishuv to secure itself; Britain's last service to Zionism was to abandon the Zionist policy.

Britain's colonial state in Palestine was extraordinarily weak. No form of "intelligence state," however strong, could have resolved Britain's conflicting commitments, or the Arab-Zionist conflict, without a firm policy about Palestine's future. Such a pathway proved elusive. The intelligence state usually was filled with effective people, even when it failed to prevent violence. Intelligence could not compensate for bad policy, but it could manage the contradictions of the mandate, temporarily and always at a price. In this way, intelligence was fundamental to British power in Palestine. For more than thirty years it kept British rule afloat. With Zionist help, it propped up British power. Without consent from the governed, only by reaching totalitarian levels could the intelligence state maintain Britain's interests in Palestine or the Middle East in perpetuity.

NOTES

Introduction

1. TNA, CO 448/36/2, "Suggested Forfeiture of Mr Joseph Davidescu's OBE," ca. 1930.

2. TNA, CO 733/456/12, 2, Alex Kellar (MI5) to Christopher Eastwood, 24.8.1945.

3. Jack Davidescu and Haviva Zemach, conversation with the author, 3 December 2011; BAZY, DP, Dalia Karpel, "Bullet in the Head," Ha'ir (Hebrew), 2.3.1990.

4. Ferris, Intelligence and Strategy, 16.

5. Andrew and Dilks, Missing Dimension.

6. Shaw, Survey of Palestine, 1:244–45.

7. Thomas, Empires of Intelligence, 3–5.

8. Thomas, Empires of Intelligence, 8.

9. Thomas, Empires of Intelligence, 4–5.

10. Thomas, Empires of Intelligence, 6.

11. Bennett, "Minimum Force"; Reis, "Myth of British Minimum Force."

12. Johnson, British Imperialism, 78, 95, 115–16, 135–36, 145–46.

1. Britain's Wartime Policies

1. French, Strategy of the Lloyd George Coalition, 38; Cornwall, Undermining of Austria-Hungary, chap. 1; Messinger, British Propaganda, chap. 11; Sanders and Taylor, British Propaganda.

2. Sheffy, British Military Intelligence, 21–22.

3. Storrs Papers, Pembroke College Cambridge, 11/3, 22.2.1915, cited in Kedourie, In the Anglo-Arab Labyrinth, 33.

4. TNA, FO 371/1973, 87396, note by Storrs 19.4.1914, cited in Kedourie, In the Anglo-Arab Labyrinth, 7.

5. Barr, Line in the Sand, 8–11.

6. TNA, CAB 24/1/51, "War Committee—Evidence of Sykes on Arab Question," 16.12.1915.

7. ISA, RG 65/P/349/28, Mark Sykes, "Memorandum on the Asia-Minor Agreement," 14.8.1917.

8. Kayali, Arabs and Young Turks, 187–88.

9. TNA, AIR 8/62, Pal. 9, The Future of Palestine. Memo circulated at first cabinet meeting of the Palestine Committee, 5.6.1923. See especially "Appendix II, Strategical Importance of Palestine."

10. Renton, "Flawed Foundations," 91; Robson, "Church, State," 458–61.

11. Bar-Yosef, "Last Crusade?," 103.

12. Huneidi, "Was Balfour Policy Reversible?"; Schneer, *Balfour Declaration*, 341.

13. Renton, "Flawed Foundations," 27–30, 34, 37; Huneidi, "Was Balfour Policy Reversible?," 36–38.

14. Paris, *Britain, the Hashemites and Arab Rule*, 39.

15. Renton, *Zionist Masquerade*, 15–17.

16. Schneer, *Balfour Declaration*, 107–23.

17. Schneer, *Balfour Declaration*, 152–65.

18. Schneer, *Balfour Declaration*, 153.

19. Ferris, "British Empire."

20. Schneer, *Balfour Declaration*, 366; Renton, *Zionist Masquerade*, chap. 5. See p. 80 (the source of the quotation) on intelligence views of Zionist influence in Russia.

21. SAD, Gilbert Clayton Papers, GB-0033-SAD, 693/13/13, Clayton to Mark Sykes, 17.12.1917; 693/13/10, Clayton to Gertrude Bell, 8.12.1917.

22. SAD, 693/13/47, Clayton to Sykes, 4.4.1918.

23. SAD, 693/13/40, Clayton to "My Dear General" (perhaps Sir Henry Wilson or Allenby), 2.4.1918.

24. TNA, FO 608/99, ff. 292–93, Weizmann to Balfour, 30.5.1918.

25. SAD, 693/13/55, Clayton to Bell, 17.6.1918.

26. SAD, 693/13/55, Clayton to Bell, 17.6.1918.

27. Ochsenwald, "Ironic Origins," 195–201; Khalidi, "Ottomanism and Arabism," 62.

28. Khalidi, *Palestinian Identity*, 38–39.

29. The Nahda is the subject of countless studies, including the classic, Hourani, *Arabic Thought*; and more recently, Hanssen and Weiss, *Arabic Thought*; Hamzah, *Making of the Arab Intellectual*; Sheehi, *Foundations of Modern Arab Identity*; and Tageldin, *Disarming Words*.

30. Dawn, "From Ottomanism to Arabism"; Kayali, *Arabs and Young Turks*, 18–21.

31. For a comprehensive study of the movements, see Tauber, *Emergence of the Arab Movements*; and Tauber, *Arab Movements*.

32. Khoury, *Urban Notables*, 63.

33. Tauber, *Arab Movements*, 62; Kayali, *Arabs and Young Turks*, 69–71, 198, 212; Khoury, *Urban Notables*, 65.

34. Khoury, *Urban Notables*, 86; Tauber, *Emergence of the Arab Movements*, 213–36.

35. Cleveland, *Islam against the West*, 7.

36. Khalidi, "Ottomanism and Arabism," 52–53, 62–64.

37. The journal's title was a nickname for Islam or its principles, meaning "the most steadfast support." Menachem Milson, Arabic-Hebrew Dictionary Based on the Ayalon-Shneier Dictionary, Hebrew University of Jerusalem, accessed 20 November 2013, http://arabdictionary.huji.ac.il. Also see Qur'an 2:256 and 31:22.

38. Kayali, *Arabs and Young Turks*, 181–82.

39. Hamzah, "Muhammad Rashid Rida."

40. Tauber, *Arab Movements*, 18; Tauber, *Emergence of the Arab Movements*, 281–82, 315–16.

41. Tauber, *Arab Movements*, 58–59.

42. Tauber, *Emergence of the Arab Movements*, 219–30, 233–34.

43. IOR, L/PS/18/B215, Ronald Storrs, "Note on Communication from the Sherif of Mecca," 19.8.1915.

44. TNA, FO 684/2, f. 28, "Memorandum: Damascus Consul," 14.8.1924.

45. IOR, MSS Eur F 112/277, Hogarth memo to WO, "Certain Conditions of Settlement with Asia," 15.11.1918.

46. IOR, MSS Eur F 112/277, Hogarth memo to WO.

47. For new research on the key courier, see Kalisman, "Little Persian Agent."

48. Tauber, *Arab Movements*, 63–65.

49. Tauber, *Arab Movements*, 61; Wagner, "British Intelligence and Arab Nationalism," 69.

50. Wilson, "Hashemites," 208–11.

51. IOR, L/PS/10/523, McMahon to Edward Grey, 12.8.1915.

52. IOR, L/PS/10/524, McMahon to Viceroy, 22.10.1915.

53. IOR, L/PS/10/523, Arthur Hirtzel, Coversheet 4024 1915, "Arabia Pan-Arab Movement Treatment of Mohammed Sherif el-Faruqi," 1.11.1915.

54. IOR, L/PS/10/524, Viceroy to India Sec., 26.10.1915.

55. Tauber, "Role of Lieutenant Muhammad Sharif Al-Faruqi."

56. IOR, L/PS/18/B247, f. 16, Arthur Hirtzel, "British Interest in Arabia," 20.1.1917.

57. Gelvin, *Divided Loyalties*, 59–62.

58. Watenpaugh, *Being Modern*, chap. 6.

59. ʿAllush, *Al-muqawamah al-ʿArabiyah fi Filastin*, 39–42.

60. TNA, FO 608/98, ff. 356–57, Storrs to Clayton, "Covering Letter, Secret," n.d., ca. 3.1919.

61. TNA, FO 608/98, J. N. Camp, "Secret—The Palestine Conference," 15.2.1919, Intelligence (B) (B probably was for internal security).

62. TNA, FO 608/98, Camp, "Secret—The Palestine Conference."

63. TNA, FO 608/98, ff. 354–55, Clayton to FO, 2.3.1919.

64. SAD, 693/13/55, Clayton to Gertrude Bell, 17.6.1918.

65. Ferris, "British Empire," 326.

66. Ferris, "British Empire," 331.

67. ISA, RG 2 M/7/12, 1a, Col. Bertie Harry Waters-Taylor to OETS Admin., 3.2.1919.

68. TNA, WO 32/21125, 17A, "Copy of Minute by Mr. Newby, MI5," 10.7.1919.

2. Intelligence, Policy, and the Emerging Modern Middle East

1. HA, 115/9, "Situation in Palestine July 1921" (probably by Herbert Samuel).

2. Pedersen, *Guardians*, 27.

3. TNA, FO, 608/98, Weizmann to David Eder, 17.12.1918.

4. TNA, FO, 608/98/9, Reg. 159, "Relations between Jews and Arabs in Palestine" and Feisal-Weizmann agreement, 16.1.1919. See also Reg. 155, for Feisal's manifesto.

5. TNA, FO, 608/98/8, "Zionism in Palestine" and minute by Mallett, 17.1.1919.

6. TNA, FO, 608/98, minute by Toynbee, "British Aid to Jews in Palestine," 17.1.1919.

7. MacMillan, *Peacemakers*, 400–402.

8. TNA, WO/106/194, 35, "Extract from a Secret Paper," ref. meeting 21.3.1919; FO 371/4179, f. 430, Derby to British Foreign Secretary Lord Curzon, 6.4.1919.

9. TNA, FO 371/4182, f. 273, Directorate of Military Intelligence (DMI) to FO, 1.9.1919.

10. Wagner, "British Intelligence and Policy," 37–39.

11. TNA, WO 106/194, 3, untitled memo by Lt. Col. (Gribbon), 12.6.1919.

12. TNA, HW 12/2, 000338, Emir Zeid, Damascus, to Emir Feisal, n.d. (intercept prepared 19.11.1919); 000337, Emir Aly, Prime Minister, Mecca, to Emir Feisal, London, 23.11.1919; 000360, Emir Feisal, Paris, to Emir Zeid, Damascus, 27.11.1919; 000404, Emir Feisal to Emir Zeid, Damascus, n.d., received 4.12.1919; 000452, Emir Feisal to Emir Zeid, Damascus, n.d. (intercept prepared 10.12.1919); 000579, Emir Feisal to Emir Zeid, Damascus, n.d., received 19.12.1919; 000599, Admral [sic] Bristol, Constantinople, to Mr. Lansing, Washington, 17.12.1919; HW 12/3, 000683, Emir Feisal to Emir Zeid, Damascus, 3.1.1920.

13. For scholarly work on British intelligence overall, including the Aaronsohns, see Sheffy, British Military Intelligence. The story of Sarah Aaronsohn's spy work, capture, and execution has been read by Israeli schoolchildren for decades. See Melman, "Legend of Sarah."

14. Jewish Museum, London, Official Record of Gallant Deeds, JML/1984.125/1984.125.T.156; Gelber, Shorshe ha-ḥavatselet, 1:12–15.

15. Gelber, Shorshe ha-ḥavatselet, 1:11.

16. Gelber, Shorshe ha-ḥavatselet, 1:12.

17. HA, 80/145/P/1, Shneerson to Zabutinsky (Jabotinsky), 15.12.1918.

18. TNA, FO 608/99, f. 385, Money to CPO (Chief Political Officer—Clayton), 15.4.1919.

19. Gelber, Shorshe ha-ḥavatselet, 1:19.

20. TNA, WO 106/189, 32, J. N. Camp, French Propaganda in Jerusalem, 2.2.1919.

21. BAZY, AAP 17/1/10, file 2, "Très Secret," from Farid, 28.11.1918; 17/1/10, file 3, handwritten note from Farid, date illegible (late 1918); 17/1/23, Lt. Alex Aaronsohn, F.I.988, "Farid Pasha El YAFI on the Political Situation," 31.12.18.

22. HA, 80/145/P/16, Report on the Present Political and Economic Attitude of the British Military Administration in Palestine, 30.4.1919.

23. TNA, FO 608/99, f. 230, Clayton to FO, 26.3.1919.

24. His connection to Aaronsohn is established in Italian documents described in Minerbi, "Angelo Levi Bianchini."

25. TNA, WO 106/190, 97, untitled ("Grubb Street informs us that . . ."), 23.4.1919.

26. TNA, FO 608/99, f. 297, Bianchini to Weizmann, n.d., ca. spring 1919.

27. Gelber, Shorshe ha-ḥavatselet, 1:20; TNA, FO 608/99, ff. 348–49, Money to GHQ, 31.3.1919.

28. TNA, FO 608/99, ff. 371–72, Clayton to FO, 2.5.1919.

29. TNA, FO 608/99, f. 270, minute by AGT, 18.4.1919.

30. TNA, FO 608/99, f. 451, Clayton to FO, 19.6.1919.

31. SAD, Clayton Papers, 693/14/17, Clayton to FO, 28.2.1919.

32. TNA, FO 608/99, f. 393 Clayton to FO, 11.5.1919.

33. ISA, RG 2/M3/9, 81, Balfour to Egypforce, Weizman to Bianchini, 15.4.1919, and 84, Clayton to OETA South, 8.5.1919; TNA, FO 608/119, ff. 46–53, Clayton to Balfour, 5.5.1919; Minerbi, "Angelo Levi Bianchini," 322–23.

34. For more on his fascinating story, see Minerbi, "Angelo Levi Bianchini."

35. Patrick, *America's Forgotten Middle East Initiative*, chap. 1.

36. ISA, RG 2/M/7/12, 38B, Jaffa governor to editor of El-Kawkab, Arab Bureau, Gresham House, Cairo, 31.5.1919; 27A, intercepted (i/c) letter from Mohamed Yusef Jamaa El Kinani, Jerusalem, to Saeed Zein El Din, Jaffa, 20.5.1919.

37. ISA, RG 2/M/7/12, 29a, "Political Propaganda," 20.5.1919; 35a, "Ragheb De-jani," 26.5.1919.

38. TNA, FO, 608/99, 18352, Gerald Spicer for Curzon to Balfour, 21.8.1919.

39. TNA, WO, 106/194, 19, FO to Col. C. French, 4.8.1919.

40. TNA, FO 608/99, ff. 476–82, J. N. Camp, Intelligence Office, Jerusalem, to Chief Political Officer GHQ Cairo, 12.8.1919.

41. TNA, FO 608/99, ff. 476–82, Camp to Chief Political Officer, 12.8.1919.

42. TNA, FO 608/99, ff. 476–82, Camp to Chief Political Officer, 12.8.1919.

43. HA, 19/mshtr/4, various letters from June through September 1919.

44. TNA, FO 608/99, ff. 476–82, Camp to Chief Political Officer, 12.8.1919.

45. TNA, FO 608/99, f. 475, French to Curzon, 26.8.1919.

46. See for example the correlation between Camp's report and CZA, Z4/3886/ii, "Jerusalem from August 19th–30th 1919."

47. TNA, FO 608/100, f. 458, memo by M. Watts Taylor, AA & QMG, GHQ Mt. Carmel, 12.8.1919.

48. TNA, FO 371/4238, 176186, intelligence, 9.1.1920.

49. TNA, WO 106/196, 15, GHQ intelligence summary, EEF, 9.4.1920; WO 106/195, 28, GHQ Egypt to DMI, 9.3.1920; WO 106/195, 18, GHQ Egypt to WO, 10.3.1920.

50. TNA, WO 106/195, 25, WO to GHQ Constantinople, 12.3.1920.

51. TNA, WO 106/195, 18, GHQ Egypt to WO, 10.3.1920.

52. Gelber, *Shorshe ha-ḥavatselet*, 1:26.

53. BAZY, AAP 17/6/12, "Jerusalem," 31.1.1920; CZA, Z4/3886/ii, "20 JM," 20.3.1920; Z4/3886/i, "Arab National Movement," 31.1.1920; L3/278, "Arab National Movement," 31.1.1920; Z4/14437, "22 JM," 22.3.1920.

54. SAD, Clayton Papers, 693/13/55, Clayton to Bell, 17.6.1918; TNA, WO 106/189, 61, Clayton to ?, 28.2.1919.

55. TNA, FO 608/99, ff. 476–82, Camp to Chief Political Officer, 12.8.1919; Matthews, *Confronting an Empire*, 144–45.

56. HA, 80/145/P/20, "Lod," 25–30.1.1920.

57. TNA, FO 141/651, British Consul Beirut to FO, 10.3.1920.

58. BAZY, AAP 17/5/13, "Secret: Arab Movement in Palestine," 19.3.1920.

59. Porath, *Emergence of the Palestinian-Arab National Movement*, 93–100.

60. Matthews, *Confronting an Empire*, 29–31.

61. TNA, WO 106/196, 41, "Nationalists and Arabs" (likely a SIS report), ff. 136–43.

62. CZA, Z4/3886/ii, "32 JM," 1.4.1920.

63. Mattar, *Mufti of Jerusalem*, 17.

64. CZA, Z4/3886/ii, "31 JM," 31.3.1920.

65. CZA, Z4/3886/ii, "32 JM," 1.4.1920.

66. CZA, Z4/3886/ii, "33 JM," 2.4.1920.

67. Porath, *Palestinian Arab National Movement*, 77–78.

68. Porath, *Emergence of the Palestinian-Arab National Movement*, 100; TNA, AIR 5/1243, Lt. Col. H. E. Braine, "Operations at Semakh April 1920," 11.6.1920; BAZY, AAP 17/5/4, "22 JA," 26.4.1920; 17/8/44, "46 JM," 26.4.1920; CZA, L3/278, "Preparation for a Revolution," 30.4.1920.

69. TNA, WO 106/196, 50, GHQ Egypt to WO, 13.5.1920.

70. Gelber, *Shorshe ha-ḥavatselet*, 1:36.

71. YYGH, Vashitz Papers, (1)15.35–95, "Transjordan (Damascus)," 3.6.1920.

72. Gelber, *Shorshe ha-ḥavatselet*, 1:36–37.

73. BAZY, AAP 17/7/44, "46 JM," 26.4.1920.

74. CZA, Z4/3886/ii, "32 JM," 1.4.1920.

75. BAZY, AAP 17/5/3, "Pogroms in Jerusalem. April 4th, 5th and 6th 1920," n.d., ca. 9–12 April 1920.

76. Friedman, *British Pan-Arab Policy*, 267.

77. Lockman, *Meinertzhagen's Diary Ruse*.

78. TNA, WO 95/4375, Waters-Taylor to Louis Bols, 16.4.1920.

79. TNA, WO 95/4375, Bols to GHQ Cairo, 21.4.1920; Weizmann, *Letters and Papers*, 1:288; Wagner, "British Intelligence and the Jewish Resistance Movement," 636.

80. Wasserstein, *British in Palestine*, 84; TNA, WO 95/4375, Walter Norris Congreve to WO, 28.4.1920.

81. TNA, WO 95/4375, Congreve to WO, 28.4.1920; Wasserstein, *British in Palestine*, 72.

82. HA, 87/Zion/17, Meinertzhagen to Weizmann, 13.5.1920.

83. TNA, FO 141/742/3, various.

3. Cause for Peace

1. CZA, Z4/3886/ii, "32 JM," 1.4.1920.

2. TNA, CO 733/13, f. 599, C. D. Brunton, GSI, "Situation in Palestine," 13.5.1921; Huneidi, *Broken Trust*, 127–28; Wasserstein, *British in Palestine*, 100–102.

3. Weizmann, *Letters and Papers*, 1:212–13, 227, papers 48 and 51; Renton, *Zionist Masquerade*, 25, 59–64, 145.

4. Lockman, *Comrades and Enemies*, 59.

5. Andrew, *Defence of the Realm*, 140–50.

6. TNA, FO 141/742/3, 4759/333, Vansittart to Curzon, 16.11.1920.

7. TNA, FO 371/6374, f. 201, G. W. Courtney, director, "Bolshevism in Palestine," 4.1.1921.

8. TNA, FO 371/6374, f. 199, minute by O. G. Scott, 15.2.1921.

9. TNA, WO 106/205, 41, "Reported Attempts to Cause Trouble in Palestine," 28.1.1921; 42, WO to GHQ Egypt, 21.2.1921.

10. TNA, WO 106/208, 32, "The Communist Party"; 26, "The Bolsheviks and the Poale Zion," 1.4.1921; f. 4, "The Bolsheviks and the Poale Zion Communists," 1.4.1921.

11. TNA, CAB 1/29, "The Poale Zion," n.d., captured document dated 25.3.1921.

12. HA, 47/466, 19176, "Extract Intel Summary 86," 31.10.1923; 19177, Clayton to Deputy Inspector General (DIG), CID, 31.10.1923.

13. HA, 47/466, 19188, AIG to DIG, 5.11.1923.

14. HA, 47/466, 19144, "Extract Jerusalem DIS," 5.10.1923; 19149, "Bolshevik Proclamation," 9.10.1923.

15. HA, 47/466, 19159, "Search at PK Club," 10.10.1923.

16. HA, 47/788, 217284, "Summary of Intelligence No. 10," 31.5.1924.

17. HA, 47/982, 158a, DCP North to Acting Inspector General (AIG), CID, 20.7.1924, and related fols.

18. HA, 47/466, 19119, David Tidhar, "Closing of the Fractzia Club," 11.8.1924; 47/983, 19133, "Communists," 26.8.1924, and attached deportation list.

19. HA, 47/986, 19369, Hubert Young to Clayton, 26.1.1924.

20. Lockman, *Comrades and Enemies*, chaps. 3–5. See p. 131 on the role of the Histadrut in breaking Jewish Communist groups.

21. TNA, FO 141/672, "Report on Political Situation in Palestine," 10.1923.

22. CZA, J15/7223, 11, Joseph Davidescu, "Report on the Muslim-Christian Association Lately," 5.4.1921.

23. TNA, WO 106/209, f. 16, "Palestine and Syria Nationalist Intrigue," Constantinople, 25.4.1921.

24. Ferris, "British Empire," 336–37.

25. ISA, RG 100/P/649/7, Samuel to Curzon, 14.11.1920.

26. BAZY, AAP 17/1/21, political notes, 14.12.1918.

27. TNA, WO 106/205, 26, W. H. Deedes, "Political Report No. 1," January 1921.

28. Pappé, *Rise and Fall*, 213–15.

29. Mattar, *Mufti of Jerusalem*, 24–26; Elpeleg, *Grand Mufti*, 7–10.

30. Pappé, *Rise and Fall*, 217–19.

31. TNA, CO, 537/852, f. 14, Deedes to John Shuckburgh, 22.11.1921.

32. ISA, RG 65/P/3051/26, 4, C. A. Mackintosh to Dept. of Immigration and Travel, Jerusalem, 8.3.1923.

33. TNA, FO 141/464, "Minute Sheet: FO to HC," 4.10.1923; CO, 537/859, 10, Young to Clayton, 14.9.1923.

34. TNA, CO 537/859, 14, Clayton to Young, 5.10.1923.

35. TNA, KV 2/2084, 1a, cross-reference, Haj Amin Husseini, 30.9.1926. "Refugees" likely refers to rebel leaders in exile and not the civilian population.

36. ISA, RG 65/P/985/19, ECPAC to NPL, 25.8.1926.

37. ISA, RG 65/P/985/16, Mary Broadhurst to Jamal al-Husseini, 16.12.1926; TNA, AIR 5/206, 68A, HC to CO, 22.2.1927.

38. TNA, AIR 5/723, 1B, "Palestine and Transjordan Intelligence Summary," 5.1926.

39. ISA, RG 100/P/649/7, Allenby to Samuel, 28.6.1920.

40. Gelber, *Shorshe ha-ḥavatselet*, 1:48–50.

41. Gelber, *Shorshe ha-ḥavatselet*, 1:41–42, 52.

42. TNA, WO 106/198, 84, Aaronsohn to Colonel [French?], 19.9.1920.

43. ISA, RG 100/P/649/7, Storrs to Samuel, 7.5.1920.

44. Cohen, *Army of Shadows*, 18–22.

45. Porath, *Emergence of the Palestinian-Arab National Movement*, 211–13.

46. TNA, FO 141/672, E. Mills, Acting District Governor, Haifa, to CS, "Political Report for Period Ending the 31st of August 1924," 6.9.1924.

47. Porath, *Emergence of the Palestinian-Arab National Movement*, 239–40.

48. TNA, FO 371/6376, 9488, "Palestine," 11.8.1921.

49. TNA, CAB 24/127, memo re. Palestine, Winston Churchill, 11.8.1921.

50. Johnson, *British Imperialism*, 135–36, 154–56.

51. ISA, RG 65/P/984/10, shorthand writer's report of conversation between Churchill and PAD at the House of Lords, 12.8.1921.

52. The term "Bayt Watani" implied an ancestral homeland, whereas "Bayt Qowmi" was a place for a nation or peoplehood. ISA, RG 65/P/984/10, shorthand writer's report, 12.8.1921.

53. ISA, RG 65/P/984/10, shorthand writer's report,12.8.1921; RG 65/P/984/10, report of conference held at CO, 22.8.1921.

54. ISA, RG 65/P/339/14, PAD to Churchill, 25.8.1921.

55. TNA, CO 537/849, f. 8, Deedes to Young, 2.8.1921.

56. YYGH, Vashitz Papers, (1)15.35–95, Kisch to Zionist Organization London, 7.11.1924.

57. Porath, *Emergence of the Palestinian-Arab National Movement*, 245–47.

58. TNA, AIR 8/62, 13, "Cabinet Committee on Palestine: General Situation in Palestine," note by Samuel, 18/7/1923.

59. TNA, CO 733/13, 37529, "The Moslem Christian Delegation from Palestine," 27.7.1921.

60. Pryce-Jones, *Treason of the Heart*, 193–95.

61. An interesting discussion of the resolution is found in Huneidi, *Broken Trust*, 161.

62. See TNA, KV2/877, Robert Gordon-Canning; KV2/834, Barry Domvile; and KV2/2084, Amin al-Husseini.

63. Mary Adelaide Broadhurst, "Women's Election Policy," *Times* (UK), 2 November 1922, Times Digital Archive.

64. CZA, Z4/42749, Lewis Namier to H. R. Lewis, 1.6.1922.

65. ISA, RG 65/P/984/10, telegram from Jamal al-Husseini to CO and NPL, 29.6.1923, and attached memoranda; "Arab Resignation from Advisory Council," n.d.

66. Pedersen, "Impact of League Oversight," 42–45; also see Pedersen, *Guardians*, 95–103.

67. TNA, FO 371/6375, E2363, Samuel to CO, 20.2.1921.

68. Pedersen, "Impact of League Oversight," 46.

69. ISA, RG 65/P/985/19, Broadhurst to Jamal al-Husseini, 8.4.1926.

70. ISA, RG 65/P/984/23, Broadhurst to al-Husseini, 7.7.1927.

71. ISA, RG 65/P/985/19, Broadhurst to al-Husseini, 30.7.1926.

72. ISA, RG 65/P/985/16, NPL to al-Husseini, 2.12.1926.

73. Compare ISA, RG 65/P/985/9, with TNA, FO 141/672, "Political Report Palestine," 9.1923.

74. TNA, FO 141/672, "Palestine Situation Report," 12.1923.

75. ISA, RG 65/P/946/15, French consul Gaston Maugras relating conversation with Clayton (handwritten German notes, copied during Second World War from French original held at Quai D'Orsay), 2.8.1924. Translation by Christian Wehrenfennig.

76. Porath, *Emergence of the Palestinian-Arab National Movement*, 242–43, quoted in Cohen, *Army of Shadows*, 58.

77. Porath, *Emergence of the Palestinian-Arab National Movement*, 243–44.

78. Porath, *Emergence of the Palestinian-Arab National Movement*, 204.

79. Shlaim, *Iron Wall*, 12–15.

4. Security, Air Control, and the 1929 (Attempted) Revolt

1. TNA, AIR 9/19, 26, "Extract from CID Paper 199-C," 13.6.1923.

2. TNA, AIR 9/19, 5, "Notes on Importance of Palestine and Transjordan . . . Role in Major War . . . ," 8.10.1926.

3. Porath, *Emergence of the Palestinian-Arab National Movement*, 258–62.

4. An example is found in ʿIzzat Darwaza's memoir, *Mudhakkirāt Muḥammad ʿIzzat Darwazah*, 1:647.

5. Porath, *Emergence of the Palestinian-Arab National Movement*, 262–67.

6. Porath, *Emergence of the Palestinian-Arab National Movement*, 269.

7. Compelling examples are also found in Townshend, "Going to the Wall," 37.

8. Mattar, *Mufti of Jerusalem*, 37.

9. Darwazah, *Mudhakkirāt Muḥammad ʿIzzat Darwazah*, 1:646–57.

10. Darwazah, *Mudhakkirāt Muḥammad ʿIzzat Darwazah*, 1:600.

11. MECA, GB165–0188, Luke Papers, 5/2, ff. 70–80, Vaʿad to HC, 2.9.1929.

12. Gelber, *Shorshe ha-ḥavatselet*, 1:67.

13. Mattar, *Mufti of Jerusalem*, 46.

14. Gelber, *Shorshe ha-ḥavatselet*, 1:58.

15. Kolinsky, *Law, Order, and Riots*, 44–46.

16. MECA, GB165–0188, Luke Papers, 5/2, ff. 4–10, C-in-C Mediterranean Fleet to Luke, 24.8.1929; RAF Amman to Luke, 24.8.1929; Egypforce to Luke, 24.8.1929; Luke to Governor Malta, 23.8.1929.

17. MECA, GB165–0188, Luke Papers, 5/2, f. 19, Brig. Dobbie to Egypforce, 26.8.1929.

18. TNA, CO 733/176/5, 9, Chancellor to CO (Lord Passfield), 20.11.1929; AIR 5/1243, 13, Playfair, *Report on the Palestine Riots*, 26.12.1929, pp. 8, 33; Kolinsky, *Law, Order, and Riots*, 51; Kolinsky, "Reorganization," 160.

19. Compiled from TNA, AIR 20.5996, Playfair and Dobbie, *Report on Palestine Riots*, 3.1930; MECA, GB165–0188, Luke Papers, 5/2, various.

20. Cohen, *Tarpaṭ*.

21. Kolinsky, *Law, Order, and Riots*, 42.

22. MECA, GB165–0188, Luke Papers, 5/2, f. 171, Dobbie to CAS, Baghdad, 5.9.1929.

23. MECA, GB165–0188, Luke Papers, 5/2, f. 144, TJFF to HQ troops and HQ, RAF, Jerusalem, 4.9.1929.

24. TNA, AIR 20/5996, Dobbie, *Narrative of Operations*, 7.10.1929, 90.

25. TNA, AIR 20/5996, Dobbie, *Narrative of Operations*, 90.

26. TNA, CO 733/190/5, 1, Chancellor to Passfield, 22.2.1930, p. 1.

27. TNA, CO 733/190/5, 1, Chancellor to Passfield, 22.2.1930, pp. 1–2.

28. TNA, CO 733/190/5, 1, Chancellor to Passfield, 22.2.1930, p. 7.

29. TNA, CO 733/190/5, 1, Chancellor to Passfield, 22.2.1930, p. 7; HQ RAF Jerusalem to Air Ministry, 15.3.1930.

30. TNA, CO 733/190/5, 1, HQ RAF Jerusalem to Air Ministry, 15.3.1930.

31. TNA, CO 733/370/9, 1, "Terrorism 1936–1937," 4.5.1938.

32. CZA, S25/22329, "Secret. Conversations with the Arab Executive during the Period following the 1929 Riots, Oct. to Nov. 1929," p. 30.

33. CZA, S25/22329, "Secret," pp. 42–45.

34. HA, 8/Klali/29, "Black Hand—Note," 9.9.1930.

35. Harouvi, *HaBoleshet khokeret*, 59.

36. Omissi, *Air Power*; Ferris, *Men, Money, and Diplomacy*, 63–66; also see chap. 2.

37. French, *British Way in Warfare*, chap. 7; Ferris, *Men, Money, and Diplomacy*, 12, 22, 24, quotation 53.

38. TNA, WO 32/5281, ff. 6–9, Churchill, "The Cabinet: Palestine and Mesopotamia," 7.5.1920.

39. TNA, CAB 1/29, Trenchard, "A Preliminary Scheme for the Military Control of Mesopotamia by the Royal Air Force," 12.3.1920.

40. TNA, WO 106/204, f. 47, Deedes to various political officers, 16.12.1920.

41. Satia, *Spies in Arabia*, 163, 246–55.

42. During the 1936 revolt, British forces asked for special permission to use tear gas, but regularly bombed and demolished Palestinian homes. TNA, AIR 2/1759, 131a, HC to CO, 25.5.1936.

43. Satia, *Spies in Arabia*, 11.

44. Churchill to the Secretary of State for India, 24 February 1922, quoted in TNA, AIR 9/19, 9, "Notes on Public Security in Palestine," 2.9.1929.

45. Compiled from TNA, AIR 8/47, 9, Air Vice Marshal Dowding, "Appreciation of Situation in Palestine," see chart (item 9 within); CO 733/176/5, f. 38, "Present Establishment of British Section of Palestine Police," in Arthur Mavrogordato, "Reorganisation British Police in Palestine," 14.11.1929; CAB 19/97, ff. 16–19, *Report of Palestine Garrison Sub-Committee, Committee of Imperial Defence*, 27.6.1930.

46. TNA, AIR 2/1212, 23a, Rees to Burnett, 4.1.1927.

47. TNA, AIR 2/1212, "Minute 38," 24.5.1928.

48. ISA, RG 65/P/946/15, French consul Gaston Maugras relating conversation with Clayton (handwritten German notes, copied during Second World War from French original held at Quai D'Orsay), 2.8.1924. Translation by Christian Wehrenfennig.

49. TNA, FO 371/6376, 9488, "Palestine," 11.8.1921.

50. TNA, CO 537/826, Meinertzhagen to Shuckburgh, 13.5.1921; minute by T. E. Lawrence, 17.5.1921.

51. TNA, CO 837/849, Deedes to Young, 2.8.1921.

52. TNA, FO 371/6375, "Military Aspect of the Present Situation in Palestine," General Staff note, 8.7.1921.

53. Ferris, *Men, Money, and Diplomacy*, 89–91.

54. TNA, AIR 9/19, 4, "Air Staff Note on Reduction of Palestine Garrison," 5.1924.

55. TNA, CO 733/53, f. 460, Air to CO, 4.5.1923; f. 600, Tudor to Chief Secretary, 18.8.1923.

56. SAD, 694/10/26, Clayton, "Memorandum on the Proposed Reduction of the British Garrison in Palestine," 19.6.1923.

57. Smith, *Roots of Separatism*, 34–35; Wasserstein, *British in Palestine*, 152; TNA, CAB 24/178, "Palestine Loan Guarantee Bill," 17.2.1926.

58. TNA, AIR 8/47, 4, "CO Proposals to Convert the Gendarmerie . . . ," 15.1.1925.

59. TNA, AIR 9/19.25, "Lord Plumer's Reorganization of the Palestine Defence Forces 1925/26," 30/12/1929; handwritten note quoting Plumer to Trenchard, 29.7.1926.

60. TNA, AIR 8/47, 26, Wing Commander Williams, FO3, to DCAS, 16.4.1930; CO 733/58.43662, WO to Treasury, 29.8.1923.

61. TNA, CO 537/864, 10, Plumer to Leo Amery, 6.5.1926.

62. TNA, FO 141/432/3, Baron George Lloyd to Gen. Richard Haking, 20.3.1926.

63. TNA, CAB 16/97, "Enclosure 5 to CID Sub-Ctee Report on Palestine Garrison," 17.1.1930, pp. 26–29.

64. ISA, RG 160/P/1946/24, Ben-Zvi, "Report on Security and Police Matters," 13.12.1928.

65. Kolinsky, "Reorganization," 157.

66. TNA, WO 32/21125, 1B, "Intelligence Service—Middle East," n.d.

67. IOR, L/PS/11/179, Samuel to Curzon, 6.10.1920; minute by LDW, 25.1.1921; FO to India Office, 22.1.1921.

68. TNA, FO 371/7770, E 506, John Shuckburgh to FO, 14.1.1922; E 1441, Shuckburgh to FO, 8.2.1922.

69. TNA, KV 4/151, "Secret Service 1922/23," 28.1.1922.

70. Gelber, *Shorshe ha-ḥavatselet*, 1:34.

71. HA, 80/145/P/4, Davidescu to Shneerson, 7.7.1920. Thank you to Yael Steinitz for helping me with the handwritten document.

72. CZA, S25/10320, Zionist Organization to Kalvarisky, 6.2.1923; Weizmann to Shlomo Kaplansky, 23.2.1923.

73. "Dr. Chaim Kalvarisky Buried in Palestine; Was Chief Exponent of Arab-Jewish Unity," Jewish Telegraphic Agency, January 21, 1947, http://www.jta.org/1947/01/21/archive/dr-chaim-kalvarisky-buried-in-palestine-was-chief-exponent-of-arab-jewish-unity; Huneidi, *Broken Trust*, 270n102, Schama, *Two Rothschilds*, 169.

74. Gelber, *Shorshe ha-ḥavatselet*, 1:55–56.

75. Thomas, *Empires of Intelligence*, 240–41.

76. TNA, KV 2/2084, 1a, cross-reference, Haj Amin Husseini, 30.9.1926.

77. MECA, GB165–0188, Luke Papers, 5/3, f. 114, "Minutes of a Conference Held in the Office of the HC," 3.10.1929, p. 3.

78. TNA, AIR, 8/47, 9, Dowding, "Note on the Future Garrison of Palestine," 25.9.1929.

79. TNA, AIR 9/19, 14, "Note on the Future Garrison of Palestine," 10.1929.

80. TNA, AIR 2/1196, 40a, AOC Iraq to Air Ministry, 22.5.1931; 27c, "Future Intelligence Organisation in Iraq," 21.7.1930.

81. Thomas, *Empires of Intelligence*, 245–46.

82. TNA, CO 935/4/2, Dowbiggin, *Report on the Palestine Police Force*, 6.5.1930, pp. 228–29.

83. TNA, CO 733/176/5, Commandant to CS, "Enclosure 1: Reorganisation of British Police in Palestine," 14.11.1929.

84. Kolinsky, "Reorganization," 162–73.

85. Kolinsky, "Reorganization," 164.

86. Omissi, *Air Power*, 67–68; TNA, CO 733/176/5, 9, Chancellor to Passfield, 20.11.1929.

---

87. TNA, CAB 16/97, "CID: Palestine Garrison Sub-Committee; Report," 27.6.1930.

88. Harouvi, *HaBoleshet khokeret*, 69.

89. TNA, CAB 16/97, 1, "CID Palestine Garrison Sub-Committee," 29.5.1930; CO 323/1113/17, Maurice Hankey, "CID: The Garrison and Responsibility for Control . . . ," 31.7.1931; CAB 16/97, f. 34, Passfield, "Enclosure 2," 1.5.1930.

90. Gil-Har, "Political Developments"; Gil-Har, "British Intelligence."

91. Gil-Har, "British Intelligence," 120.

92. Jeffery, *MI6*, 276–77, 283–84.

93. Pedersen, "Impact of League Oversight," 49–51.

94. TNA, CO 733/180/1, 80, Draft Passfield to PM, 11.8.1930; IOR L/PS/10/1315, CID Police Summaries.

95. Thomas, *Empires of Intelligence*, 240.

96. Kroizer, "From Dowbiggin to Tegart," 121–22, 128.

97. Incidentally, al-Imam became one of Davidescu's informants in 1937.

98. CZA, S25/22329, "Secret," pp. 58–59.

99. See "On nous mande de Jérusalem," "Dernieres nouvelles télégraphique," *L'Avenir illustré*, 12 December 1929, p. 2, Historical Jewish Press, National Library of Israel, accessed 26 December 2018, http://jpress.nli.org.il; "Palestine Inquiry: A Sheikh's Evidence," *Times* (UK), 5 December 1929. Khalil Taha and his son were assassinated by the mufti's supporters in September 1936 for proposing an alternative to the general strike; see Cohen, *Army of Shadows*, 106–7.

100. TNA, CO 448/36, throughout.

101. Gelber, *Shorshe ha-ḥavatselet*, 1:106.

102. Kolinsky, *Law, Order, and Riots*, 100–101.

103. Friling, *Arrows in the Dark*, 279.

104. Harouvi, "Reuven Zaslani," 32–33; Eshed, *Reuven Shiloah*, 16–24.

105. Wagner, "Britain and the Jewish Underground."

5. British Intelligence, the Mufti, and Nationalist Youth

1. Cohen, *Britain's Moment in Palestine*, 229–40.

2. Kupferschmidt, *Supreme Muslim Council*, 66–77, app. 3; Matthews, *Confronting an Empire*.

3. Hourani, "Ottoman Reform"; Dawn, "From Ottomanism to Arabism"; Khoury, *Urban Notables*, of which a helpful synthesis is found in Gelvin, "'Politics of Notables.'"

4. Khalidi, "Ottomanism and Arabism"; Kayali, *Arabs and Young Turks*.

5. Matthews, *Confronting an Empire*, 2.

6. Seikaly, *Men of Capital*.

7. Swedenburg, *Memories of Revolt*; Khalaf, *Politics in Palestine*, 67–68.

8. In 2015, this led the Israeli prime minister to suggest that the mufti had inspired the Final Solution. Jodi Rudoren, "Netanyahu Denounced for Saying Palestinian Inspired Holocaust," *New York Times*, October 21, 2015, http://www.nytimes.com/2015/10/22/world/middleeast/netanyahu-saying-palestinian-mufti-inspired-holocaust-draws-broad-criticism.html.

9. Elpeleg, *Grand Mufti*, 41.

10. Mattar, *Mufti of Jerusalem*, 66–67.

11. Pappé, *Rise and Fall*, 255–57.

12. Cohen, *Britain's Moment in Palestine*, 240.

13. Wagner, "British Intelligence and Policy," see appendix.

14. Matthews, *Confronting an Empire*, 78.

15. ISA, RG/65/P/985/47, "Syrian Information Bureau," throughout; RG/65/P/985/16, Arslan to Jamal al-Husseini, 21.10.1925.

16. Cleveland, *Islam against the West*, 52–54.

17. Cleveland, *Islam against the West*, 52.

18. Matthews, *Confronting an Empire*, 31; Tauber, *Emergence of the Arab Movements*, 115.

19. McMeekin, *Berlin-Baghdad Express*, 172–79.

20. Matthews, *Confronting an Empire*, 31; Elpeleg, *Grand Mufti*, 3.

21. Cleveland, *Islam against the West*, 58.

22. TNA, CO 733/184/3, various. Intelligence on Canning was collected in Palestine, but made known to the cabinet and the Committee for Imperial Defence. See TNA, CAB 24/209, 0035, "Appendix," 28.11.1929, p. 10.

23. TNA, CO 733/184/3, 34, Carter, Scotland Yard, to Home Office, 31.3.1930.

24. CZA, J105/7, Tidhar to Kisch, handwritten note, 23.3.1930.

25. TNA, AIR 23/405.19a, "Weekly Appreciation Summary 7," 18.2.1931.

26. Unreliable land tax revenue was a longstanding problem. See Bunton, *Colonial Land Policies*, chap. 4; see also Matthews, "Pan-Islam or Arab Nationalism?"

27. IOR, L/PS/10/1315, "Political Summary," 3.3.1931.

28. IOR, L/PS/10/1315, CID to CS, 22.12.1931.

29. IOR, L/PS/10/1315, "Summary No. 21," 26.5.1931.

30. IOR, L/PS/10/1315, "No. 27," 28.7.1931; "No. 29," 25.7.1931.

31. IOR, L/PS/10/1315, CID to CS re. 3/32, 26.1.1932; Matthews, *Confronting an Empire*, 118.

32. IOR, L/PS/10/1315, CID to CS re. 3/32, 26.1.1932.

33. Mattar, *Mufti of Jerusalem*, 48.

34. Matthews, *Confronting an Empire*, 65.

35. Matthews, *Confronting an Empire*, 56–60.

36. TNA, KV 2/2084, 4A, "Cross Reference—Haj Amin," 17.6.1930.

37. Matthews, *Confronting an Empire*, 77.

38. IOR, L/PS/10/1315, "No. 32," 14.8.1931; "No. 34," 26.8.1931.

39. IOR, L/PS/10/1315, "Weekly 31," 5.8.1931.

40. IOR, L/PS/10/1315, "Weekly 52," 30.12.1931.

41. IOR, L/PS/10/1315, f. 431, "CID Weekly Summary 1/32," 14.1.1932.

42. Matthews, "Pan-Islam or Arab Nationalism?," 7–8.

43. Elpeleg, *Grand Mufti*, 32–39; Matthews, *Confronting an Empire*, 119–22. (Matthews here blurs the distinction between YMMAs and the Youth Congress.)

44. Matthews, *Confronting an Empire*, 175–76.

45. MECA, GB165–0168, Luke Papers, 5/2, f. 82, C. C. Troops Palestine to Air Ministry, 2.9.1929; f. 102, Chief Secretary to High Commissioner, report received 1115 hours, 2.9.1929; UK Government, "Report by His Majesty's Government."

46. Matthews, *Confronting an Empire*, 154.

47. IOR, L/PS/10/1315, "31/32," 10.8.1932.

48. HA, 8/klali/30b, "Battle of Hittin," 28.8.1932.

49. IOR, L/PS/10/1315, CID to CS 35/32, 9.9.1932.

50. IOR, L/PS/10/1315, "37/2," 21.9.1932.

51. Matthews, *Confronting an Empire*, 272.

52. Matthews, *Confronting an Empire*, 56–57.

53. HA 47/747, f. 307, Commandant to DSP South, 26.11.1929.

54. HA 47/747, f. 314, "Extract from DIS 69," 23.4.1930; f. 318, "DSP South to Commandant," 10.8.1930.

55. IOR, L/PS/10/1315, "Weekly 31," 5.8.1931.

56. Matthews, *Confronting an Empire*, 122–23.

57. IOR, L/PS/10/1315, "37/2," 21.9.1932.

58. IOR, L/PS/10/1315, CID to HC 13/33, 22.4.1933.

59. IOR, L/PS/10/1315, CID to HC 20/33, 10.8.1933.

60. IOR, L/PS/10/1315, "8/33," 10.3.1933.

61. TNA, CO 732/53/3, 15, Wauchope to CO, 30.1.1932.

62. IOR, L/PS/10/1315, CID to CS, 9.2.1932.

63. IOR, L/PS/10/1315, f. 388, "CID Weekly Summary 12/32," 30.3.1932.

64. See, for instance, Cohen, *Army of Shadows*, 70, 179.

65. IOR, L/PS/10/1315, "Summary 26," 30.6.1931; "No. 20," 19.5.1931; "No. 21," 26.5.1931.

66. Cohen, *Army of Shadows*, 59–61.

67. Kolinsky, *Law, Order, and Riots*, 100.

68. IOR, L/PS/10/1315, ff. 630–34, CID to CS, "Enclosure to Political Summary February 1931," 3.3.1931.

69. IOR, L/PS/12/3343, "CID Summary 13/34," 20.9.1934; "CID 14/34," 15.10.1934.

70. IOR, L/PS/12/3343, "CID 14/34," 15.10.1934; "12/34," 28.8.1934; "10/34," 14.7.1934.

71. IOR, L/PS/12/3343, "CID 8/35," 20.04.1935.

72. IOR, L/PS/12/3343, "CID 2/35," 21.1.1935.

73. TNA, FO 141/489, "Papers on Islamic Congress," enclosures 3 and 4, 25.1.1932.

74. CZA, S25/22735, "ASI Summary," 3.4.1935.

75. Cleveland, *Islam against the West*, 147–49.

76. Fiore, *Anglo-Italian Relations*, 56–57, 97; Arielli, *Fascist Italy*, 29–34, 71–72.

77. The origin of this term is uncertain. It was probably used to recall the soldiering prowess of "original" Arabs of the Dawasir tribe, similar to the way that "Qahtaniya" was a reference to the "original" Qahtan tribes. It was likely linked to mythology around Dawasir cavalry from pre-Islamic times. Ṭabarī, *History of Al-Tabari*, 79–80; IOR, L/PS/12/3343, "CID 12/35," 5.8.1935.

78. IOR, L/PS/12/3343, "CID 11/35," 27.6.1935; "CID 13/35," 24.8.1935.

79. IOR, L/PS/12/3343, "CID 13/34," 20.9.1934.

80. TNA, KV 2/2084, 24a, Cx88500, "Palestine: Miscellaneous," 21.7.1938, p. 3.

81. CZA, S25/22249, Sasson to Arab Office, 14.2.1935. Identity of Shanti from Gelber, *Shorshe ha-ḥavatselet*, 1:121.

82. Cleveland, *Islam against the West*, 81–83.

83. IOR, L/PS/12/3343, "CID 11/34," 6.8.1934; L/PS/10/1315, "CID 6/33," 18.2.1933; "CID 17/33," 20.6.1933.

84. CZA, S25/22745, Arslan to al-Husseini, translated letter, 20.2.1935.

85. CZA, S25/22735, "ASI summary," 3.9.1935.

86. CZA, S25/22735, "ASI," 6.12.1935.

87. CZA, S25/22735, "Letter from CID," 21.3.1935; TNA, CO 732/68/4, 2, Hall to CO, 11.5.1935.

88. CZA, S25/22735, "CID extract," 14.3.1935.

89. CZA, S25/22735, "ASI Summary," 2.10.1935.

90. IOR, L/PS/12/3343, "CID 16/35," 30.10.1935.

91. CZA, S25/22735, "Extract from RAF Weekly Intel Summary," 25.10.1935.

92. CZA, S25/22735, "From CID," 30.10.1935.

93. CZA, S25/22735, "ASI Monthly Summary," 1.11.1935.

94. CZA, S25/22735, "ASI Monthly Summary," 22.11.1935.

95. TNA, FO 141/489, minute, Loraine to Lancelot Oliphant, 5.1.1932; AIR 23/405, 24b, Loraine to Oliphant, 12.6.1931.

96. Johnson, *British Imperialism*, 89.

97. Wagner, "Whispers from Below," 446.

6. Intelligence, Security, and the Road to Rebellion

1. Lockman, *Comrades and Enemies*, 50–53.

2. Lockman, *Comrades and Enemies*, 202–7.

3. CZA, S25/22735, "Police: Deportation of Hauranis," 12.4.1935; "Deportation of Hauranis," 2.9.1935; IOR, L/PS/12/3343, "CID 12/34," 28.8.1934.

4. Lockman, *Comrades and Enemies*, 217–20.

5. Lockman, *Comrades and Enemies*, 207, 222–33.

6. Lockman, *Comrades and Enemies*, 240–47.

7. ISA, RG 69/P/935/36, David HaCohen letters of appreciation, Bernard Paget, CinC to HaCohen, 19.2.1946; [Brig.] Jack Evetts to HaCohen, 24.3.1939; K. W. Blackburne to HaCohen, 11.9.1938; Air Marshal Park to HaCohen, 21.10.1944.

8. Lockman, *Comrades and Enemies*, 220–21.

9. IOR, L/PS/12/3343, "CID 7/35," 9.3.1935.

10. IOR, L/PS/10/1315, "CID 14/32," 27.4.1932; "CID 43/32," 2.11.1932.

11. IOR, L/PS/12/3343, "CID 4/36," 10.3.1936.

12. TNA, KV 5/16, 2a, "Cross Reference Histadruth re. Communism," 8.11.1937.

13. Wagner, "Britain and the Jewish Underground," 23.

14. Shapira, *Land and Power*, 178.

15. Shapira, *Land and Power*, 184, 187–88.

16. Shindler, *Triumph of Military Zionism*, 86–92, 107–15, 143–47.

17. Gelber, *Shorshe ha-ḥavatselet*, 1:59.

18. CZA, J105/19, "Outline of Program for the Improvement of Jewish-Arab Relations," 27.2.1930.

19. Credit and my thanks to John Ferris for his help with this paragraph. TNA, FO 371/13784, E 3200, *Report by SIS "Eastern Department" to FO*, 21.6.1929.

20. TNA, FO 371/12278, E 3134/G, AOC Iraq to Air Ministry 1/438, 9.6.1927; E 3324, "C" to Nevile Bland, C/2664, 9.8.1927; AIR 23/433, Air Ministry to AOC Iraq, 1.2.1928; MECA, GB165–0298, MSS, *Fifty Years in Asia*, 130–55.

21. IOR, L/PS/10/1315, CID to CS re. 29/31, 25.7.1931; CID to CS re. 30/31, 29.7.1931.

22. HA, 8/klali/29, f. 49, "Public Movements & Propaganda," 8.1931.

23. TNA, AIR 2/1568, 1B, A. T. Barker, "Enclosure 1," 19.10.1931.

24. HA, 8/klali/29, f. 54, 24.10.1931.

25. HA, 8/klali/30b, f. 360, "Secret," 3.8.1932.

26. YYGH, Vashitz Papers, (2)15.35–95, "Information from Z'Y," 30.3.1933. Z may refer to Israel Zablodovsky (Amir), a Haganah district commander and intelligence hand.

27. TNA, AIR 2/1568, "Albert John (A.J.) Kingsley-Heath–Hagana," 19.7.1932. Forwarded by Wauchope, 6.8.1932.

28. CZA, S25/22735, "Smuggling of Firearms," 10.1934.

29. IOR, L/PS/10/1315, "CID 4/34," 12.2.1934.

30. CZA, S25/22735, "ASI," 2.1935.

31. IWM, Clarke Papers, 2, *Memoir*, 485–86.

32. HA, 47/145, ff. 1495–1500, OAG to CID, 13.11.1935; CID to X2, 21.12.1935.

33. By 1939, the Haganah had about twenty thousand static and ten thousand mobile troops. Those ranks swelled by several thousand during the revolt, and even more dramatically during the war.

34. CZA, S25/22740, "Extract from Beirut Liaison Officer—Arms Traffic," n.d.

35. CZA, S25/22735, Capt. Rice, "Memorandum," n.d.

36. HA, 47/76, "Jewish Military Activities in Poland" (in French), 26.7.1934; HA, 47/145, Warsaw to CO, 10.11.1935; Shindler, *Triumph of Military Zionism*, 154–59.

37. HA, 47/76, ff. 1493–94, "OPH?, XO4?, Haifa Port to CID," 8.11.1935.

38. CZA, S25/22735, "Smuggling of Arms by Jews from Trans-Jordan," 25.11.1935.

39. CZA, S25/22737, "Extract from Meeting at Gov't Office," 23.10.1935.

40. CZA, S25/22737, "From Colonial Office," 8.11.1935; "Letter to Three Arab Leaders," 10.11.1935.

41. Ofer, *Escaping the Holocaust*, 7–11.

42. IOR, L/PS/10/1315, "CID 27/33," 19.12.1933.

43. IOR, L/PS/12/3343, "CID 11/34," 6.8.1934.

44. IOR, L/PS/12/3343, "CID 12/34," 28.8.1934.

45. HA, 47/1035, 7a, "Extract Dis 178/34," 31.8.1934.

46. IOR, L/PS/11/201, 3992, Samuel to CO, "Press Censorship," 4.8.1921; ISA, RG 15/M/5145/1, "Weekly Confidential Summary of Information and Opinion in the Press," 1.1928–11.1928; ISA, RG 28/M/1951/4, "Postmaster General to Director of Customs," 30.5.1938.

47. HA, 47/747, "Jaffa DIS," 3.4.1932; "Jaffa DIS," 2.8.1931.

48. HA, 47/1035, "CID to CS re. Eviction of Arab Wadi Hawareth," 20.6.1933.

49. Gelber, *Shorshe ha-havatselet*, 1:105–7.

50. Gelber, *Shorshe ha-havatselet*, 1:106.

51. IOR, L/PS/10/1315, CID to CS re. 7/32, 23.2.1932.

52. Sanagan, "Teacher, Preacher, Soldier, Martyr," 344. I am grateful to Mark Sanagan for sharing with me his then-unpublished paper on the Nahalal murders.

53. IOR, L/PS/10/1315, "CID 6/33," 18.2.1933.

54. IOR, L/PS/10/1315, "CID 29/32," 27.7.1932.

55. IOR, L/PS/10/1315, CID to CS re. 2/33, 11.1.1933.

56. IOR, L/PS/10/1315, "CID 20/33," 10.8.1933.

57. Weiss, "Transfer Agreement"; Shindler, *Triumph of Military Zionism*, 175–80.

58. Shindler, *Triumph of Military Zionism*, 175–80.

59. ISA, RG 130/mfa/4373/7, Domvile to Zaslani, 9.6.1934.

60. IOR, L/PS/10/1315, "CID 9/34," 15.6.1934.

61. Gorney, "Voluntaristic Zionist System," 554.

62. CZA, S25/22735, "ASI," 2.5.1935; IOR, L/PS/12/3343, "CID 6/35," 27.2.1935.

63. TNA, CO 733/250/7, 9, Wauchope to Philip Cunliffe Lister, 13.3.1934; A., RGB Spicer to Wauchope, 29.11.1934; B., Spicer to Wauchope, 5.12.1934.

64. Shaw, *Survey of Palestine*, 1:185.

65. IOR, L/PS/10/1315, "CID 24/33," 7.10.1933.

66. IOR, L/PS/10/1315, "CID 24/33," 7.10.1933.

67. IOR, L/PS/10/1315, "CID 25/33," 23.10.1933.

68. IOR, L/PS/10/1315, "CID 24/33," 7.10.1933; "CID 25/33," 23.10.1933.

69. IOR, L/PS/10/1315, "CID 25/33," 23.10.1933.

70. TNA, FO 141/699/9, HC Palestine to HC Egypt, 13.10.1933; *Musa Kazim Husseini Being Beaten by a British Policeman, Jaffa 1933*, photograph, 27 October 1933, Institute of Palestine Studies, Photograph Collection 81/144, https://en.wikipedia.org/wiki/File:Musa_Kazim_Jaffa_1933.jpg#filelinks.

71. TNA, FO 141/699/9, Hall to Loraine, 14.10.1933; Egypforce to HC Palestine, 14.10.1933.

72. MECA, GB165-0101, Faraday Papers, 1/3, "Police Dispositions for Friday 27 October 1933," 25.10.1933.

73. Gelber, *Shorshe ha-ḥavatselet*, 1:61, 115–16.

74. Gelber, *Shorshe ha-ḥavatselet*, 1:118.

75. TNA, FO 141/699/9, GSI Egypt to First Secretary Cairo, 1.11.1933.

76. TNA, FO 141/699/9, RAF Headquarters, Cairo, to the Chancery, the Residency, Cairo, "Situation—Palestine," 2.11.1933.

77. TNA, FO 141/699/9, Jerusalem to Cairo, 1.11.1933.

78. TNA, HO 144/22592, Guy Liddell to F. A. Newsam, Home Office, 13.11.1933.

79. IOR, L/PS/10/1315, "CID 8/34," 26.5.1934.

80. IOR, L/PS/10/1315, "3/34," 30.1.1934; "1/34," 5.1.1934; "27/33," 19.12.1933.

81. ISA, RG/65/P/986/39, Farquharson to Musa Kazim, 14.12.1933.

82. IOR, L/PS/12/3343, "10/34," 14.7.1934.

83. TNA, FO 141/699/9, AOC Middle East to Chancery, Cairo, 6.11.1933.

84. IWM, Simonds Papers, *Pieces of War*, 10.

85. IWM, Simonds Papers, *Pieces of War*, 25.

86. Ferris, "'FORTITUDE' in Context," 119–20.

87. TNA, CO 323/1248/13, *Report on the Internal Security Exercise*, 6.1934.

88. CZA, S25/22735, Wauchope, "Speech on Public Security," n.d.

89. CZA, S25/22735, "ASI Summary," 22.11.1935.

90. CZA, S25/22735, AS [Alan Saunders?] to Assistant Chief Secretary, handwritten note, 5.12.1935.

91. CZA, S25/22735, "ASI Summary," 22.11.1935.

92. CZA, S25/22735, "Air Intelligence Weekly Summary," 13.12.1935.

93. Qawuqji and Qasimiyah, *Mudhakkirat Fawzi al-Qawuqji*, 10–14.

94. Qawuqji and Qasimiyah, *Mudhakkirat Fawzi al-Qawuqji*, 10–14.

95. IOR, L/PS/12/3344, HC to CO, 20.4.1936.

96. Qāsimīya, al-ʿAẓma, and al-ʿAẓma, *Ar-Raʿīl al-ʿarabī al-auwal*, 66–67.

97. HA, 47/770, 58, "DIS Nablus Extract," 23.3.36; 59a, "Jaffa DIS Extract," 24.3.36.

98. IOR, L/PS/12/3343, DIG, CID to CS, 11.4.1936.

99. Zuʿaytir, *Yawmīyāt Akram Zuʿaytir*, 42–43.

100. Zuʿaytir, *Yawmīyāt Akram Zuʿaytir*, 54.

101. Sanagan, "Teacher, Preacher, Soldier, Martyr," 348–49.

102. Sanagan, "Teacher, Preacher, Soldier, Martyr," 350.

103. TNA, FO 684/8, MacKereth to Wauchope, 26.11.1935.

104. HA, 47/770, "Extract Jaffa DIS," 30.11.1935.

105. HA, 47/1033, f. 031, "Haifa DIS Extract—Arab Youth Congress," 21.12.1935; f. 029, ASP Haifa, "New Armed Gangs—Hikmet el-Namleh," 29.11.1935.

7. The Arab Revolt

1. IOR, L/PS/12/3343, "CID 4/36," 10.3.1936.

2. IOR, L/PS/12/3343, "CID 4/36," 10.3.1936, p. 2.

3. IOR, L/PS/12/3343, "CID Summary 2/36," 18.2.1936, pp. 4–5.

4. IOR, L/PS/12/3343, "CID 7/36," 1.4.1936.

5. IOR, L/PS/12/3343, "CID 9/36," 6.5.1936.

6. "Macdonald Explains Status of Royal Commission," Jewish Telegraphic Agency, 27 May 1936, http://www.jta.org/1936/05/27/archive/macdonald-explains-status-of-royal-commission; "Royal Commission to Probe Palestine Disorders, Commons Told," Jewish Telegraphic Agency, 19 May 1936, http://www.jta.org/1936/05/19/archive/royal-commission-to-probe-palestine-disorders-commons-told.

7. See note 6. Also see CZA, S25/22704, Auni Abdul Hadi to HC, 14.5.1936; Auni Abdul Hadi to CS, 12.5.1936.

8. Gelber, *Shorshe ha-ḥavatselet*, 1:145–47.

9. Gelber, *Shorshe ha-ḥavatselet*, 1:146–47. Dajani was assassinated on 12 October 1938 by the mufti's agents.

10. Matthews, *Confronting an Empire*, 253.

11. Gelber, *Shorshe ha-ḥavatselet*, 1:187–88.

12. IOR, L/PS/12/3344, HC to CO, 2.5.1936; CZA, S25/22726, Wauchope to ʿAbdullah, 10.6.1936.

13. CZA, S25/22726, Wauchope to CS, 2.5.1936.

14. CZA, S25/22726, "Intelligence Summary (Police)," 8.6.1936.

15. CZA, S25/22704, "Minutes of Meeting Held at Gov't Offices," 11:00 a.m., 14.5.1936. Present were the high commissioner, the chief secretary, his assistant, and the HC's private secretary.

16. HA, 80/153p/9, "Meeting Shertok and Wauchope," 19.5.1936.

17. HA, 80/153p/9, "Meeting Shertok and Wauchope," 19.5.1936.

18. YYGH, Vashitz Papers, 2/15.35–95, Shertok to Wauchope, 20.5.1936.

19. CZA, S25/22768, "Minutes of Executive Council Meeting," 21.5.1936.

20. IOR, L/PS/12/3343, "CID 10/36," 21.5.1936.

21. HA, 8/klali/38, Part 2, ? to District Commissioner Jaffa, 23.5.1936; ? to DIG, 9.6.1936; TNA, AIR 2/1759, 131a, HC to CO, 25.5.1936.

22. CZA, S25/22768, "Notes by CS on Letter to HC from Treasurer," 30.5.1936.

23. Hughes, "Banality of Brutality," 322; Gavish, "Old City of Jaffa."

24. TNA, CO 733/317/1, 13, "Despatch by Air Vice Marshal Peirse: Part II—26 April to 16 May 1936."

25. Parsons, *Commander*, chap. 3.

26. CZA, S25/22708, Baghdad to Eden (FO), 25.6.1936.

27. Hughes, "Banality of Brutality," 324.

28. IOR, L/PS/12/3343, "CID 14/36," 18.8.1936.

29. ISA, RG 65/P/986/36, "Jamal, President PAP, to CO, Times, Morning Post . . . Archbishop Canterbury, National [Political] League," n.d. [late October 1936].

30. TNA, CO 733/285/21, Farquharson to Baldwin, 20.12.1935; India Office to CO, 18.12.1935.

31. See throughout ISA, RG 65/P/3220/17, especially "The Palestinian Arab Case," in *Great Britain and the East*, 2.7.1936, correspondence between Ghory and Jamal.

32. IOR, L/PS/12/3343, "CID 11/36," 23.6.1936.

33. TNA, AIR 2/1813, 2a, Air Intelligence to FO Eastern Department, "Italian Propaganda in Palestine," 9.6.1936.

34. IOR, L/PS/12/3343, "CID 11/36," 23.6.1936, p. 5.

35. IOR, L/PS/12/3343, "CID 14/36," 18.8.1936, p. 2.

36. CZA, S25/22704, "Note on My Interview with His Eminence the Mufti," 9.9.1936.

37. CZA, S25/22784, "Most Secret—Note from G.," 15.7.1936. G may be the initial of the mole.

38. IOR, L/PS/12/3343, 9, "CID Summary 14/35," 28.9.1935.

39. CZA, S25/22735, "ASI Summary," 1.11.1935.

40. CZA, S25/22726, Jeddah to HC Palestine, FO, 30.4.1936.

41. TNA, HW 12/203, 65196, Yasin to King, 29.4.1936.

42. CZA, S25/22726, Jeddah to HC Palestine, FO, 30.4.1936.

43. IOR, L/PS/12/2118, "CID," 24.8.1935.

44. TNA, HW 12/204, 65317, King to Minister, 15.6.1936.

45. TNA, HW 12/201, 65398, King to Minister, and reply, 21.6.1936.

46. CZA, S25/22726, CO to HC, 7.7.1936.

47. TNA, HW 12/207, 66083, King to Minister, 30.8.1936.

48. TNA, HW 12/207, 66083, King to Minister, 30.8.1936.

49. TNA, HW 12/207, 66134, Minister to King, 2.9.1936.

50. TNA, HW 12/207, 66155, King to Minister, 24.7.1936; decrypted 5.9.1936.

51. Provence, *Last Ottoman Generation*, 234–37.

52. HA, 87/Zion/9, Shertok, "Note of a Conversation with Two RAF Officers," 27.8.1936.

53. HA, 87/Zion/9, Shertok, "Conversation with Buss and Sofiano (Intel Officers)," 27.8.1936; IOR, L/PS/12.3343, "CID to CS re. Report 15/36," 1.9.1936; Kedourie, "Great Britain and Palestine," 103–4.

54. TNA, HW 12/207, 066194, the King, Riyadh, to the Saudi Minister, London, 7.9.1936; 066083, the Saudi-Arabian Minister, London, to the King, Riyadh, 28.8.1936; 066281, the King, Riyadh, to the Saudi Minister, London, 15.9.1936.

55. IOR, L/PS/12/3343, "CID 16/36," 28.9.1936.

56. TNA, HW 12/207, 066134, the Saudi-Arabian Minister, London, to the King, Riyadh, 2.9.1936.

57. CZA, S25/22771, "Comments by High Commissioner on Air Vice-Marshal Peirse's Secret Memorandum of 20.8.36," 22.8.36; TNA, CO 733/317/1, f. 207, "Appendix A—Peirse Memo," 20.8.1936.

58. CZA, S25/22726, CO to HC, 10.10.1936.

59. IOR, L/PS/12/3343, "CID 17/36," 16.10.1936.

60. IOR, L/PS/12/3343, "CID 16/36," 28.9.1936; TNA, HW 12.208, 066428, London to Riyadh, 25.9.1936.

61. IOR, L/PS/12/3345, "GSI No. 2," 6.10.1936.

62. TNA, HW 12/211, 67463, Arslan and Jabri to King, 11.12.1936.

63. TNA, HW 12/207, 066376, the King, Riyadh, to the Saudi Representative, Baghdad, 31.8.1936; IOR, L/PS/12/3343, "CID 16/36," 28.9.1936.

64. TNA, WO 191/73, K. C. Buss, "Secret No. 1," n.d.

65. IOR, L/PS/12/3343, "CID 16/36," 28.9.1936.

66. CZA, S25/22784, CO to HC, 13.10.1936.

67. CZA, S25/22704, CO to HC, 14.10.1936.

68. TNA, CO 733/317/1, 1, Wauchope to Ormsby Gore, 17.10.1936.

69. IOR, L/PS/12/3343, "CID 18/36," 7.11.1936.

70. HA, 8/153p/11a, F. H. Kisch, "Interview with Group Captain Buss (Chief Intelligence Officer) at Army HQ," 7.11.1936.

71. IOR, L/PS/12/3343, "CID 18/36," 7.11.1936.

72. IOR, L/PS/12/3343, "CID 19/36," 20.11.1936.

73. CZA, S25/22769, HC to CO, 29.12.1936.

74. IOR, L/PS/12/3343, "CID 20/36," 12.12.1936.

75. IOR, L/PS/12/3343, "CID 1/37," 4.1.1937; TNA, HW 12/211, 67350, "Intercept: Ibn Saud to London," 1.1.1937; ISA, RG 65/P/3056/37, royal commission 57th meeting, 13.1.1937; 58th meeting, 13.1.1937.

76. IOR, L/PS/12/3343, "CID 11/37," 5.7.1937.

77. IOR, L/PS/12/3343, "CID 12/37," 14.7.1937; "CID 13/37," 2.8.1937.

78. HA, 115/25, MacKereth to Albert John Kingsley-Heath (CID), 17.8.1937; HA, 80/50p/35, Eliyahu Epstein, Arab Bureau Intelligence from Damascus, source ʻayin ʻayin, 27.8.1937.

79. Gelber, Shorshe ha-ḥavatselet, 1:208.

80. TNA, FO 684/10, MacKereth to FO, 15.9.1937; "MacKereth: Memo," 14.9.1937; "X" to MacKereth, 13.9.1937, annexes 5 and 6.

81. Gelber, Shorshe ha-ḥavatselet, 1:210.

82. Gelber, Shorshe ha-ḥavatselet, 1:210–11; HA, 8/klali/103, Galili records, Arab Bureau Intelligence, "Joseph Informs," 30.8.1937.

83. HA, 80/141p/1, "List of Arab Moderates Assassinated and Assaulted during Recent Months," 17.9.1937.

84. HA, 47/757, ff. 276–497, "Haifa," 20.9.1937; HA, 115/97, "GSI. I (a) Summary," 1.10.1937, p. 5.

85. IOR, L/PS/12/3343, "CID 16/37," 15.10.1937.

86. TNA, HW 12/220, 069440, George Wadsworth to Washington, 2.10.1937.

87. CZA, S25/22768, "Executive Council Decision," 8.10.1937.

88. IWM, Simonds Papers, *Pieces of War*, 43–44.

89. IWM, Clarke Papers, 2, *Memoir*, 551–52, 588.

90. IOR, L/PS/12/3343, "CID 17/37," 9.11.1937; CZA, S25/22768, "Meeting at Office of OAG," 5.11.1937, p. 11.

91. IOR, L/PS/12/3348, Sir John Shuckburgh to Leonard D. Wakely, secret report on mufti activities in Syria received from Jewish Agency, 16.11.1937. On French surveillance, see Thomas, *Empires of Intelligence*, 203–7, 220.

8. Military Intelligence and the Arab Revolt

1. CZA, S25/22393, Domvile to Zaslani, 22.10.1937.

2. Kroizer, "From Dowbiggin to Tegart," 129.

3. Hughes, "Palestinian Collaboration," 311.

4. Hughes, "Palestinian Collaboration," 313.

5. TNA, AIR 2/1761, 95a, AOC to Air Ministry, 9.7.1936.

6. TNA, WO 33/1436, Appendix A, "Combined Staff," part of "Information for Commanders of Reinforcing Troops," n.d. (ca. August 1936).

7. IWM, Evetts interview, reel 3.

8. IOR, L/PS/12/3343, "CID 7/37," 10.5.1937.

9. IOR, L/PS/12/3343, "CID 8/37," 28.5.1937.

10. Jeffery, *MI6*, 283–84.

11. TNA, AIR 2/1244, General Staff HQ, Palestine, *Military Lessons of the Arab Rebellion in Palestine, 1936*, 2.1938, p. 45. On Clarke's authorship, see IWM, Clarke Papers, 1, "Note on Qualifications," n.d. (written with his CV after 1945, possibly in the 1970s as part of a book pitch).

12. TNA, CO 733/317/1, f. 182, app. 3, "Op Instructions," 24.6.1936; TNA, CO 732/81/10, 25, "GSI Summary 22/38," 4.11.1938; CZA, S25/22738, Foley, "Military Operational Standing Orders," 16.9.1938, part C.

13. Thomas, *Empires of Intelligence*, 245–46.

14. IWM, Clarke Papers, 2, *Memoir*, 546.

15. TNA, AIR 2/1244, General Staff HQ, Palestine, *Military Lessons*, p. 42.

16. IWM, Clarke Papers, 2, *Memoir*, 557–58.

17. CZA, S25/22678, "Conferences," 9–10.6.1936.

18. CZA, S25/22768, "Note of Situation Conference," 13.6.1936.

19. TNA, CO 733/317/1, appendix A to appreciation dated 20.8.1936.

20. TNA, AIR 2/1244, General Staff HQ, Palestine, *Military Lessons*, pp. 51–52.

21. IWM, Clarke Papers, 2, *Memoir*, pp. 571–72.

22. TNA, CO 733/317/1, 3c, "Memo of Comments by HC on Dill's Report," 15.9–30.10.1936.

23. TNA, AIR 2/1244, General Staff HQ, Palestine, *Military Lessons*, pp. 161–62; IOR, L/PS/12/3343, "CID 16/36," 28.9.1936. This story is told in gripping detail in Parsons, *Commander*, chap. 3.

24. IWM, Clarke Papers, 1, Evetts to Clarke, 15.9.1936. Credit to Matthew Hughes for his help with the troop numbers.

25. TNA, WO 32/4174, 9a, "Instructions," 7.9.1936.

26. TNA, WO 282/4, 7a, Dill to Air Vice Marshal Christopher Lloyd Courtney, 28.9.1936.

27. TNA, WO 33/1436, "Part IV: Present Intelligence System," in "Information for Commanders of Reinforcing Troops," August 1936; CZA, S25/22740, ? to CS, n.d. (ca. 10.1936).

28. Eshed, *Reuven Shiloah*, 29–31.

29. MECA, GB165–0279, Teague Papers, part 3, p. 122, diary entry 19.6.1937; "Social and Personal," *Palestine Post*, 7.5.1939, p. 2. His name also appears on distribution lists for CID summaries.

30. TNA, KV 3/317, 108a, Vernon Kell to Goldsmith, 4.1.1938; 116a, Kell to Goldsmith, 18.3.1938. I had previously erroneously identified him as the banking heir, MP, and hotelier Frank Goldsmith. I am grateful to Zac Goldsmith and Dido Goldsmith for access to their family photographs, which helped me clear this up.

31. TNA, WO 32/21125, 21a, MI2 to FO, 17.10.1919. Also see other items in file.

32. TNA, AIR 23/810, "Notes on Emergency in the Near East September 1935 to June 1936," 15.7.1936, p. 14; WO 282/5, 6a, Lt. Gen. Weir to Dill, 17.2.1937; FO 371/21838, E6646, "Proposal for Combined Intelligence Bureau for Middle East," 31.10.1938.

33. Ferris, "'FORTITUDE' in Context," 120, 131–32. For example, TNA, KV 4/305, 2B, GOC-in-C, Middle East, to War Office, 17.11.1939, reveals Wavell's role in 1939; TNA, CAB, 104/72, 51A, "CID 36 Meeting Minutes," 25.5.1939; 6A, "Note by DDI, Air Ministry," 14.11.1938.

34. Ferris, "'Usual Source,'" 84–85.

35. Wagner, "British Intelligence and the Jewish Resistance Movement"; Wagner, "Whispers from Below."

36. IOR, MSS Eur C235/2, Tegart memoir, 291.

37. TNA, WO 191/90, GSO, British Forces Palestine, *The Development of the Palestine Police Force under Military Control*, 6.1939, app. D.

38. MECA, GB165–0281, Tegart Papers, 4/6, *Diary*, 23.12.1937.

39. Gelber, *Shorshe ha-ḥavatselet*, 1:81, 112, 197.

40. HA, 87/zion/10, "Minute of Interview with the DIG CID," 2.10.1937.

41. Zuʿaytir, *Yawmīyāt Akram Zuʿaytir*, 14.

42. MECA, GB165–0281, Tegart Papers, 4/2a, untitled unaddressed letter by Tegart, 12.10.1937.

43. IOR, MSS Eur, C152/5, Wedgwood Benn to Lord Irwin, 21.11.29.

44. MECA, GB165–0281, Tegart Papers, 4/6, *Diary*, 30.12.1937.

45. Elpeleg, *Grand Mufti*, 48.

46. MECA, GB165–0281, Tegart Papers, 4/6, *Diary*, 29–30.12.1937.

47. MECA, GB165–0281, Tegart Papers, 4/6, *Diary*, 23.12.1937; 4/7, *Diary*, 7.2.1938; Lachman, "Arab Rebellion and Terrorism," 83; Cohen, *Army of Shadows*, 135.

48. Hughes, "Palestinian Collaboration," 296.

49. CZA, S25/22744, various 1936; HC to British resident Amman (Cox), 1.1938.

50. Cohen, *Army of Shadows*, 143.

51. MECA, Tegart Papers, 2/3, H. M. Foot, Assistant District Commissioner, Samaria, "Note on Recent Terrorist Activity," 24.12.1937.

52. IOR, MSS Eur C235/2, Tegart memoir, 255–56.

53. TNA, CO 733/383/2, 13, Harold MacMichael to CO, 4.8.1938. The RMP failed, but a mechanized Police Mobile Force came into being in 1944 to combat Jewish terrorism.

54. IOR, MSS Eur C235/2, Tegart memoir, 273–74.

55. IOR, MSS Eur C235/2, Tegart memoir, 278.

56. CZA, S25/22753, "Record of Meeting on Public Security," 7.1.1938.

57. CZA, S25/22753, "Record of Meeting on Public Security," 7.1.1938.

58. MECA, Tegart Papers, 2/3, Tegart? to Battershill, 2.1.1938.

59. MECA, Tegart Papers, 4/6, *Diary*, 2.1.1938.

60. MECA, Tegart Papers, 4/6, *Diary*, 25–26, 28.12.1937.

61. MECA, Tegart Papers, 2/3, "Minutes of Meeting," 28.1.1938.

62. Further details on the campaign are found in TNA, CO 732/81/9, 10, "GSI Serial 8/38," 22.4.1938; "GSI Serial 9/38," 6.5.1938; MECA, Tegart Papers, 2/3, "Present Situation," 3.5.1938.

63. CZA, S25/22768, "Minutes Pub-Sec Meeting," 10.6.1938.

64. ISA, RG 65/P/3056/37, Clarke, "Response to GOC," 1.7.1937.

65. MECA, Tegart Papers, 2/3, "Notes on Meeting with CS," 31.12.1937.

66. TNA, WO 191/90, GSO, British Forces Palestine, *Development of the Palestine Police Force*, 9–10, 14, 21.

67. Kroizer, "From Dowbiggin to Tegart," 128; Kevin Connolly, "Charles Tegart and the Forts That Tower over Israel," BBC, September 9, 2012, http://www.bbc.co.uk/news/magazine-19019949; Kroizer, "'Back to Station Control.'"

68. Kroizer, "'Back to Station Control,'" 96, 104, 115–16, 119, 128.

69. ISA, RG 65/P/3056.37, D. W. Clarke, "Conference at Secretariat," 28.5.1938; MECA, Tegart Papers, 3/2, DIG(A) to Tegart, 18.2.1938; ISA, RG 65/P/3056/37, *Final Report by Sir Charles Tegart on the Closing of the Northern and Eastern Frontiers of Palestine*, 9.6.1938 (note costs on p. 12); MECA, Tegart Papers, 3/2, verso f. 56, handwritten notes on section B of fence by Tabgha, n.d. (ca. February 1938).

70. CZA, S25/22762, "Note," 28/3/1938.

71. CZA, S25/22753, "Pubsec Meeting," 24.6.1938.

72. CZA, S25/22753, "Minutes of a Meeting on Public Security," 2.5.1938.

73. ISA, RG 65/P/3059/9, "Preliminary Instructions . . . ," 11.5.1938; "Force HQ Warning Order," 14.5.1938; RG 65/P/3058/20, Clarke, "Operation Order No. 1," 18.5.1938.

74. IOR, Microfilm M2313, Wingate Papers, Ritchie, "Force Intelligence Instruction No. 1," 20.5.1938.

75. ISA, RG 65/P/3056/37, *Final Report*; Clarke, "Conference at Government Offices," 19.5.1938.

76. MECA, Tegart Papers, 4/4, Tegart to GOC, 15.7.1938.

77. Khalidi, "Palestinians and 1948."

78. IWM, Clarke Papers, 2, *Memoir*, 556–57.

79. TNA, CO 732/81/9, 17, "GSI Serial 14/38," 15.7.1938.

80. IWM, Clarke Papers, 2, *Memoir*, 591.

81. Adam and Rivlin, *Kesher amits*, 107.

82. Anglim, "Orde Wingate." Many thanks to Simon Anglim for sharing this paper.

83. CZA, S25/22743, "Interview Given by A/C.S. (Mr. Moody) to Mr. Ben Zvi, Chairman of the Vaad Leumi on the 6th July 1938," 6.7.1938.

84. IOR, Microfilm M2313, Wingate Papers, Ritchie to Wingate, 25.5.1938.

85. HA, 87/zion/28, Clarke, "Training of Supernumeraries," 2.6.1938.

86. HA, 87/zion/27, Gordon, "Notes to Circular on Training Supernumeraries," 3.7.1938.

87. Hughes, "Terror in Galilee," 591; Hughes, "Palestinian Collaboration," 308.

88. TNA, WO 191/90, GSO, British Forces Palestine, *Development of the Palestine Police Force*, app. E.

89. Cohen, *Army of Shadows*, 145–55; Gelber, *Shorshe ha-ḥavatselet*, vol. 1, chap. 18.

90. HA, 80/141p/1, MBH (Hexter) to Shertok, 23.5.1938.

91. TNA, CO 732/81/9, 16, "GSI Serial 13/38," 1.7.1938.

92. HA, 80/50p/35, "Arab Bureau Intel," 27.8.1937; TNA, FO 684/10, MacKereth to FO, 19.10.1937.

93. Gelber, *Shorshe ha-ḥavatselet*, 1:236–38.

94. TNA, KV 2/2084, 32a, "Tannous' Mission to Lebanon," 20.9.1938; 33a, "Mufti's Organization in Lebanon," 7.10.1938.

95. TNA, CO 732/81/10, 24, "GSI Serial 21/38," 21.10.1938.

96. Hughes, "Palestinian Collaboration," 298.

97. HA, 8/klali/2, part 3, *Untitled Report—T/A No. 63*, with note to Ezra Danin, 11.11.1938; CZA, S25/22734, "Armed Gangs 48/38" (probably GSI), 15.11.1938.

98. TNA, CO 732/81/10, 25, "GSI Serial 22/38," 4.11.1938.

99. IOR, Microfilm M2313, Wingate Papers, Danin, *Documents and Portraits*, 150–51.

100. Hughes, *Britain's Pacification of Palestine*, chap. 7, esp. 253, 271.

101. See TNA, FO 371/23242, HC to CO, 3.12.1938; MECA, PPOCA, G6/24, "Re-Taking Jerusalem," various memoirs; TNA, CO 732/81/10, 25, "GSI 22/38," 4.11.1938, and "GSI 21/38," 21.10.1938; and the colorful account in IWM, Simonds Papers, *Pieces of War*, 49–52. Other narrative sources from National Library of Israel, Historical Jewish Press, http://jpress.nli.org.il/; *Palestine Post*, front pages between 16 and 23 October 1938.

102. IOR, L/PS/12/3343, "CID 4/38," 1.11.1938.

103. TNA, CO 732/81/10, "GSI 24/23," 2.12.1938, p. 13.

104. Hughes, "Palestinian Collaboration," 300.

105. TNA, CO 732/81/10, 27, "GSI 24/38," 2.10.1938.

106. TNA, CO 732/81/10, 27, "GSI 24/38," 2.10.1938.

107. HA, 47/1177. Throughout is raw correspondence. This material and related assessments are visible in staff intelligence material in CZA, S25/22732.

108. TNA, CO 732/81/10, 26, "GSI 23/38," 18.11.1938; 27, "GSI 24/38," 2.12.1938.

109. CZA, S25/22191, "Shakib Arslan on the Economic and Defence Power of the Arabs . . . ," 15.11.1938.

9. Intelligence, Ibn Saʿud, and the White Paper Policy

1. Thomas, *Empires of Intelligence*, 258.

2. Porath, *Palestinian Arab National Movement*, 277–81; Kedourie, "Great Britain and Palestine."

3. Porath, *Palestinian Arab National Movement*, 279–80.

4. Wasserstein, *Britain and the Jews of Europe*, 353.

5. Wasserstein, *Britain and the Jews of Europe*, 351.

6. Cohen, *Palestine, Retreat from the Mandate*, 66-85; Cohen, *Palestine to Israel*, 49.

7. Cohen, *Palestine to Israel*, 97.

8. Cohen, *Palestine to Israel*, 98.

9. Cohen, *Palestine, Retreat from the Mandate*, 38–49.

10. Cohen, "British Mandate in Palestine," 89; Cohen, *Palestine, Retreat from the Mandate*, 67.

11. Said Zahlan, *Palestine and the Gulf States*, 21.

12. Said Zahlan, *Palestine and the Gulf States*, 20–24.

13. Kedourie, "Great Britain and Palestine," 154.

14. Kedourie, "Great Britain and Palestine," 162–63.

15. Kedourie, "Great Britain and Palestine," 153.

16. Kedourie, "Great Britain and Palestine," 154.

17. TNA, HW 12/217, 68731, i/c King to Saudi Minister Damascus, 10.7.1937.

18. Kostiner, "Britain and the Challenge," 141.

19. Leatherdale, *Britain and Saudi Arabia*.

20. Goldberg, "Origins of British–Saudi Relations," 695–98.

21. ISA, RG 65/P/3059/24, Ibn Saʿud delegation papers, FG Peake, 24.3.1928, app. 6; Ferris, "Small Wars and Great Games," 219; Ferris, " 'Internationalism of Islam,' " 72; Fletcher, *British Imperialism*, chap. 3.

22. TNA, AIR 5/1244, *Report on the Operations of "SOUFORCE" in Southern Transjordan from 14 June 1932 to 2 September 1932*, 28.9.1932.

23. IOR, L/PS/10/1315, "CID 32/32," 17.8.1932; TNA, AIR 5/1244, *Report on the Operations*; HA, 8/klali/30b, M[oshe].Sh[ertok]., "Intel on Hejaz Revolt," 19.7.1932.

24. TNA, AIR 2/2210, E 6320/22/31, from FO, 8.11.1937; and minute 5.

25. CZA, S25/22776, Extract FO to Jeddah, 15.2.1935.

26. CZA, S25/22735, "ASI Intelligence," 2.5.1935.

27. CZA, S25/22776, Bullard to Eden, 2.10.1936.

28. These divisions had affected the Syro-Palestinian congress since the early 1920s. Bailony, "Transational Rebellion," 183–84. My gratitude to Bailony for sharing her dissertation.

29. Zamir, " 'Missing Dimension' "; Landis, "Syria and the Palestine War"; Porath, "Abdallah's Greater Syria Programme."

30. IOR, L/PS/12/2118, "CID," 24.8.1935.

31. TNA, WO 106/1594b, "MA Conference, June 1937: Statement by MI2," 22.6.1937, p. 6.

32. TNA, HW 12/218, 69021, Saudi representative, Damascus, to King, Riyadh, 13.7.1937.

33. TNA, HW 12/217, 68756, various i/cs, *Palestine Report—Ibn Saud Views*, 20.7.1937.

34. CZA, S25/22776, "2 Tels. from Alexandretta," 13.9.1937; "Minute by OAG," 16.9.1937; TNA, HW 12/219, 69255, Muqbil al Muhusn, al Serabati – Hsin al Safr, al Timimi – Tulk, al Shaban – Sawd, al Sad al Hwin, to King, Riyadh, 13.8.1937.

35. TNA, HW 12/219, 69279, King to Damascus, 13.8.1937.

36. TNA, HW 12/219, 69216, Saudi representative, Damascus, to King, Riyadh, 23.8.1937.

37. CZA, S25/22768, from Jeddah, 28.8.1937.

38. CZA, S25/22776, Jeddah to FO, 13.9.1937.

39. HA, 115/97, "'I' Summary," 1.10.1937; TNA, CO 732/79/4, Glubb to Amman, 15.8.1937.

40. CZA, S25/22776, "Extract from Major Glubb's Report," 19.1937.

41. TNA, HW 12/221, 69763, King, Riyadh, to Ibn Sulaiman, Taif, 5.10.1937; CZA, S25/22776, HC to Jeddah, 28.9.1937; TNA, HW 12/219, 69307, King, Riyadh, to Ibn Zeid, Zat al Haj, 18.8.1937; HW 12/220, 69590, Emir of Tebuk to King, Riyadh, 20.9.1937.

42. TNA, HW 37/1, London to King, 30.9.1937.

43. TNA, HW 12/220, 069576, Saudi Minister to King, 15.10.1937.

44. TNA, HW 12/220, 69533, King, Riyadh, to Saudi Minister, London, 7.10.1937.

45. TNA, CAB 24/273/6, cp281/37, FO, "Palestine," 19.11.1937, p. 6; CAB 24/273/14, cp289/37, CO, "Policy in Palestine," 1.12.1937.

46. Said Zahlan, *Palestine and the Gulf States*, 22.

47. TNA, FO 684/10, MacKereth to Rendel, 16.11.1937.

48. TNA, CO 733/381/5, Loraine to Anthony Eden, 28.12.1937.

49. TNA, HW 12/223, 70266, Minister London to King, 31.12.1937. The parentheses with a question mark are original and represent a probable solution to a corruption in transmission.

50. TNA, HW 12/223, 70295, King to London, 2.1.1938.

51. IOR, L/PS/12/3346, 8414, Bullard to FO, 15.12.1937.

52. Pedersen, "Impact of League Oversight," 57–61.

53. Cohen, *Palestine to Israel*, 101.

54. Quoted in Kedourie, "Great Britain and Palestine," 168. Kedourie describes the strikethrough in the original.

55. Kedourie, "Great Britain and Palestine," 169.

56. TNA, HW 12/223, 70422, Ibn Saʿud to Imam Yahya, 25.1.1938.

57. TNA, KV 2/2084, 11a, "Miscellaneous Arab Information," 4.2.1938.

58. IOR, L/Mil/7/10827, "Conference at CO," 7.9.1938.

59. TNA, FO 371/21838, Measures to Influence Minor Powers and Arab States, 61st meeting, 23.9.1938.

60. TNA, CO 733/386/13, Palestine discussions, 1st meeting, 7.10.1938; 9th meeting, 12.10.1938.

61. TNA, CAB 104/8, Committee on Palestine, 3rd meeting, 14.11.1938.

62. TNA, CAB 104/8, Committee on Palestine, 3rd meeting, 14.11.1938.

63. TNA, CO 732/85/1, "Measures to Influence Arab States . . . ," draft, 24.1.1939; second draft, 30.1.1939; Leslie Hollis, *Attitude of the Arab World*, 6.1.1939.

64. TNA, CO 733/410/2, 5, "Summary of Procès-Verbaux of Meeting in Cairo of Arab and Egyptian Delegates Etc. regarding Palestine," 29.4.1939, p. 2.

65. Kochavi, *Post-Holocaust Politics*, 59.

66. TNA, HW 62/21, untitled and unsigned memorandum, 21.11.38. My thanks to John Ferris for this discovery.

67. TNA, HW 12/237, 74058, King to Faysal, 17.3.1939.

68. TNA, HW 12/237, 74115, King to Faysal, 19.3.1939.

69. TNA, HW 12/237, 74093, Faysal, London, to King, Mecca, 21.3.1939; 74094, Faysal, London, to King, Mecca, 22.3.1939.

70. TNA, HW 12/237, 74144, King, Riyadh, to Faysal, London, 22.3.1939.

71. TNA, CO 733/410/6, ff. 16–27, "Modification 1," 22.3.39.

72. TNA, HW 12/237, 74117, Faysal, London, to King, Riyadh, 23.3.1939; 74145, Faysal, London, to King, Riyadh, 24.3.1939.

73. TNA, HW 12/237, 74163, Tofiq, London, to Iraqi Foreign Office, Baghdad, 24.3.1939.

74. Segev, *One Palestine, Complete*, 449.

75. TNA, HW 12/238, 074218, Iraqi Rep., Cairo, to FM, Baghdad, 31.3.1939.

76. TNA, HW 12/238, 074350, "Palestine: Doctor Weizmann's Offer to Egyptian Premier," 18.4.1939 (i/c 14.4.39).

77. TNA, HW 12/238, 074305, "Palestine: Further Arab Discussions," 13.4.1939.

78. TNA, HW 12/238, 074359, "Palestine: Emir Feisal's interview with M. Bonnet," i/c 29.3.1939.

79. TNA, HW 12/238, 074472, "Palestine: Ibn Saud's Message to Mufti," 27.4.1939.

80. TNA, HW 12/238, 074403, George Wadsworth, Jerusalem, to Secretary of State, Washington, 21.4.1939; 074503, "Palestine: Emir Faisal's Report to Ibn Saud," 27.4.1939.

81. TNA, WO 106/1594B, 13a, MI2, "Note on Probable Attitude in the Event of Great Britain Being Involved in a European War . . . ," 21.4.1939.

82. TNA, HW 12/239, 074525, "Palestine: Suggested Visit of Delegate to Ibn Saud," 2.5.1939 (i/c 28.4.1939).

83. TNA, CO 733/410/2, 5, "Summary of Procès-Verbaux," 29.4.1939.

84. TNA, CO 733/410/2, 5, "Summary of Procès-Verbaux," 29.4.1939.

85. TNA, HW 12/239, 074558, untitled, 4.5.1939 (i/c 2.5.1939).

86. TNA, CO 733/410/16, 4, Lampson to FO, 29.4.1939; 6, FO to Lampson, 1.5.1939; 9–10, FO to Lampson, 26.4.1939 and reply.

87. IOR, R/15/1/335, f. 19/163 II (C 77), Bahrain to Bushire, 7.5.1939.

88. IOR, R/15/2/165, ff. 130–36, Political Agent, Bahrain, to King of Saudi Arabia, 6.5.1939.

89. IOR, R/15/2/165, f. 130, FO to Ibn Sa'ud, 6.5.1939.

90. TNA, HW 12/239, 074665, "Palestine: Ibn Saud's Attitude," 15.5.1939; n.b., the original text vaguely refers to "the explanation from Cairo."

91. TNA, CO 733/410/2, 5, "Summary of Procès-Verbaux," 17.5.1939.

92. TNA, HW 12/239, 074667, Iraqi Representative, Cairo, to Foreign Minister, Baghdad, 15.5.1939.

93. TNA, HW 12/239, 074689, Iraqi Representative, Cairo, to Foreign Minister, Baghdad, 17.5.1939.

94. TNA, HW 12/237, 74072, Iraqi Consul, Beirut, to the Iraqi Legation, London, 17.3.1939.

95. TNA, HW 12/239, 074724, "Palestine: Attitude of the Arab Higher Committee," 20.5.1939.

96. TNA, FO 371/23269, E7409, Bullard to Halifax, 24.10.1939.

97. TNA, CO 733/426/11, 3, Bullard to Halifax, 2.12.1939.

98. TNA, CO 733/426/11, J. E. Shuckburgh, minute 16, 9.7.1940.

99. TNA, CO 733/426/11, 17 & 18, No. 2 W/T coy Sarafand to WO, 9.7.1940.

10. The Consequences of the White Paper

1. HA, 80/141p/1, Reuven [Zaslani] to Eliyahu [Golomb], London, 28.2.1939.

2. This is a summary based on previous chapters; Gelber, *Shorshe ha-ḥavatselet*, vol. 1; and Shindler, *Triumph of Military Zionism*, 189–98.

3. CZA, S25/22731, Arthur Giles to Chief Secretary re. Daily Summary 51/38, 18.7.1938.

4. Shindler, *Triumph of Military Zionism*, 202–5; Hoffman, *Anonymous Soldiers*, 76–79; CZA, S25/22731, "Daily Summary 48/38," 5.7.1938.

5. TNA, KV 5/34, 1b, SI [Secret Intelligence], "Palestine: The New Zionist (Revisionist) National Army," 17.1.1939.

6. TNA, KV 5/34, 3b, C to MI5, 9.6.1939.

7. Harouvi, *HaBoleshet khokeret*, 141, 144–45.

8. Harouvi, *HaBoleshet khokeret*, 146.

9. HA, 115/97, 40–44, SOI, "Political Situation," 19.1.1940; 45–46, SOI, Appendix, "Narrative of Jewish Disturbances following the Publication of the Land Sales Restriction Ordinance on 28th February," 14.3.1940.

10. HA, 115/97, 52–55, "Summary of Intelligence (SOI)," 14.3.1940.

11. HA, 115/97, 56–60, "SOI," 28.3.1940.

12. HA, 115/97, 67, "SOI," 25.4.1940.

13. The best discussion of this issue is Friling, *Arrows in the Dark*, vol. 1, esp. 6–8, 23–34, 77–81.

14. HA, 115/97, 71, "SOI," 24.5.1940.

15. HA, 115/97, 73–77, "SOI," 8.6.1940.

16. Harouvi, "CID in Palestine," 212–13; TNA, FO 921/153, Jerusalem to Cairo, 29.9.44.

17. HA, 87/zion/1, Lt. Col. C. B. St. Lawrence to A. S. P. Owen, Taps and District Superintendents, 17.8.1939.

18. CZA, S25/22788, "Operations-Jew-Policy," Adjutant, 2nd Battalion, Rifle Brigade, Safad, 29.11.1939.

19. CZA, S25/22736, "Minutes of Security Committee Meeting," 11.4.1939.

20. TNA, CO 733/393/18, Barker to HC, 10.11.1939; Wavell to WO, 4.11.1939.

21. TNA, HS 3/209, Ben-Gurion, "Conversation Notes MacDonald, Ben Gurion, Downie," 16.11.1939.

22. TNA, HS 3/209, Ben-Gurion, "Conversation Notes MacDonald."

23. TNA, CO 733/415/25, MacDonald to MacMichael, 29.2.1940.

24. TNA, CO 733/422/1, note by FIRST NAME Luke, "Illicit Stocks of Arms," 17.7.1940; table 30.6.1940.

25. TNA, CAB 67/4/25, Malcolm MacDonald to War Cabinet re. "WP (G) (40) 17," 29.1.1940; CAB 67/4/1917, Malcolm MacDonald, "WP (G) (40) 17," 1.1940.

26. TNA, FO 371/24569, f. 129, J. M. Martin to C. G. Eastwood, 29.5.1940.

27. TNA, CAB 65/5/39, "War Cabinet 39(40). Conclusions," 12.2.1940.

28. TNA, FO 371/24569, f. 129, J. M. Martin to C. G. Eastwood, 29.5.1940; f. 117, MacDonald to MacMichael, 24.5.1940; f. 118, MacMichael to MacDonald, 24.5.1940; f. 122, Lloyd to PM, 28.5.1940.

29. Quoted in Ofer, *Escaping the Holocaust*, 23.

30. NARA, RG 165, entry 77, box 758, report no. 336, G2-USAFIME, *General Security Information in Syria, Palestine & Egypt*, 1.9.1943.

31. TNA, CO 733/409/27, throughout.

32. HA, 87/zion/10, "Short Note of Dr. Weizmann's Conversation with 'G' DNI, Admiralty, December 1939."

33. HA, 87/zion/10, "Short Note of Interview with General Sir Edmund Ironside, CIGS, War Office," 14.11.1939.

34. Gelber, *Shorshe ha-ḥavatselet*, 1:290–92, 2:507, 548–50, 563–75.

35. Wagner, "Whispers from Below," 445.

36. Gelber, *Shorshe ha-ḥavatselet*, 2:468.

37. TNA, FO 1093/330, "Minute by Lincoln," 16.4.1943.

38. Wagner, "Britain and the Jewish Underground," 62.

Conclusion

1. Darwin, *Empire Project*, 473–75; Johnson, *British Imperialism*, 155–56.

2. Wagner, "British Intelligence and the Jewish Resistance Movement"; Wagner, "Whispers from Below."

BIBLIOGRAPHY

Manuscript and Archival Sources

Beit Aaronsohn, Zichron Ya'akov (BAZY)
    DP—Davidescu Papers
    AAP—Alexander Aaronsohn Papers
Ben-Gurion Institute, Ben-Gurion University of the Negev (BGA)
    David Ben-Gurion Archives—Chronological fonds
Central Zionist Archives, Jerusalem (CZA)
    J15—Jewish Colonization Association
    J105—Joint Bureau
    L3—Zionist Commission
    S25—Political Department of the Jewish Agency
    Z4—Central Office for the World Zionist Organization and Jewish
        Agency, London
Haganah Archives, Tel Aviv (HA)
    8—Intelligence Service (territorial)
    19—Notarim, Jewish Settlement Police, and SNS
    47—CID Microfilms
    80—Private Archives
    87—Documentation from other Israeli archives
    115—Intelligence Service (British department)
Imperial War Museum, London (IWM)
    A. C. Simonds Papers
    D. W. Clarke Papers
    John Evetts, interview by Conrad Wood, 1979, http://www.iwm.org.
        uk/collections/item/object/80004411.
India Office Records, British Library, London (IOR)
    L/Mil/7/10827 Reinforcements for Palestine
    L/PS/10/1315 Palestine: Police Summaries
    L/PS/11/179 Political and Secret Annual Files
    L/PS/12/2118 Pan-Islamic Congress, 1933–35; activities of Shaukat
        Ali, the mufti of Jerusalem, and others

L/PS/12/3343 Political Situation: Police Summaries, July 1934 to
    November 1938

L/PS/12/3344 Arab-Jewish Disturbances, 1936: Situation Reports

L/PS/12/3345 Arab-Jewish Disturbances, 1936: War Office Summa-
    ries, Nos. 1–2, 4

L/PS/12/3346 Disturbances and Anti-Jewish Riots: Reactions in For-
    eign Countries

Microfilm M2313 Wingate Papers

MSS Eur C152/5 Halifax Collection

MSS Eur C235/2 Sir Charles Augustus Tegart Papers

Israel State Archives, Jerusalem (ISA)

RG 2 Mandatory Government

RG 15 Propaganda Administration

RG 28 Rail and Port Administration

RG 65 Abandoned Documents

RG 69 Jewish Lawyers

RG 100 Herbert Samuel Archive

RG 130 Israeli Foreign Office

RG 160 Yitzhak Ben-Zvi Collection

Jewish Museum, London

JML/1984.125/1984.125.T *Official Record of Gallant Deeds*

Middle East Centre Archive, Oxford (MECA)

GB165-0101 J. A. M. Faraday Papers

GB165-0188 Luke Papers

GB165-0224 Palestine Police Old Comrades Association (PPOCA)

GB165-0281 Tegart Papers

GB165-0298 Geoffrey Wheeler Papers

GB165-0279 Teague Papers

National Archives and Records Administration, College Park, MD (NARA)

RG 165—Administrative Files of the War Department, Military Intel-
    ligence Division

National Archives at Kew, London (TNA)

AIR—RAF and Air Ministry

2—Registered Files

5—Air Historical Branch

8—Department of the Chief of the Air Staff: Registered Files

9—Directorate of Operations and Intelligence and Directorate of
    Plans

20—Papers Accumulated by the Air Historical Branch

23—RAF Overseas Commands: Reports and Correspondence

CAB—Cabinet Office
  1—Miscellaneous
  16—Committee of Imperial Defence
  19—Special Commissions to Enquire into the Operations of War
    in Mesopotamia (Hamilton Commission) and in the Darda-
    nelles (Cromer and Pickford Commission)
  24—War Cabinet and Cabinet: Memoranda
  67—War Cabinet Memoranda
  104—Supplementary Registered Files
CO—Colonial Office
  323—Colonies, General: Original Correspondence
  448—Honours: Original Correspondence
  537—Confidential General and Confidential Original
    Correspondence
  732—Middle East Original Correspondence
  733—Palestine Original Correspondence
  935—Confidential Print Middle East
FO—Foreign Office
  141—Embassy and Consulates, Egypt: General Correspondence
  371—Political Departments
  608—Peace Conference, British Delegation
  684—Damascus Consulate
HO—Home Office
  144—Registered Papers, Supplementary
HS—Special Operations Executive
  3—Africa and Middle East Group: Registered Files
HW—Government Code and Cypher School
  12—Decrypts of Intercepted Diplomatic Communications
  37—Diplomatic Decrypts Passed to the Secret Intelligence Service
    for Distribution
KV—Security Service
  2—Personal Files
  3—Subject Files
  4—Policy Files
  5—Organization Files
WO—War Office
  32—Registered Files
  33—Reports, Memoranda and Papers
  95—First World War and Army of Occupation War Diaries
  106—Directorate of Military Operations and Military Intelligence

191—Peacetime Operations Abroad, War Diaries and Headquarters Records
282—Field Marshal Sir John Greer Dill: Papers
Sudan Archives, Durham (SAD)
Gilbert Clayton Papers
Yad Ya'ari, Givat Haviva (YYGH)
Yosef Vashitz Papers

Printed Primary Sources

Adam, Monya, and Gershon Rivlin. *Kesher amits: Me-'Alilot Sherut ha-kesher shel ha-"Haganah."* Tel Aviv: Ministry of Defence, 1986.

Darwazah, Muḥammad. *Mudhakkirāt Muḥammad 'Izzat Darwazah, 1305 H-1404 H/1887 M-1984 M: Sijill ḥāfil bi-masīrat al-ḥarakah al-'Arabīyah wa-al-qaḍīyah al-Filasṭīnīyah khilāla qarn min al-zaman.* 6 vols. Beirut: Dar al-Gharb al-Islami, 1993.

Ḥairīya Qāsimīya, Nabīh al-'Aẓma, and 'Ādil al-'Aẓma. *Ar-Ra'īl al-'arabī al-auwal: Ḥayāt wa-aurāq Nabīh wa-'Ādil al-'Aẓma.* London: Riyāḍ ar-Raiyis, 1991.

Qawuqji, Fawzi, and Khayriyah Qasimiyah. *Mudhakkirat Fawzi al-Qawuqji, 1890–1977.* Damascus: Dar al-Numayr; Beirut: al-Ruwad, 1995.

Shaw, J. V. W. *A Survey of Palestine: Prepared in December 1945 and January 1946 for the Information of the Anglo-American Committee of Inquiry.* 3 vols. Jerusalem: Government of Palestine, 1946. http://www.palestineremembered.com/Acre/Books/Story831.html.

Tidhar, David. *Crime and Criminals in Palestine.* Jerusalem: n.p., 1924.

——. *Entsiklopedyah le-halutse ha-Yishuv u-vonav: Demuyot u-temunot.* 1947–70. Touro College Libraries. http://www.tidhar.tourolib.org.

United Kingdom Government. *Report by His Majesty's Government in the United Kingdom of Great Britain and Northern Ireland to the Council of the League of Nations on the Administration of Palestine and Trans-Jordan for the Year 1932.* Palestine: League of Nations, December 31, 1932. https://unispal.un.org/DPA/DPR/unispal.nsf/0/73F844E0122D6772052565D80053B611.

Weizmann, Chaim. *The Letters and Papers of Chaim Weizmann.* Series B. 2 vols. New Brunswick, NJ: Transaction Books, 1983.

Zu'aytir, Akram. *Yawmīyāt Akram Zu'aytir: Al-Ḥarakah Al-Waṭanīyah Al-Filasṭīnīyah, 1935–1939.* Beirut: Mu'assasat al-Dirāsāt al-Filasṭīnīyah, 1980.

Secondary Sources

'Allush, Naji. *Al-muqawamah al-'Arabiyah fi Filastin (1917–1948).* 2nd ed. Beirut: Dār al-Ṭalī'ah, 1970.

Andrew, Christopher. *The Defence of the Realm: The Authorized History of MI5.* London: Allen Lane, 2009.

Andrew, Christopher, and David Dilks. *The Missing Dimension: Governments and Intelligence Communities in the Twentieth Century.* Basingstoke: Macmillan, 1984.

Anglim, Simon. "Orde Wingate and Anglo-Jewish Military Cooperation in the Arab Revolt of 1936–39—Myth versus Reality." Unpublished paper, n.d. Microsoft Word file.

Arielli, Nir. *Fascist Italy and the Middle East, 1933–40*. New York: Palgrave Macmillan, 2010.

Bailony, Reem. "Transnational Rebellion: The Syrian Revolt of 1925–1927." PhD diss., University of California, 2015.

Barr, James. *A Line in the Sand: Britain, France and the Struggle That Shaped the Middle East*. London: Simon and Schuster, 2011.

Bar-Yosef, Eitan. "The Last Crusade? British Propaganda and the Palestine Campaign, 1917–18." *Journal of Contemporary History* 36, no. 1 (2001): 87–109.

Bennett, Huw. "Minimum Force in British Counterinsurgency." *Small Wars & Insurgencies* 21, no. 3 (2010): 459–75.

Bunton, Martin P. *Colonial Land Policies in Palestine, 1917–1936*. Oxford: Oxford University Press, 2007.

Cleveland, William L. *Islam against the West: Shakib Arslan and the Campaign for Islamic Nationalism*. Modern Middle East Series 10. Austin: University of Texas Press, 1985.

Cohen, Hillel. *Army of Shadows: Palestinian Collaboration with Zionism, 1917–1948*. Berkeley: University of California Press, 2008.

——. *Tarpaṭ : Shenat ha-efes ba-sikhsukh ha-Yehudi-ʿArvi*. Jerusalem: Keter, 2013.

Cohen, Michael J. *Britain's Moment in Palestine: Retrospect and Perspectives, 1917–1948*. Abingdon: Routledge, 2014.

——. "The British Mandate in Palestine: The Strange Case of the 1930 White Paper." *European Journal of Jewish Studies* 10, no. 1 (2016): 79–107. https://doi.org/10.1163/1872471X-12341287.

——. *Palestine, Retreat from the Mandate: The Making of British Policy, 1936–45*. New York: Holmes and Meier, 1978.

——. *Palestine to Israel: From Mandate to Independence*. London: Cass, 1988.

Cornwall, Mark. *The Undermining of Austria-Hungary: The Battle for Hearts and Minds*. New York: St. Martin's, 2000.

Darwin, John. *The Empire Project: The Rise and Fall of the British World-System, 1830–1970*. Cambridge: Cambridge University Press, 2009.

Dawn, C. Ernest. "From Ottomanism to Arabism: The Origin of an Ideology." *Review of Politics* 23, no. 3 (1961): 378–400.

Elpeleg, Zvi. *The Grand Mufti: Haj Amin Al-Hussaini; Founder of the Palestinian National Movement*. London: Frank Cass, 1993.

Eshed, Haggai. *Reuven Shiloah: The Man behind the Mossad; Secret Diplomacy in the Creation of Israel*. Translated by David Zinder and Leah Zinder. New York: Frank Cass, 2005.

Ferris, John. "The British Empire vs. the Hidden Hand: British Intelligence and Strategy and 'the CUP-Jew-German-Bolshevik Combination,' 1918–1924." In *The British Way in Warfare: Power and the International System, 1856–1956*, edited by Keith Neilson and Greg Kennedy, 325–46. Farnham, UK: Ashgate, 2010.

——. "'FORTITUDE' in Context: The Evolution of British Military Deception in Two World Wars, 1914–1945." In *Paradoxes of Strategic Intelligence: Essays in*

Honor of Michael I. Handel, edited by Richard K. Betts and Thomas G. Mahn-ken, 112–58. London: Frank Cass, 2003.

——. *Intelligence and Strategy: Selected Essays.* London: Routledge, 2005.

——. "'The Internationalism of Islam': The British Perception of a Muslim Menace, 1840–1951." *Intelligence and National Security* 24, no. 1 (2009): 57–77.

——. *Men, Money, and Diplomacy: The Evolution of British Strategic Policy, 1919–26.* Ithaca, NY: Cornell University Press, 1989.

——. "Small Wars and Great Games: The British Empire and Hybrid Warfare, 1700–1970." In *Hybrid Warfare: Fighting Complex Opponents from the Ancient World to the Present,* edited by Williamson Murray and Peter R. Mansoor, 199–224. New York: Cambridge University Press, 2012.

——. "The 'Usual Source': Signals Intelligence and Planning for the Eighth Army 'Crusader' Offensive, 1941." *Intelligence and National Security* 14, no. 1 (1999): 84–118.

Fiore, Massimiliano. *Anglo-Italian Relations in the Middle East, 1922–1940.* Burlington, VT: Ashgate, 2010.

Fletcher, Robert. *British Imperialism and "the Tribal Question": Desert Administration and Nomadic Societies in the Middle East, 1919–1936.* Oxford: Oxford University Press, 2015.

French, David. *The British Way in Warfare, 1688–2000.* London: Unwin Hyman, 1990.

——. *The Strategy of the Lloyd George Coalition, 1916–1918.* Oxford: Oxford University Press, 2002.

Friedman, Isaiah. *British Pan-Arab Policy, 1915–1922: A Critical Appraisal.* New Brunswick, NJ: Transaction, 2010.

Friling, Tuvia. *Arrows in the Dark: David Ben-Gurion, the Yishuv Leadership, and Rescue Attempts during the Holocaust.* 2 vols. Madison: University of Wisconsin Press, 2005.

Gavish, Dov. "The Old City of Jaffa, 1936—A Colonial Urban Renewal Project" [in Hebrew]. *Eretz-Israel: Archaeological, Historical and Geographical Studies* 17 (1983): 66–73.

Gelber, Yoav. *Shorshe ha-ḥavatselet: Ha-modiʻin ba-yishuv, 1918–1947.* 2 vols. Tel Aviv: Ministry of Defence Publications, 1992.

Gelvin, James L. *Divided Loyalties: Nationalism and Mass Politics in Syria at the Close of Empire.* Berkeley: University of California Press, 1998.

——. "The 'Politics of Notables' Forty Years After." *Middle East Studies Association Bulletin* 40, no. 1 (2006): 19–29. https://doi.org/10.2307/23062629.

Gil-Har, Yitzhak. "British Intelligence and the Role of Jewish Informers in Palestine." *Middle Eastern Studies* 39, no. 1 (2003): 117–49. https://doi.org/10.1080/0026 3200412331301617.

——. "Political Developments and Intelligence in Palestine, 1930–40." *Middle Eastern Studies* 44, no. 3 (2008): 419–34. https://doi.org/10.1080/00263200802021574.

——. "Zionist Policy at the Versailles Peace Conference: Setting the Northern Border of Palestine." In *A New Jewry? America since the Second World War,* edited by Peter Y. Medding, 8:153–67. Studies in Contemporary Jewry. New York: Oxford University Press, 1992.

Goldberg, Jacob. "The Origins of British–Saudi Relations: The 1915 Anglo–Saudi Treaty Revisited." *Historical Journal* 28, no. 3 (1985): 693–703.

Gorney, Yossef. "The Voluntaristic Zionist System in Trial" [in Hebrew]. In *Toldot Ha-Yishuv Ha-Yehudi Be-'Ereṣ-Yiśra'el: Me-'az Ha-ʿaliyah Ha-Ri'shonah. Teḳufat Ha-Mandaṭ Ha-Briṭi*, edited by Moshe Lissak, Anita Shapira, and Gavriel Cohen, 551–647. Jerusalem: "Daf-Noy," 1994.

Hamzah, Dyala. *The Making of the Arab Intellectual (1880–1960): Empire, Public Sphere and the Colonial Coordinates of Selfhood.* New York: Routledge, 2012.

——. "Muhammad Rashid Rida (1865–1935) or: The Importance of Being (a) Journalist." In *Religion and Its Other: Secular and Sacral Concepts and Practices in Interaction*, edited by Heike Bock, Jörg Feuchter, and Michi Knecht, 40–63. Chicago: University of Chicago Press, 2009.

Hanssen, Jens, and Max Weiss, eds. *Arabic Thought beyond the Liberal Age: Towards an Intellectual History of the Nahda.* Cambridge: Cambridge University Press, 2016.

Harouvi, Eldad. "The CID in Palestine, 1918–1948." PhD diss., University of Haifa, 2002.

——. *HaBoleshet khokeret: HaCID B'Eretz Yisrael, 1920–1948.* Kochav-Yair, Israel: Porat, 2011.

——. "Reuven Zaslani (Shiloah) and the Covert Cooperation with British Intelligence during the Second World War." In *Intelligence for Peace: The Role of Intelligence in Times of Peace*, edited by Hési Carmel, 30–48. London: Frank Cass, 1999.

Hoffman, Bruce. *Anonymous Soldiers: The Struggle for Israel, 1917–1947.* New York: Knopf, 2015.

Hourani, Albert. *Arabic Thought in the Liberal Age, 1798–1939.* Cambridge: Cambridge University Press, 1983.

——. "Ottoman Reform and the Politics of Notables." In *Beginnings of Modernization in the Middle East: The Nineteenth Century*, edited by William R. Polk and Richard L. Chambers, 41–68. Chicago: University of Chicago Press, 1968.

Hughes, Matthew. "The Banality of Brutality: British Armed Forces and the Repression of the Arab Revolt in Palestine, 1936–39." *English Historical Review* 124, no. 507 (2009): 313–54.

——. *Britain's Pacification of Palestine: The British Army, the Colonial State, and the Arab Revolt, 1936–1939.* Cambridge: Cambridge University Press, 2019.

——. "Palestinian Collaboration with the British: The Peace Bands and the Arab Revolt in Palestine, 1936–9." *Journal of Contemporary History* 51, no. 2 (2016): 291–315.

——. "The Practice and Theory of British Counterinsurgency: The Histories of the Atrocities at the Palestinian Villages of al-Bassa and Halhul, 1938–1939." *Small Wars & Insurgencies* 20, no. 3 (2009): 528–50.

——. "Terror in Galilee: British-Jewish Collaboration and the Special Night Squads in Palestine during the Arab Revolt, 1938–39." *Journal of Imperial and Commonwealth History* 43, no. 4 (2015): 590–610.

Huneidi, Sahar. *A Broken Trust: Herbert Samuel, Zionism and the Palestinians, 1920–1925.* London: I. B. Tauris, 2001.

——. "Was Balfour Policy Reversible? The Colonial Office and Palestine, 1921–23." *Journal of Palestine Studies* 27, no. 2 (1998): 23–41. https://doi.org/10.2307/2538282.

Jeffery, Keith. *MI6: The History of the Secret Intelligence Service, 1909–1949.* London: Bloomsbury, 2010.

Johnson, Robert. *British Imperialism*. New York: Palgrave, 2003.

Kalisman, Hilary Falb. "The Little Persian Agent in Palestine: Husayn Ruhi, British." *Jerusalem Quarterly*, no. 66 (2016): 65–86.

Kayali, Hasan. *Arabs and Young Turks: Ottomanism, Arabism, and Islamism in the Ottoman Empire, 1908–1918*. Berkeley: University of California Press, 1997.

Kedourie, Elie. "Great Britain and Palestine: The Turning Point." In *Islam in the Modern World*, edited by Elie Kedourie, 93–170. New York: Holt, Rinehart and Winston, 1980.

——. *In the Anglo-Arab Labyrinth: The McMahon-Husayn Correspondence and Its Interpretations, 1914–1939*. London: Frank Cass, 2000.

Khalaf, Issa. *Politics in Palestine: Arab Factionalism and Social Disintegration, 1939–1948*. Albany: SUNY Press, 1991.

Khalidi, Rashid. "Ottomanism and Arabism in Syria before 1914: A Reassessment." In *The Origins of Arab Nationalism*, edited by Rashid Khalidi, 50–72. New York: Columbia University Press, 1991.

——. *Palestinian Identity: The Construction of Modern National Consciousness*. New York: Columbia University Press, 1998.

——. "The Palestinians and 1948: The Underlying Causes of Failure." In *The War for Palestine: Rewriting the History of 1948*, edited by Eugene L. Rogan and Avi Shlaim, 12–36. Cambridge: Cambridge University Press, 2007.

Khoury, Philip S. *Urban Notables and Arab Nationalism: The Politics of Damascus, 1860–1920*. Cambridge: Cambridge University Press, 2003.

Kochavi, Arieh J. *Post-Holocaust Politics: Britain, the United States and Jewish Refugees, 1945–1948*. Chapel Hill: University of North Carolina Press, 2001.

Kolinsky, Martin. *Law, Order, and Riots in Mandatory Palestine, 1928–35*. London: Macmillan, 1993.

——. "Reorganization of the Palestine Police after the Riots of 1929." *Studies in Zionism* 10, no. 2 (1989): 155–73. https://doi.org.10.1080/13531048908575953.

Kostiner, Joseph. "Britain and the Challenge of the Axis Powers in Arabia: The Decline of British-Saudi Cooperation in the 1930s." In *Britain and the Middle East in the 1930s: Security Problems, 1935–39*, edited by Michael Joseph Cohen and Martin Kolinsky, 128–43. Basingstoke: Macmillan in association with King's College, London, 1992.

Kroizer, Gad. "'Back to Station Control': Planning the 'Tegart' Police Fortresses in Palestine." *Kathedra*, no. 111 (2004): 95–128.

——. "From Dowbiggin to Tegart: Revolutionary Change in the Colonial Police in Palestine during the 1930s." *Journal of Imperial and Commonwealth History* 32, no. 2 (2004): 115–33. https://doi.org/10.1080/03086530410001700426.

Kupferschmidt, Uri M. *The Supreme Muslim Council: Islam under the British Mandate for Palestine*. Leiden: Brill, 1987.

Lachman, Shai. "Arab Rebellion and Terrorism in Palestine: 1929–39; The Case of Sheikh Izz al-Din al-Qassam and His Movement." In *Zionism and Arabism in Palestine and Israel*, edited by Sylvia G. Haim and Elie Kedourie, 53–100. London: Frank Cass, 1982.

Landis, Joshua. "Syria and the Palestine War: Fighting King 'Abdullah's 'Greater Syria Plan.'" In *The War for Palestine: Rewriting the History of 1948*, edited by Eugene L. Rogan and Avi Shlaim, 176–204. Cambridge: Cambridge University Press, 2007.

Leatherdale, Clive. *Britain and Saudi Arabia, 1925–1939: The Imperial Oasis*. London: Frank Cass, 1983.

Lockman, J. N. *Meinertzhagen's Diary Ruse: False Entries on T. E. Lawrence*. Grand Rapids, MI: Cornerstone, 1995.

Lockman, Zachary. *Comrades and Enemies: Arab and Jewish Workers in Palestine*. Berkeley: University of California Press, 1996.

MacMillan, Margaret. *Peacemakers: The Paris Conference of 1919 and Its Attempt to End War*. London: J. Murray, 2001.

Mattar, Philip. *The Mufti of Jerusalem: Al-Hajj Amin Al-Husayni and the Palestinian National Movement*. New York: Columbia University Press, 1988.

Matthews, Weldon. *Confronting an Empire, Constructing a Nation: Arab Nationalists and Popular Politics in Mandate Palestine*. London: I. B. Tauris, 2006.

——. "Pan-Islam or Arab Nationalism? The Meaning of the 1931 Jerusalem Islamic Congress Reconsidered." *International Journal of Middle East Studies* 35, no. 1 (2003): 1–22. https://doi.org/10.1017.S0020743803000011.

McMeekin, Sean. *The Berlin-Baghdad Express: The Ottoman Empire and Germany's Bid for World Power, 1898–1918*. London: Penguin, 2011.

Melman, Billie. "The Legend of Sarah: Gender Memory and National Identities." *Journal of Israeli History* 21, no. 1–2 (2002): 55–92.

Messinger, Gary S. *British Propaganda and the State in the First World War*. Manchester: Manchester University Press, 1992.

Minerbi, Yitzhak. "Angelo Levi Bianchini U-Fe'iluto BaMizrach (1918–1920)." *HaTzionut* 1 (1970): 296–356.

Ochsenwald, William. "Ironic Origins: Arab Nationalism in the Hijaz, 1882–1914." In *The Origins of Arab Nationalism*, edited by Rashid Khalidi, 189–203. New York: Columbia University Press, 1991.

Ofer, Dalia. *Escaping the Holocaust: Illegal Immigration to the Land of Israel, 1939–1944*. New York: Oxford University Press, 1990.

Omissi, David E. *Air Power and Colonial Control: The Royal Air Force, 1919–1939*. Manchester: Manchester University Press, 1990.

Pappé, Ilan. *The Rise and Fall of a Palestinian Dynasty: The Husaynis, 1700–1948*. London: Saqi, 2010.

Paris, Timothy J. *Britain, the Hashemites and Arab Rule, 1920–1925: The Sherifian Solution*. London: Frank Cass, 2003.

Parsons, Laila. *The Commander: Fawzi al-Qawuqji and the Fight for Arab Independence, 1914–1948*. New York: Hill and Wang, 2016.

Patrick, Andrew. *America's Forgotten Middle East Initiative: The King-Crane Commission of 1919*. London: I. B. Tauris, 2015.

Pedersen, Susan. *The Guardians: The League of Nations and the Crisis of Empire*. Oxford: Oxford University Press, 2015.

——. "The Impact of League Oversight on British Policy in Palestine." In *Britain, Palestine and Empire: The Mandate Years*, edited by Rory Miller, 39–66. Burlington, VT: Ashgate, 2010.

Porath, Y. "Abdallah's Greater Syria Program." *Middle Eastern Studies* 20, no. 2 (1984): 172–89. https://doi.org/10.1080/00263208408700579.

——. *The Emergence of the Palestinian-Arab National Movement, 1918–1929*. London: Frank Cass, 1974.

——. *The Palestinian Arab National Movement: From Riots to Rebellion*, vol. 2, *1929–1939*. London: Frank Cass, 1977.

Provence, Michael. *The Last Ottoman Generation and the Making of the Modern Middle East*. Cambridge: Cambridge University Press, 2017.

Pryce-Jones, David. *Treason of the Heart: From Thomas Paine to Kim Philby*. New York: Encounter Books, 2011.

Reis, Bruno C. "The Myth of British Minimum Force in Counterinsurgency Campaigns during Decolonisation (1945–1970)." *Journal of Strategic Studies* 34, no. 2 (2011): 245–79.

Renton, James. "Flawed Foundations: The Balfour Declaration and the Palestine Mandate." In *Britain, Palestine and Empire: The Mandate Years*, edited by Rory Miller, 15–38. Burlington, VT: Ashgate, 2010.

——. *The Zionist Masquerade: The Birth of the Anglo-Zionist Alliance, 1914–18*. Basingstoke: Palgrave Macmillan, 2007.

Rivlin, Gershon, and Aliza Rivlin. *Zar lo yavin: Kinuye-seter ba-yishuv ha-yehudi be-Erets-Yiśra'el*. Tel Aviv: Ministry of Defence Publications, 1988.

Robson, Laura. "Church, State, and the Holy Land: British Protestant Approaches to Imperial Policy in Palestine, 1917–1948." *Journal of Imperial and Commonwealth History* 39, no. 3 (2011): 457–77. https://doi.org/10.1080/03086534.2011.598751.

Said Zahlan, Rosemarie. *Palestine and the Gulf States: The Presence at the Table*. New York: Routledge, 2009.

Sanagan, Mark. "Teacher, Preacher, Soldier, Martyr: Rethinking 'Izz al-Din al-Qassam." *Die Welt des Islams* 53, no. 3–4 (2013): 315–52. https://doi.org/10.1163/15685152-5334P0002.

Sanders, Michael, and Philip M. Taylor. *British Propaganda during the First World War, 1914–18*. London: Macmillan, 1982.

Satia, Priya. *Spies in Arabia: The Great War and the Cultural Foundations of Britain's Covert Empire in the Middle East*. Oxford: Oxford University Press, 2008.

Schama, Simon. *Two Rothschilds and the Land of Israel*. New York: Knopf, 1978.

Schneer, Jonathan. *The Balfour Declaration: The Origins of the Arab-Israeli Conflict*. New York: Random House, 2010.

Segev, Tom. *One Palestine, Complete: Jews and Arabs under the British*. London: Abacus, 2002.

Seikaly, Sherene. *Men of Capital: Scarcity and Economy in Mandate Palestine*. Stanford, CA: Stanford University Press, 2015.

Shapira, Anita. *Land and Power: The Zionist Resort to Force, 1881–1948*. Stanford, CA: Stanford University Press, 1999.

Sheehi, Stephen. *Foundations of Modern Arab Identity*. Gainesville: University Press of Florida, 2004.

Sheffy, Yigal. *British Military Intelligence in the Palestine Campaign, 1914–1918*. London: Frank Cass, 1998.

Shindler, Colin. *The Triumph of Military Zionism: Nationalism and the Origins of the Israeli Right*. New York: I. B. Tauris, 2006.

Shlaim, Avi. *The Iron Wall: Israel and the Arab World*. London: Penguin, 2001.

Smith, Barbara J. *The Roots of Separatism in Palestine: British Economic Policy, 1920–1929*. Syracuse, NY: Syracuse University Press, 1993.

Swedenburg, Ted. *Memories of Revolt: The 1936–1939 Rebellion and the Palestinian National Past*. Fayetteville: University of Arkansas Press, 2003.

Ṭabarī. *The History of Al-Tabari: The Sasanids, the Lakhmids, and Yemen*. Albany: SUNY Press, 1999.

Tageldin, Shaden M. *Disarming Words: Empire and the Seductions of Translation in Egypt*. Berkeley: University of California Press, 2011.

Tauber, Eliezer. *The Arab Movements in World War I*. New York: Routledge, 1993.

——. *The Emergence of the Arab Movements*. London: Frank Cass, 1992.

——. "The Role of Lieutenant Muhammad Sharif Al-Faruqi—New Light on Anglo-Arab Relations during the First World War." *Asian and African Studies* 24, no. 1 (1990): 17–50.

Thomas, Martin. *Empires of Intelligence: Security Services and Colonial Disorder after 1914*. Berkeley: University of California Press, 2007.

Townshend, Charles. "Going to the Wall: The Failure of British Rule in Palestine, 1928–31." *Journal of Imperial and Commonwealth History* 30, no. 2 (2002): 25–52.

Wagner, Steven. "Britain and the Jewish Underground, 1944–46: Intelligence, Policy and Resistance." MA thesis, University of Calgary, 2010.

——. "British Intelligence and Arab Nationalism: The Origins of the Modern Middle East." In *The First World War and Its Aftermath: The Shaping of the Modern Middle East*, edited by T. G. Fraser, 63–76. London: Gingko Library, 2015.

——. "British Intelligence and Policy in the Palestine Mandate, 1919–1939." DPhil thesis, University of Oxford, 2014.

——. "British Intelligence and the Jewish Resistance Movement in the Palestine Mandate, 1945–46." *Intelligence and National Security* 23, no. 5 (2008): 629–57.

——. "Whispers from Below: Zionist Secret Diplomacy, Terrorism and British Security Inside and Out of Palestine, 1944–47." *Journal of Imperial and Commonwealth History* 42, no. 3 (2014): 440–63. https://doi.org/10.1080/03086534.2014.895136.

Wasserstein, Bernard. *Britain and the Jews of Europe, 1939–1945*. New York: Oxford University Press, 1979.

——. *The British in Palestine: The Mandatory Government and Arab-Jewish Conflict, 1917–1929*. Oxford: Blackwell, 1991.

Watenpaugh, Keith David. *Being Modern in the Middle East: Revolution, Nationalism, Colonialism, and the Arab Middle Class*. Princeton, NJ: Princeton University Press, 2014.

Weiss, Yf'aat. "The Transfer Agreement and the Boycott Movement: A Jewish Dilemma on the Eve of the Holocaust." *Yad Vashem Studies* 26 (1998): 129–72.

Wilson, Mary C. "The Hashemites, the Arab Revolt, and Arab Nationalism." In *The Origins of Arab Nationalism*, edited by Rashid Khalidi, 204–21. New York: Columbia University Press, 1991.

Zamir, Meir. "The 'Missing Dimension': Britain's Secret War against France in Syria and Lebanon, 1942–45—Part II." *Middle Eastern Studies* 46, no. 6 (2010): 791–899. https://doi.org/10.1080/00263206.2010.520412.

INDEX

Page numbers in *italics* refer to figures, tables, and maps.

Teague, John, 190, 192, 197, 259
Tegart, Charles, 105, 188, 190, 198–209, 211, 214, 264–65
Tel Hai, 51
Temporary Additional Police (TAP), 206, 253, 255
terrorism, 17, 181, 183, 202, 236, 256, 265; Arab, 428; Jewish, 247–53, 291n53; urban, 211
Thomas, Martin, 102, 221
Tidhar, David, 62, 116
Tisha B'Av demonstrations, 84, 87
topography, 92
Toynbee, Arnold, 40
Transjordan, 48, 230–31; 1929 riots and, 88, 91; Arab revolt and, 167, 197; British security and, 82, 94–95, 99; Hashemites in, 221; partition proposal and, 180, 225; RAF intelligence and, 97; Saudi Arabia and, 227–28
Transjordan Frontier Force (TJFF), 91, 95–96, 99, 103–4, 146, 157, 194–95, 205, 225, 227
translations, 237
Trenchard, Hugh, 94–95
Trumpeldor, Joseph, 51
Tudor, Henry Hugh, 98
Tulkarm, 58, 182, 207, 211
Turkey, 36, 51, 231, 245. See also Ottoman Empire
Turkish movements, 51–52, 67

'Ulema (Muslim scholars), 64–65, 170
United Nations, 209; War Crimes Commission, 111–12
United States, 33, 39–40, 44–45, 47
'Usifyia, 217

Va'ad Leumi (National Council), 69–70, 73, 86
Vansittart, Robert, 61
village occupation scheme, 206–7, 208
villages: defensive militias, 214–17; intelligence on, 197; rebel attacks on, 201–2, 204, 214–18; SNS raids on, 212–13 (see also Special Night Squads)
village watchmen, 100
Vivian, Valentine, 155

Wafdist independence revolt, 49, 266
Wahba, Hafez, 173, 175–76, 230–33, 242
Wahhabi movement, 40, 227, 234
Wailing Wall dispute, 83–84, 87, 102, 107
Waqf, 83, 85, 201
War Office, 99; intelligence, 49–50, 101, 195

Wasserstein, Bernard, 222–23
Waters-Taylor, Bertie Harry, 55–56
Wauchope, Arthur, 110, 125, 130, 134, 136, 147, 149, 151, 156–57, 160, 163–67, 169, 171–74, 177–79, 185–86, 194, 203, 225, 263–64, 266
Wavell, Archibald, 156, 189, 198, 203, 254
Wedgewood, Josiah, 140
Weizmann, Chaim, 24–26, 34, 38–41, 43, 49, 56–57, 60, 70, 72–73, 76, 109, 151, 224, 234–35, 237, 239, 246, 255, 257–58, 263, 428. See also Feisal-Weizmann agreement
Western Wall dispute, 83–84, 87, 102, 107
Wheeler, Geoffrey, 141
White Paper policy (1939), 234–35, 237–39, 243, 261, 265, 267–68; consequences of, 246–60; end of Zionist policy, 12–13, 17, 220–21; explanations of, 221–26; publication of, 244
Wilenski, Nahum, 214
Wilkin, Tom, 250, 252
Wilson, Mary, 31
Wilson, Woodrow, 19, 39–40, 45
Wingate, Orde, 190, 203, 207, 212–13, 248, 253, 258–59, 265
wireless communications, 3, 105, 193, 201, 207, 212, 259
Woodhead Commission, 219, 222, 236
workers, Arab, 55, 137; Arab nationalism and, 50–51; political parties and, 138–40
World War, First, 18–21, 235, 252; Arab policy, 27–30; British intelligence and, 1–2, 4; intelligence during, 100; Palestine and, 21–23; peace conference, 39–41; Zionist policy, 23–27
World War, Second, 6, 17, 139, 251, 256–59, 265; appeasement and, 223; intelligence during, 198; Jewish immigration to Palestine during, 2, 145, 150, 152; Middle East and, 220, 229–30. See also Nazi Germany
World Zionist Organization, 252

X2, 105
XX system, 193, 195

Yacoubi, Joseph, 149
Yagur murder, 137, 149
Yahya, Imam, 129, 163–64, 174–75, 228, 235
Yasin, Yusuf, 173
Yemen, 16, 129, 163–64, 174, 230
Yishuv (Jewish community in Palestine). See Arab-Jewish cooperation; Arab-Jewish tensions; Jewish immigration;